I0801389

A Pictographic Naxi Origin Myth from Southwest China

A PICTOGRAPHIC NAXI ORIGIN MYTH FROM SOUTHWEST CHINA

An Annotated Translation

Duncan Poupard

LEIDEN UNIVERSITY PRESS

Cover design: Andre Klijsen
Cover illustration: Naxi hero Coqssei-leel'ee being lifted into the heavens by a white crane.
Lay-out: Crius Group

Every effort has been made to obtain permission to use all copyrighted illustrations reproduced in this book. Nonetheless, whosoever believes to have rights to this material is advised to contact the publisher.

ISBN 978 90 8728 427 5
e-ISBN 978 94 0060 469 8 (e-PDF)
https://doi.org//10.24415/9789087284275
NUR 522

© Duncan Poupard / Leiden University Press, 2023

All rights reserved. Without limiting the rights under copyright reserved above, no part of this book may be reproduced, stored in or introduced into a retrieval system, or transmitted, in any form or by any means (electronic, mechanical, photocopying, recording or otherwise) without the written permission of both the publisher and the editors of the book.

Acknowledgements

My thanks go to dongba He Guisheng of Ludian township for his patient reading of what can be considered an idiosyncratic manuscript, and He Lingyu for her tireless assistance in transcription and interpretation. Without their hard work, this book would not have been possible. The editing process benefited immensely from the careful and critical reading of Li Lan. The translation work was generously supported by the Sino-British Fellowship Trust. All errors are, of course, my own.

Contents

Part One: Introduction	**9**
Words as pictures	11
The Naxi and their literature	16
Elise Scharten, Naxi translator	20
The translation method	23
Why another translation?	28
What to watch out for when reading	29
The *chelggvq* purification ceremony	37
Part Two: Annotated Translation	**41**
Dramatis Personae	43
Cover page	45
Panel 1-1 — 1-10	47
Panel 2-1 — 2-13	58
Panel 3-1 — 3-9	73
Panel 3-10, 4-1 — 4-9	84
Panel 5-1 — 5-10	95
Panel 6-1 — 6-9	107
Panel 7-1 — 7-8	118
Panel 8-1 — 8-10	127
Panel 9-1 — 9-9	138
Panel 10-1 — 10-9	149
Panel 11-1 — 11-9	159
Panel 12-1 — 12-7	171
Panel 13-1 — 13-7	181
Panel 14-1 — 14-11	191
Panel 15-1 — 15-10	204
Panel 16-1 — 16-7	214
Panel 17-1 — 17-11	223
Panel 18-1 — 18-9	235
Panel 19-1 — 19-8	245
Panel 20-1 — 20-10	253

Panel 21-1 — 21-10 266
Panel 22-1 — 22-10 279
Panel 23-1 — 23-12 290
Panel 24-1 — 24-10 302
Panel 25-1 — 25-10 314
Panel 26-1 — 26-8 325
Panel 27-1 — 27-7 336
Panel 28-1 — 28-11 345
Panel 29-1 — 29-11 354
Panel 30-1 — 30-9 365
Panel 31-1 — 31-8 374
Panel 32-1 — 32-8 384
Panel 33-1 — 33-3 393

References 395

Appendix 1: The Scharten manuscript 397

Appendix 2: The Scharten translation (sample) 415

Part One

Introduction

Words as pictures

It is sometime in the early 1930s, deep within the alpine pastures and high mountain peaks of the land of the Naxi people. In this remote Himalayan region of southwest China, a Dutch missionary, Cornelia Elisabeth (Elise) Scharten, sits in the open courtyard of an old wooden house with a local Naxi "sorcerer", a ritual specialist who can commune with the spirit world. The ritualist is reciting from an ancient manuscript written in pictographs. After pausing and discussing the meaning of certain words (they are talking in the Tibeto-Burman Naxi language, for Elise Scharten has been living here for over fifteen years, and is already fluent), Scharten types an English translation using her typewriter, a technological marvel in this remote mountain town on the ancient "Tea Horse Road". This typewritten manuscript would become the first cover-to-cover translation of the most important Naxi myth: the origin story of mankind, a tale of incest, a cataclysmic flood, and a hero's quest to win the hand of a divine bride. Once complete, the original pictographic manuscript and its translation were taken back to Scharten's native Netherlands, where they have lain untouched in a museum archive for almost a century. Now, with modern technology, we can bring this old Naxi manuscript, along with its oral reading and typewritten translation, back to life.

Starting in the late nineteenth century, unusual pictographic books began to flow from a remote corner of southwest China into the libraries of the western world. At first this flow was nothing more than a mere trickle, a few curios sent home by French Catholic missionaries, but by the early twentieth century, they were being acquired in their hundreds and thousands, bought up in bulk by renowned plant hunters and explorers, and filling up shelves in such venerated institutions as the Library of Congress, the British Library and the German State Library at Marburg. This was a literature that could no longer be ignored, or, in the words of Austrian writer Felix Braun, "eine literarische Entdeckung, die fortan in der Geschichte der Weltliteratur nicht mehr ubersehen werden kann" (Koc 1969). What made these books so attractive? For one, they possessed the air of mystery that came with being "magical" books almost indecipherable to all but a select few ritual specialists, but perhaps more importantly, they were written in what looked like an ancient form of picture writing.

These are books where the written events unfold on the page visually. Rather than just reading descriptions of heroic deeds, the reader actually *sees* the protagonists perform them: but they are not picture books, for the pictures on these pages are themselves words. Take the sentence "The man takes his arrow and bow and kills the tiger". Now compress the nouns, verbs and other syntax words into two (or at least what looks like two) graphs, and you might get something like this:

Figure 1. A simplified reading: man shoots tiger.
Collection Nationaal Museum van Wereldculturen.
Coll.no. RV-4175-26, detail.

The imagery is relatively clear: a horned figure aiming an arrow at a tiger, the animal represented by its head alone. Perhaps this looks something like a primitive comic book – but a comic book still relies on the words to be read alongside the pictures. What if the words were also the pictures? This is the allure of the Naxi "dongba" script, a logographic writing system that emerged centuries ago as a form of picture writing, and which later developed into a script that is still in use today to record the religious stories of the Naxi, a Tibeto-Burman people who live amidst the high mountains of the extended Himalayas in southwest China. This is the world's only fully logographic writing system still alive today, a form of writing in which one single graph can equate to a whole word, or sometimes even a whole sentence.

But how do we go about *reading* these graphs that look like pictures? How do you compose complicated syntax in such a script? This is where the difficulties really begin. Writing is, ordinarily, a linear process of moving from one word to the next in a regimented fashion. In the dongba script of the Naxi, especially as it is traditionally composed in the ritual literature, there is no fixed order of the graphs on the page, and they are often arranged in intricate, ideographic collages. To compound matters further, some words are written and not read, while many are read and not written. There is in general a looser relationship between the written and the spoken word than the reader is probably used to.

The two graphs in Figure 1 above *could* read:

Naxi: la / kail / zhuaq / nee / kail[1]
Word for word: tiger / shoot / man / topicalizer / shoot
English translation: [When it comes to] the shooting of the tiger, the man does the shooting

This means that those two graphs are read as five syllables (in already very concise ritual language). The man and the bow represent all at once the verb "*kail*" (to shoot), which is

[1] Reading by He Yuncai (YSMGZCGB 1986, 249).

read twice, and the noun "*zhuaq*" (man). The fact that this figure as written has horns and an elephant's trunk (in what are admittedly very abstract forms) also indicate that this is the Naxi culture hero Coqssei-leel'ee, the only man to survive a great flood in Naxi myth. His name is not read out in this section; in this way the graph, by virtue of those adornments on the figure's head, portrays even more information than a formulaic reading presents (in Saussurean terminology, it is a "motivated" sign). The source marker *nee*, a grammatical particle crucial to the syntax because it identifies the agent of the action, is not written at all, and must be supplied from memory. The non-linear connection between the written and the spoken word has led some scholars to call dongba script a "phraseographic" writing (*yuduan wenzi* 语段文字), wherein one single graph can represent an entire phrase.[2]

The second major problem is that a great number of the graphs are, as they are used in the manuscripts, not what they at first seem: they lose their "motivation" (the degree to which a symbol actually looks like what it is supposed to represent). Take the following graph as an example:

Figure 2. Zzee'laq-epv.
Collection Nationaal Museum van Wereldculturen.
Coll.no. RV-4175-26, detail.

Now, you might see the resemblance of this head to the tiger's head in Figure 1 and think "Aha! What we have here is surely an anthropomorphic tiger wearing some kind of robe!", and that *is* precisely what is depicted, but it is not the meaning of this graph, it is not how it is read. This is the graph denoting the maternal grandfather of mankind, the god, Zzee'laq-epv, who is depicted as a robed, seated tiger. He was not, in fact, a tiger; the tiger's head is used merely phonetically. When we see the tiger, we know in this case that the name of this individual includes the syllable "*la*", the Naxi word for tiger, here just the second syllable in the deity's name: Zzee'**laq**-epv (read in the falling tone).

This is what is known as the rebus principle, one of the great leaps forward in the technology of writing (and coincidentally what marks Naxi dongba as essentially a phonetic, not a pictographic script). Even so, the dongba script is almost universally known as a "pictographic"

[2] See for example Wang Yuanlu (1988, 162).

writing system (see the title of this very book!) despite its overt reliance on the rebus principle, presumably because there is a certain appeal to talking about pictographs that remind us of the mystical past of the written word, and it is also more convenient than bombarding the reader with such academic jargon as "logographic" (where each graph represents a word, and is not limited to a single syllable) or "morpho-syllabic" (where each graph represents a single monosyllabic morpheme). The simplest explanation, perhaps, is this: the dongba script, like the Chinese script, is comprised of *evolved* pictographs, with the caveat that the Naxi script remains fossilized in an earlier stage of evolution compared to Chinese writing. This means that, by virtue of being made almost obsolete by the encroaching influence of Chinese, the dongba graphs have retained more of their original pictorial quality.

The dongba script can be used to write fully syntactic texts such as land contracts, diary entries, and colophons appended to ritual manuscripts where the dongba lament their old age and the passing of time.[3] In its most traditional form, however, this writing is characterized by its semi-oral nature, by the "gaps" that need to be filled in. Without already knowing the story that a manuscript relates, it would be very difficult to put the graphs into any kind of syntax (the grammar words, such as auxiliary particles, are often not written). All this means that the books are essentially indecipherable mysteries for anyone approaching them *in isolation*. Reading these texts, then, requires context. This context is usually supplied by someone who already knows the stories and the rites, i.e., a "dongba", the very ritual specialists after which the script was named.

The dongba are the mediators between the human world, the spirit world, and the divine. They officiate the religious ceremonies of the Naxi, ensuring that both man- and spirit-kind retain their harmonious relationship. It is the remit of the dongba to fill in the "gaps" of the written manuscript, and a proficient dongba well-versed in the tradition could perhaps elaborate at length upon any given section of text. When faced with a situation like this, where a handful of written graphs can be embellished to tell a longer story episode, we can understand how the early western commentators might have suggested that the Naxi dongba script was not a "full" writing system. The intrepid missionaries and explorers of the nineteenth century who were first to come into contact with this writing almost couldn't conceive of it as "writing" at all: they were stuck in linear, logocentric modes of thought, innately suspicious of anything that claimed to be writing but that didn't seem to accurately transcribe speech. Père Desgodins of the Missions-Etrangères de Paris, one of the first Westerners to encounter the Naxi script, wrote in an 1882 letter to the Tibetologist Terrien de Lacouperie that "These hieroglyphics ... are not, properly speaking, a writing" (1894, 47). This blanket, orientalist

[3] A colophon to a manuscript written by dongba He Nianheng of Baidi includes the lines: "I hope there'll be more days left for me, and if so, I will visit that village [where I conducted this ceremony] again one day. May the cranes fly among the clouds, and may the wild geese wander by the riverside, I'll be there again one day," see Yang (2008, 243).

appraisal can still be seen in some contemporary scholarship on the Naxi. But denying the Naxi script the status of writing "proper" is misleading, an ideological position tied too closely to a linear understanding of writing as a technology. If we posit that non-linear writing can exist, then the "gaps" in a Naxi manuscript do not indicate a *lost* presence, but merely another kind of presence, a non-logocentric presence. Think of it like this: the spaces can themselves be read, or, in other words, the spaces can be filled with words by virtue of those words that *have* been written down. In the same way that a parent may give an impromptu performance when reading a children's book, perhaps inserting extra dialogue to match a particularly vivid picture, the dongba extemporise during a performance where necessary. In this way the Naxi dongba script is still writing, just not writing as we normally understand it. The Naxi books can be read, and if they can be read, then they can be translated into other languages.

It wasn't until the Austro-American botanist explorer, Joseph Rock (1884–1962) began his expeditions into China's mountainous southwest in the early twentieth century that the world began to have some idea what the Naxi books contained. Rock, famous for being the *National Geographic* magazine's "man in China" in the 1920s and 30s, was captivated by the ritual books he found in the possession of the Naxi religious specialists (the "dongba") while plant hunting in China's borderlands. Rock went on to devote the remaining years of his life to the translation of these books that contained such a treasure house of knowledge, a corpus of literature that, for Rock, offered tantalising glimpses at the indigenous religion of pre-Buddhist Tibet.

Rock, a voracious autodidact, appreciated an intellectual challenge: this was a script that, by the time he first encountered it in the 1920s, nobody had previously deciphered (aside from some exploratory, incomplete translations conducted via Chinese by French scholars and explorers). This vast corpus of ritual literature was essentially unexplored territory, and this was where Rock liked to tread. Through his assiduous collecting and cataloguing, and not without controversy,[4] he preserved thousands of these texts in collections now spread throughout the western world. Unfortunately, this legacy has not yet been fully developed by western scholars. Rock's passing in 1962 marked the abrupt end of a nascent European Naxiology:[5] his work was completed by scholars unfamiliar with Naxi in adjacent disciplines such as Tibetology and Sinology.

[4] In China, Joseph Rock's legacy has undergone a radical transformation. During the Cultural Revolution, he was branded an imperialist spy, and criticized for "stealing" thousands of historical manuscripts – an entire corpus of minority religious literature (YNDXLSYJS 1976, 2). In China today, his legacy is celebrated, and he is heralded as one of the progenitors of Naxi studies. Somewhat ironically, his legacy in the west has continued on an opposite trajectory, and his work is treated with some scepticism by anthropologists and Sinologists alike.

[5] Naxiology can be defined as a specialized discipline that involves the in-depth philological study of the Naxi literature. "The death of J. F. Rock has left research on the Nakhi, an ethnic group of about 175,000 people in the province of Yün-nan, in a stage when it was just about to develop into a distinctive specialized discipline" (Prunner 1969, 100).

In the story of western "Naxiology", which is very much a history of these unusual manuscripts and their translation, Rock is not the only protagonist (although he no doubt wished to believe he was). Indeed, there were other unsung translators who encountered the Naxi and attempted to bring their manuscripts, and the stories contained within them, to the western world. The translator whose work forms the core of this book, Elise Scharten (1876-1965), was a Dutch Pentecostal missionary, and like the early Jesuits in China, she was convinced of the need to spread the Christian message amongst the Chinese and non-Han minority peoples of that country. But she also took an interest in the Naxi ritual literature, and this interest led to the creation of a unique translation of a central Naxi origin story that has, until now, lain undisturbed in a Dutch museum archive. Elise Scharten's most valuable contribution to Naxiology is this full, cover-to-cover translation of the Naxi *Coqbbertv* (loosely, the *Origin and Migration of Mankind*) myth, completed before Rock published any of his own full translations. But let us first take a step back. What exactly are these "pictographic" books, and how do we read them?

The Naxi and their literature

Unfortunately for those who approach the books in the western collections, the Naxi manuscripts cannot be understood when they are divorced from the context of their creation and performance. So, who are the Naxi? They are, at least by Chinese standards, a numerically small ethnic group, with a population of around 330,000, most of whom live in and around the picturesque Lijiang basin in the Himalayan foothills of northwest Yunnan province. The Naxi language is usually classified within the Tibeto-Burman language family, but it is writing among the Naxi that has given them a certain level of cultural cachet that is perhaps not commensurate with the size of their population. Besides generally writing standard Chinese with Chinese characters, they have two native scripts for recording their own language, one phonetic and the other primarily logographic (touted by the Chinese authorities as "the world's last living pictographs"). The traditional Naxi name for this script is *serjel lvjel*, literally "wood record, stone record",[6] which scholars suggest points to the earliest materials used for recording the characters, that is, writing is defined as marks made on wood and stone. It is today more commonly known by its Chinese name, *dongbawen* 东巴文, "dongba script", after the dongba themselves, and a straight translation of the colloquial Naxi phrase, *dobbaaq tei'ee*, "dongba writing". There is another mode of writing known as *geba*, which is entirely syllabic, and shares more in common with the syllabic modern Yi script than logographic dongba script. To illustrate the difference between a logographic script and a syllabic script, take the word "Naqxi" (Naxi): in dongba script, this word is represented by one single graph, and read "Naqxi", with two syllables: . This is a figure of a person, and the sheaf of rice on

[6] Here the abstract verb is depicted via a rebus: while we have two graphs derived from pictographs, a tree and a lump of stones, the verb *jel*, to record, is portrayed with the graph for bracelet, *jjiuq*, used as a rebus, and read "*jel*".

their head indicates the pronunciation (*xi*, person). We know it is not just any person, but a Naxi person, because the head is coloured black (*naq*, black). One graph therefore represents two syllables. In the geba script, the same word, "Naqxi", would be written with two graphs, one to represent each syllable: 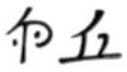 The first graph is "*na*" (without the falling tone, as geba graphs do not represent any specific tone), and the second "*xi*". In geba, each distinct graph represents one syllable only. When placed together, they are read "Naqxi", the context indicating which tones are required. Table 1 shows the same word across all the major scripts used to write Naxi.

Table 1. Script diversity in Lijiang

Script	Example
Simplified Chinese	纳西
Hanyu pinyin	Nàxī
Modern Naxi pinyin	Naqxi
Rock's romanization[7]	¹Na-²khi
Dongba script (logographic)	
Geba script (syllabic)	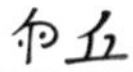

While rare, manuscripts can be written entirely in geba. The majority of the Naxi books are predominantly written in dongba, but it is altogether possible for a text to mix the two systems. As we shall see, Scharten's *Coqbbertv* manuscript features a number of geba graphs, used by the composer of the manuscript as a kind of shorthand (for the dongba graphs are usually more complex).

The Naxi religion and its ritual specialists are both known as *dobbaq*, Chinese "dongba 东巴", which is either derived from the Tibetan *stonpa*, meaning "teacher" (according to Rock 1963, 87), or more likely the Tibetan Bonpo, the priests from whom the dongba ritualists likely inherited many ritual manuscript traditions.[8] The dongba religion therefore shares elements of the early Tibetan religion (what many scholars label "Bon"), but also draws from Tibetan Buddhism, Taoism, and Confucianism, to differing degrees. It is a complex admixture of beliefs and ritual practices. The dongba have no temples, instead conducting their rites in designated clearings adjacent to the mountain villages or in the courtyards of the households which have requested a ceremony. They pass their knowledge from father to son (during

[7] Despite being anachronistic, some of Rock's transcriptions persist to this day: notably "Na-khi" (Naxi) and "dto-mba" (dongba). For these general terms I use standard Chinese pinyin as is convention, and for other Naxi words I use Naxi pinyin.

[8] The prolific Chinese Naxiologist Yang Fuquan has discussed the connection between *dobbaq/stonpa* and *bonpo* (possibly rendered into Naxi as "*biu bbiuq*") at length, see Yang (2012, 298-334).

the Cultural Revolution, this chain of patrilineal transmission was cut for a generation, but there are now a number of dongba training schools in Lijiang where the tradition is taught to any students who are willing to learn). A dongba must be proficient at performing major rites such as funerals, appeasing the nature spirits, and exorcising malevolent entities. These rituals require the recitation of the Naxi ritual literature, written left to right on coarse, locally-produced paper and bound into small, rectangular volumes. The majority of the extant Naxi ritual texts are written in the dongba script, a script that has stuck very close to its pictographic roots – direct representation of the thing itself. The dongba script has an inventory of several thousand graphs, which can be combined in a near infinite number of ways to create noun and verb phrases. Joseph Rock's 1963 dictionary, for example, lists over 3,000 graphs but is by no means exhaustive.

Nobody knows exactly how many texts make up the body of Naxi literature as a whole, or even exactly how far back the script dates. Lijiang authorities have estimated that around 1,000 separate manuscript traditions exist, but new ritual traditions are still being discovered in manuscript collections stored around the world. Li Lin-ts'an believed that the dongba script could not have predated the Tang dynasty (618 – 907 CE), and that it could not have emerged any later than the Ming Dynasty (1368-1644 CE). The earliest dated manuscript is from the 13th century. There are well over 30,000 individual dongba manuscripts stored in various library collections around the world. Rock, alongside other less prolific collectors, preserved these manuscripts in the west, essentially for nobody to read; as the British anthropologist Anthony Jackson has said, "The irony is that the freely-available [Naxi] mss. in the West cannot be read by Western scholars!" (1989, 137). This is the somewhat dire state of affairs when it comes to western Naxiology as a discipline.

We cannot access the content of the books without being able to first *read* them. In this, Naxiology shares a similar fundamental linguistic barrier to that of Sinology: just as Sinologists must first master the Chinese literary language, requiring a long and demanding training "that can seldom be combined with the acquisition and cultivation of another discipline" (Leys 2013, 317), so too must Naxiologists learn Naxi and the dongba script. Therein lies the rub. If, as with Sinology, the Naxiological field is restricted linguistically, the problem is that it is even more difficult to master the Naxi literary language than it is the Chinese; so much so that Rock was the only westerner to have done so (with a prodigious amount of assistance from native informants). As Klaus Janert, the Sanskrit scholar who attempted to finish the cataloguing of Rock's Naxi manuscripts in Germany after his death, once said, "Rock was the first and the only European so far who learned to read the pictographical script of the Dtombas as well as their syllabic characters and to interpret the Nakhi texts" (Rock 1965, xv). Elise Scharten (of whom Janert was most likely unaware, for Rock never wrote about her) interpreted a text, but she did so via a translation into vernacular Naxi from a local informant, for there is little evidence she could read the dongba script. She was fluent in colloquial Naxi, but not literate in the written ceremonial register.

The first task of any true Naxiologist, then, is to learn the language. This in itself would certainly also require a long training, but even knowledge of Naxi and the dongba script does not give us direct access to the ritual texts – they are always being read in translation. When read, the texts have to be translated ad-hoc from the semi-oral mode of ritual composition into an oral performance. The Naxi manuscripts' semi-oral nature (many scholars, following Rock, have labelled them "mnemonic" texts; see for example Michaud, Zhong and He [2017]), means that anyone wishing to really *read* these manuscripts must first be familiar with the oral traditions behind them, something which takes, at perhaps a conservative estimate, a decade of single-minded study with an inheritor of the oral tradition (the most learned of which have long since passed away), and in any case would still not equip one with the necessary training to memorise all of the ritual traditions in the Naxi corpus.

What is required, therefore, is the assistance of a dongba ritualist well versed in the oral traditions. Rock hired a number of such local informants (and he dedicated his Naxiological magnum opus, a two-volume compendium of translations of and bibliographic notes on Naxi manuscripts, the *Na-Khi Naga Cult and Related Ceremonies*, to these "Na-khi teachers"). This makes the translation of a Naxi text a time-consuming and expensive affair and precludes the existence of one true "translation", for each dongba will give an idiosyncratic reading dependent upon their own memory. To put it simply, translation in the Naxi dongba context is fraught with the indeterminacy of reading. It is highly improbable that a dongba will give the exact same performance of a book twice, and when the book is unfamiliar to them, i.e., from outside of their own oral inheritance, they will read it much less fluently, or perhaps distort the written text with the influence of their own memory.

Joseph Rock realised that the voluminous undertaking of translating the Naxi texts would take more than his lifetime, but he felt nevertheless that this was his mission, spurred in the belief that if he were not to translate these books, the knowledge contained within would be lost forever: "A very few years more and the Na-khi books will be undecipherable, and no matter how many and how complete dictionaries may be available they will remain closed books, no Rosetta stone would prove of value" (1952, 18). Rock's more pessimistic prognostications have not (yet) come to pass: the Naxi manuscripts are not, even in the twenty first century, closed books. At least when it comes to the more common manuscripts, we can still access readings, and we can get toward some semblance of "translation", as this book aims at showing. I hesitate to suggest, as Jackson's student at Edinburgh, Pan Anshi (1998), has done, that we can rely on Rock's work alone to perform translations of any Naxi book, for Rock did not translate all their literature as he had hoped, and in any case relying on Rock alone would mummify what is supposed to be a living oral tradition. We can, however, still find learned dongba in the Naxi areas, and by using the vast body of Naxiological scholarship left by Rock, Li Lin-ts'an and other Chinese and western scholars, we can come to a fuller understanding of the contents of these manuscripts.

Before we can do anything serious with these texts, such as exploring the Naxi religious beliefs or examining the philological practices of the dongba, we must understand the books, and this necessitates various layers of translation (from semi-oral ritual manuscript to spoken Naxi, from the literary language of the old books to the modern vernacular, and finally from Naxi to a more accessible language such as Chinese or English). While most of the manuscripts stored in the western world (in places such as the Library of Congress, the Harvard-Yenching Library and the John Rylands Library in Manchester) have lain dormant, unused and untranslated, a number of intrepid individuals have chosen to attempt translations since the late nineteenth century. It is the intent of this book to explore one particular manuscript and its previously forgotten translation in detail, at once contributing to the discipline of western Naxiology and attempting to highlight the contribution of the forgotten missionary translator Elise Scharten.

Elise Scharten, Naxi translator

Elise Scharten (1876-1965) was a pioneering Dutch missionary who has been almost completely omitted from the history of the Naxi people, and of translation studies as a whole.[9] This obscurity is remarkable, for Scharten was the first person to produce a complete translation of a Naxi ritual text (the focus of this book). Despite Rock's pre-eminence in Naxiological circles, it was Scharten who was the first to fully translate a Naxi ritual text, and her translation work fills a gap in the translation history of the Naxi manuscripts. Scharten was helping interested parties (notably the Scottish plant hunter George Forrest) to understand these unusual manuscripts from the early 1920s. In fact, we can see Scharten's work as the link between the early translation attempts of the late 19th century and the larger-scale translation projects that would follow. Scharten translated three Naxi ritual texts, in full or in part.[10] Two translations were sent to George Forrest, one of which has been identified in the John Rylands Library Naxi collection. I have previously said that the handwritten draft translation of Mo-So 6 at the John Rylands Library was one of these two translations (Poupard 2018), but upon further analysis it is unlikely to be the case. I thank Michael Friedrich for correcting this oversight (2023, 294). The third is a typescript translation, stored in the Rijksmuseum voor Volkenkunde, part of the Nationaal Museum van Wereldculturen in the Netherlands, and it is this translation that is particularly noteworthy, as it is a complete rendition of a central Naxi manuscript, and a translation conducted without the mediating influence of the Chinese language. These are

[9] For a more complete introduction to Elise Scharten as a Naxi-English and English-Naxi translator, see Poupard (2018), from which parts of this section have been adapted and updated.

[10] A tentative list of Scharten's extant translations is as follows (her Naxi-English translations are undated). Naxi-English: *The Book to Invite the Spirit*. Mo-So Manuscripts Collection, John Rylands Library, Manchester (a partial translation of a Naxi text that tells of the origin of a warrior god). *Manuscript Scharten*. Nationaal Museum van Wereldculturen, Leiden, RV-4175-26 (a translation of the Naxi creation myth). English-Naxi: *Na-hsi Mark*. (Shanghai, British & Foreign Bible Society, 1932). *Na-hsi Catechism*. (Shanghai, British & Foreign Bible Society, 1933). *Na-hsi Hymnbook*. (Shanghai, British & Foreign Bible Society, 1933).

important documents: many libraries and museums around the world have collections of Naxi manuscripts, but very few possess full translations of these books. Scharten spoke Naxi but would not have been literate in dongba writing, or familiar with the rituals, making a dongba informant a necessity for her translation process.[11]

Dutch scholar of Pentecostal history Cornelis van der Laan (2008) has written an authoritative account of Elise Scharten's life and missionary work, and I will only summarise a couple of main points here. Cecil Polhill, himself a missionary to China from 1885-1900, established the Pentecostal Missionary Union (PMU) on 9 January 1909. In 1911, the PMU began work in Kunming, Southwest China. Scharten, born in Amsterdam in 1876, was among the first few missionaries to be sent to the region, arriving with the second group in 1912 (Arie and Elsje Kok, also of Amsterdam, were the first, arriving in 1910). The Dutch missionaries had a calling for Tibet, but as Tibet was closed to foreign visitors, they were assigned to Lijiang. The PMU quickly established a church in Lijiang. Van der Laan wrote how Scharten seems to be among the first foreigners to become proficient in the Naxi language (van der Laan 2008, 351). Rock apparently became friends with Scharten sometime during this period, but she does not write of this friendship in her diaries. In September 1945, the political situation in China forced the missionaries to leave Lijiang.

Scharten's first recorded translation works were two draft translations of Naxi manuscripts for George Forrest (1873-1932). Upon his request, she sent him two original books alongside their abridged translations. These are perhaps the first direct translations into English of Naxi texts (there had previously been partial translations into French, by Charles Eudes Bonin [1896], Prince Henri d'Orleans [1898] and Jacques Bacot [1913]). Scharten writes in a letter dated 21 Nov 1922, "I hope you will be able to make out what the pictures in the book mean through the translation".[12] Translation seems to have been pleasant work for her, as she states, "Please, don't thank me any more for the work, for it has been quite a pleasure to me to do the same." Scharten then offers further assistance if required, "Perhaps you will find a moment to look up the Mo-su's books. Perhaps there is something which has to be explained. If so, gladly I will do so."[13] During the early 1920s, Scharten must have been one of, if not the only, westerner fluent in the Naxi language, but even so, these early translations seem to have been

[11] Yu Suisheng has published a letter written by the dongba He Huating and written in dongba script that mentions how Rock came to hire his services (Yu 2003, 271). Any assistance Scharten may have had has gone uncredited. Modern Chinese translations are usually attributed to a dongba who reads the performance, as well as the translator(s) responsible for the Chinese version.

[12] Letter from Scharten to Forrest dated 21 Nov 1922, Mo-So Manuscripts Collection, Acc. Book XI f.24, John Rylands Library, Manchester.

[13] Here Scharten refers to the Naxi by their earlier name, the Mosuo. Mosuo/Moso/Mo-so (Chinese 摩梭/麼些) are all names given to the Naxi before they were "officially named" as an ethnic group in China's nationwide ethnic group classification project that took place after 1949.

carried out via Chinese, that is, there was an intermediary stage of a translation relay, from Naxi, then to Chinese, then to English.

Perhaps Scharten's most overlooked contribution to Naxi studies is her full translation of the *Coqbbertv* manuscript – the Naxi creation myth that tells of how a heroic Naxi ancestor wed his heavenly bride. This is a central myth of the Naxi people, a story that has become an essential part of contemporary Naxi cultural identity.[14] The translation would have been completed with the assistance of a Naxi dongba, with Scharten translating from the oral explication. At ten A4 pages of typescript,[15] it is a 'full' translation of the written Naxi manuscript, and in fact the lengthiest translation of a Naxi text to have been completed up to that point.

The translation is a close match to the written graphs, suggesting that her Naxi informant was not performing and elaborating much upon the text, merely providing an interpretation of the writing on the page. This gives us an excellent opportunity to investigate the connection between the written and the "spoken" word when reading the Naxi manuscript – we can match Scharten's rendition with the graphs on the page, because the translation does not add much in the way of extra detail or context. The story itself contains the Naxi cosmogony and anthropogenesis, beginning with the creation of the earth and a flood that leaves only one survivor, the protagonist and Naxi culture hero, Coqssei-leel'ee, who embodies all that is best in men. The story then concerns how Coqssei-leel'ee came to find a celestial bride. The hero's name is romanised as "T'so-rze-le-hgeh" by Scharten, and 'T'so dze llü ghüh' by Rock, which shows an almost uncanny similarity in the use of consonant sounds (and is most likely a coincidence). The *Coqbbertv* is the single most-translated Naxi story, and it has been re-translated and re-interpreted in many Chinese publications, starting from 1946, with Li Lin-ts'an (only published in 1957), followed by Fu Maoji in 1948, and Zhou Rucheng in 1963. Chinese translation work picked up again in the 1980s with the coming of the era of reform and opening up, and there are many contemporary versions. Scharten's translation, however, was the first to be completed, and to this day no complete English translation of a single *Coqbbertv* manuscript tradition has been published.

14 Emily Chao notes that the *Coqbbertv* (or the variant name, *Coqbbersa*, that she uses) has become "one of the most important, if not *the* most important" dongba texts (2012, 82), used to represent the entirety of Naxi culture and history. Despite this present-day cultural cachet, knowledge of the myth was not widespread among lay Naxi in 1990s Lijiang (*ibid.*, 83). It must have nevertheless been highly valued by Scharten's Naxi informants in the early 1930s, however, as this is the only manuscript selected for a full translation. Chao connects the privileging of the origin myth with the creation of an essentialized "dongba culture" during the late twentieth century, and efforts to solidify a homogenous "Naxi" ethnicity.

15 A letter from a Pentecostal missionary in Lijiang and published in the missionary newsletter, *Confidence*, mentions Scharten's typewriter, which was evidently a source of fascination to the Naxi locals at the time. "It is amusing to learn some of their ideas of England. Miss Scharten has a typewriter which the teacher really thought was an English printing press. But when I told him they could print the book he held in England in about five minutes he was more than surprised, and would hardly believe it" (Andrews 1923, 88). This helps us to surmise that Scharten's translations were indeed carried out at her home in Lijiang.

The original source Naxi manuscript used by Scharten likely dates back to the late-nineteenth to early-twentieth century, and bears some similarity to a manuscript translated by Li Lin-ts'an in 1946. It was probably written by a Lijiang dongba, as some of the graphs on the early pages are coloured, generally known to be a Lijiang affectation, and at certain points in the text, syllabic graphs are used instead of dongba logographs (the syllabic "geba" graphs are primarily seen in Lijiang and its environs). The unpublished draft translation is not dated, but we can ascertain that the translation was completed in Lijiang between 1924 and 1934, before Scharten travelled back to the Netherlands on furlough. The reasons for this are twofold: firstly, it follows the early, more concise translation attempts of separate manuscripts that were sent to George Forrest, translations that do not reveal any prowess at spoken Naxi. Secondly, it was given to the museum alongside fifteen Naxi ritual texts in 1936. Coincidentally, Rock published his own summary translation of the Naxi creation myth in 1935, suggesting that work on translating this important Naxi religious text was carried out almost concurrently by both Rock and Scharten. Rock's early translation is more of an overarching explanation of the text and its underlying traditions, while Scharten's is a more straightforward translation of one particular manuscript – notable for its completeness, as earlier Naxi translations were only partial.

Her work on the *Coqbbertv* makes her the starting point of a translating lineage that extends to the present day, but Scharten's pioneering work has, for almost a century, found no audience. Nevertheless, Scharten was, pre-1949, the longest-residing western resident of Lijiang, and the first dedicated translator both into and out of Naxi from English. She was by all accounts a hard-working and kind missionary, but she was also a pioneer of Naxi studies and missionary translation, a field at the time almost completely dominated by men. This book is an attempt at reclaiming something of that lost audience: by publishing her draft translation of the *Coqbbertv*, no doubt her crowning achievement in Naxi-English translation, alongside a presentation of the original manuscript, with a full exegesis and updated translation, we can carry this manuscript tradition into dialogue with the present. The Naxi ritual texts are a treasure trove of myths and legends accumulated over centuries, told and re-told in each performance, and translations like the one presented herein are part of an intertextual retelling that allows the tradition to survive and be rediscovered in a new time and place.

The translation method

The translation presented in this book owes most to the detailed ethnographic translations of Joseph Rock. After some early, piecemeal attempts at translating the Naxi ritual texts during the late nineteenth and early twentieth centuries, Naxi scholarship as we know it began in earnest with Rock, who spent many years between 1922-1949 in southwest China, either in the provincial capital of Kunming, or holed up at the foot of the Jade Dragon snow range. He eventually published full translations of several Naxi ritual traditions, alongside a plethora of other anthropological and bibliographical works. His published translations first appeared in 1935, with the retelling of the story of the flood. Prior to this, however, Elise Scharten had already finished a complete translation of the same Naxi story, a version that can be read alongside the source manuscript that she collected while working as a missionary in Lijiang. Despite hers being the first cover-to-cover translation of a ritual manuscript, Scharten never published her work. This book revisits Scharten's translation, adopting some of the translation methodology that Rock later created, finally putting these two Naxiologists in conversation with one another.

While Rock's first published translations were no more than concise summaries of the stories he discovered within the Naxi manuscripts, he later developed a more extensive, anthropological style of translation. This meant recording in exacting detail the phonetic reading given by a dongba and then embarking upon a full written commentary. The first translation to use this method was published in 1937 as *The birth and origin of Dto-mba Shilo, the founder of Mo-so shamanism, according to Mo-so manuscripts*, a seminal work on Dobbaq-sheel'lo, the mythical founding father of the dongba religion. Just two years later he published the monograph-length *Romance of Ka-ma-gyu-mu-gki: a Na-khi tribal love story translated from Na-khi pictographic manuscripts*, which he believed to be the most lyrical and beautiful of the stories contained within the Naxi books. In 1948 he published a translation of the most important Naxi ceremony, the sacrifice to heaven. After he was compelled against his will to leave China in 1949 because of the changing political situation, he continued with his Naxiological endeavours. He worked on multi-volume works such as the *Na-khi-English Encyclopaedic Dictionary* in two volumes, and the *Na-khi Naga Cult and Related Ceremonies*, also in two volumes. Since Rock's time, Chinese translations of Naxi texts have flourished, but western Naxiology floundered, and while we have seen several translations and attempts at engaging with this corpus of texts, there have been no studies that engage fully with the source manuscripts.

This is to be expected, for Rock's method of translation (as discussed in Rock 2002, 186) was a laborious one. He presented the texts in a number of additive layers: the original text (via a line drawing), followed by a transcription into a romanisation system of his own devising (inclusive of tone marks), then translation (sometimes split between a word-for-word and a literal translation) and finally an explanation of the text, syntax and detailed exegesis of the graphs themselves. This was, in effect, a "five-way" translation that produced worthwhile results. Under this method, the text undergoes a series of movements, or translations: from the original to the transcription, then written translation, before arriving at a full explanation. This meant that Rock's translations allowed for unparalleled access to the world of the Naxi literature, but only if the reader could stomach all those annotations and comments. In Rock's time, producing translations and getting them printed was an exceedingly costly business, most notably as he liked to present the manuscript he was translating in line illustrations to accompany the exegesis. Rock says he drew these images "in Chinese ink on stiff paper, uniform size" (Rock 2002, 197); they were then reproduced on zinc plates and the images were printed simultaneously with the text.

The layers of translation had to be carefully prepared. Rock would work with his informant, who for many years was dongba He Huating. The young dongba would first copy out each page of a manuscript in his own delicate calligraphy. He would then perform a reading for Rock, who jotted this down in a system of transcription that he had himself invented. The next stage was a translation from the ritual language to the vernacular. This was then translated into Chinese, and Rock then produced the final version in English, alongside detailed notes on the graphs themselves (see Mueggler 2011, 273-274). This elucidation makes the method even clearer: we go from copies of the original to a phonetic transcription, to a colloquial Naxi reading, to a translation into Chinese, only then into English. The crucial final component was the philological analysis, a "double-backing" that serves as the real code to understanding the graphs.

In this book I take cues from Rock's method, providing first a digital recreation of each individual panel of the manuscript, labelling the graphs in the order in which they are read, as they are often read out of the traditional left-to-right order. I then provide a key to the pronunciation of the graphs in Naxi pinyin and a phonetic reading of the panel itself,[16] followed by several "translations": a word-for-word translation, Elise Scharten's original translation, a new, modern rendition of my own, and exegetical notes that bring in wider scholarship on the Naxi or explain the reading process. Rock reproduced each page at a time and dealt with the panels one by one in a following explanation, but this method involved a lot of aforementioned "double-backing", of moving from exegesis back to the line drawing and then forwards again, often across multiple pages. I attempt to solve this inconvenience by showing each panel in the Naxi script (the panels of a manuscript are separated by vertical lines, and frequently indicate a discrete intonation unit, or story episode composed of several such units) and providing an individual analysis before moving on to a recreation of the following panel in the same manner. This admittedly turns reading the translation into a gruelling task, but one which hopefully highlights the textuality of the manuscript in greater detail.

[16] It should be stressed here that the reading is based upon a modern interpretation by a contemporary dongba, in conjunction with the phonetic readings separately recorded by Li Lin-ts'an and He Yuncai. The phonetic readings presented in this book are by no means definitive, and simply provide guidelines for *one possible* oral performance. I use Naxi pinyin instead of IPA firstly for the practical reason that He Guisheng, the dongba who provided a reading of this text, and He Lingyu, my Naxi language informant in Lijiang, themselves both use this system. Secondly, and more importantly, it allows the reader to look up the Naxi words in various contemporary dictionaries and reference works, all of which are arranged alphabetically according to Naxi pinyin. By far the most useful reference work is the *Naqxi neif Habaq shelzoteeq* [Naxi-Chinese dictionary] by He Xueguang 和学光, in six volumes, published by the Naxi culture promotion committee in Lijiang in 2013. A more readily-accessible resource is Thomas Pinson's 2012 dictionary.

Because no such work can conceivably be completed by someone from outside the Naxi tradition, I am indebted to dongba He Guisheng 和桂生 of Ludian township (鲁甸乡) in Lijiang for his patient reading and exegesis which has been crucial to the new translation presented in this book, as well as his student He Lingyu, who performed valuable work on the ground, recording and transcribing the dongba's readings. He Guisheng has been taking dongba disciples since 2004, and has established a centre for the inheritance and transmission of dongba culture in his native village. It should be noted that He's readings often diverge from the writing on the page itself, as the dongba are wont to perform a recital in line with the books from their own oral tradition that they have already committed to memory. The manuscript being translated is a historical one, and its provenance is unknown, but any significantly divergent readings are highlighted in the notes. As an example, when reading page two of the manuscript, which describes the genesis of the great god Iggvq-ogeq (Naxi: ), He Guisheng briefly recounts the origin of Iggvq-dinal (Naxi: ), a malevolent deity who is the dualistic counterpart of the benevolent god Iggvq-ogeq, despite the name Iggvq-dinal or the deity's origin *not* being recorded in the written text. He Guisheng adds two intonation units totalling some twenty-seven syllables to the reading. Iggvq-dinal is completely absent from Scharten's original translation, just as it is absent from the written manuscript. The transcription and translation presented herein are informed by He Guisheng's contemporary reading, but this is only one source among many: the readings of He Guisheng are taken into consideration alongside published translations of similar manuscript traditions. Rock published two different translations of this origin myth: the first, appearing in 1935, is a short summary that appeared in a scholarly journal. The second is another summary that appeared in his 1952 *Na-Khi Naga Cult* (675-688), but that does share some DNA with the Scharten manuscript, for it is also related to the *chelggvq* purification rite. The version by Taiwanese scholar and prominent early Naxiologist Li Lin-ts'an is a classic "four-way translation" (the "four ways" are the original manuscript, IPA notation, direct translation, free translation) carried out with the assistance of a young dongba, He Cai. This translation has proven to be a valuable reference, although many of He Cai's readings appear to be at odds with the written manuscript Li presented. The reading by He Yuncai, recorded in IPA transcription and translated into Chinese by He Fayuan (see YSMGZCGB 1986) as part of a Chinese minority literature translation project that would eventually result in the publication of a one-hundred-volume "complete" collection of translations, has also been consulted (alongside the English translation by Charles McKhann in his 1992 PhD thesis, which draws from this rendition, as well as Rock's translations). Finally, another contemporary translation can be found in volume 39 of the *Annotated Collection of Naxi Dongba Manuscripts* (Kunming, Yunnan renmin chubanshe, 1999). Other translations exist, but those not consulted are primarily "literary" re-imaginings that have little to do with the original manuscripts.

I have combined these sometimes divergent readings with my own textual research to reconstruct a simulacrum of the reading that engendered Scharten's translation.[17] The key element that makes Rock's translations stand apart is their intertextuality. He was aware that the books did not stand in isolation; he knew that each manuscript was a tributary of a particular tradition. While Rock's intertextuality dealt with numerous manuscript sources, the translation in this book is an intertextual rendition taking into account the *translations* of similar manuscript traditions. Thus armed with the work that has been completed over the second half of the twentieth century, we can revisit Scharten's early translation.

Scharten's translation is perhaps overly concise, in that it offers the reader no context for what is transpiring beyond the pages which are populated by very few written words. Her translation sticks very closely to the words written on the page, mostly ignoring potentially elaborate readings. It is also written in often questionable English, which has been preserved in the transcription, with some very minor spacing edits. To complicate matters further, she could not actually read the dongba script. But we can be sure that she *did* know fluent Naxi, and further, she was able to secure the services of a dongba to perform a reading of the manuscript for her. This oral recitation was the real "source text" of her translation. By working backwards (i.e., utilising the process of "back translation") combined with an analysis of the graphs on the page, we can make some approximations as to what that reading might have been, and "resurrect" this early performance of an old manuscript.

As a simple example, early in the manuscript the story of a heavenly chicken is related. This chicken lays eggs that hatch into a pantheon of deities and ritual practitioners. At first, this chicken is unable to fly up high into the heavens (see panel 2-10). Only in Scharten's translation do we read about the chicken's feathers falling across the earth: in other versions (including the contemporary reading of this manuscript), feathers are not mentioned, despite the textual clues pointing to falling feathers on the page itself. It can be said, therefore, that Scharten's translation offers the reader valuable glimpses into an early performance of the Naxi origin myth as it pertains to a particular ceremonial tradition (the purification rite), made prior to any of the published translations available today.

[17] As such, and this should be emphasised, all mistakes that appear within these pages are entirely my own.

Why another translation?

If we already have English translations of the Naxi origin myth, then why, the reader may rightly ask, do we need another one? Beyond T.S. Eliot's oft-repeated maxim that "each generation must translate for itself", there are a number of more practical reasons. No translation of the *Coqbbertv* in English has connected the story to the actual ritual at hand. This translation showcases the Naxi origin myth as it relates in particular to the *chelggvq* (purification) ceremony. Rock's translation in the *Na-Khi Naga Cult* covers only twelve pages, and is merely a summary of the story, while McKhann's translation comes primarily from a manuscript that belongs to the "sacrifice to the wind" ceremonial tradition, and as such the final pages refer specifically to the expelling of various malicious spiritual presences. As Rock says, "There are only few ceremonies during which Ts'o mběr t'u [Coqbbertv] is not chanted, but as already remarked each ceremony has its own particular Tso'o mběr t'u, the main facts of the story remain however unchanged" (1935, 65). Although the main story beats remain the same, what does change is the ritual setting. Jackson noted that the origin myth plays a pivotal role in the ritual structure of the Naxi because it is "used as a charter: the ending is simply adjusted to ratify the particular rites that are to be performed" (Jackson 1975, 212). Scharten's *Coqbbertv* manuscript is a distinct retelling that includes an emphasis on the details of the *chelggvq* purification rite. The last page of the manuscript describes a prototypical performance of such a ceremony, including the ritual altar and paraphernalia, and even the animals used for a ritual sacrifice, which include a chicken, a duck, and the centrepiece, a black goat. Further, in Scharten's translation the dongba Chelshul-jiqbber  (Scharten romanises this name as "T'she-su-chi-mbehr") appears for the first time in English. This legendary dongba is summoned specifically during the purification ceremony and is depicted as a robed figure with the head of a yak (a phonetic for the final syllable in his name, *bber*).

Further, and most importantly, no translation of the *Coqbbertv* in English has ever attempted a detailed graph-by-graph analysis. Rock's translations are both summaries, and McKhann's is a translation based upon other translations and with no single manuscript source in particular. The real key to understanding the Naxi texts, as Rock's most successful translations show, is to allow the reader to navigate that fine line between orality and literacy that they represent, and this requires an in-depth explication of the graphs that appear on the manuscript pages, alongside the words that a dongba chants when reading them, and an explanation of how the oral and the written interact (including, perhaps, a discussion of what is written and what is not written, what is read and what is not read, and a philological examination of the manuscript text). It is for this reason that I invite the reader to use the translation as a guide with which to navigate the mostly uncharted realm of the Naxi scriptworld.

What to watch out for when reading

There is an organic fluidity to Naxi dongba writing that is born from being unrestrained by orthographic rules. Entire phrases can be left out, summoned back into the manuscript by the power of memory alone. The dongba do not have to make sure that each graph is the "right" size. No schoolmasters are present to scold a dongba who writes a graph too ebulliently, the ink crossing over a dividing line marker. There are no barriers between the words or sentences – or perhaps more accurately we can say that the barriers are pushed back, to form rectangular spaces of irregular length but more or less fixed height, and the words can appear at differing sizes anywhere within this 2D space, creating loose, cartouche-like episodes in which the words, the "characters", are free to interact with one another in different ways within said space. Here, then, we have free range words, not the battery-farmed rigidity of alphabetic or morphosyllabic composition. Given this lack of rules, and a general refusal of the dongba to standardise (e.g. which graphs to use as phonetic borrowings), the uniformity in how the texts are composed is still quite remarkable. It has been possible to recreate the entire Coqbbertv manuscript using standardised digitised graphs, with only a handful of exceptions. The basic graphic inventory of the digital recreation is based on the Naxi script input method editor, Edongba, which uses a font based upon the graphs contained within Fang Guoyu's 1981 dictionary. To recreate graphs that do not appear in this input editor, I have used Li Lin-ts'an's 2001 dictionary (a reprint of an earlier 1972 edition). Thus, all the graphs in the recreated manuscript have their provenance in these two dictionaries, none have been drawn from "scratch". The digital recreation is meant to mirror the original manuscript, but not to be an exact copy. Some graphs have been edited slightly in terms of size and position, but, when consulting the original manuscript, it should still be readily apparent which graphs are which in the digital recreation.[18]

Reading each panel is akin to solving an intricate philological jigsaw puzzle. Working out how the graphs connect with each other, and with the oral performance, is the key to solving this puzzle. On the most basic level, the Naxi manuscripts are read left to right, panel to panel; sometimes panels continue on subsequent lines or pages. For some very brief panels (usually four graphs or less), I have combined two panels into one individual analysis.

The phonetic readings provided herein, alongside the word-for-word translations, are intended to be a *rough guide only*. The phonetics do not recreate a full oral performance of the text, but a reconstruction of a single possible reading, with an emphasis first and foremost on the written manuscript. The idea is to try to connect potential readings with both the original translation and the graphs on the manuscript page. To do this, each graph has been numbered. This allows the reader to quickly identify what each graph represents, because

[18] The possibilities of using digital technology to study the Naxi dongba script haven been explored in an article by Xu Duoduo (2023).

each panel has its own key to the graphs contained within, and to follow the reading, because the graphs that appear on the page are highlighted in bold in the phonetic reconstruction.

Figure 3. Top: The sacred mountain is constructed, Collection Nationaal Museum van Wereldculturen. Coll.no. RV-4175-26, detail.
Bottom: Digital recreation of the same panel (panel 7-4).

Consider the panel in Figure 3 (top) which shows the construction of the Naxi sacred mountain. Contrast with the digital recreation (bottom, panel 7-4 in the translation). Here the mountain and the materials used to build it emerge before our very eyes: the first graph to be read appears in the middle-right of this panel: the sacred mountain itself (labelled "1"), with its stepped base and angular faces. The reader may then consult graph number 1 in the graph-by-graph analysis and learn that it is read "Jjiuqnal-sheel'lo", the name of the sacred mountain.

The transcription reveals that this five-syllable name accounts for the first intonation unit of this panel. We then move to the left to read the next two graphs (silver and gold), followed by graph 4, a ploughshare that indicates via the rebus principle the verb "to build". We then jump beyond the mountain to the final two graphs (turquoise and carnelian). The numbers represent *as accurately as possible* the intended reading order of the oral performance, but it must be borne in mind that sometimes words are repeated several times and only written once. In this case, the verb "to build" appears in two intonation units, attached to each pair of materials, but is only written once. This method of numbering the graphs has some precedent: A single panel of a manuscript was presented in this way in Tatsuo Nishida's introduction to the Naxi and their script (2001, 105), but that was merely used for illustrative purposes. To aid the reader decipher the manuscript reproduced within this book, the idea of numbering the graphs has been taken to its natural conclusion – every single graph that appears in the manuscript is labelled, even obscure ones without definitive readings.

Basic character classification

Assuming that the Naxi "pictographs" are all pictures of things is a common misconception. In fact, scholars usually borrow the first five categories from Xu Shen's 许慎 ancient classification method for Chinese writing, the *liu shu* 六书 "six writings", to classify dongba graphs. Bear in mind, however, that these categories are all more fluid in dongba script than they are in Chinese.

i) Simple pictographs

Many graphs are simple visual depictions of what they are intended to denote. A common example is *xi*, person, a stick figure with arms and legs. Contrast this with the more abstract Chinese graph for person, *ren* 人, a somewhat more unfortunate stick figure with only its legs remaining, but that is still classified as a pictograph. Some pictographs can be drawn with such simplicity they almost seem to lose their pictographic nature, while others can be elaborate artistic depictions. Many pictographs are written in exacting detail when important events are depicted. In panel 32-2, we see the bundle of green branches being burned on a fire, smoking out (*shul*) the demons of impurity (*chel*). Immediately following this, there is a striking depiction of a goat, head and tail raised, tied to a wooden peg, awaiting sacrifice. This is the most important offering to the gods and is therefore drawn in full.

Figure 4. The ritual scene: burning the branches (left), the sacrificial goat tied to the peg (right). Collection Nationaal Museum van Wereldculturen. Coll.no. RV-4175-26, detail.

From the final page of the manuscript, and again on the back cover (albeit somewhat more indistinctly drawn), we can see a leopard, depicted in full, after the manuscript proper has finished. These two depictions are no longer occupying space within any particular panel, but are instead roaming free across the page.

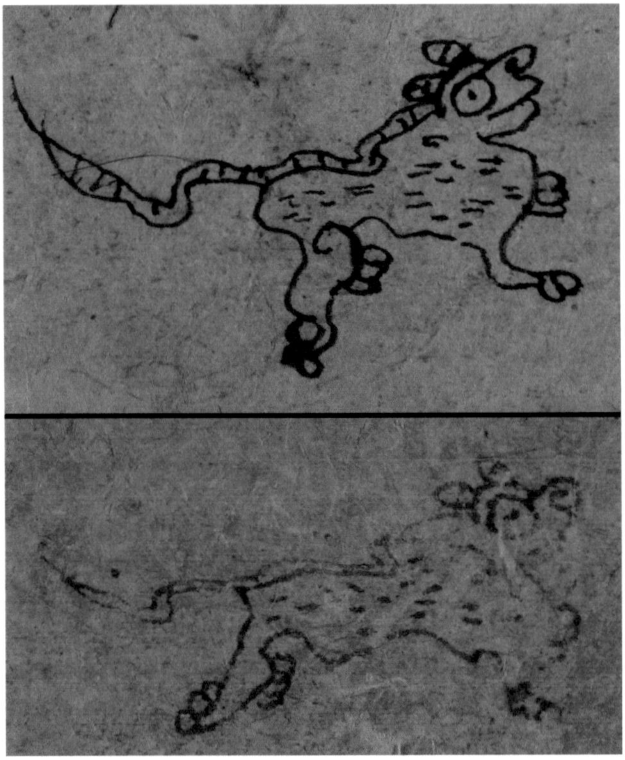

Figure 5. Leaping leopards.
Collection Nationaal Museum van Wereldculturen.
Coll.no. RV-4175-26, detail.

The leopard, *rhee*, is also a pictograph (identified by its distinctive spots and long tail), although in a manuscript proper it would likely be depicted with only its head, a conventional shorthand for writing animals: . I have encountered two related possibilities for the purpose of this final leopard. Both agree that it is a marker of the ceremony at hand, *chel ggvq*. According to He Guisheng, impurities are often termed *chel neiq rhee*, "the unclean and impure", meaning that the leopard indicates the impurity to be expelled in the ceremony. Li Lin-ts'an suggests a different possibility, indicating that *rheeq*  (read with the falling tone), a leopard's head and a stick, can be used to mean "beat", as in "beat or expel ghosts", and the graph is used in purification rites (2001, 149). In both cases the leopard signifies impurity, although in the latter it is explicitly connected with the *removal* of impurity. What at first looks like a simple pictographic, decorative depiction, then, takes on a deeper symbolic meaning. In some sense the leopard becomes a shorthand for the purification ceremony as a whole, and a clear marker to any dongba of the contents of this book. It might already be clear, then, that the term "simple pictographs" is a bit of a misnomer, for they are anything but.

ii) Simple ideographs

The simple ideographs are not pictographs, because they are not direct representations of a thing (i.e. a loom or a pig), but rather abstract symbols that represent an *idea*. Take for example the graph *shuaq* , "high", its meaning indicated by two horizontal lines marking a high point atop a vertical line.

iii) Compound ideograms

Some graphs are combinations of two independent elements, fused together into a new compound. The principle is similar to how in Chinese person + tree can become *xiu* 休, rest (a person resting against a tree), only in Naxi this principle is much more freeform. Some of these compounds are highly conventional. "Tea" is a tealeaf inside a cup, *leil* a combination of the two graphs. To drink tea, *leil teeq* , is a person drinking a tea leaf inside a cup, combining three graphs ideographically. Compound ideograms may also contain phonetic elements: snow tea, *goq leil* (lit. "alpine meadow tea"), is a tealeaf atop an alpine meadow, but there is a needle (*goq*) inside the meadow, its presence indicating the pronunciation of meadow "*goq*" .[19]

It is also possible for a dongba to simply invent new compounds by combining graphs that would originally be written separately. Take *haisheeq meeltv* , a gold walking stick, which is depicted by a pictograph of a walking stick, with the graph for "gold", *hai*, superimposed on top of it (panel 11-6): thus we know instantly that the walking stick is made out of gold. Ordinarily this could be written with the two characters in adjacent positions. Similarly, the "red cow" in panel 30-3 is a cow's head with the graph for red, *hiuq* (depicting roaring flames) written inside the beast's neck: . These are by no means standardized combinations, but they are nevertheless instantly recognizable as compound ideograms. These compounds can be much more involved: not just the combination of two graphs, but whole dioramas can become compound graphs in their own right, a chicken lays atop a nest of eggs, figures move into houses, husband and wife talk with one another face-to-face, speech lines emerging from their mouths and meeting in the middle. The graphs become animated within the world of the text. Some scholars have attempted to differentiate between certain kinds of compound (usually in terms of how conventional they are), but I find this to be an exercise in futility; the imposition of a taxonomic framework upon a writing that fundamentally resists it. The joy of reading the dongba script – if you can get past the frustration commensurate with non-linear writing – is knowing that there are no real boundaries between words. The writing, just like the readings it engenders, is always in a state of flux.

[19] Snow tea (Chinese *xuecha* 雪茶) is an herbal tea made from *Thamnolia vermicularis*, a white worm lichen found in Yunnan, mostly at an altitude of around 4,000 metres.

iv) Phono-semantic compounds

Phono-semantic compounds, graphs that combine phonetic and semantic information, are extremely common. *Aiq* , a cliff, is a depiction of a cliff with a chicken poking its beak in from the bottom corner. This is not to say that chickens live in the cliffs; the chicken's head tells us that the graph is read *aiq*, because chicken in Naxi is *aiq*. The fluidity of the script however means that any dongba can invent their own such compounds, adding phonetic markers to simple pictographs that already have formulaic pronunciations. Take the cat depicted in panel 28-7, for example. Normally the cat's head is read *halleiq* , with two syllables, but in this manuscript a phonetic marker has been added, the upturned moon, read *hal* and originally meaning "night" . Together with the cat's head, it becomes a phonetic marker for the first syllable of *halleiq*, and the two graphs (originally pictographs) together become a "new" phono-semantic compound.

v) Rebus (phonetic loan) characters

As mentioned at the beginning of this book, one of the greatest difficulties encountered when reading the dongba script is the fact that it is not strictly pictographic. There is a preponderance of phonetic loan graphs: graphs that are not used for their semantic value, but are instead used only for their phonetic value. One of the most common is *tvq*, originally a trough, bucket, or container. This graph is hardly ever used for its literal, pictographic meaning. Most of the time it instead indicates an emergence, or an arrival, and is read in the level tone, *tv* (indeed, it is used in the title of the *Coqbbertv* to mean "origin").

Figure 6. Arriving home.
Collection Nationaal Museum van Wereldculturen.
Coll.no. RV-4175-26, detail.

In Figure 6, the "bucket" graph appears at the bottom of a house, indicating an arrival home. The other two graphs are also rebuses: *ye* (tobacco) and *goq* (a needle), used to represent *yegoq*, "home". Because these phonetic loans are so common, context is crucial. Take the following two graphs: 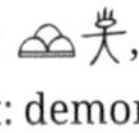, read *lvceeq*, these are literally "rock demons", which means what you might expect: demons that have dominion over the rocks. This is the literal reading.

However, when read *lvceel* (reading the second syllable with a high tone instead of a falling tone), the two graphs mean instead "gravestone". The correct interpretation of the graphs is governed entirely by context.

The geba syllabic graphs

Even armed with all this information, there is still the need to approach the text cautiously. The reader should first make themselves aware of certain unique characteristics of the Naxi dongba script. At a basic level, it's important to know the context of the story when trying to read a manuscript written in the traditional ceremonial register, and even single graphs in isolation can be a minefield of varying readings. What look like simple pictures of things could mean something else entirely. This is compounded by the two different systems of writing at play: logograms and syllabograms. Consider this dongba graph: , read "*ceiq*". It is used as a numeral in logographic dongba script and (normally) means "ten". But add a small dot to the m and we get , a geba syllabic graph that simply stands for the syllable "*la*", and is most commonly used phonetically in proper names or as the grammatical particle *la*, indicating "also". But you don't even need to add a dot for there to be confusion: there is a geba graph that looks *almost exactly the same* as *ceiq* above: , read not "*la*" but "*ai*". And even if you think  means "ten", then you'll be saddened to hear that it's used interchangeably with another graph, , read *xi* (the graphic form derived from Chinese *shi* 十, ten), which means one hundred, and the two are frequently used idiosyncratically for both ten *and* one hundred. Understanding of the graphs therefore is dependent upon having knowledge of the context surrounding the graph – if you don't know the context, it becomes mostly guesswork.

The geba phonetic graphs are generally considered to be later inventions (although Rock argued that they antedated the dongba graphs). They are rarely found in manuscripts that are from the heartlands of Naxi dongba culture to the north and northeast of Lijiang, along the historic migratory route traversed by the Naxi ancestors. In this manuscript, the geba graphs often appear as later additions, see for example panel 27-4, where a deity's name is added in geba around the other graphs that were probably written earlier.

Sometimes a geba graph is used in place of a dongba graph that had been used earlier on in the text. As an example, in panel 25-8 there is the dongba graph for tower, *tal* , used as a phonetic loan for *tal*, to be able. This is a very common phonetic loan. In a later panel (26-1), the same word is not represented by the tower, but by a geba syllabic graph that is read *ta* , and the reader has to supply the high tone (*tal*) as geba graphs do not indicate tone. From this example we can see that the dongba graphs might make for better phonetic loans, because it is possible to choose a homonym with a matching tone. But it isn't always so easy; sometime graphs that are not exact homonyms – near or even not-so-near homonyms – are used. This may involve some guesswork when it comes to reading the text, and I have labelled such graphs with a question mark in parentheses where they appear in the text. See for example panel 25-7, where the graph *no* , down or soft feathers, is perhaps used phonetically for the preposition *nieq,* "in".

Semantic vs phonetic readings

A related issue is found in instances where graphs are read literally in one panel and then phonetically in the next, or even within the same panel. Take panel 5-3, where the graph for rain, *heeq* , appears twice. The first time it is actually not read *heeq*, but *ruq*, summer – this means that it is used semantically, not phonetically, because summer is the rainy season in Lijiang. To complicate things further, the second time is appears in the same panel, it *is* read *heeq*, as rain – "in summer, the rains..."

Also, for purposes of diversifying what can be a repetitive ceremonial register, sometimes different phonetic loan graphs are used to represent the same word: a shoulder blade  and a ghost with hair sticking on end , are both used as phonetic borrowings for the past tense of the verb, "to come" (see panel 25-10). Graphs can also be read semantically. In panel 6-4, the graph *bberq*, yak is used to denote not the yak itself, but simply the head. This is because most animal graphs are written using only the head as a form of pictographic shorthand, the rest of the animal is present but not written. However, if the head is meant, then the same graph can simply be read semantically as *gv*, "head" and the animal to which the head belongs is obvious, but not actually read out.

Written, but not read

I have already discussed the issue of the "gaps" left in the written text; the feature that marks the manuscripts as semi-oral. But there is a related issue to this: alongside graphs that are not visibly written but that should still be read, we have graphs that are written and that are not read.

In panel 10-4 the brothers pair up with their sisters and have intercourse, which generates impurity (see Figure 7). In the manuscript we see an ideographic compound comprised of *jjiq*, house, *ddeiq*, to have sexual intercourse (two figures copulating inside the house), and *chel*, unclean (a vapour over their heads). The reading only references the incestuous intercourse via euphemism, both the house (*jjiq*) and the impurity (*chel*) are not read out. Fu Maoji (1982) notes how common an occurrence this is in "picture writing" and suggests that picture writing should be distinguished from "pictographic writing", the latter being a more advanced stage of development where one graph represents one syllable. Fu is here referring to morpho-syllabic writing; "picture writing" must, by its definition alone, be pictographic. Further, I argue that Naxi dongba script can be both at once syllabic and ideographic.

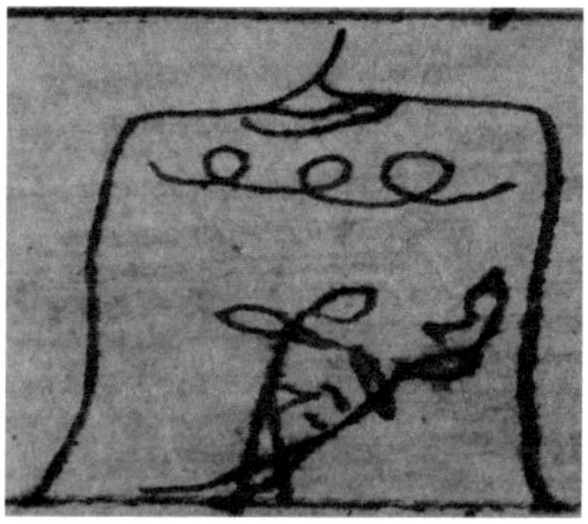

Figure 7. Incestuous relationships engendering impurity. Collection Nationaal Museum van Wereldculturen. Coll.no. RV-4175-26, detail.

Sometimes figures appear in the manuscript either as interlocutors, as people being spoken to, or as people being referred to in the third person, but they are not mentioned in the oral performance. Nevertheless, they are still "present" in the story, and on the page, whether the words are read or not. The "actors" move through the pages as if they have a life of their own. Mueggler (2022, 3) has written of a similar understanding when it comes to the Nuosu writing: "When abstracted from the glottographic function of the script, these forms could appear as discrete but mutating things, or *bodies*, which can be seen moving through any page." There is therefore a constant tension between the shadow and light, what can be seen and what cannot be seen, what can be read but is not read. What one does see is bound inextricably to what one does not. From a linear perspective of reading, ambiguity is rampant. In this sense we must be able to divorce the graphs from the spoken reading, with the caveat that this separation is only partial: the graphs are not always part of the oral recitation, but they are always part of the story-world that the text has created, they exist on the pages as a presence whether they are specifically mentioned or not.

The *chelggvq* purification ceremony

The manuscript contained within this book belongs to an ancient Naxi ceremonial tradition: *chelnaggvq*, the ceremony for the purification of a place or a house. To put the performance of the manuscript in its proper context, it is perhaps worthwhile to say something about this purification rite and how it is performed. Before a large-scale ceremony such as the *svqggvq* (propitiating the nature spirits) is conducted, the site of the ceremony is cleansed of impurity, or "*chel*". "*Chel*" can mean a physical impurity, such as faeces or household waste, but it can also indicate spiritual impurity, such as immorality and evil.

To rid the household or ceremonial ground of this impurity, the demons of impurity, *chelceeq* , have to first be invited (the figure to the left is a ghost or demon, *ceeq*, a person with their hair standing on end, holding a lump of impurity, read *chel*: this has been suggested variously to be a depiction of a foetus, or swirling vapour, or even an intestinal tract). The demons are then propitiated and finally driven away; only then will the spirits attend the main ceremony. The purification ceremony is itself a large affair and many manuscripts are performed (a total of 51 manuscripts is suggested in Xi and Zhao [2009], making undoubtedly for a rather gruelling undertaking), but the number depends on how many books the officiating dongba possesses.

According to Joseph Rock, the first thing prepared in the ceremony is an improvised chapel, usually located in the centre room of the house. Other sources suggest that the entire ceremony be conducted in a flat, open field (Xi and Zhao 2009, 299). In the chapel, three painted scrolls are hung behind an altar: Dobbaq-sheel'lo, the archetypal ritual practitioner and founding father of the Naxi religion goes in the centre, to the left is a deity known as "Zotv-ggesserq Yemaq", who controls the *chel* demons and the *chelnaqggvq* ceremony. To the right of the altar, an image of "Tvchee Yemaq" is placed.

Figure 8. "Zotv-ggesserq Yemaq"

The Yemaq are protective spirits of a martial proclivity: their purpose is to fight demons. They are analogous in many respects to the Tibetan *wer-ma* བྱེར་མ་, a class of minor deities in the Bon religion, sometimes translated as "warrior spirits". Of Zotv-ggesserq, we know that his body is covered in flames, and that he lives at the border between the white land of the gods and the black land of the demons (Rock 1952, 138-139). Rock goes into quite some detail on his provenance, but suffice to say, once he appears, "the demons vanish like snow on a lake".

Figure 9. "Tvchee Yemaq".

Tvchee Yemaq is the first of all the Yemaq. His body is white, and he is dressed in tiger's skin from the waist down. He holds in his hands a trident and a sword (Rock 1952, 136-7). Tvchee Yemaq is depicted in the Tibetan style in an early work of Naxiology by Tibetologist Jacques Bacot (1913, plate XIV). Note how the Yemaq are depicted in dongba script in Figures 8 and 9: first, on the left-hand side, the names of both these Yemaq deities are written phonetically with rebuses. Just as Jean-François Champollion discovered – by deciphering the name "Ramses" – that Egyptian names could be written phonetically in hieroglyphs, so it goes for the names in dongba "pictographs". These phonetic graphs are complemented on the right-hand side by a much more visual depiction, a pictograph that is simply read "Yemaq". They have the heads of lions, and the wings and tails of powerful birds.

Now comes the ritual proper. Some opening prayers are chanted (alongside the "throwing the grain" rite) on the first evening, and incense is burned before the aforementioned banners. The first manuscripts to be chanted are those concerning burning sacrificial incense, lighting the lamps, inviting the gods, and investing oneself with the power of the gods (see Xi and Zhao 2009, 301).

In Rock's account, the ritual field is erected in the courtyard of the home (traditional Naxi homes in Lijiang consist of a main building flanked by two side buildings, with a central, open-air courtyard). In the area of the courtyard that faces north, the gates of the gods are erected (made from juniper or pine). There is one main gate and five gates that lead to the houses of the *chel* demons. The main gate is some two metres high and one metre wide, enough for someone to walk through.

Either side of the main gate are the white stones of Dduq and wooden ritual slats, the one representing Dduq is placed to the left, the one representing Seiq is placed to the right (these two deities, the Naxi house gods, are central figures in the story told by the manuscript translated in this book). Five willow sticks are also used, three on one side and two on the other. Other descriptions note the use of a pot containing pure water, and bowls containing milk and animal blood. In front of the main gate is a bench upon which offerings are placed. A black hemp cloth is put on top of the bench, this represents the black bridge that the *chel* demons can use to cross over into this realm. Wooden effigies, acting as "guards", are placed by the gates to the *chel* demons.

Lit charcoal is put into a bowl, and flour and pork fat are put on top of it. This generates an unpleasant smell that attracts the *chel* demons. This offering is placed before the central tree of the *chel* demons (there are three *chel* trees, a species of fir [*Abies Forrestii*]). More manuscripts are chanted on the following day. These will include the origin of impurity, the migration of mankind (i.e. the manuscript translated in this volume) and the story of the white bat's search for the scriptures. Specific manuscripts dealing with the eradication of impurity then follow. Bundles of green branches are lit by two dongba ritualists. The branches burn with white smoke, which cleanses the area of impurities. A sacrificial animal (in the case of our manuscript, a black goat, although Rock states that a white goat was used) is tied up south of the central *chel* gate, and a chicken tied beside the rightmost gate (see Figure 4 for a depiction of the burning branches and sacrificial goat). In the more ancient past, a cow was used for the blood sacrifice (Rock 1952, 627-628). The animals are sacrificed at the end of the ceremony. The stomach and heart of the goat are presented to the Yemaq protective deities, and the blood and meat are offered to the *chel* demons, who thus propitiated, will no longer cause the human world to be polluted. A microcosm of this ritual appears at the end of Scharten's *Coqbbertv* manuscript, on pages 31 and 32.

Part Two

Annotated Translation

Dramatis Personae

These are some of the most important recurring characters in the story, presented in order of appearance, first as they are written in the original manuscript, then as they appear in the digital recreation, followed by their name and a brief English introduction:

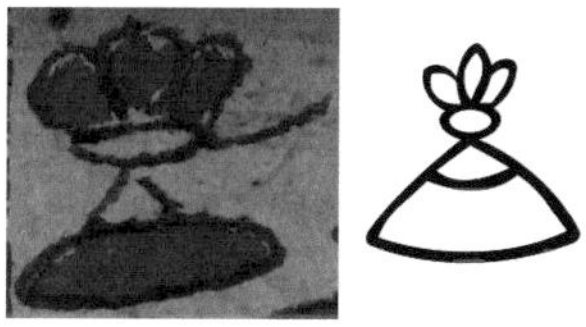

Dduq, male deity, husband of Seiq. Identified by his headdress.

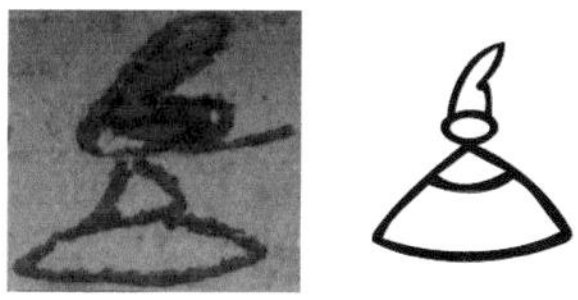

Seiq, female deity, wife of Dduq. Identified by her headdress.

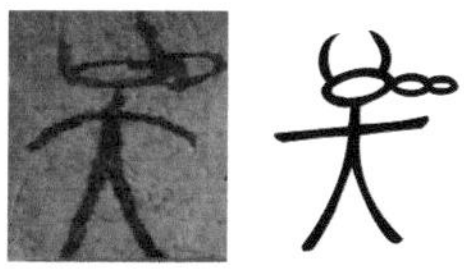

Coqssei-leel'ee, pre-flood ancestor of mankind, husband of Ceilheeq-bbvbbeq. Identified by the pronounced elephant trunk (indicating *coq*, the first syllable of his name).

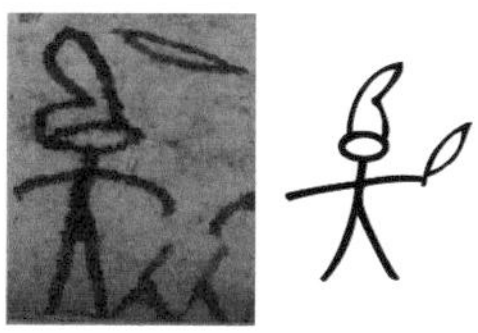

Ceilheeq-bbvbbeq, divine daughter of Zzee'laq-epv and wife of Coqssei-leel'ee. Identified by the leaf (*cei*) and perhaps also teeth (*heeq*), the first two syllables of her name.

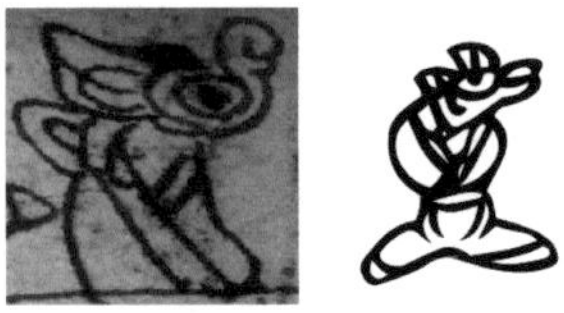

Zzee'laq-epv, grandfather deity, a celestial being who gave his daughter's hand in marriage to Coqssei-leel'ee. Identified by the tiger's head (second syllable of his name).

Chelshul-jiqbber, a ritual practitioner who specialises in expelling demons of impurity. Identified by the yak's head, *bber* (last syllable of his name)

Cover page

Graph-by-graph

1. **biuq**, to chant, a seated ritualist, mid-chant.
2. **ggeq**, a raised platform or bench.
3. **chel**, twisting intestines, indicating “unclean”.
4. **ggvq**, a bear, here used phonetically for *ggvq*, to overcome, as the second syllable of the ceremony name: *chel ggvq* (purification).
5. **coq bber**, a compound graph, consisting of Coqssei-leel’ee, represented by a man with an elephant’s head (read *coq* and here a metonym for humankind in general), and the verb “to go”, *bber*, represented by the pronounced left foot moving across the land.
6. **tvq**, literally bucket, here used phonetically to indicate *tv*, appear, here meaning an emergence or origin.
7. **oq**, grain, a large store of grain, here used phonetically for *oq*, thus, so.
8. **mei**, female, here used as a final particle.

Transcription
chel / ggvq / coq / bber / tv / oq / mei
unclean / overcome / humankind / go / origin / thus / particle

Scharten translation
From where mankind comes?

New translation
Purification ceremony: The emergence and migration of humankind

Notes
The first two graphs on the left, coloured in red on the original manuscript and unlabeled in the key above, are not strictly part of the title: they represent a dongba (*dobbaq*), seated upon a raised platform or bench (*ggeq*), with sound emerging from his mouth. This figure, read *biuq* (to chant), announces the title of the book. Most dongba will not read them, but they still carry meaning beyond mere decoration, for they indicate that this is a Naxi religious manuscript, and that a recitation by a dongba is about to commence.

Scharten translates only the title of the ritual that is the focus of this book, not the name of the wider ceremony. "*Chelggvq*" is the name of the ceremony for the purification of either a place or a home. Prior to the performance of a large rite the ceremonial ground is purified of *chel*, or uncleanliness. If this is not done, the *svq* nature spirits (or other deities) will not attend. This particular book recounts the story of the flood (i.e. the first great purification). Note here the graph used to depict *chel* (graph 3) is a looping line, according to Rock either indicative of the human intestine (which is unclean), or "a decayed part of a body showing tendons" (1937, 176). A variant form more commonly found is the graph . For Fang Guoyu, both graphs indicate swirling vapour (see Fang and He 1981, 263), although Rock has also suggested two differing interpretations for the commonly-seen  graph, either a human embryo (for any woman with child is considered *chel*, or unclean, see Rock 1935, 73), or simply a pictograph of human excrement (1952, 634). The final two graphs of the title page can be roughly translated as "thus is it so", with *oq* being "thus", and *mei*, an emphatic final particle. These two graphs are often seen appended to titles of Naxi manuscripts.

1-1

Graph-by-graph

1. **ddvperq**, the white conch. This graph indicates the call to prayer, and is often vocalised not by its denotative meaning, but as an elongated "O". One of the eight auspicious symbols borrowed from Tibetan Buddhism.
2. textual caret imported from Tibetan manuscript traditions used as a section marker. Not a graph that represents language, and therefore not read.
3. **la**, tiger. Animals are often depicted by a drawing of their head, and are distinguished by various identifying features: horns, whiskers etc. In this case, specifically the tiger's stripes. Here the graph is used to represent the idea of ancestors and past epochs (possibly relating to ancient customs of totemic tiger worship).
4. **me**, not, negation, could be a representation of an empty trap, or possibly the last quarter of the waning moon.
5. **sher**, seven, here with no specific meaning, or perhaps as a phonetic borrowing for the verb *shel*, to speak.

Transcription

a / **la** / **me** / **sher** / ni
oh / ancient / not /spoken / day

Scharten translation

From the very beginning

New translation

Oh, in a time not spoken,

Notes

The manuscript beings with a conch: this is not read out as a word, but is vocalized as a long "o", somewhat reminiscent of a call to prayer indicated by the blowing of a conch shell. What follows to the right (the second glyph on the page, but not labelled) is not a written graph but a textual caret, derived from the Tibetan *yig mgo*, that indicates the beginning of the book. The oral formula *a la me sher ni* is an opening sentence common to many manuscripts and is perhaps the Naxi tradition's most famous and easily identifiable oral formula. It is uttered in a unit of either five syllables, as it is here, or its variant, *e ni la sher ni*, or the seven syllable *a la me sher be thee rheeq*, all with essentially the same meaning. The formula is usually represented in the written text as a tiger's head. It can sometimes be written metonymically with the tiger's head alone, or each syllable can be written. Here, the opening syllable *a-* , an exclamation (and visually an utterance emerging from a mouth), and the final syllable *ni* (often written by using the graph for sun, ), are not written. Nevertheless, the five syllables are all read. He Jiren explains the whole unit as simply meaning "before", and the tiger as representing the ancient Naxi pronunciation for "and", *la*. His word-for-word translation of the five-syllable phrase is "yesterday and the day before yesterday" (2006, 3). The tiger graph may point to antiquity, i.e. a time of old no longer spoken of. Concerning graph 3, the negation (one of the most common graphs in this or any Naxi manuscript), Li Lin-ts'an suggests the following evolution of graphic depictions of the "waning moon", ending in the familiar "*me*", "not":  (see Li 2001, 10).

1-2

Graph-by-graph

1. **mee**, the high heavens, heaven. The graph originally depicts a kind of mushroom, but is often used for sky or heaven.
2. **lee**, a louse, here used phonetically to represent the idea of the earthly world.
3. **hoq**, a constellation, here used phonetically for the verb *hol* (in the high tone), to mix.
4. **gv**, literally garlic, here used phonetically to indicate *gvl*, the verb "to be able".
5. **rheeq**, time. Here depicted by drops of water, possibly representing the passage of time.

Transcription

mee'lee / hoq / gvl / rheeq

heaven and earth / mix / able / time

Scharten translation

the heavenly spirit made all kinds of things

New translation

In the time when heaven and earth were mixed together,

Notes

The Naxi *mee'lee* is interpreted by Scharten as "the heavenly spirit", likely as a contraction of Mee'lee-ddeezzi, one of the great gods of the Naxi pantheon. Here, however, *mee'lee* simply indicates heaven and earth: i.e. "in the time when the heavens and earth had not yet been separated".

1-3

Graph-by-graph

1. **Dduq**, the male spirit. Perhaps equivalent to the Chinese notion of *yang* 阳. Here depicted singing.
2. **Seiq**, the female spirit. Perhaps equivalent to the Chinese *yin* 阴. Here depicted singing.
3. **hoq**, literally rib bones, used here phonetically to indicate the verb *hoq* "to sing",
4. **gv**, literally garlic, here used phonetically to indicate *gvl*, the verb "to be able".
5. **rheeq**, time.

Transcription

Dduq / Seiq / hoq / gvl / rheeq

deity / deity / sing / able / time

Scharten translation

On earth the spirit spoke.

New translation

In the time when Dduq and Seiq were able to sing,

Notes

Dduq and Seiq are two of the highest spirits in the Naxi pantheon, representing male and female energies. Rock says that Dduq embodies "the male active principle" while Seiq "the passive principle" (1952, 121). In ritual practice, they are often represented using rocks known as Dduqlv; the Dduq rocks are taken from the cliff face and the Seiq rocks from the riverbed, then they are placed either side of an entrance to a house. In this way, they act as "door gods". These two spirits always appear in the manuscripts as a pair, like the energies of *yin* and *yang* which they represent.

Scharten's translation sees them as a single entity, the "spirit" who is speaking. These two spirits *are* depicted here as speaking, as we can see the speech emanating from their mouths. It is said that the Dduq and Seiq spirits once sang in unison, but, now transformed into stones guarding Naxi entryways, they no longer need to sing. Some modern annotated translations suggest that the *hol* indicates "to drive (livestock)", i.e. that just as the shepherd brings order to their flock, these two spirits are, in some distant mythical past, responsible for bringing order to the universe.

1-4

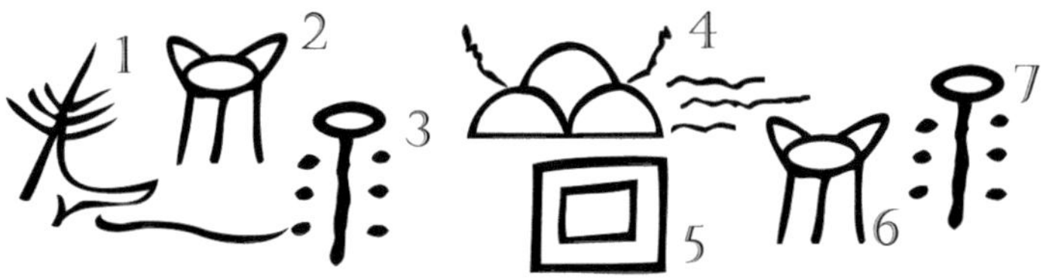

Graph-by-graph

1. **ser zzeeq jji**, this is a compound graph read with three syllables. *Ser*, meaning "wood" or "tree", *zzeeq* meaning "grow", and *jji* meaning "walk"; that is, the trees grew feet and walked.
2. **gv**, literally garlic, here used phonetically to indicate *gvl*, the verb "to be able".
3. **rheeq**, time. Drops of water, possibly representing the passage of time.
4. **lv ggee**, *lv* meaning "stone", *ggee* meaning "split", hence the stones split open.
5. **tal**, literally tower, used phonetically for the verb "to speak".
6. **gvl**, to be able.
7. **rheeq**, time.

Transcription

ser zzeeq jji / gvl / rheeq
tree grow walk / able / time
lv / ggee / tal / gvl / rheeq
stone / split / speak / able / time

Scharten translation
The trees could walk.
The stones could open their mouth.

New translation
In the time when the trees grew feet and walked, when the stones split open and spoke.

Notes
This panel indicates a time of great antiquity in Naxi myth, when it is said that the very trees could wander the earth, and the stones themselves could open their mouths and speak. McKhann has linked this formula to the inseparability of nature/culture in early Naxi thought: "the Naxi dongba ritual texts speak endearingly of a time long past 'when trees could walk and rocks could talk'" (2017, 383).

1-5

Graph-by-graph
1. **zheel**, soil, surrounded by wavy movement lines, which suggest shaking, or perhaps an earthquake: *liulliu* (to shake).
2. **lv**, stone (three stones piled atop one another).
3. **rheeq**, time.

Transcription
zheel / **lv** / **liulliu** / tv / chee / **rheeq**
soil / stone / shake / appear / that / time

Scharten translation
The earthglobe could move.

New translation
When the stones of the earth shook.

Notes

Here, to make a seven-syllable intonation unit, there are two words not written: *tv*, to appear, and *chee*, a demonstrative, "that". Li Lin-ts'an's source manuscripts has the movement lines also surrounding the stone, otherwise they are identical. Scharten takes *zheel lv*, the soil and the stones, together to mean "the earthglobe", and the quaking becomes in her version "movement".

1-6

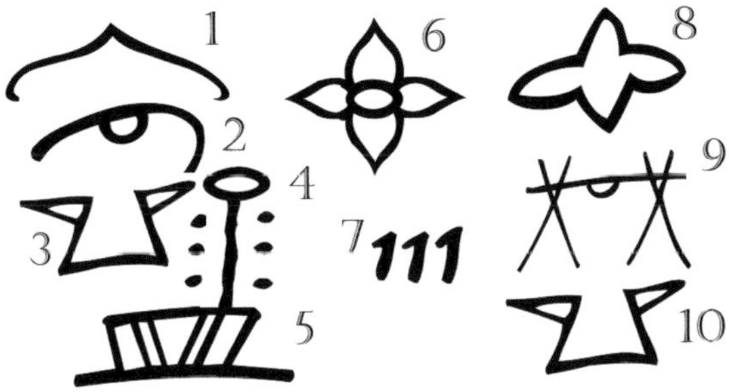

Graph-by-graph

1. **mee**, the heavens, the sky, the curved vault of heaven.
2. **me**, a negation.
3. **tvq**, a bucket, used phonetically to indicate *tv*, appear.
4. **rheeq**, time.
5. **ddiuq**, the earth.
6. **waq**, a graph depicting a precious blue-green stone, i.e. turquoise, used phonetically for *waq*, archaic term for "shadow".
7. **seel**, three.
8. **siuq**, kind, type.
9. **ga**, this graph depicts a swing, here used for the preposition "before".
10. **tvq**, a bucket, used phonetically to indicate *tv*, appear.

Transcription

mee / la / **me** / **tv** / see / chee / **rheeq**
heavens / even / not / appear / imperfect aspect particle / this / time
ddiuq / la / **me** / ku / see / chee / **rheeq**
earth / even / not / split / imperfect aspect / this / time
mee / neiq / **ddiuq** / **waq** / ee / mei / **seel** / **siuq** / **ga** / nee / **tv**
heavens / and / earth / shadow / good / nominalizer / three /kinds / before / ablative marker / appear

Scharten translation
All these things were, but heaven and earth were not yet created.

New translation
In the time when the heavens had not appeared and the earth had not been split open, there first appeared three good shadows of them both.

Notes
The first five graphs are here called upon in this reading to form two intonation units. In this regard certain words are made use of twice, "The heavens did not appear that time, the earth had not been split that time". The second half of this panel begins the recounting of how, in the earliest time, there was nothing but goodly shadows of the fundamental elements of the universe. In McKhann: "Before Heaven and Earth appeared, there first appeared the three good kinds of shadow of each" (1992, 84-85). Scharten's translation does not include this final intonation unit, instead skipping directly to the next panel. Graph 6, *waq* (turquoise) can also be read *herq*, green, or indeed a combination of both: *waqherl*, turquoise-green.

1-7

Graph-by-graph

1. **bbi**, the sun (archaic).
2. **me**, a negation.
3. **tvq**, a bucket, used phonetically for *tv*, appear.
4. **leiq**, the moon (archaic).
5. **waq**, archaic term for "shadow", originally a graph depicting a precious blue-green stone.
6. **seel**, three.
7. **siuq**, kind, type.
8. **ga**, this graph depicts a swing, here used for the preposition "before".
9. **tv**, to appear.

Transcription

bbi / la / **me** / **tv** / see / chee / rheeq
sun / even / not / appear / imperfect aspect / this / time
leiq / la / **me** / **tv** / see / chee / rheeq
moon / even / not / appear / imperfect aspect / this / time
bbi / neiq / **leiq** / **waq** / ee / mei / **seel** / **siuq** / **ga** / nee / **tv**
sun / and / moon / shadow / good / nominalizer / three / kind / before / ablative marker / appear

Scharten translation

In heaven only the shadow of sun and moon were there, the echos in three different kinds.

New translation

In the time when the sun had not appeared and the moon had not appeared, there first appeared three good shadows of them both.

Notes

Once again, the first four graphs are called upon in this reading to form two intonation units. The now-familiar graph for "time" is no longer written, but is still read.

1-8

Graph-by-graph

1. **geeq**, the stars.
2. **me**, a negation.
3. **tvq**, a bucket, used phonetically for *tv*, appear.
4. **ssaq**, a planet. Depicted by a planetary body leaving a trail through the cosmos.
5. **seel**, three.
6. **siuq**, kind, type.
7. **ga**, this graph depicts a swing, here used for the preposition "before".
8. **tv**, to appear.

Transcription

geeq / la / **me** / **tv** / see / chee / rheeq
stars / even / not / appear / imperfect aspect / this / time
ssaq / la / **me** / **tv** / see / chee / rheeq
comets / even / not / appear / imperfect aspect / this / time
geeq / neiq / **ssaq** / waq / ee / mei / **seel** / **siuq** / **ga** / nee / **tv**
stars / and / moon / shadow / good / nominalizer / three / kind / before / ablative marker / appear

Scharten translation

No ~~The~~ stars, only thier shadow and echo in three different ways.

New translation

In the time when the stars had not appeared and the planets had not appeared, there first appeared three good shadows of them both.

Notes

The formulaic panels continue, this time with stars and planets more generally instead of our sun and moon. Scharten only notes down stars, and has made a correction on the manuscript to add in the negation. The Naxi *ssaq* means planet(s), but this name is also given to demons who cause eclipses of the sun and moon by devouring them, suggesting the Naxi had some rudimentary knowledge of astronomy (Rock 1948, 73).

1-9

Graph-by-graph

1. **jjuq**, a mountain.
2. **me**, a negation.
3. **tvq**, a bucket, used phonetically for *tv*, appear.
4. **loq**, a valley. Depicted by a body of water (a river).
5. **waq**, shadow.

6. **seel**, three.
7. **siuq**, kind, type.
8. **tv**, to appear.

Transcription

jjuq / la / **me** / **tv** / see / chee / rheeq
mountains / even / not / appear / imperfect aspect / this / time
loq / la / **me** / **tv** / see / chee / rheeq
valleys / even / not / appear / imperfect aspect / this / time
jjuq / neiq / **loq** / waq / ee / mei / **seel** / **siuq** / **ga** / nee / **tv**
mountains / and / valleys / shadow / good / nominalizer / three / kind / before / ablative marker / appear

Scharten translation

No ~~The~~ mountains, only their shadow and echos in three different ways.

New translation

In the time when the mountains had not appeared and the valleys had not appeared, there first appeared three good shadows of them both.

Notes

Once again Scharten simplifies this section, only noting down mountains. The graph depicting "valleys" is attached to the mountain, but is a non-standard form; "valley" is usually written , depicting water running down a valley.

1-10

Graph-by-graph

1. **ser**, wood, a tree.
2. **me**, a negation.
3. **tvq**, a bucket, used phonetically for *tv*, appear.
4. **lv**, stone. Depicted by three stones piled up.

5. **waq**, shadow.
6. **seel**, three.
7. **siuq**, kind, type.
8. **tvq**, a bucket, used phonetically for *tv*, appear.

Transcription

ser / la / **me** / **tv** / see / chee / rheeq
trees / even / not / appear / imperfect aspect / this / time
loq / la / **me** / **tv** / see / chee / rheeq
rocks / even / not / appear / imperfect aspect / this / time
ser / neiq / **loq** / waq / ee / mei / **seel** / **siuq** / **ga** / nee / **tv**
tree / and / rocks / shadow / good / nominalizer / three / kind / before / ablative marker / appear

Scharten translation

No trees and stones, only their shadows and achos in three different ways.

New translation

In the time when the trees had not appeared and the stones had not appeared, there first appeared three good shadows of them both.

Notes

Another repetition of the formula, with trees and stones now mentioned in an interesting compound graph, with a tree growing out of a rock formation. In some versions of this story (e.g. McKhann 1992) this is omitted, as stones and forests are connected with the mountains and the valleys of the earlier panel.

2-1

Graph-by-graph

1. **ggee**, chew (a jaw with teeth). Here the graph is used phonetically for *ggeel*, 'true'.
2. **neif**, and. The graph depicts a heart, *nee*, but it is most likely read *neif*, as the conjunction.
3. **me**, not, negation.
4. **ggeel**, true. The two graphs (3 and 4) are read together, *me ggeel*, i.e. 'not true/real'.
5. **tvq**, a bucket, used phonetically for *tv*, appear.

Transcription
ggeel / neif / me / ggeel / tv
true / and / not /true / appear

Scharten translation
Some of the true things were changed in false

New translation
The true and false appeared.

Notes
This simple panel is primarily interesting for its use of the heart graph, *nee*, to stand in for the conjunction *neif*, and. We will see in a following panel (2-3) the re-substitution for the amaranth leaf, *neif*, also a rebus, but one much closer phonetically to the Naxi "and". The heart graph here is a noteworthy anomaly that points to the non-standard, idiosyncratic nature of these phonetic borrowings. "True" and "not true" are two sides of the same coin and "not true" does not imply some sort of deception. McKhann suggests that the "Judeo-Christian opposition between 'good' and 'evil' is closer to the sense of the relationship implied here" (1992, 85).

2-2

Graph-by-graph

1. **zeiq**, a malevolent spirit, used phonetically for *zzeiq*, real.
2. **nee**, heart, used phonetically for *neif*, the conjunction "and".
3. **me**, not, negation.
4. **zzeiq**, real. The two graphs (3 and 4) are read together, *me zzeiq*, i.e. "not real".
5. **tvq**, bucket, used phonetically for *tv*, appear.

Transcription

zzeiq / neif / me / zzeiq / tv
real / and / not /real / appear

Scharten translation

And some of the real things were changed in unreal

New translation

The real and unreal appeared.

Notes

This panel acts as a continuation of the previous one, where we now have "real" instead of "true", and its counterpoint, the "unreal". McKhann suggests that these terms are probably of Buddhist origin. A dongba might append one more similar intonation unit after this one: *shuq neif me shuq tv* (the clean and the unclean appeared). This is not included in the manuscript.

2-3

Graph-by-graph

1. **ggeel**, true.
2. **neif**, and. The graph is the amaranth leaf, here used as a phonetic for the conjunction.
3. **zeiq**, malevolent spirit, used phonetically for *zzeiq*, real.
4. **nee**, heart, here used as a phonetic for the topicalizer, *nee*.
5. **bee**, artemisia, used as a phonetic for the first syllable of the verb, *beebabbei* (to transform).
6. **ba**, a frog's head, used a phonetic in the three-syllable verb.
7. **bbei**, a farm tool, used here semantically to indicate the verb "to do", used as a phonetic as the final syllable of the verb.

Transcription

geel / neif / zeiq / nee / beebabbei
true / and / real / topicalizer / to make a change (sexual intercourse)

Scharten translation

These two things come in friction

New translation

The true and the real came together in union.

Notes

Scharten's "come in friction" is most certainly a euphemism for the act of copulation, a sexual union that leads to the creation of something new. The Naxi phrase, *beebabbei*, essentially means intercourse. It is one of the most frequently recurring words in the Naxi texts, and is often written with the compound graph . Here we see two phonetic loans, with the addition of a semantic component (*bee* and *ba*, the artemisia and frog, with the semantic *bbei*, the farm tool working the earth to represent "do/make/perform"). The semantic component was probably a later addition. In the Chinese translations (as a general rule), this word for sexual intercourse is not translated directly, but instead with a euphemism, *zuo bianhua* 做变化 (make a change). There is another, more pictorially direct, Naxi graph for *beebabbei*, which shows a man and a woman mid-coitus:

, a graph that could be read *ddeiq*, and that we will see later on in the text (see panels 10-4 and 11-8). Whichever graph is used, the meaning is still clear: sex. In fact, the phrase can have two meanings (both interrelated): to have sexual intercourse, to produce, to come into being through sexual intercourse; and also to cause something to appear, to cause an apparition, via magic.

2-4

Graph-by-graph

1. **oq herq bbu**, bright green stone (a turquoise gemstone emitting light).
2. **tvq**, bucket, used phonetically for *tv*, appear.
3. **bee**, artemisia, used phonetically for the first syllable of the verb, *beebabbei*.
4. **ba**, a frog's head, used phonetically in the three-syllable verb.
5. **bbei**, to do, used phonetically as the final syllable of the verb,
6. **Iggvq-ogeq**, a great god of the Naxi pantheon.
7. **tvq**, bucket, used phonetically for *tv*, appear.

Transcription
o herq / bbu / ddeeq / lv / la / **tv**
green / bright / great / stone / also / appear
bbu / ddeeq / lv / la / **beebabbei**
bright / great / stone / too / transform
Iggvq-ogeq / tv
great god / appear

Scharten translation
And because of this there arises a bright precious stone. This precious stone arises and proceed two people, named o-kgeh and eh-kgeh.

New translation
And there came forth a bright green stone. This stone then transformed into the great god, Iggvq-ogeq.

Notes

What Scharten writes as “o-kgeh” and “eh-kgeh” here are not two people, but the one great god, Iggvq-ogeq, written in Naxi with the graph , which seems to share some commonality with the Tibetan mantric syllable and sacred sound, Om ཨོཾ. Rock calls him “^{2}O-^{1}gko-^{2}aw-^{1}gko. The first great cause” (Rock 1972, 40). He is never directly figured in a pictographic graph, instead he is only depicted with the graph that resembles the Tibetan letter. He seems to be tied at the top of the Naxi pantheon with the great god, Saqyi-weddei . Sometimes Iggvq-ogeq comes first, at other times, Saqyi weddei is the first to be mentioned. Rock notes that “It is related that the Na-khi deity Ssaw yi wua de which corresponds in all probability to the Tibetan Shen rezigs sPpyan ras gzigs meditated on the existence of O which is O gko aw gko and the latter became a reality” (1937, 67). This panel could be followed by the story of the birth of the evil counterpart to Iggvq-ogeq, Iggvq-dinaq, whose name is written with the Tibetan letter *na*, meaning black. Iggvq-dinaq is the original evil and enemy of Iggvq-ogeq. In Naxi myth, every good being has an evil counterpart. Such a section may be read “*Me ggee neif me zzeiq nee beeba bbei, o naq lv la tv*” (the false and unreal came together to create a black opal), “*o naq lv la nee beebabbei, Iggvq dinaq tv*” (and the black opal changed into Iggvq dinaq). The emergence of Iggvq-dinaq occurs in panel 3-8 of the Scharten manuscript.

2-5

Graph-by-graph

1. **bee**, artemisia, used phonetically for the first syllable of the verb, *beebabbei*.
2. **ba**, a frog’s head, used phonetically as a phonetic in the three-syllable verb.
3. **bbei**, to do, used phonetically as the final syllable of the verb,
4. **mee lee zhul gv perq**, “a white light in the space between heaven and earth” (i.e. in the world), a composite graph of the heavens emitting light, with the graph for white *perq*, appended below.
5. **perq**, white (part of the above compound). The etymology of the graph is unclear. Li suggests that it depicts the verb *perq*, to untie, and shows a string being untied (2001, 278-9). I believe it was originally a glyph (not a pictograph) depicting a Tibetan deity and resembling perhaps a Tibetan letter, later adopted as the conventional graph for “white”.
6. **tvq**, bucket, used phonetically for *tv*, appear.

Transcription
Iggvq-ogeq / nee / **beebabbei**
great god / topicalizer / transform
mee lee zhul gv perq / yi / tei / nee / **tv**
white place in between heaven and earth / emphatic / here / topicalizer / appear

Scharten translation
These two arises and proceed a bright white thing.

New translation
Iggvq-ogeq transformed into a white light that shone over the world, in between heaven and earth.

Notes
The "bright white thing" of Scharten's rendition is something akin to a divine light that emerges from a divine transformation and shines over the world. In some way this can be compared to the biblical proclamation, "Let there be light".

2-6

Graph-by-graph
1. **bee**, artemisia, here used phonetically for the first syllable of the verb, *beebabbei*.
2. **ba**, a frog's head, here used phonetically in the three-syllable verb.
3. **bbei**, to do, here used phonetically as the final syllable of the verb.
4. **perq**, white.
5. **gv**, egg.
6. **tvq**, bucket, used phonetically for *tv*, appear.

Transcription
mee lee zhul gv per / nee / **beebabbei**
white place in between heaven and earth / topicalizer / transform

gv / **per** / ddee / lvl / **tv**
egg / white/ one / measure word / appear

Scharten translation
This thing arises and becomes a white egg.

New translation
The light transformed into a white egg

Notes
This panel follows the transformation formula, beginning with what was created in the previous panel, namely the divine light, now coalescing into a single white egg. The words *ddee*, one, and *lvl*, a measure word for rock-shaped objects, are not written.

2-7

Graph-by-graph

1. **bee**, artemisia, here used as a phonetic for the first syllable of the verb, *beebabbei.*
2. **ba**, a frog's head, here used as a phonetic in the three-syllable verb.
3. **bbei**, to do, here used as a phonetic as the final syllable of the verb.
4. **aiq**, chicken, here depicted by the animal's head alone.
5. **perq**, white. Fang Guoyu suggests that this graph is borrowed from *perq*, to untie a knot (1981, 322).
6. **ddal**, to chop, here used as a phonetic for *ddaq*, an emphatic particle.
7. **tvq**, bucket, used phonetically for *tv*, appear.

Transcription
gv / perq / ddee / lvl / **beebabbei**
egg / white / one / measure word / transform
aiq / **perq** / ddee / **ddaq** / **tv**
chicken / white/ one / emphatic / appear

Scharten translation

This thing arises and proceed a white chicken.

New translation

The egg transformed into a white chicken.

Notes

When it comes to the old riddle of the chicken and the egg, the Naxi know that the egg came first. He Guisheng gives the reading of the second intonation unit as "*ai per ddee qu tv*" (a group of white chickens appeared), taking the pointed graph above the trough (i.e., graph 6) to be *qul*, , an awl, but in this case a phonetic for *qu*, meaning "group" or "flock". Having consulted various other translations, only one chicken ever emerges from the egg. I therefore suggest that the graph is to be read as *ddaq*, an emphatic which implies agency in the second or third person (i.e. attributing agency in this case to the egg). Scharten's reading concurs with the interpretation of there being only one chicken.

2-8

Graph-by-graph

1. **aiq**, chicken, here depicted by the animal's head alone.
2. **perq**, white.
3. **mi**, fire, here used as a phonetic for the noun, *miq*, name. This is a phonetic loan in Naxi from the Chinese *ming* 名, name.
4. **zeel**, a bundle of sticks, here used as a phonetic for the verb, to name.
5. **xi**, a sheaf of rice, here used a phonetic for xi, person.
6. **me**, a negation
7. **nge**, oneself, a figure pointing to themselves.
8. **mi**, fire, used phonetically for *miq*, name.

Transcription

aiq / **perq** / tee / ddee / mei / **miqzeel** / **xi** / **me** / jjuq

chicken / white / that / measure word (animals) / name / person / not / have
nge / **miq** / nge / lei / zeel
self / name/ self / particle used before verbs / to name

Scharten translation
There was none to give this white chicken a name.
Afterwards it gave itself the following name:

New translation
There was nobody to give this white chicken a name, so it named itself,

Notes
This panel is slightly convoluted if we look at the order in which the graphs are read. The white chicken is represented by the second and third graphs of the left-hand column, and the verb, to name, *zeel*, is represented by the bottom graph (graph 4) and used twice in this panel, it is however only read once. The verb of the second intonation unit, *jjuq*, to have, is not written. In the manuscript, graph number 7, *nge* ("oneself"), appears to be mis-written as *niul* , to shake.

2-9

Graph-by-graph

1. **Dduq**, a male god of benevolence, a distant ancestor of mankind. The graph written here actually more closely resembles the general term for god, *heiq*.
2. **ggeq**, a bench, used phonetically for *gge*, the possessive particle.
3. **ee**, svastika, here used as a phonetic for the first syllable of a proper name.
4. **yuq**, a variant of the geba phonetic .
5. **maq**, butter, here used as a phonetic in the proper name.
6. **cal**, to bite (salt entering a mouth), here perhaps incorrectly written for *zeel*, to name.
7. **maq**, a phonetic.
8. **mi**, fire, used phonetically for *miq*, name.

Transcription
Dduq / gge / Eeyuq-ee**maq** / lei / miq / **zeel**
Name of a deity / of / name of the chicken / emphatic particle / name / to name
Eeyuq-ee**maq** / lei / **miq** / bbei
proper name / particle / name / make

Scharten translation
Ggeh-yu-kgeh-ma

New translation
Eeyuq-eemaq of Dduq was what it named itself, this was the name it took.

Notes
This panel reveals the name that the chicken gave itself. Rock translates this as "Du (Muan llü du ndzi) gave it the name ghügh yu ghügh ma" (1937, 67), however all other versions agree that this is not the name that the deity Dduq gave it (for we are told in the previous panel that it named itself), rather that Dduq forms *part* of the name, i.e., this is the chicken that belonged to one of the first ancestors of the Naxi: Dduq. Indeed, we have the possessive particle, *gge*, in the manuscript below the deity himself. This deity, Dduq, is glossed in Rock as Meeleel-dduqzzeeq: "Muan llü du ndzi often called only Du, is perhaps equivalent to the Chinese god of longevity the Shou shen 寿神. The Chinese always depict him with a very high forehead, and so do the Na-khi in their religious manuscripts" (ibid.). The manuscript shows simply a god, Dduq is more properly written with a narrow headdress: . Of particular note is the proper name of the chicken itself. Rock's "ghügh yu ghügh ma" is clearly phonetically equivalent to Scharten's "Ggeh-yu-kgeh-ma", and indeed we see this very name in He Yuncai's reading and He Fayuan's translation (1986, 154). In the manuscript read by He Yuncai, the four-syllable name is written with only three graphs, *ee yuq maq* , the extra "*ee*" must be inserted by the reader. The problem with the Scharten manuscript is the repetition of butter, *maq* – the name should by all accounts feature only one "maq" syllable. A direct phonetic reading of the five graphs (3-7) would be *ee yuq maq cal maq*; this is not a variant name for the chicken, but instead something interesting is going on with graph 6, what looks like *cal*, to bite, but is probably meant to be *zeel*, the verb meaning "to name" (which can be written with the graph *zeel* , meaning "to gag", a bundle entering a person's mouth). The copyist of the manuscript probably confused these two graphs, for *cal* depicts salt entering a mouth, *zeel* is a bundle. This means that the final two graphs (7 and 8) probably represent another intonation unit, i.e., graph 7 (*maq*) is used by itself to represent the entire name, Eeyuq-eemaq.

2-10

Graph-by-graph

1. **mee**, heaven.
2. **zzeq**, to fly, a bird in flight.
3. **me**, not, a negation.
4. **ggee**, to chew. Here used phonetically for *geeq*, to fall.

Transcription

mee / shuaq / **zzeq** / **me** / zeil
sky / high /fly / not / all around
fv / **geeq** / ddiuq / **me** / zeil
feather / fall / earth / not / all around

Scharten translation

It tells itself, you must not fly high, so that your feathers will fly on earth

New translation

It did not fly high into the sky and its feathers did not fall around the earth

Notes

This is a cryptic panel, for there are a number of divergent readings across the literature, some of which are quite lengthy, while the Scharten manuscript only provides four written graphs. The general idea, obscured somewhat in Scharten's original translation, is one of impotence: the chicken cannot fly. For this panel He Guisheng gives the reading: "zzeqzzeq mee shua gu nee lei zzeq hee / mee niuq lei me da / coco ddiu lo lei co hee / ddiu lo lei me da" ("It wanted to fly up into the sky, but could not reach the heavens, it wanted to jump on the earth but could not reach the ground"). This is similar to He Yuncai's 1986 version (as translated by McKhann): "Oh, Eeiuq-eemaq! It had wings and could hover, but it could not fly up to the high heavens. It had feet and could jump, but it could not jump down to the low earth" (McKhann 1992, 86). The major difference here is the addition of an extra intonation unit at the beginning, "Eeiuq-eemaq nee", in He Yuncai's version. Rock (1935) provides a slightly different rendering, replacing jumping with crowing: "The chicken tried to fly towards heaven but could not reach it. It tried to crow but could not. (68).

None of these readings account for graph 4, the verb *geeq*, to fall, one of only four graphs in this panel, and one that probably represents the second intonation unit in its entirety. This graph is normally (i.e. by Fang and Li) explained as a jaw with teeth, but Rock says it depicts (quite abstractly) a ripe fruit which has opened and then fallen to the ground. Scharten's version of this second intonation unit, "feathers will fly on earth", reduplicates the verb "fly" from the first intonation unit, but I believe she means "fall on earth". The closest we get to understanding what the verb "fall" is doing here in any of the annotated translations is from Li Lin-ts'an's version, as his manuscript also contains the *ggeeq* graph: "Eeiuq-eemaq, flew up high into the sky, but the sky stretches up and up and it could not reach the top, it scattered leaves on the earth, but the leaves could not cover all the world" (1966, 27-28). Li records the reading of *geeq* for the same graph that appears in the Scharten manuscript, but in the context of leaves falling to the ground. Therefore, with reference to Li's translation I have attempted to recreate the reading Scharten would have been given here, which seems to take the *geeq* as the chicken's own feathers, not leaves, falling to the ground.

2-11

Graph-by-graph

1. **zzeq**, to fly.
2. **gv**, garlic, a phonetic loan for the verb *gvl*, "to be able".
3. **me**, not, a negation.
4. **co**, to dance. A figure mid-dance.
5. **me**, not.

Transcription

zzeq / **gvl** / **zzeq** / **me** / ni
fly / to be able /fly / not / want
co / **gvl** / **co** / **me** / ni
dance / to be able / dance / not / want

Scharten translation

When you can fly, you must not fly. When you can spring, you must not spring

New translation

It could not fly, and it could not jump.

Notes

Here the theme of impotence and incompleteness is continued. Rock records a fairly similar rendition with one important addition, the chickens travelling to a different land: “It then arrived at the land Tsü hö dü mba and thence could neither fly nor hop” (1935, 68). The chicken is, at this point, in some kind of limbo. Scharten appears to take the final verb *ni*, “to want”, as an imperative, while other versions seem to take it merely as a reinforcement of the verb *gvl*, to be able to.

2-12

Graph-by-graph

1. **liu**, a spear with a rounded tip.
2. **me**, not, a negation.
3. **ni**, the numeral two, here used phonetically for the verb, *ni*, that usually means “to want”, but here takes the sense of “to be able”.
4. **ggai’ler**, a cuirass made from animal hide.
5. **dder**, a bamboo mat, here used phonetically for the verb “to place on” (e.g. to put something on someone).
6. **zziddeeq**, compound graph representing a chieftain (figure with hair on either side of the head) and minor official (the object in the figure’s hand with curved tip)
7. **me**, not.
8. **lv**, a pile of stones, here used phonetically for the idea of working together closely.

Transcription

liu / tal / zeeq / **me** / **ni**
spear / tip / upright / not / able
ggai'ler / **dder** / me / ni
armour / to place on / not / able
zziddeeq / **lvl** / **me** / ni
chieftain / minor official / to work together / not / able

Scharten translation

When you want to waer an armour, you must not wear in the wrong way. When you see a high person, dont hate him.

New translation

The spear tips could not be raised upright, the armour could not be worn, the chieftains and minor officials could not work together.

Notes

In this panel we now begin to see the problems experienced in the wider world – before things have been fully formed – in three parallel intonation units: the weapons are deficient, the armour is unwearable, and the leaders are not working in harmony. Scharten does not translate the first intonation unit, and Rock omits the third, saying "there was neither lance nor armour" (68), while McKhann has "there were no headmen to attend to matters...spears could not pierce, armour could not protect" (1992, 86). Scharten's translation, while idiosyncratic, does record the verb "worn" for the armour, which appears in the manuscript as the graph *dder*, meaning "to put on". Rock (1955, 5) discusses Naxi armour, of which he himself was able to attain several pieces, in detail: "The ^{1}Na-^{2}khi armor does not consist of large pieces of leather covering the chest and back as was in use during the Nan chao kingdom, but of hundreds of laminae laced together with leather thongs; the armor is a sleeveless coat but has pauldrons which protect the shoulders and upper arm".

Graph 6 above is of particular interest, as it appears to be a compound graph of the headman, *zzi*, holding a distorted spear. From its curved tip, this spear is probably an incorrectly written form of the graph *ddeeq* , meaning minor official, as this graph appears individually in Li's manuscript beneath *zzi*, or chieftain. He Guisheng gives the reading "*zziddeeq*" for the compound graph.

2-13

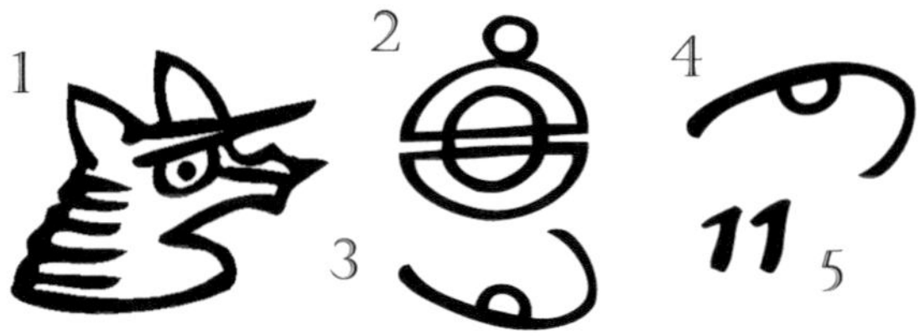

Graph-by-graph

1. **rua**, a horse, depicted by its head and mane.
2. **juq**, an iron bell.
3. **me**, not.
4. **me**, not.
5. **ni**, to be able.

Transcription

rua / **juq** / rerq / **me** / **ni**
horse / bell / to make a noise / not / able

Scharten translation

When you see a horse, don't begin to cacle.

New translation

The horse bells did not ring out.

Notes

Note here the extra "*me*" negation in the mid-bottom of this panel, it is likely a mistake, and He Guisheng does not read it. Scharten's version continues to read like advice being given to the chicken, whereas other translations all speak in more general terms. The corresponding panel in Li Lin-ts'an's manuscript (1978, 26) has only three graphs, the horse, the bell and the negation, but he translates these graphs "马蹄铁掌订不成" [the horseshoe cannot be fitted]. I presume this to be an outlying reading by his dongba assistant, He Cai. If we posit that Scharten misheard the word *juq* "bell" and took it instead for the verb, *liuq* "to look", we can see how she arrived at a graph-by-graph reading like "horse see make noise don't".

3-1

Graph-by-graph

1. **biuq**, a dongba, here seated and mid-chant.
2. **paq**, a female diviner (also read *saipaq*), depicted by the graph for white, *perq*, perhaps above an outstretched hand, or a depiction of blood (*sai*).
3. **me**, not.
4. **oq**, grain (the graph shows a barnful of grain), here used as a phonetic for *oq*, power.

Transcription

biuq / neif / **paq** / **me** / **oq** / mei
dongba / and / female diviner / no / [to have] power / final particle

Scharten translation

A sorcerer and a witch must have no work together

New translation

The dongba and the *saipaq* diviners had no power.

Notes

This panel, a continuation of the narrative of impotency from the end of the previous page, has several different interpretations. For Rock, this reads "and the ²dto-¹mba and ²Llü-¹bu could not chant or cast horoscopes correctly" (1952, 677), whereas McKhann has "and the [male] priests and [female] shamans had no powers" (1992, 86). The "female shamans", *paq*, are here represented by the graph for white, *perq*.

Closest to Scharten's "A sorcerer and a witch must have no work together" is perhaps the version by He Yuncai and He Fayuan, who take the final three syllables, *oq me niq*, to mean "the dongba and the witch cannot work together" (154). The operative word here is, I believe, *oq*, represented graphically by a barnful of grain. If we take it to mean *oq*, power, then we arrive at the reading of He Cai, "*Biuq paq oq me ni*", which Li Lin-ts'an translates to "the sorcerer and the wizard have no power", echoing the interpretation of both Rock and Mckhann. He Guisheng gives an altogether different interpretation of the *oq* (and the preceding negation): *me oq mei*, "if it were not for", taking *oq* to mean "if", i.e. if it were not for the dongba and the sorceress, [then we would not know about all this]. This understanding is not reflected in any of the other translations, but the formulation *me oq mei* does appear in Rock in association with Dobbaq-sheello, "If it were not for [Dobbaq-sheello]...etc." (1965, 203). This makes some sense, as at this point in the narrative the dongba and the female diviners do not yet exist. In any case I follow the majority here and translate "*oq*" as power, i.e. "[they] have no powers", for, as McKhann notes, this section of the myth is all about impotency and the lack of ability to do things correctly (1992, 86): at this point, the world has not yet properly formed. He Guisheng's reading is however a close reflection of the manuscript *as written*.

3-2

Graph-by-graph

1. **aiq**, a chicken, mid-flight.
2. **mee**, heaven.
3. **jiq**, clouds (a pictograph).
4. **perq**, white.
5. **gv kol**, a nest. The graph shows many eggs (*gv*), a plenitude indicated by the dots, inside a nest.
6. **ddiuq**, the earth, here with tufts of verdant grass growing atop it.
7. **herq**, green, a borrowing from the graph *waq* for turquoise/jade (hence, green in colour).
8. **gv kol**, a nest.
9. **gv**, egg.
10. **perq**, white.
11. **ggv**, nine. The number nine is usually depicted by nine marks in three rows of three, here the marks are replaced by eggs.

Transcription

Eeiuq-eemaq / tee
name of the chicken / it

mee / gge / **jiq** / **perq** / zzerl / lei / **gvkol** / bbei
sky / of / cloud / white / to pluck out / particle / nest / make
ddiu / gge / ssee / **herq** / zzerl / lei / yilkeq / bbei
earth / of / grass / green / pluck / particle / blanket / make
ssee / herq / **gv kol** / loq
grass / green / nest / in
gv / perq / ggv / zzeeq / gvq / lei / ji
egg / white / nine / pairs / lay (eggs) / particle / put

Scharten translation
Heaven prepares for the chicken, named Greh-yü-kge-ma a nest in the grass, and in that nest came three pairs of eggs.

New translation
The chicken Eeiuq-eemaq plucked white clouds from the sky to make a nest, and plucked fresh grass from the earth to make the bedding. In the nest of green grass, it laid many pairs of white eggs.

Notes
This panel is, perhaps more than most, an imagistic poetic collage rather than a sequence to be read literally. The first intonation unit is that of the chicken's name, which is not written, although the chicken itself is depicted. Both depictions of "nest" on the page are idiosyncratic, for the first nest in the illustration above I have used the common graph in Fang's dictionary (1981, 165). In the manuscript itself, the pair of eggs are covered in this nest by faint lines that presumably indicate the soft grass used as bedding material. He Guisheng's reading has the grass as the "blanket", which echoes the written text here.

Scharten's translation omits the clouds entirely. Quite how Scharten arrives at "three pairs of eggs" is unclear, as the text continues by enumerating twelve distinct pairs, and we have in the first nest (under the chicken) a pair of eggs, and above the second depiction of nest (represented in shorthand by a mere concave line) nine eggs laid out in three parallel rows, hence nine pairs. The number three *was* probably part of the original reading, for the other translations all agree that the chicken uses three clouds and three tufts of grass for its bedding.

He Guisheng suggests that "nine" should be translated as "many", for nine is often merely metaphorical and indicates a great number. Indeed, this is borne out here, for the manuscript goes on to show twelve distinct pairs of eggs.

3-3

Graph-by-graph

1. **gv**, egg (two eggs are written).
2. **perq**, white, a phonetic borrowing for Paiq, a god associated with the Tibetans.
3. **saiq**, a deity associated with the Bai people of Dali. Fang Guoyu suggests the graph may have evolved from the Naxi *sai* , blood.
4. **tvq**, bucket, here read *tv*, to emerge.
5. **gv**, egg (two eggs).
6. **gga**, the god of victory. Depicted here by a battle flag.
7. **wuq**, commander, a high-ranking military official, depicted here by the phonetic, which is a bowl of rice used as an offering.
8. **tv**, to emerge.
9. **o**, a protective deity.
10. **heiq**, a great god.
11. **tv**, to emerge.

Transcription

juq / gge / tee / ddee zzeeq / **paiq** / neif / **saiq** / **tv** / heq
before / of / this / pair / name of a deity / and / name of a deity / emerge / go
tee / ggv / mei / ddee zzeeq / **gga** / neif / **wuq** / **tv** / heq
this / after / topicalizer / pair / name of a deity / and / name of a deity / emerge / go
tee / ggv / mei / ddee zzeeq / **o** / neif / **heiq** / **tv** / heq
this / after / topicalizer / pair / name of a deity / and / name of a deity / emerge / go

Scharten translation

The first pair of eggs brought forth white and yellow. White is the one, who opens the heaven and the yellow means to open the earth. The second pair the god of governing, the general and the officer. The third pair brought forth the two gods of harvest.

New translation

From the first pair came the gods of heaven and earth, Paiq and Saiq. From the second pair, the spirits of victory, Gga and Wuq. From the third pair, the gods O and Heiq emerged.

Notes

Now the eggs have begun to hatch, and the Naxi pantheon is revealed. The first graphs in the panel are the two eggs, but they are not read as such: instead, the dongba reads the words *ddee zzeeq* (one pair), which would be written **1** . The first pair of gods is Paiq and Saiq, the nine male creators of the heavens and the seven female creators of the earth, respectively (Rock 1952, 91). Next are the Gga, the gods of victory, and their caretakers, i.e. lesser officers, the Wuq. The third pair of eggs hatches to reveal O and Heiq, greater gods who always follow the Gga and Wuq but who are not associated with any specific powers. Scharten claims they are the gods of harvest, but it is almost certain she mistook the combined names of O and Heiq for the demigod Oq-mei-heiq, the god of grain and harvest. McKhann gives detailed information about these gods and their roles in Naxi society (1992, 87-88).

3-4

Graph-by-graph

1. **Dduq**, male deity.
2. **Seiq**, female deity.
3. **tvq**, a bucket, used phonetically for *tv*, emerge.
4. **gv**, egg (two eggs are written).
5. **gvl**, the able, a phonetic loan using the graph for garlic, *gv*, a pictograph of a head of garlic.
6. **see**, the wise, a phonetic loan using the graph for wood, *ser*, a pictograph of a tree branch.
7. **tv**, to emerge.

8. **gv**, egg (two eggs).
9. **lerl**, one who can measure, a phonetic loan using the graph for to measure, *lerl*, a pictograph of a ruler.
10. **chel**, one who can survey, a phonetic loan using the graph for unclean, *chel*. This is the geba graph, perhaps derived from an intestine.
11. **tv**, to emerge.

Transcription

tee / ggv / mei / ddee zzeeq / **Dduq** / neif / **Seiq** / **tv** / heq
this / after / topicalizer / pair / name of a deity / and / name of a deity / emerge / go
tee / ggv / mei / ddee zzeeq / **gvl** / neif / **see** / **tv** / heq
this / after / topicalizer / pair / the able / and / the wise / emerge / go
tee / ggv / mei / ddee zzeeq / **lerl** / neif / **chel** / **tv** / heq
this / after / topicalizer / pair / measure / and / survey / emerge / go

Scharten translation

The fourth pair brought forth man and woman.
The fifth one, one who is able to every thing and who knows every thing. The sixth brought forth the measurement.

New translation

From the next pair came Dduq and Seiq, male and female principles. From the next pair, the able and the wise emerged. From the following pair, the one who could measure, and the one who could survey.

Notes

In this panel the pairs of eggs continue to hatch. Dduq and Seiq are Naxi deities who protect the people. They are associated with male and female principles or energies, and are perhaps related to the Chinese *yin* and *yang*, hence Scharten's translation "man and woman". From the next two pairs emerge not deities, but people who are the paragons of wisdom and ability, or the skills of measurement and surveying. These graphs are frequently written with phono-semantic compounds where the phonetic appears above a seated figure, for example the second pair, *gvl* and *see*: , but in this case only the phonetics are used.

3-5

Graph-by-graph

1. **gv**, egg (two eggs).
2. **zziddeeq**, chieftain-official (compound graph).
3. **tvq**, a bucket, used phonetically for *tv*, emerge.
4. **gv**, egg (two).
5. **biuq**, dongba.
6. **paq**, female diviner.
7. **tv**, to emerge.

Transcription

tee / ggv / mei / ddee zzeeq / **zzi** / neif / **ddeeq** / **tv** / heq
this / after / topicalizer / pair / chieftain / and / official / emerge / go
tee / ggv / mei / ddee zzeeq / **biuq** / neif / **paq** / **tv** / heq
this / after / topicalizer / pair / dongba / and / diviner / emerge / go

Scharten translation

The seventh brought forth the principles, The eighth created priests, sorcerer

New translation

From the next pair came chieftains and officials, and from the next pair, the dongba and the female diviners.

Notes

Two more pairs of eggs hatch, this time seeing the emergence of office-holders – “a headman and his subordinate” (Rock 1952 677) – and then the religious specialists.

3-6, 3-7

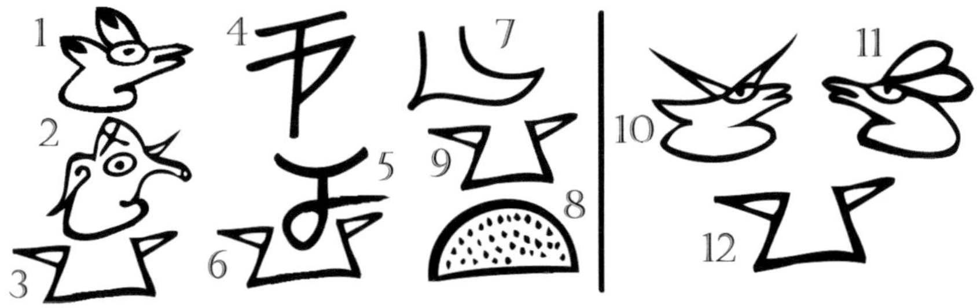

Graph-by-graph

1. **zzi**, a jackal, phonetic loan for *zzi*, people (in general).
2. **coq**, elephant, phonetic loan for *coq*, humanity.
3. **tvq**, a bucket, used phonetically for *tv*, emerge.
4. **perq**, white.
5. **naq**, black.
6. **tv**, to emerge.
7. **be**, sole of the foot, loan graph for Be, an east Tibetan people from Muli, Sichuan.
8. **oq**, grain. Phonetic loan for O, a Tibetan people from Eya, Sichuan.
9. **tv**, to emerge.
10. **neeq**, a sheep, used here to indicate livestock.
11. **to'lei**, a rabbit, here used metonymically to indicate *xu*, wild beasts.
12. **tv**, to emerge.

Transcription

tee / ggv / mei / ddee zzeeq / **zzi** / neif / **coq** / **tv** / heq
this / after / topicalizer / pair / people / and / humanity / emerge / go
tee / ggv / mei / ddee zzeeq / **perq** / neif / **naq** / **tv** / heq
this / after / topicalizer / pair / white / and / black / emerge / go
tee / ggv / mei / ddee zzeeq / **Be** / neif / **Oq** / **tv** / heq
this / after / topicalizer / pair / name of a tribe / and / name of a tribe / emerge / go
tee / ggv / mei / ddee zzeeq / **neeq** / neif / **xu** / **tv** / heq
this / after / topicalizer / pair / livestock / and / wild animals / emerge / go

Scharten translation

The nineth brought forth the people of the earth, black and white, Hsi-fan and Li-su. Domestic and wild beasts,

New translation

Then came the people of the world, the black and white tribes, the "Be" and "O" peoples. Then came the domestic and the wild animals.

Notes

Now the people of the world emerge, followed by the beasts. It is unclear which people exactly are referred to by "black" and "white", although white could be Tibetans (who live near the foot of the "white hill" in the mytho-geography of the Naxi) and the black the Naxi (*naq* = black, *xi* = person). Scharten's characterization of the "O" as "Li-su" is probably inaccurate. He Guisheng posits the "Oq" as a phonetic loan for "*wuq*", slaves/servants, I here follow Rock's interpretation of the "O" as a tribe neighbouring the Tibetan peoples (whom he called Hsi-fan 西番 after the Chinese fashion) of Muli.

3-8

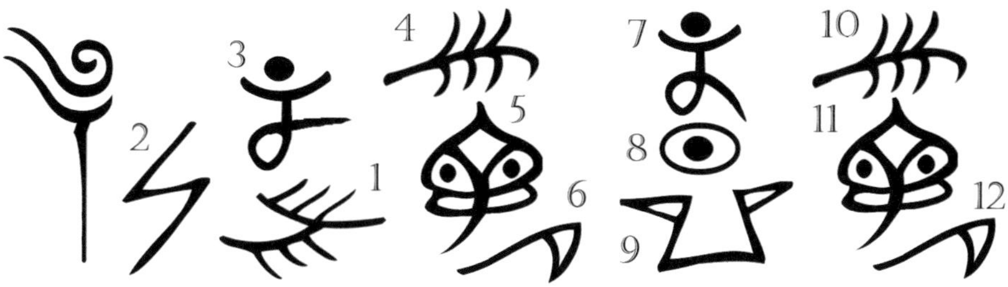

Graph-by-graph

1. **mai**, tail, used phonetically for *mail*, after.
2. **cherl**, generation, represented perhaps by a broken stick (or one generation branching off into another).
3. **Iggvq-dinaq**, a malevolent deity.
4. **bee**, artemisia, phonetic for the first syllable of the verb, *beebabbei* (to transform).
5. **ba**, a frog's head, second syllable of *beebabbei.*
6. **bbei**, to do, final syllable of *beebabbei.*
7. **Iggvq-dinaq**.
8. **gv naq**, a black egg.
9. **tvq**, a bucket, used phonetically for *tv*, emerge.
10. **bee**, first syllable of *beebabbei* (to transform).
11. **ba**, second syllable of *beebabbei.*
12. **bbei**, final syllable of *beebabbei.*

Transcription
tee / ggv / **mail** / ddee / **cherl** / **Iggvq-dinaq** / **beebabbei**
this / after / next / one / generation / deity / transform
gv / **naq** / ddee / lvl / **tv**
egg / black / this / one / emerge
gv / naq / **beebabbei**
egg / black / transform

Scharten translation
Afterwards a man comes, named: I-kuh-ti-na and he creates a black egg. This black [egg] arises and proceed a black chicken.

New translation
In the following generation, Iggvq-dinaq transformed into a black egg, and that egg hatched.

Notes
This panel begins with a textual caret, derivative of the Tibetan *yig mgo*, that indicates the beginning of a new episode. Here the antithesis of the great god Iggvq-ogeq appears, a black deity known as Iggvq-dinaq. His name is written with the graph for black, *naq*, with an additional black mark above it. The second time his name appears (graph 7 above), it is not necessarily read out. The birth of Iggvq-dinaq is truncated here: at first the false and the unreal come together to create a black orb, from which comes a black gem, that becomes an evil breath. From this breath comes Iggvq-dinaq (McKhann 1992, 89).

3-9

Graph-by-graph
1. **aiq naq**, black chicken (the black dot on the breast indicates its colour).
2. **mi**, fire, used phonetically for *miq*, name.
3. **xi**, rice, used phonetically for *xi*, person.
4. **me**, negation.
5. **Mee'leel-seeqzzee**, a demon king. Here simplified to *seeq*.
6. **bbei**, to do, a farm tool.

7. **Fvljji-ainaq**, the black chicken (now named).
8. **gv kol**, nest (with black eggs inside).

Transcription
aiq / **naq** / ddee / mei / tv
chicken / black / one / particle / emerge
miq / zeel / **xi** / **me** / jjuq
name / to name / person /not / have
wu / miq / wu / lei / zeel
self / name / self / particle used before verbs / to name
seeq / gge / Fvljji-ainaq / lei / miq / **bbei**
malevolent spirit / possessive / name of the chicken / again / name / to do
Fvljji-ainaq / beebabbei
name of the chicken / to transform
gv / naq / ggv / zzeeq / tv
egg / black / nine / pair / to emerge

Scharten translation
There was none to give it a name, but afterward it gives itself a name: Fu-chia-ai-nae. Heaven prepares it a nest in the grass, where nine pairs of eggs are created.

New translation
Nobody gave it a name, so the black chicken named itself Fvljji-ainaq of Seeq. Fvljji-ainaq laid nine pairs of black eggs.

Notes
The first time the chicken appears (graph 1), it is simply a "black chicken", but the second time (graph 7), it is read as Fvljji-ainaq, its proper name, as its name has by then been revealed. The black chicken belongs to the demon king Mee'leel-seeqzzee, the enemy of Mee'leel-dduqzzee. He Guisheng expands the story to mirror the creation of the nest, the black chicken taking black grass to create its nest etc.

He Guisheng suggests that the unlabeled graph, the awl beside the first graph that looks quite a bit like a dagger, could be read *qu* and indicate a group of chickens. I have not included this in the translation as none of the other versions indicate any more than one chicken.

3-10, 4-1

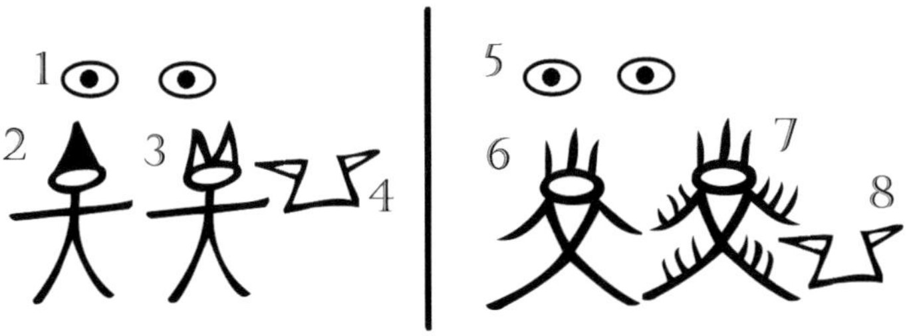

Graph-by-graph

1. **gv naq**, a black egg (two eggs are depicted).
2. **ddvq**, a malevolent spirit.
3. **zeiq**, a malevolent spirit.
4. **tvq**, a bucket, used phonetically for *tv*, emerge.
5. **gv naq**, a black egg (two eggs are depicted).
6. **mu**, a malevolent water spirit.
7. **eeq**, a malevolent water spirit.
8. **tv**, emerge.

Transcription

juq / gge / tee / ddee zzeeq
before / of / this / pair
ddvq / neif / **zeiq** / **tv** / heq
Spirit / and / spirit / emerge / go
tee / ggv / mei / ddee zzeeq
that / after / particle / pair
mu / neif / **eeq** / **tv** / heq
spirit / and / spirit / emerge / go

Scharten translation

The first pair of black eggs, proceed, two evil spirits.
The second brought forth the evil spirit of the waters.

New translation

From the first pair, the ddvq and zeiq spirits came forth.
From the second pair came the mu and eeq spirits of the waters.

Notes

Now it is the turn of the black eggs to hatch, out of which emerge all manner of not-so-pleasant entities. The black eggs (graphs 1 and 5) are referred to as pairs "*zzeeq*", and not read as literally "black egg". The first entities to emerge are the ddvq and the zeiq, malevolent spirits that frequently appear as a pair throughout the ritual tradition.

The ddvq, deriving from the Tibetan *bdud* བདུད, are black with pointed heads. The zeiq, Tibetan *btsan* བཙན, are red in colour, are frequently seen riding horses, and have split heads. Rock implies that these head shapes are merely distinctive headpieces (1952, 90), while Fang Guoyu suggests that the demon's heads themselves are thus shaped (1981, 358).

In the second panel we see malevolent spirits that live in bodies of water. "It is believed that people who are drowned, either accidentally or by committing suicide, come into the power of the ^{2}Mun ^{1}Ghügh demons" (Rock 1952, 93). A ceremony to appease them involves throwing a live chicken into the water, as payment for the souls that have become trapped in their watery realm.

4-2

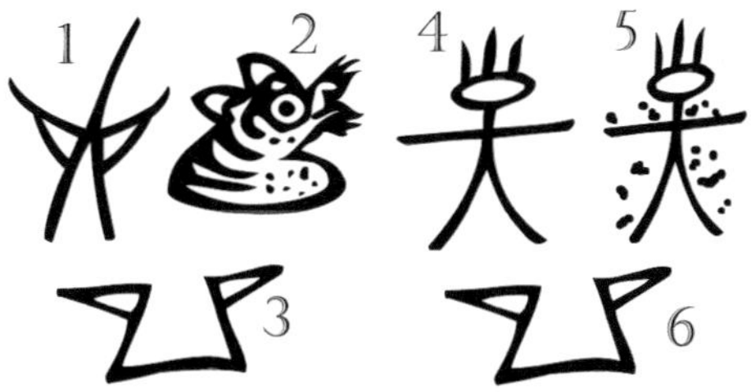

Graph-by-graph

1. **derq**, a malevolent spirit.
2. **la**, tiger's head, here a borrowing for *laq*, a malevolent spirit.
3. **tvq**, a bucket, used phonetically for *tv*, emerge.
4. **ceeq**, a malevolent spirit.
5. **niuq**, a malevolent spirit.
6. **tv**, emerge.

Transcription

tee / ggv / mei / ddee zzeeq
that / after / particle / pair
derq / neif / **laq** / **tv** / heq
spirit / and / spirit / emerge / go
ceeq / neif / **niuq** / **tv** / heq
spirit / and / spirit / emerge / go

Scharten translation

The third brought forth the guost of one, who has not been judged.

New translation

From the next pair came the derq and the laq, the ceeq and the niuq.

Notes

Now are revealed the final two pairs of evil spirits. The derq are headless demons, frequently associated with the laq: "Any person dying unattended, killed by falling rocks or trees, by lightning, in battle, devoured by wild beasts, etc., becomes a [1]Dtěr demon" (Rock 1972, 261). Scharten's "one who has not been judged" likely refers to a derq ghost of someone who died in unusual circumstances. In the manuscript, the laq are depicted by a tiger's head alone, but they have their own phono-semantic compound with the tiger's head atop the derq graph: . The last ghost (graph 5) is an enigma. He Guisheng reads it as "yeq", a demon of suicide, usually depicted , and this reading is borne out in the more contemporary manuscripts (i.e. a Coqbbertv manuscript written by dongba He Guowei in 2004 in the author's possession). Rock states however that the ceeq are "always associated" with the "niuq", perhaps revealing an evolution in the tradition. Graph 5 above is perhaps an alternate form of *niuq*  (see Fang and He 1981, 358), a trembling ghost.

4-3

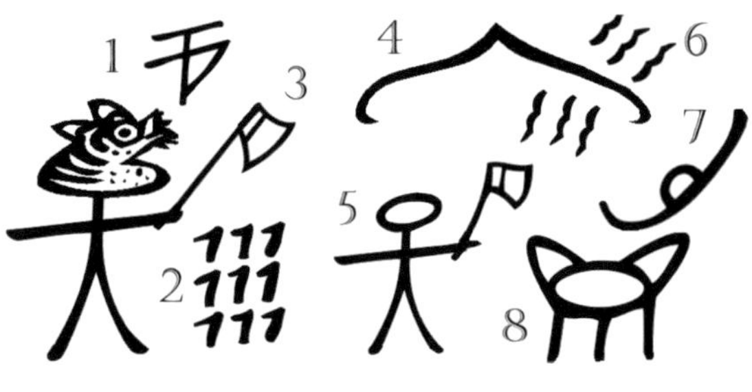

Graph-by-graph

1. **pv'laq**, gods. Indicated by two phonetic loans: white (*perq*), and tiger (*la*).
2. **ggv**, nine.
3. **bbei**, to do, make. First syllable of *bbeigv*, brothers.
4. **mee**, heaven.
5. **beelzhee**, an artisan. A figure wielding a tool (an axe).
6. **mee liulliul**, a shaking sky.
7. **me**, negation.
8. **gv**, garlic, loan for *gvl*, to be able.

Transcription

pv'laq / **ggv** / **bbei**gv / **mee** / tv / **beelzheel** / lei / bbei / zhee
gods / nine / brothers / heaven / open / artisan / particle / do / point, instruct
mee liulliul / la / tv / **me** / **gvl**
sky shaking / even / open / not / able

Scharten translation

Nine gods were not able to open heaven, for there was thunder lightning.

New translation

Nine male gods were to be the artisans that opened up the heavens, but the sky shook, and they were unable to do so.

Notes

To open up the skies is an important step in the creation story. The nine brother gods have this duty, and they were to be the "artisans" that achieved such a feat, although thwarted at this first attempt. The word for artisan, *beelzheel*, has a standard graph, a figure with a robe and headdress holding an axe: . The manuscript, however, shows a much-simplified graph. Sky, *mee*, is read twice, but one graph here doubles up as the first "heavens" and also the second noun phrase, the shaking sky. Other manuscript traditions have two separate graphs, e.g. in He Yuncai and He Fayuan (YSMGZCGB 1986, 158)

4-4

Graph-by-graph

1. **laq**, gods.
2. **mil**, girl, woman.
3. **sher**, seven.
4. **ddiuq**, the earth.
5. **ku**, a door. Phonetic loan for *ku*, to open.
6. **zheellv niuniu**, earthquake.
7. **ku**, door (to open).

8. **me**, negation.
9. **she**, syllabic graph derived from Chinese *shang* 上 (up), no semantic meaning.

Transcription
laqmi / **sher** / meiheiq / **ddiuq** / **ku** / beelzheel / lei / bbei / zherq
female gods / seven / sisters / earth / open / artisan / particle / do / point, instruct
zheellv niuniu / **ku** / **me** / gvl
earthquake / open / not / able

Scharten translation
Also nine virgins were not able to open earth, for there was earthquake in the earth.

New translation
Seven sister gods were to be the artisans that opened up the earth, but the ground shook, and they were unable to do so.

Notes
In another highly visual collage, the seven sister gods are tasked with opening up the earth. The final graph (9) is a geba phonetic syllable, *she*; He Guisheng does not read it, instead using the formulaic verb, *gvl*, to be able, as in the previous panel. He also suggests that "seven" is indicative not of a literal number, but, like the number nine, merely a number used to indicate the idea of "many". Scharten's "nine virgins" is clearly a simple error, considering the "seven" is prominently written.

4-5

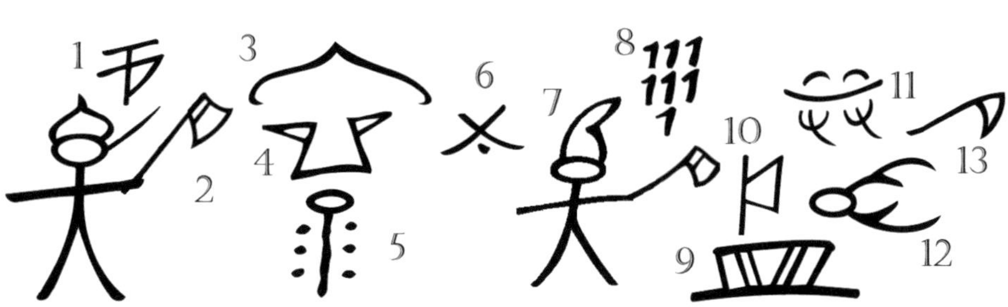

Graph-by-graph
1. **pv'laq**, gods.
2. **bbei**, to do, make. Perhaps first syllable of *bbeigv*, brothers, or indicative of *beelzheel*, artisans.
3. **mee**, heaven.

4. **tvq**, a bucket, used phonetically for *tv*, emerge.
5. **rheeq**, drops of water, “time” (the passage of).
6. **la**, syllabic graph, first syllable of *lamil*, female gods.
7. **mil**, woman. The axe indicates that the female deities are working on creating the earth.
8. **sher**, seven.
9. **ddiuq**, the earth.
10. **ku**, door, to open.
11. **mie**, eyes. First syllable of *mieggeeq*, vast.
12. **ggee**, to chew. Second syllable of *mieggeeq*, vast.
13. **bbei**, to do.

Transcription
pv’laq / ggv / **bbei**gv / **mee** / **tv** / beelzheel / lei / tv / heq
gods / nine / brothers / heaven / open / artisan / particle / do / go
lamil / **sher** / meiheiq / **ddiuq** / **ku** / **mieggeeq** / lei / **bbei** / heq
female gods / seven / sisters / earth / open / vast / particle / do /go

Scharten translation
Afterwards there were seven man- and seven women gods, who were able to open heaven and earth.

New translation
The nine brothers were able to open up the heavens, and the seven sisters were able to open up the earth.

Notes
While Scharten’s translation suggests a different set of gods, these are the same deities of the previous panels, only now successful in creating the heavens and the earth. Graph 5, *rheeq*, is not read by He Guisheng, it may be a substitute for the verb, *heq*, “to go”. The *rheeq* graph also appears in Li Lin-ts’an’s manuscript, but was not read by his dongba assistant, He Cai, either. Graphs 1 and 2 can be considered a single compound graph: *Pv’laq ggv bbeigv*, “the nine brother gods”. The omission of the numeral nine and the inclusion of the seven, associated with the sister gods, may have led Scharten to use the same figure for both.

4-6

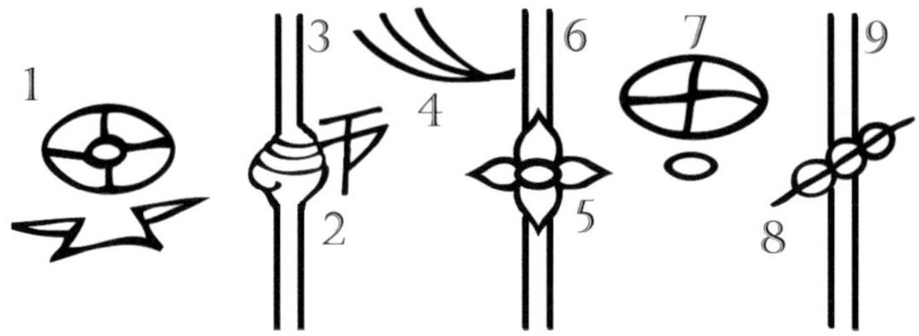

Graph-by-graph

1. **nimeitv**, "sun emerge", i.e., east.
2. **ddvperq**, white conch.
3. **dvlrer**, column.
4. **yicheemee**, the bottom of a watercourse: south.
5. **waqherq**, turquoise gemstone.
6. **dvlrer**, column.
7. **nimeiggvq**, visually "sun egg", the egg (*gv*) is used phonetically for *ggvq*, meaning fall, hence "sun fall", i.e., west.
8. **chuq**, carnelian gemstone.
9. **dvlrer**, column.

Transcription

Jjiuqnal-sheello / **nimeitv / ddvperq / dvlrer** / ceel / lei / ji
sacred mountain / east / white conch / column / erect / particle / put
Jjiuqnal-sheello / **yicheemee / waher / dvlrer** / ceel / lei / ji
sacred mountain / south / turquoise / column / erect / particle / put
Jjiuqnal-sheello / **niemeiggvq / chuqna / dvlrer** / ceel / lei / ji
sacred mountain / west / black carnelian / column / erect / particle / put

Scharten translation

In the earth there appeared a white spiral univalve shell pole, in the south there appeared a pole of precious stones and in the west one of coral.

New translation

To the east, the sacred mountain was supported with a column of white conch. To the south, with a column of turquoise, and to the west, with a column of black carnelian.

Notes

The mytho-geography of the Naxi religion now comes into view: the sacred mountain, the Naxi *axis mundi* Jjiuqnal-sheello, is in the centre of the world (although not yet depicted on this page), and, towards the cardinal directions, giant columns of different gemstones that help to support the heavens are erected by the nine brothers and seven sisters. For an in-depth discussion of these gemstone bulwarks and their significance, see Li (2007, 122-128). This panel is prefaced by a double line, perhaps indicating a stronger break, and the start of a new part of the text. He Guisheng adds to the written text with an oral reading that comes directly before this section: because of the storms and earthquakes, the gods had difficulty opening the heavens and the earth, and so in order to stabilize the cosmos the ritual specialists, alongside the able and the wise, all came together to decide what to do. At this conference it was decided that the cosmos would be propped up by columns of precious material.

4-7

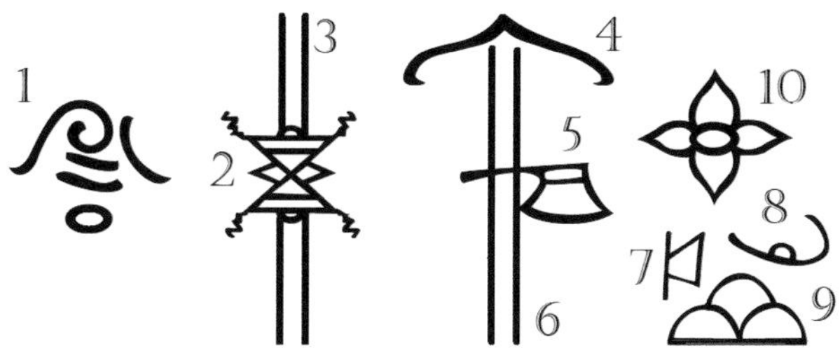

Graph-by-graph

1. **hu**, syllabic graph, indicating **hoggv'loq** north.
2. **haiq**, gold, here read *haisheeq*, yellow gold.
3. **dvlrer**, column.
4. **mee**, heaven.
5. **shuq**, an axe, borrowing for "iron".
6. **dvlrer**, column.
7. **ku**, to open.
8. **me**, negation.
9. **lv**, stones, loan for *lvq*, enough.
10. **waq**, turquoise.

Transcription

Jjiuqnal-sheello / **hoggv'loq** / **haisheeq** / **dvlrer** / ceel / lei / ji
sacred mountain / north / gold / column / erect / particle / put
Jjiuqnal-sheello / **mee** / neif / ddiuq / liuggv / **shuq**perq / **dvlrer** / ceel / lei / ji
sacred mountain / heaven / and / earth / in between / white iron / column / erect / particle / put
mee / **ku** / **me** / **lvq** / **waq** / nee / lei / zhul / seiq
heaven / open / not / enough / jade / agent marker / particle / mend / final particle

Scharten translation

In the north there appeared a golden and silver pole, in the midst an iron pole, but material was not enough and used therefore precious stones.

New translation

To the north, the sacred mountain was supported with a column of gold. In the centre between heaven and earth, a column of iron was erected. Where the heavens were not opened fully, jade was used to fill in the gaps.

Notes

Graph 1 is a geba syllabic graph, *hu*, which is an unusual way of indicating *hoggv'loq*, north. The He Yuncai manuscript has two syllabic graphs for the same words (*hu* and *lo*), suggesting that the use of syllabic graphs here is traditional. The dongba graph for north represents the top part of a watercourse: 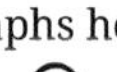. Li Jingsheng (2009) has suggested that this graph indicates a historical migration south from the source of a major river.

4-8

Graph-by-graph

1. **ddiuq**, the earth.
2. **ku**, door, to open up.
3. **me**, negation.
4. **lv**, stones, borrowing for *lvq*, enough.
5. **haiq**, a gold brooch, gold.

Transcription

ddiuq / ku / me / lvq / haiq / nee / lei / yeq / seiq

earth / open / not / enough / gold / agent marker / particle / to plaster (i.e., a wall) / final particle

Scharten translation

For the earth there was also not enough material and they used silver and gold.

New translation

To the north, the sacred mountain was supported with a column of gold. In the centre between heaven and earth, a column of iron was erected. Where the earth was not opened fully, gold was used to fill in the gaps.

Notes

Potholes in the newly carved out earth are now filled in (in this case, the verb *yeq* is used, “to plaster [as in a wall])” with gold. The verb is not written in this manuscript, but the He Yuncai text records the phonetic loan graph, *yeq*  (tobacco, or perhaps a high alpine plant, see Li [2001, 200]. Rock believed that the graph indicated wilted leaves, as an ideograph for *yeq*, wilted).

4-9

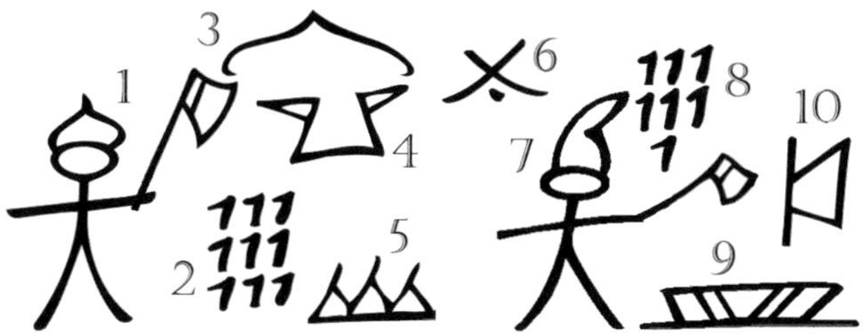

Graph-by-graph

1. **pv’laq**, deities.
2. **ggv**, nine.
3. **mee**, heaven.
4. **tv**, to open out.
5. **hiuq**, red (like fire).
6. **la**, syllabic graph, first syllable of *lamil*, female gods.
7. **mil**, woman.
8. **sher**, seven.
9. **ddiuq**, the earth.
10. **ku**, door, to open up.

Transcription

pv’laq / **ggv** / bbeigv / **mee** / **tv** / beelzheel / lei / bbei / heq
deities / nine / brothers / heaven / open / artisan / particle / become / go
lamil / **sher** / meiheiq / **ddiuq** / **ku** / **mieggeeq** / beelzheel / lei / bbei / heq
female deities / seven /sisters / earth / open / vast / artisans / particle / become / go

Scharten translation

Afterwards nine gods finished creating heaven and nine virgins created earth.

New translation

Thus the nine brother gods opened up the heavens and the seven sister gods levelled out the earth.

Notes

This is a repetitive panel that closely mirrors panel 4-5. It acts as a confirmation before the story continues – the nine brother gods and seven sister gods thus became the artisans who opened out the heavens and levelled out the earth. Of particular note is graph 5 (*hiuq*, red), not read by He Guisheng or (apparently) Scharten's dongba. It could possibly be a borrowing for the final verb *heq*, to go.

5-1

Graph-by-graph

1. **ddee**, one.
2. **cherl**, generation (the graph represents a broken stick).
3. **aiq**, chicken.
4. **gv**, egg.
5. **mai**, tail, loan for *mail*, after.
6. **bbei**, snow, semantic loan for *ceil*, winter.
7. **seel**, three.
8. **hei**, month.
9. **bbei**, snow.
10. **bbvq**, to incubate, an egg in a nest.
11. **tvq**, a bucket, used phonetically for *tv*, emerge.
12. **me**, negation.

Transcription

tee / ggv / gge / **ddee** / **cherl** / lei / ggv / nieq
this / after / possessive / one / generation / particle / attain / at that time
aiq / gge / **gv** / **mail** / tee / ddee /liu
chicken / possessive / egg /after / that / one / measure word for egg
cee / mei / **cee seel hei**
winter / topicalizer / winter three months
bbei / nee / seel / ha / bbvq
snow / adverbial marker / three / night / hatch
bbvq / lei / **tv**/ **me** / ni
hatch / particle / emerge / not / want

Scharten translation

The third egg, the last one of the chicken, was hidden in the snow for three days. It could not proceed any thing, because of this.

New translation

In the generation that followed, the last egg that the chicken laid was incubated in the snow during the three months of winter for three days, but did not hatch.

Notes

Note the visual resemblance between graphs 8 and 10, which are probably a purposeful mirroring: the moon and the egg in a nest. Graphs 6 and 9 are the same, but the former is read *ceil* (winter), while the latter is read *bbei*, snow. McKhann here offers this translation "In the generation of [the god] Dduq, Eeiuq-eemaq laid her last egg; it was a very troublesome egg…" (1992, 91).

5-2

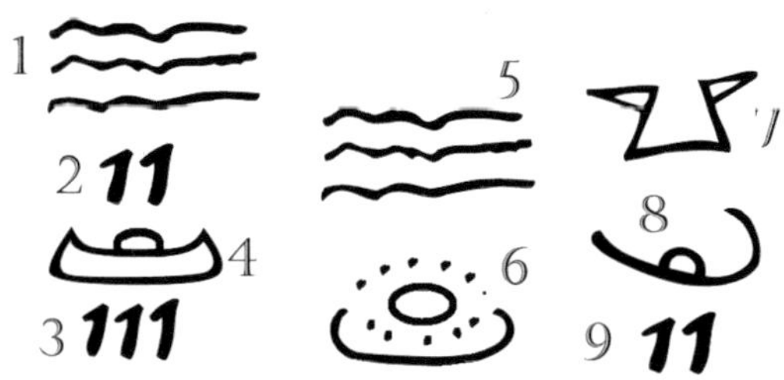

Graph-by-graph

1. **her**, wind, semantic loan for *meeniq*, spring.
2. **ni**, two, phonetic loan for *meeniq*, spring.
3. **seel**, three.
4. **hei**, month.
5. **her**, wind.
6. **bbvq**, to incubate.
7. **tvq**, a bucket, used phonetically for *tv*, emerge.
8. **me**, negation.
9. **ni**, two, phonetic loan for *ni*, to want.

Transcription

niq / mei / **niqseelhei**

spring / topicalizer / spring three months

her / nee / seel / ha / **bbvq**

wind / adverbial marker / three /night / hatch

bbvq / lei / **tv**/ **me** / **ni**

hatch / particle / emerge / not / want

Scharten translation

In the spring the high winds hindered the chicken to come out of the egg.

New translation

During the three months of spring, the egg was incubated in the wind for three days, but it didn't hatch.

Notes

Spring is traditionally the season of high winds. Both graphs 1 and 2 can here be read as "*niq*", spring. The first is a semantic loan, for spring is the season of high winds, while the second is a phonetic loan, borrowing the pronunciation for two, *ni*. Either the phonetic loan is in this case somewhat superfluous, or we can consider both graphs together to form a single graph: a phono-semantic compound. Graph 9 is another "two", and a *different* phonetic loan, this time for *ni*, to want.

5-3

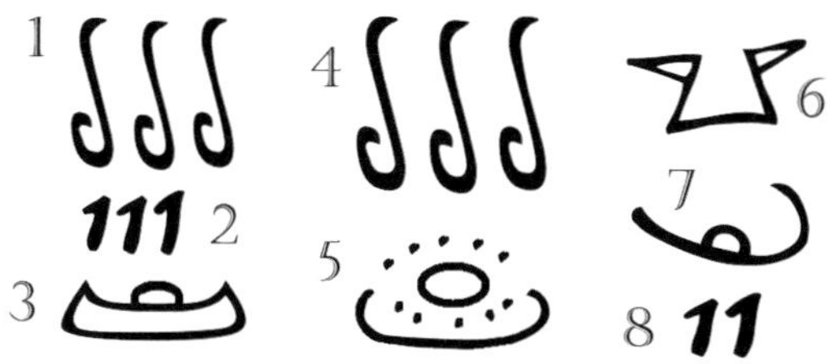

Graph-by-graph

1. **heeq**, raindrops, hence rain, semantic loan for *ruq*, summer (the month of the summer rains).
2. **seel**, three.
3. **hei**, month, a moon.
4. **heeq**, rain.
5. **bbvq**, an egg in a nest, to incubate.
6. **tvq**, a bucket, used phonetically for *tv*, emerge.
7. **me**, negation.
8. **ni**, two, phonetic loan for *ni*, to want.

Transcription

ruq / me / **ruqseelhei**

summer / topicalizer / summer three months

heeq / nee / seel / ha / **bbvq**
rain / adverbial marker / three /night / hatch
bbvq / lei / **tv** / **me** / **ni**
hatch / particle / emerge / not / want

Scharten translation
In the summer the heavy rains are a hindrance.

New translation
During the three months of summer, the egg was incubated in the summer rains for three days, but it didn't hatch.

Notes
Summer is the rainy season in the Himalayan foothills of southwest China, therefore rain is the symbol used to depict summer graphically. In this panel the rain graph is used twice, both as a semantic loan word (to portray the idea of "summer", graph 1) and literally, the pictograph of rain drops indicating rain itself (graph 4).

5-4

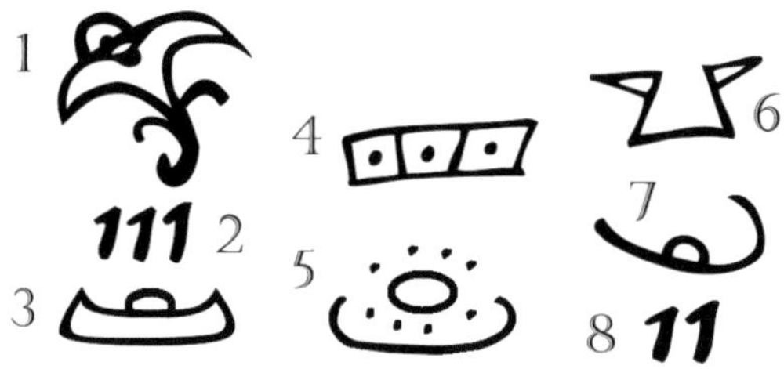

Graph-by-graph
1. **bbaq**, flower, semantic loan for *chul*, autumn.
2. **seel**, three.
3. **hei**, month.
4. **zhee**, soil.
5. **bbvq**, an egg in a nest, to incubate.
6. **tvq**, a bucket, used phonetically for *tv*, emerge.
7. **me**, negation.
8. **ni**, two, phonetic loan for *ni*, to want.

Transcription
chul / mei / **chulseelhei**
autumn / topicalizer / autumn three months
zhee / nee / seel / ha / **bbvq**
soil / adverbial marker / three /night / hatch
bbvq / lei / **tv** / **me** / **ni**
hatch / particle / emerge / not / want

Scharten translation
In the autumn neaither for it was put in the earth.

New translation
During the three months of autumn, the egg was incubated in the soil for three days, but it didn't hatch.

Notes
Autumn is traditionally the season where the flowers bloom in the high alpine meadows, hence the flower used as a semantic loan for *chul*, autumn. Here the egg is incubated in the fertile soil of the autumn season for three days, but still it refused to hatch.

5-5

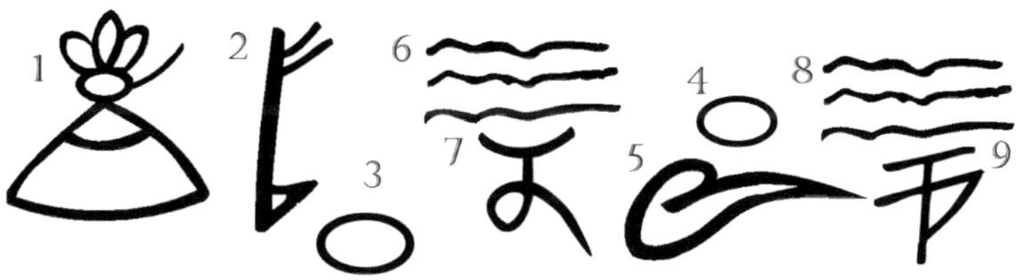

Graph-by-graph
1. **Dduq**, male deity.
2. **meeltv**, walking stick.
3. **gv**, egg.
4. **gv**, egg.
5. **heel**, ocean.
6. **her**, wind.
7. **naq**, black.
8. **her**, wind.
9. **perq**, white.

Transcription
Me / heeq / Dduq / me / heeq
not / peace / deity / not / peace
Mee'leel Dduq epv / nee / **meeltv** / yuq / lei / **gv** / lei / paq
Grandfather Dduq / topicalizer / walking stick / take up / particle / egg / particle / hit (wildly)
gv / yuq / jjuq / gv / gvl
egg / take up / mountain / top / throw
jjuq / gv / jjiq / nieq / heq
mountain / top / water / into / go
jjiq / naq / heel / nieq / heq
water / large / sea / in / go
gv / yuq / **heel** / nieq / rhuq
egg / take up / sea / into / drop
wai / nee / **her** / **naq** / tv / yi / nee / **her** / **perq** / tv
left / adverbial marker / wind / black / rise / right / adverbial marker / wind / white / rise

Scharten translation
Becaude the chicken could not come out of its self, the god of heaven got angry. He takes a stick and wants to throw the egg in the sea. From the left and the right a big wind is blowing and carries the egg in the sea, where it is carried to and fro.

New translation
And the god Dduq was not at all pleased; he took up his stick and thwacked the egg so that it plopped into a stream on top of a mountain, where the waters swelled and carried it down into the ocean. From the left came a black wind, and from the right blew a white wind.

Notes
Nine graphs here account for He Guisheng's reading of 48 syllables across seven intonation units. Some parts must be recited completely from memory, such as the opening line concerning how angry the god became at the egg's temerity in refusing to hatch (i.e. what incited him to strike it with his stick like an oversized golf ball – and straight into a water hazard, no less!); the mountain and the stream are also not written. While Scharten does explain the god's anger, the divine egg thwack is missing; in her reading, the winds blow the egg directly into the sea. In the He Yuncai manuscript, Dduq and his walking stick do not appear at all (160-161).

5-6

Graph-by-graph

1. **ai**, cliff (the chicken's head, *aiq*, acts as a phonetic marker).
2. **bbu**, bright (a light emanating outward).
3. **tvq**, a bucket, used phonetically for *tv*, emerge.
4. **zzee**, to eat (in this case, lean meat going into a person's mouth).
5. **eseeq**, father. Wood (*ser*) acts as phonetic marker atop the head.
6. **yuq**, sheep, phonetic loan for *yuq*, to be born (with), to live.
7. **shul**, comb (of a chicken), represented by the chicken's head.
8. **me**, negation.

Transcription

gv / perq / her / nee / muq / lei /ai /nieq / gvl
egg / white / wind / subject marker / blow / particle / cliff / into / throw
ai / gv / **bbu** / sso / ddee / gvl / **tv**
cliff / top / light / bright / one / measure word / appear
Reqzzee-bbubbv / lei / mi / bbei
name / particle / name / make
eseeq / **shul** / **yuq** / zherq
father / comb (chicken) / born (with) / to cause, make
shul / see / lei / me / yuq
comb / first / particle / not / born (with)

Scharten translation

It was thrown on the shore and through its fall, there came out a man, named Peh-puh. On his forehead was a cresh, for he was the chicken's generation.

New translation

The white wind blew the egg onto a cliff, where it hatched into a bright light. A being appeared [from within], with the name of Reqzzee-bbubbv. Now, its father's generation grew combs atop their heads, but this being had no comb.

Notes

The egg hatches into something else, something *other*: This being is merely described as "strange" and given no name in He Yuncai's reading (161). Scharten calls it Peh-puh, but He Guisheng ascribes to it the name Reqzzee-bbubbv (presumably graph 4, to eat, is a shorthand for this). The "father" in the text would be the generation of chickens that hatched the egg, who all had combs on their heads, but this being does not. There is a dedicated graph for a chicken's comb in the script, , but it is not used here (we get instead the chicken's head peeking somewhat cheekily in from the end of the page, graph 7).

5-7

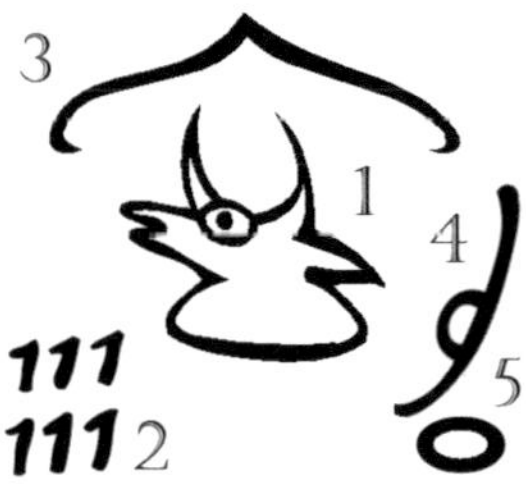

Graph-by-graph

1. **ko**, horns (the head of a horned animal).
2. **chual**, six.
3. **mee**, heaven.
4. **me**, negation.
5. **gv**, egg. Probably a phonetic loan for *gvl*, to be able.

Transcription

ko / see / lei / yuq / ceeq
egg / first / again / born (with) / come
ko / nee / **mee** / dvl / bee / **me** / **gvl**
horn / topicalizer / heaven / to prop up / go / not / able

Scharten translation

On his head he had horns, but they were too long, and because of this, he coul not do any work.

New translation

It grew horns, but the horns could not support the heavens.

Notes

He Guisheng's reading of the second intonation unit of this panel is "*ko yuq mee dvl hee*", or, "it grew horns that could prop up the heavens". This reading ignores the final two graphs of the manuscript, which suggest an inability (an inability that is present in Scharten's translation). He Yuncai's reading suggests "*me ni*", unable [to reach the heavens], which I alter to "*me gvl*" (also "unable") based upon the final graph, an egg, *gv*, and probably a borrowing for *gvl*, to be able. There is no readily apparent explanation for graph 2, *chual* (six): all readings suggest "*see*", "first", which can be depicted using the graph for three (*seel*).

5-8

Graph-by-graph

1. **mil**, woman, here read *elmei*, a respectful term for mother.
2. **rheq**, claw.
3. **me**, negation.
4. **be**, foot, more accurately the sole of a foot.
5. **ddiuq**, the earth.
6. **me**, negation.
7. **ba**, a frog's head. Probably a borrowing for *bal*, to dig.
8. **me**, negation.
9. **ku**, door, loan for *ku*, to open or flatten out.

Transcription

emei / **rheq** / yuq /zherq
mother / claw / born (with) / to cause, make
rheq / see / lei / **me** / yuq
claw / first / again / not / born (with)
be / see / lei / yuq / ceeq
foot / first / again / born (with) / come
be / nee / **ddiuq** / me / **bal** / ddiuq / me / **ku**
foot / topicalizer / earth / not / dig / earth / not /flatten out

Scharten translation

The older mother seemed to have the claws of a bird, but it was the sole of a man. She was not able to create the earth.

New translation

Its mother's generation grew claws on their feet, but it was not born with claws. It instead grew feet, but the feet could not dig into and flatten out the earth.

Notes

McKhann translates this panel as "it could not use its feet to grab the earth" (1992, 91). Graph 4, *be*, is more literally the "sole (of the foot)", hence Scharten's translation. "Sole" is more commonly written  (Li 2001, 129).

5-9

Graph-by-graph

1. **mil**, woman, here read *elmei*, a respectful term for mother.
2. **no**, fine feathers.
3. **me**, negation.
4. **fv**, hair.
5. **sher**, seven, used phonetically for *sher*, to appear.
6. **req**, grass.
7. **me**, negation.
8. **gv**, egg, used phonetically for *gvl*, to be able.

Transcription

elmei / **no** / yuq / zherq
mother / fine feathers / born (with) / to cause
no / see / lei / **me** / yuq
fine feathers / first / again / not / born (with)
fv / see / lei / yuq / **sher**
hair / first / again / born (with) / appear

fv / nee / **req** / keel / req / geeq / zherq / **me** / **gvl**
hair / topicalizer / grass / cover / grass / fill / cause / not / able

Scharten translation

The mothers generation used to have feathers of birds, but they were changed in hairs of sheep and pigs. Although they were long, it was not possible to cover the earth.

New translation

Its mother's generation grew downy feathers, but it was not born with such feathers. It instead grew hair, but the hair could not cause the grass to grow and cover the land.

Notes

Graph 6 in the manuscript at first looks like a variant or poorly written form of the geba syllabic graph *"yu"* , which can be used for the verb *"yuq"* (to live, be born with) in the panel. Comparing the graphic form with a graph in the first panel on page 8 of the manuscript, however, it becomes clear that graph 6 is in fact a somewhat crude pictographic depiction of "grass". In this context, the green grass represents fertility and the multiplication of the species.

5-10

Graph-by-graph

1. **jjiq**, house, used semantically for *we*, village.
2. **gvl**, an able man (cloves of garlic are a phonetic marker).
3. **me**, negation.
4. **see**, a wise man (the branch on the head acts as a phonetic marker).
5. **me**, negation.

Transcription

we / gv / **gvl** / sso / jjiu
village / head (top) / able / man / have
gvl / nieq / lei / milddo

able / to / again / ask
gvl / nee / lei / shel / mei
able / topicalizer / come / speak / final particle
gvl / la / **me** / gvl / zeel
able / also / not / able / reported speech marker
we / gai / **see** / sso / jjiu
village / in front / wise / man / have
see / nieq / lei / milddo
wise / to / again / ask
see / nee / lei / shel / mei
wise / topicalizer / come / speak / final particle
see / la / **me** / see / zeel
know / also / not / know / reported speech marker

Scharten translation
In the house hhere is man, who is able to do any thing. One comes to him and asks: do you know, why these things all are and he answers: no.

New translation
At the end of the village lived an able man. He was asked [by this strange horned creature] why all this came to be, and he was unable to answer. In front of the village lived a wise man. He was asked why all this came to be, and he did not know the answer.

Notes
Five graphs become 38 syllables spread across eight intonation units, so there is much here that is not written. Specifically, who exactly is coming to ask the able and the wise men about the creature who was just born from the final egg, and what was the question? McKhann has the questioner as the strange creature itself, and the question "what kind of creature am I?". He Guisheng does not explain who is asking, but the question is hinted as "how can this creature be killed?". Considering the first two panels of page six, I follow McKhann's interpretation here, but still keep the question general: how did this all come to be? Special attention should be paid to graph 2, which at first looks like a *zeiq* ghost with a split head, , but the top of the head is in fact two cloves of garlic, making it a phono-semantic compound. The graph is normally written with the whole bulb of garlic (and roots) above a seated person: .

6-1

Graph-by-graph

1. **ho**, ribs, used phonetically for the first syllable of *hoggv'loq*, north.
2. **ggv**, geba phonetic, second syllable of *hoggv'loq*.
3. **lloq**, geba phonetic, third syllable of *hoggv'loq*.
4. **Dduq**, male deity.
5. **shuq**, iron, an axe.
6. **perq**, white.
7. **bberq**, yak, here bellowing.
8. **meegeel**, a shaking sky [thundering sky].
9. **hiuq**, red [like fire], perhaps used phonetically for *hiu*, wild beast.
10. **meerherq**, dragon.

Transcription

hoggv / ho**lloq**ddiuq / **Dduq** / gai / lei / milddo
north / north land / deity / before / again / ask
me / heeq / Dduq / me / heeq
not / peaceful / deity / not / peaceful
Dduq / nee / **shuq** / **perq** / shu / lei / ceeq
deity / topicalizer / axe / white / wield / particle / come
yuq / lei / bberq / gv / diu
take up / particle / yak / head / hit
bberq / **bbaq** / **meegeel** / heq
yak / bellow / heaven-shake / go
waher / **meerherq** / leegeel / niuniu / teif ni ggv
turquoise / dragon / earth-quake / shake / like that

Scharten translation

The god of the earth, Peh-p'uh, kills a cow with his ax, it begins first to low a little and afterwards like a thunder.

New translation

In the north, Dduq was asked. Dduq became angry, taking up his white axe and lopping off the beast's head. And the beast bellowed like a green dragon so that the heavens and the earth shook.

Notes

Graphs 2 and 3 are almost unreadable on the manuscript, but they are nevertheless clearly variants of the two geba phonetic graphs that can be used to write the word *hoggv'loq*, north. The strange being is here depicted with the graph for yak, primarily because of its long horns. Graph 9, red/fire, is an enigma: the dragon is a turquoise one, as all the readings seem to agree (except for Scharten, who omits the metaphor in her somewhat confused translation), and the graph does not appear in other manuscript traditions. I believe it may indicate a wild beast, *hiu*, but in any case, He Guisheng does not read it. His reading of this panel incorporates the shaking of the earth described in the following panel.

6-2

Graph-by-graph

1. **yichee**, south, the bottom section of a watercourse.
2. **Seiq**, female deity.
3. **ggaiq**, a sword.
4. **bberq**, a yak, bellowing.
5. **leegeel**, the shaking earth.
6. **lv**, stones (here depicted shaking).

Transcription

yichee / yimeeddiuq / **Seiq** / gai / lei / milddo
north / north land / deity / before / again / ask
me / heeq / Seiq / me / heeq
not / peaceful / deity / not / peaceful
Seiq / nee / **ggaiq** / bbei / shu / lei / ceeq
deity / topicalizer / axe /white / wield / particle / come

yuq / lei / **bberq** / gv / ddal
take up / particle / yak / head / chop

Scharten translation
The goddess of the south also kills a cow with a knife. The cow begins to low first a little, and afterwards like an earthquake.

New translation
In the south, Seiq was then asked. Seiq became angry, taking up her sword and chopping off the beast's head.

Notes
He Guisheng does not mention the ground shaking (clearly represented in graphs 5 and 6). This detail was covered in the previous panel. In fact, the beast being killed here in some versions causes an earthquake akin to that of a golden elephant (similar to the green dragon in the previous panel), see Li Lin-ts'an's translation (1978, 32).

6-3

Graph-by-graph
1. **bberq**, yak.
2. **xil**, tongue.
3. **mixil sheeherq**, rainbow.
4. **liuq**, look. Here used to indicate "eyes", *mieq*.
5. **nee**, geba phonetic character, representing *nee*, a topicalizer.
6. **bbaq**, a flower. Used phonetically for the second syllable of *mibbaq*, spark.
7. **dol**, pictographic representation unclear. Second syllable of *ciuldol*, to sparkle.

Transcription
xil / nee / lilloq / mei
tongue / topicalizer / stick out (the tongue) / emphatic particle
mixil sheeherq / teif ni ggv

rainbow / like that
mieq / **nee** / lilloq / mei
eyes / topicalizer / stick out / emphatic particle
mibbaq / ciuldol / teif ni ggv
sparks / sparkle / like that

Scharten translation

When she kills it, it puts out its tongue and at the same time, in the sky there appears a rainbow. Also it moves its eyes and it is like the lightning.

New translation

The creature's tongue rolled out, glowing like a rainbow, and its bulging eyes shot sparks of fire.

Notes

"Rainbow" is here read *mixil sheeherq* in the traditional register, literally something like "big tongue yellow green", i.e. a rainbow is envisaged as a large, yellow and green tongue that appears in the sky. The modern word for rainbow is *mee'leelheeljjiq*.

6-4

Graph-by-graph

1. **bberq**, yak (a yak's head). Here used semantically for *gv*, head [of the yak].
2. **mee**, heaven.
3. **gv**, egg. Here used phonetically for *geel*, to burn as an offering.
4. **ee**, skin. A skinned animal (with tail).
5. **ddiuq**, the earth.
6. **gv**, egg. Representing *geel*, to burn as an offering.

Transcription

gv / nee / **mee** / **geel** / heq
head / topicalizer / heaven / burn as an offering / go

ee / nee / **ddiuq** / **geel** / heq
skin / topicalizer / burn as an offering / go

Scharten translation
Its horns are sacrificed to the god of heaven and its skin to the mother of earth.

New translation
Its head was offered to the heavens, and its skin to the earth.

Notes
Now the creature has been slain (twice!), its constituent parts are divided up and used as offerings. The "egg" graph, *gv*, is used in this panel and the ones following as a phonetic borrowing (albeit not a directly homophonous one) for the word "*geel*", in this case a ritualistic burning.

6-5

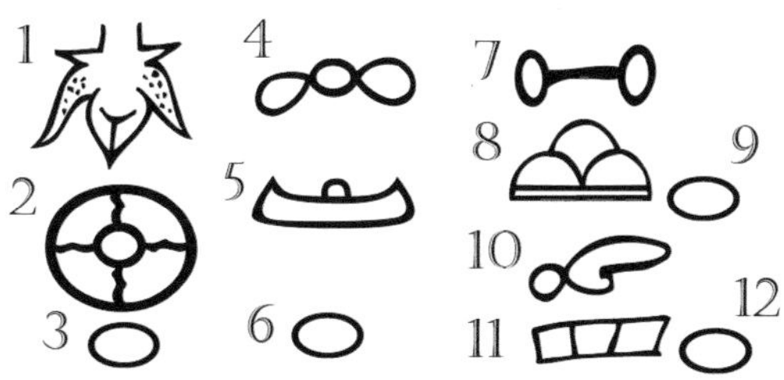

Graph-by-graph

1. **cherl**, lung.
2. **bbi**, the sun.
3. **gv**, egg. Here used phonetically for *geel*, to burn as an offering.
4. **serl**, liver.
5. **leiq**, the moon.
6. **gv**, egg.
7. **o**, bone.
8. **lv**, stones.
9. **gv**, egg.
10. **nal**, flesh (archaic).
11. **zhee**, soil.
12. **gv**, egg.

Transcription
cherl / nee / **bbi** / **geel** / heq
lung / topicalizer / sun / burn as an offering / go
serl / nee / **leiq** / **geel** / heq
liver / topicalizer / moon / burn as an offering / go
o / nee / **lv** / **geel** / heq
bone / topicalizer / stones / burn as an offering / go
nal / nee / **zhee** / **geel** / heq
flesh / topicalizer / soil / burn as an offering / go

Scharten translation
Its lungs to the sun, its liver to the moon; its bones to the stones; its meat to the clay.

New translation
Its lungs were offered to the sun, and its liver to the moon.
Its bones were offered to the stones, and its flesh to the soil.

Notes
The sacrificial offering of the beast's innards continues in formulaic fashion. He Yuncai's text uses the graph for gallbladder, *geel*, as a phonetic loan for *geel*, to burn as an offering (1986, 164). It is much closer phonetically than the *gv* (egg) used here. While this manuscript simply uses a pictograph for liver, *serl*, there is a phono-semantic compound for this graph in Fang (1981, 255): , a pictograph of a liver with a phonetic component on top (*ser*, wood).

6-6

Graph-by-graph
1. **saiq**, deity. Used phonetically for *sai*, blood.
2. **jjiq**, water.
3. **gv**, egg. Here used phonetically for *geel*, to burn as an offering.
4. **bbv**, intestines.

5. **ree**, road.
6. **gv**, egg.
7. **fv**, hair.
8. **ddiuq**, earth. Here used to represent *ssee*, grass (i.e. the grass growing on the earth is meant).

Transcription

saiq / nee / **jjiq** / **geel** / heq
blood / topicalizer / water / burn as an offering / go
bbv / nee / **ree** / **geel** / heq
intestine / topicalizer / road / burn as an offering / go
fv / nee / **ssee** / **geel** / heq
hair / topicalizer / grass / burn as an offering / go

Scharten translation

Its blood to the streams; its bowels to the big road; its hairs to the gras

New translation

Its blood was offered to the waters, its intestines to the roads, and its hair to the grass.

Notes

There is a graph for blood, *sai* , but the manuscript instead employs a phonetic loan. The astute reader will note the difference between the manuscript and the digital recreation above where it pertains to graph 4: the manuscript shows a single wavy line; the Naxi graph above derived from Fang (1981) has a double line which rhymes visually with the depiction of road in graph 5, perhaps providing a reminder of why it is the intestines that are sacrificed to the roads.

6-7

Graph-by-graph

1. **hoq**, ribs.
2. **aiq**, cliff.
3. **mai**, tail.

4. **zzerq**, tree.
5. **gv**, egg.
6. **bberq**, yak. Specifically, the front half of a yak: "*bberq ggu ggeq zzoq lo*".
7. **hu**, syllabic graph, indicating **hoggv'loq** north.
8. **gv**, egg.
9. **bberq**, yak. Specifically, the back half of a yak: "*bberq mai mail zzoq lo*".
10. **yicheemee**, south.
11. **yi**, geba syllabic graph. First syllable of *yicheeme*, south.
12. **gv**, egg.

Transcription

hoq / nee / **aiq** / geel / heq
ribs / topicalizer / cliff / burn as an offering / go
mai / nee / **zzerq** / **geel** / heq
tail / topicalizer / tree / burn as an offering / go
bberq / ggu / ggeq / zzoq lo / **hoggv'loq** / Dduq / **geel** / heq
yak / body / genitive / half / north / deity / burn as an offering / go
bberq / mai / mail / zzoq lo / **yicheemee** / Seiq / **geel** / heq
yak / tail / after / half / south / deity / burn as an offering / go

Scharten translation

Its breastbones to the mountains, its tail to the trees. When it was killed it was cut in two halves; the front part was offered to the north; the back part to the south.

New translation

Its ribs were offered to the cliffs and its tail to the trees, its front half was offered to Dduq and its back half to Seiq.

Notes

Graphs 6 and 9 both represent half of a full-body depiction of a yak. The graphic depictions have no fixed phonetic value, and must simply be glossed as "the top half of the yak" or "the bottom half of the yak", as we can see in the transcription. This represents the concise, visual nature of ideographic writing. Graph 11 is redundant: a rare geba syllabic graph that repeats the first syllable of *yicheemee*, south. It is probably employed for emphasis.

6-8

Graph-by-graph

1. **hoq**, ribs.
2. **wai**, left. A figure pointing to their left.
3. **muq**, cattle. First syllable of name Muqchuai-waiyilsee.
4. **seel**, a grass. Final syllable of name Muqchuai-waiyilsee.
5. **gv**, egg. Used phonetically for *geel*, to burn as an offering.
6. **yi**, right. A figure pointing to their right.
7. **rhuq**, horse. First syllable of name Rhuqchuai-yiqyilsee.
8. **chaq**, to milk. Milk entering a pitcher. Used phonetically for *chuai*, second syllable in name Rhuqchuai-yiqyilsee.

Transcription

bberq / **hoq** / **wai** / tee / bieq
yak / ribs / left / that / side
Muqchuai-waiyil**see** / **geel** / heq
proper name / burn as an offering / go
bberq / hoq / **yi** / tee / bieq
yak / ribs / right / that / side
Ruqchuai-yiqyilsee / geel / heq
proper name / burn as an offering / go

Scharten translation

The leftside ribs were offered to the east; and the right ones to the west.

New translation

The ribs of its left side were offered to Muqchuai-waiyilsee in the east.
The ribs of tis right side were offered to Ruqchuai-yiqyilsee in the west.

Notes

In He Guisheng's reading, meat from the beast's right side is offered alongside the ribs of the left side, but other versions suggest that the ribs are divided into two sections. The names are obscure in this panel: for He Guisheng, they are protective deities. For He Yuncai, however, they may be place names that represent directions, which directions exactly being unknown (1986, 275). Scharten's translation reveals a possible answer: east and west (this would make sense, seeing as the previous panel dealt with the north and south). Similarly, the appearance of deities Dduq and Seiq in the previous panel would indicate that perhaps the proper names here are also deities, as He Guisheng attests.

6-9

Graph-by-graph

1. **ddiuq**, the earth. Last syllable of "*zzijjeq-la'ler ddiuq*", oral formula meaning "the vast earth where the people live".
2. **gv**, garlic. Used phonetically for *gvl*, an able person.
3. **see**, wood. Used phonetically for *see*, a wise person.
4. **zzeeqggu**, to discuss. Two intersecting lines indicating speech.
5. **gv**, egg. Possibly used phonetically for final syllable of *zzeeqggu*, to discuss.

Transcription

zzijjeq-la'ler **ddiuq**
the vast earth where the people reside
gvl / neif / **see** / **zzeeqggu**
the able / and / the wise / discuss

Scharten translation

On earth there was red earth.

New translation

On the vast earth where the people live, those with ability conferred with those who were wise.

Notes

Once again those with ability and those who are wise make an appearance, via their phonetic loan graphs: but interestingly the loans (garlic and wood) are here seen “discussing” with one another, the “speech” lines emerging from each and meeting in the middle, emblematic of the verb *zzeeqggu*, which is usually written with two figures producing such speech lines: . The oral formula “*zzijjeq-la’ler ddiuq*”, the vast earth where the people live, is usually represented by a compound graph, a jackal (phonetic component) atop the land (semantic component): , but is here simplified to simply the lower component.

7-1, 7-2

Graph-by-graph

1. **lerl**, one who can measure, a compound ideograph of a person holding a ruler, *lerl.*
2. **chel**, one who can survey, phono-semantic compound of a person holding the graph for unclean, *chel.*
3. **zzi**, chieftain.
4. **ddeeq**, official, elder.
5. **biuq**, a dongba, here seated and speaking.
6. **paq**, female diviner, here depicted by a compound of *perq*, white and *sai*, blood.

Transcription

lerl / neiq / **chel** / zzeeqggu
measure / and / survey / discuss
zzi / neif / **ddeeq** / zzeeqggu
the chieftains / and / the elders / discuss
biuq / neiq / **paq** / zzeeqggu
dongba / and / diviner / discuss

Scharten translation

The one, who is able to do every thing, convers with one, who knows every thing. The workman with the farmer, the servant with his principal. The diviner with the witch.

New translation

The measurers conferred with the surveyors and the chieftains with the elders. The dongba conferred with the female diviners.

Notes

For the pairings in the first panel we have compound graphs instead of simple borrowings, that is, the "people" emerge (with their phonetic or semantic clues), and again the conferring is represented by the simple speech lines that emanate from their mouths. In the first panel here, Scharten has three pairs of people, but it is unclear where the "workman" and the "farmer" emerge from: presumably she was given a more elaborate reading. In the second panel, Scharten translates *paq* as "witch", no doubt because the female prognosticators, the *saipaq*, were traditionally female, and are often depicted in the manuscripts as having flowing, unkempt hair.

7-3

Graph-by-graph

1. **lvnaq**, black stone.
2. **seel**, three.
3. **bul**, to carry.
4. **zhee**, soil.
5. **seel**, three.
6. **bul**, to carry.
7. **ddvperq-fvlssei**, white conch.
8. **bul**, to carry.
9. **ngvq**¸silver (an earring).
10. **haiq**, gold (a brooch)
11. **yi**, geba syllabic, first syllable of *yisal*, some.
12. **sal**, breath, used phonetically for *sal*, some.
13. **bul**, to carry.
14. **waq**, turquoise.
15. **chuq**, carnelian gemstone
16. **yi**, geba syllabic, see above.
17. **ko**, horn. Used phonetically for *ko*, some.
18. **bul**, to carry.

Transcription

lvnaq / **seel** / lv / **bul**
black stones / three / measure word / carry
zheenaq / **seel** / cherl / **bul**
black soil / three / measure word / carry
ddvperq-fvlssei / **bul**
white conch / carry
ngvq / **haiq** / **yisal** / **bul**

silver / gold / some / carry
waq / chuq / yiko / bul
turquoise / carnelian / some / carry

Scharten translation
Alltogether they want to create a high mountain, named: K'uen-luen. Two of them are named: Ü-lu and Ü-kong. One mason brings three stones, an other brings three pieces of clay; an other a white spiral univalve; an other gold and silver; others presious stone and silver.

New translation
And so the people came carrying three black stones and three chunks of black soil, as well as the white conch, silver, gold, turquoise and carnelian.

Notes
After the discussion during which everyone conferred with everyone else, it was decided to further shore up the holy mountain to properly secure peace and harmony in the world. So now the construction materials are brought forward: stones and clay (soil), alongside precious gemstones. Scharten introduces this panel with explication not present in the written manuscript (importantly suggesting that this marks the creation of the sacred mountain, while in other versions they are simply conducting maintenance work upon it). He Guisheng simply follows the writing in his recital, with no introduction. Note graphs 11 and 16, geba graphs that appear in slightly unusual places in comparison to the order in which they are actually read.

7-4

Graph-by-graph

1. **Jjiuqnal-sheello**, the sacred mountain.
2. **ngvq**, silver.
3. **haiq**, gold.

4. **ceel**, ploughshare, used phonetically for *ceel*, to build.
5. **waq**, turquoise.
6. **chuq**, carnelian gemstone (a string of carnelian beads).

Transcription
Jjiuqnal-sheello
sacred mountain
ddee / pa / **ngvq** / neif / **haiq** / nee / **ceel** / lei / ji
one / side / silver / and / gold / topicalizer / build / particle / place
ddee / pa / **waq** / neif / **chuq** / nee / ceel / lei / ji
one / side / turquoise / and / carenlian / topicalizer / build / particle / place

Scharten translation
They wanted to create a quare mountain, at one side there were placed gold and silver; and at the other side precious stones and coral.

New translation
One side of the sacred mountain was built up with gold and silver, and another side with turquoise and carnelian.

Notes
A very ideographic composition, this panel could be read as a compound graph almost unto itself, the first component to be read being the mountain in the middle, then the precious metals to the left, and the precious stones to the right. The only concession to more syntactic writing is the appearance of the verb *ceel*, "to build", by way of a rebus (the ploughshare), but this is still a graph that echoes the shape and pointed tip of the sacred mountain.

7-5

Graph-by-graph
1. **qi**, thorn, used phonetically for *qi*, to protect.
2. **me**, negation.

3. **da**, horse. First syllable of *dabee*, collective name of nine divine brothers.
4. **ggv**, nine.
5. **da**, horse.
6. **lv**, stones.
7. **ggv**, nine.
8. **qi**, to protect.

Transcription
beel / jjiu / la / **qi** / **me** / jju
build / have / again / protect / not / have
dabee / **ggv** / zzo / nee
name of deity / nine / men / topicalizer
da / **lv** / **ggv** / liu /**qi**
name / stone / nine / measure word / protect
da / lv / ggv / liu / nee
one / side / turquoise / and / carenlian / topicalizer / build / particle / place

Scharten translation
They rired nine white horses and nine black ones.

New translation
There were builders, but no one to guard it.
And so the nine divine brothers protected nine divine stones,

Notes
The materials to shore up the sacred mountain have arrived, and there are masons to do the construction work. Now we are told who will be on guard during this process. The Naxi "*dabee*", represented by graph 3 (horse is colloquially read *ruaq*, but here the horse head is read "*da*" from the Tibetan *lta*, horse), is the name given to nine divine brothers who are said to have protective powers. They do not appear in He Yuncai (1986), and Li Lin-ts'an notes down the pronunciation "*dabiu*", but with the footnote "[I] do not know what this is" (1978, 33). It would appear that the reading given to Scharten was simply connecting the two horse heads with the two numerals, but ignoring the other graphs.

7-6

Graph-by-graph

1. **rhee**, leopard.
2. **la**, tiger.
3. **wa**, five.
4. **qi**, thorn, used phonetically for *qi*, to protect.
5. **Ddvperq-seiggee**, the lion who is white as a conch (graphically formed from a lion with a white conch on its forehead). The last two syllables are loaned from the Tibetan seng-ge, lion. This is the mythical lion of Tibet as depicted in paintings, it is white with a green mane and tail.
6. **qi**, to protect.
7. **haiq**, gold.
8. **coq**, elephant, with trunk and decorative headdress.
9. **qi**, to protect.
10. **Jjeqga-naqbbv**, a deity (Rock call this figure a "giant" [1952, 684]).
11. **jjeq**, unclear pictograph. According to Rock, "the origin of the symbol is obscure, it is said to represent a mould for casting gold and silver ingots" (1939, 63). Here used phonetically for *jjeq*, first syllable of the name Jjeqga-naqbbv.
12. **ga**, good. Graphic borrowing from Tibetan *ka*, second syllable of the name Jjeqga-naqbbv.
13. **qi**, to protect.

Transcription

da / lv / ggv / liu / nee / **rhee** / **la** / **wa** / bbei / **qi**
"da", a name / stones / nine / measure word / topicalizer / leopard / tiger / five / did / protect
rhee / la / wa / bbei / nee / **Ddvperq-seiggee** / **qi**
leopard / tiger / five / did / topicalizer / white conch lion / protect
Ddvperq-seiggee / nee / **Hai**sheeq-**coq**ssei / **qi**
white conch lion / topicalizer / divine elephant beast / protect
Haisheeq-coqssei / nee / **Jjeqga-naqbbv** / **qi**
divine elephant / topicalizer / deity / protect
Jjeqga-naqbbv / nee / Jjiuqnal-sheello / qi
deity / topicalizer / sacred mountain / protect

Scharten translation
Five panters, five tigers, and one lion.
One elephant and a man, named: Dyeh-kae-nae-puh. All worked at the mountain.

New translation
And the nine divine stones protected the five leopards and tigers, the five leopards and tigers protected the divine lion of the white conch, the divine lion of the white conch protected the divine golden elephant, the divine golden elephant protected the god Jjeqga-naqbbv, and, finally, Jjeqga-naqbbv protected the sacred mountain Jjiuqnal-sheello.

Notes
Now the protective daisy chain continues, with various guardian deities listed in a row. The final protective spirit is the figure Jjeqga-naqbbv, whose name can be written with one single graph (as in graph 10) or spelled out phonetically. The first two syllables of his name are repeated (graphs 11 and 12), they merely serve as a phonetic reminder to the reader. According to He Guisheng, he is renowned for his great strength.

7-7

Graph-by-graph
1. **Jjiuqnal-sheello**, the sacred mountain.
2. **ngvq**, silver.
3. **haiq**, gold.
4. **qi**, thorn, used phonetically for *qi*, to protect.
5. **waq**, turquoise.
6. **chuq**, carnelian gemstone, a string of carnelian beads.
7. **qi**, to protect.

Transcription
Jjiuqna-lsheello
sacred mountain
ddee / pa / **ngvq** / neif / **haiq** / nee / **qi**

one / side / silver / and / gold / topicalizer / protect
ddee / pa / **waq** / neif / **chuq** / nee / **qi**
one / side / turquoise / and / carenlian / topicalizer / protect

Scharten translation

Gold and silver were given to build the mountain, and precious stones.

New translation

One side of the sacred mountain was protected with gold and silver, and another side with turquoise and carnelian.

Notes

This panel is almost identical to panel 7-4, except the verb here changes from "to build" to "to protect". The mountain is not just built up with precious materials, but also protected by them.

7-8

Graph-by-graph

1. **dvl**, a four-pronged stick with an egg inserted at its top, used during the sacrifice to heaven ceremony to ward off evil that descends from the sky. Used phonetically for *dvl*, to prop up.
2. **me**, negation.
3. **herq**, rain. Here used instead of *rher*, dew.
4. **perq**, white.
5. **mi**, fire. Used phonetically for first syllable of *miperq*, frost.
6. **dvl**, to prop up.
7. **herq**, rain.
8. **perq**, white.
9. **jjiq**, water (three waters).
10. **dvl**, to prop up.
11. **zhee**, soil.
12. **see**, three.
13. **dvl**, to prop up.

Transcription

qi / jjiu / la / **dvl** / **me** / jju
protect / have / again / prop up / not / again
rher / **perq** / seel / tiel / nee / **mi**perq / see / ddie / **dvl**
dew / white / three / drop / topicalizer / frost / three / particle / prop up
miperq / see / ddie / nee / **heeq** / **perq** / see / hoq / dvl
frost / three / particle / topicalizer / rain / white / three / measure word for water / prop up
heeq / perq / see / hoq / nee / **jjiq**ceil / see / hoq / **dvl**
rain / white / three / measure word / topicalizer / stream / three / measure word / prop up
jjiqceil / see / hoq / nee / **zhee** / naq / **see** / cherl / **dvl**
stream / three / measure word / topicalizer / soil / black / three / clump / prop up

Scharten translation

Because of the many workers, unity had to be made. Three pieces of ice were united with dew; white rain with three streams; three black pieces of earth [...continued in next panel]

New translation

There were guards for the mountain, but nothing to prop it up.
And so, three drops of white dew propped up three flakes of frost. The frost propped up three showers of white rain. The rain propped up three streams, and the streams propped up three clumps of black soil.

Notes

Graph 3 should be written *rher* , dew, but instead whoever composed the manuscript has used *heeq*, rain. The reader will note in particular two different methods of expressing numbers in Naxi script: first and most commonly with numerals, as we might expect (graphs 12 and 15, “three”), and secondly (and more primitively) by simply repeating the graph the required number of times. In this way, three streams are depicted by three graphs for “water” (graph 9).

8-1, 8-2

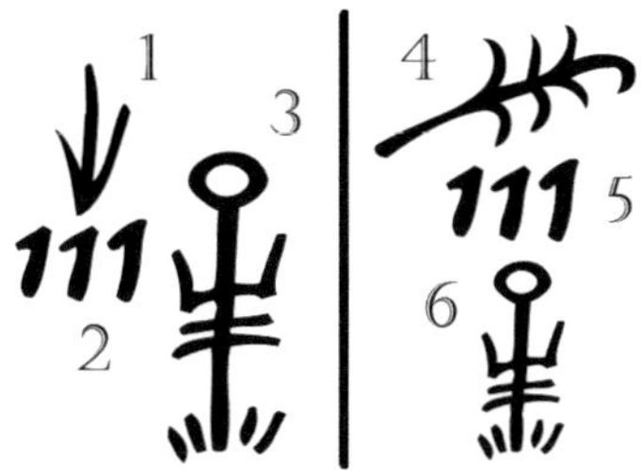

Graph-by-graph

1. **req**, grass.
2. **seel**, three.
3. **dvl**, to prop up.
4. **bee**, artemisia.
5. **seel**, three.
6. **dvl**, to prop up.

Transcription

zhee / naq / seel / cherl / nee / **req** / her / **seel** / zzerq / **dvl**
soil / black / three / clump / topicalizer / grass / green / three / measure word for plants / prop up
req / her / seel / zzerq / nee / **bee**ceil / **seel** / zzerq / **dvl**
grass / green / three / shoots / topicalizer / artemisia / three / measure word / prop up

Scharten translation

[...]with three dry stocks of grass. Three artemisias...

New translation

The soil propped up three shoots of green grass, and the grass propped up three artemisia plants.

Notes

As noted previously, the numeral "three" in these panels should not be taken literally: we are not talking about three handfuls of soil, but instead rather a great deal of earth, for three symbolizes a plenitude. It is unclear why the author of the manuscript segregates these very short panels: Scharten links them together in her translation. Scharten only translates literally what is on the page, that is, three stalks of grass and three artemisias, but the oral performance retains a slightly more elaborate formulaic structure.

8-3

Graph-by-graph

1. **zzerq**, tree.
2. **ga**, good, graphic loan from Tibetan letter *ka*.
3. **seel**, three.
4. **zeiq**, malicious spirit. Possibly used phonetically for *zzerq*, tree, not read.
5. **zzerq**, tree.
6. **dvl**, to prop up.
7. **to**, pine.
8. **perq**, white.
9. **seel**, three.
10. **dvl**, to prop up.

Transcription

beeceil / seel / zzerq / nee / **zzerq / ga / seel / zzerq / dvl**
artemisia / three / measure word / topicalizer / tree / good / three / measure word / prop up
zzerq / ga / seel / zzerq / nee / **to / perq / seel** / zzerq / **dvl**
tree / good / three / measure word / topicalizer / pine / white / three / measure word / prop up

Scharten translation

[...]with three wild chestnut-trees; three wild chestnut trees with three firtrees.

New translation

The artemisias propped up three good trees, and the three good trees propped up three white pines.

Notes

Scharten records the first tree in this panel as a chestnut, and it does indeed resemble such a tree in the manuscript, with its pronounced leaves, cf. *bbee* . He Guisheng reads the graph simply as *zzerq*, tree. The variant for *zzerq* can be seen in graph 5. Graph 4, *zeiq* (a malicious spirit), is an anomaly here, and I think it is probably used as phonetic loan for *zzerq*, tree, as this panel has nothing to do with such spirits. He Guisheng simply ignores the graph.

8-4

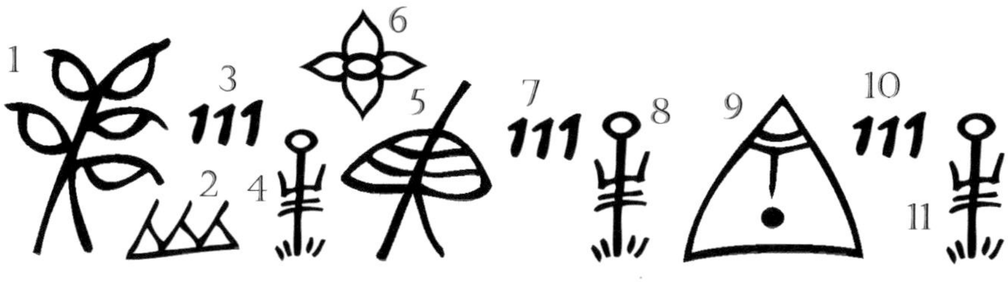

Graph-by-graph

1. **bbee**, chestnut tree.
2. **hiuq**, red (as flame).
3. **seel**, three.
4. **dvl**, to prop up.
5. **xiul**, cypress tree.
6. **herq**, green (like turquoise).
7. **seel**, three.
8. **dvl**, to prop up.
9. **jjiuq naq**, a black mountain (or a large mountain). The black dot in the centre of the graph gives the second syllable, *naq*.
10. **seel**, three.
11. **dvl**, to prop up.

Transcription

to / perq / seel / zzerq / nee / **bbee / hiuq / seel** / zzerq / **dvl**
pine / white / three / measure word / topicalizer / chestnut / red / three / measure word / prop up
bbee / hiuq / seel / zzerq / nee / **xiul / herq / seel** / zzerq / **dvl**
chestnut / red / three / measure word / topicalizer / cypress / green / three / measure word / prop up
xiul / herq / seel / zzerq / nee / **jjiuq / naq / seel** / jjiuq / **dvl**
cypress / green / three / measure word / topicalizer / mountain / black / measure word / prop up

Scharten translation

Three red chestnuts trees with three golden cypresses; three high mountains…

New translation

The pines propped up three red chestnut trees, and the chestnuts propped up three green cypresses, which in turn propped up three great mountains.

Notes

The props of the sacred mountain continue to be enumerated, with each element building upon the prior. Of note is graph 9, *jjiuq naq*, which can be understood as a "large mountain", the *naq*, usually meaning "black", here indicating large in size.

8-5

Graph-by-graph

1. **ai naq**, a black cliff. The chicken's head is a phonetic marker (*aiq* = chicken), and the black dot is read *naq*.
2. **seel**, three.
3. **dvl**, to prop up.
4. **Jjiuqnal-sheello**, the sacred mountain.
5. **gv**, egg.
6. **mee**, heaven.
7. **me**, negation.
8. **liulliu**, to shake.
9. **ddiuq**, the earth.
10. **me**, negation.
11. **liulliu**, to shake.

Transcription

jjiuq / naq / seel / jjiuq / nee / **ai / naq / seel** / jjiuq / **dvl**
mountain / black / three / measure word / topicalizer / cliff / black / three / measure word / prop up
ai / naq / seel / jjiuq / nee / **Jjiuqnal-sheello / dvl**
cliff / black / three / measure word / topicalizer / sacred mountain / prop up
gv / nee / **mee** / dvl / mee / juq / **me / liulliu**
top, head / topicalizer / heaven / prop up / heaven / direction / not / shake

kee / nee / **ddiuq** / tvl / ddiuq / juq / **me** / **liulliu**
foot / topicalizer / earth / step on / earth / direction / not / shake

Scharten translation

...with three cliffts.

When the mountain was finished, its top reached heaven, dosnt speak; its foot reaches earth, but also earth dosnt speak.

New translation

The three mountains propped up three great cliffs, and the cliffs propped up the sacred mountain.

At its peak, it touched the heavens, and the heavens did not shake. At its foot, it reached the earth, and the earth did not shake.

Notes

Some manuscripts have the sacred mountain (graph 4) planted atop the earth (graph 9), its tip reaching the heavens, in what is a slightly more ideographic representation of this panel.

8-6

Graph-by-graph

1. **dvl**, to prop up.
2. **bbuq**, pig, used phonetically for *bbuq*, to shoulder responsibility.
3. **me**, negation.
4. **elyuq**, monkey, used phonetically for the first two syllables of the name Elyu-miqyu.
5. **mi**, fire, used phonetically for the third syllable of the name Elyu-miqyu.
6. **bbaq**, flower, used phonetically for the second and fourth syllable of the name Mibbaq-labbaq.
7. **laq**, hand, used phonetically for the third syllable of the name Mibbaq-labbaq.
8. **bbuq**, pig, used phonetically for *bbuq*, to shoulder responsibility.

Transcription
dvl / jju / la / **bbuq** / **me** / jju
prop up / have / particle / oversee / not / have
Elyu-miqyuq / bbuq
name / oversee
Miyuq-**labbaq** / **bbuq**
name / oversee

Scharten translation
All have worked unitedly, and every one did his work. A-yü-mi-yü, Mi-yü-la-pu.

New translation
There were props, but nobody to bear responsibility for the mountain. And so there was Elyuq-miqyu and Miqyu-labbaq who kept watch.

Notes
Now begins a list of the beings who were in charge of keeping watch over the sacred mountain. The texts all differ as to the exact phonetics of the proper names; I have aimed to recreate the original as much as possible (for the second name, Miqyu-labbaq, He Guisheng reads "Miba-laqba"). He Yuncai and Scharten both list five names, Li Lin-ts'an has six (this manuscript also lists six names). For the sake of brevity, McKhann omits this entire section, noting simply that "different kinds of animals are called upon to keep watch" (1992, 93).

8-7

Graph-by-graph
1. **bbaq**, flower, used phonetically for second syllable of name Labbaq-gvla.
2. **gv**, garlic, used phonetically for third syllable of name Labbaq-gvla.
3. **yeq**, tobacco, used phonetically for third syllable of name Gulbbaq-yeqbbaq.

4. **bbuq**, pig, used phonetically for *bbuq*, to shoulder responsibility, oversee.
5. **see**, tree, used phonetically for the third syllable of the name Kvlla-seebbaq.
6. **bbaq**, flower, used phonetically for the fourth syllable of the name Kvlla-seebbaq.
7. **perq**, white, used phonetically for the first syllable of the name Perqbee-leilmaq.
8. **bee**, artemisia, used phonetically for the second syllable of the name Perqbee-leilmaq.
9. **meetv**, walking stick (?). Perhaps used as a corrupted form of geba graph *ma*, for final syllable of name Perqbee-leilmaq.
10. **bbu**, geba syllabic graph, used for *bbuq*, to shoulder responsibility, oversee.

Transcription

La**bbaq-gv**la / bbuq
name / oversee
Gulbbaq-**yeq**bbaq / **bbuq**
name / oversee
Kvlla-**seebbaq** / bbuq
name / oversee
Perqbee-leil**maq** / **bbuq**
name / oversee

Scharten translation

Ku-pa-pa-ku-yü; Ku-pa-sahr; Pehr-peh-la-ma.

New translation

There was Labbaq-gvla and Gulbbaq-yeqbbaq to keep watch over the mountain. And there was Kvlla-seebbaq and Perqbee-leilmaq too.

Notes

This panel is yet another microcosm of the difficulties of reading the Naxi books: it appears quite at random which syllables of the listed names actually appear, sometimes one or two (or, if we're lucky, even three), other times only the third syllable out of four is written, etc. The verb *bbuq* is written twice, once in dongba script (graph 4, via a rebus), once in geba syllabic script (graph 10), but is read four times in total. Graph 9 is unusual and has not been read by He Guisheng, nor does it appear in the other texts. It may be a corrupted form of the geba *ma*: 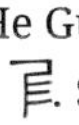. Scharten lists three names out of the four written, she has probably combined the first two into one.

8-8

Graph-by-graph

1. **Dduq**, male divinity, the *yang* principle.
2. **Seiq**, female divinity, the *yin* principle.
3. **ga**, good, phonetically used for *ga,* strength or power.
4. **ddeeq**, large. Rock, in typical botanist mode, suggests that the graph represents the fruits of *Machilus bournei* Hemsl.
5. **bbu**, geba syllabic graph, used for *bbuq*, to shoulder responsibility.

Transcription

Dduq / Seiq / ga / ddeeq / bbuq
deity / deity / strength / large / shoulder

Scharten translation

The god, Ndu-se has very much strength to carry.

New translation

Dduq and Seiq, with their great power, oversaw the mountain.

Notes

Scharten conflates Dduq and Seiq as one god, and appears to translate the *bbuq*, to oversee (i.e. the same as in previous panels) as *bbu,* to carry on the shoulder – probably influenced by *ga ddeeq*, "great strength".

8-9

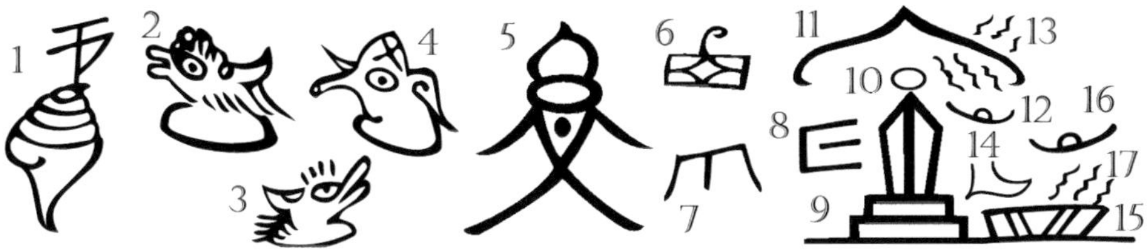

Graph-by-graph

1. **Ddvperq**, white conch.
2. **seiggee**, lion (loanword from Tibetan seng-ge).
3. **bbuq**, pig, used phonetically for *bbuq*, to shoulder responsibility.
4. **coq**, elephant.
5. **Jjeqga-naqbbv**¸a deity
6. **jjeq**, perhaps a mold. Used phonetically for the first syllable of the name Jjeqga-naqbbv.
7. **ga**, good. Graphic borrowing from Tibetan *ka*, second syllable of the name Jjeqga-naqbbv.
8. **bbuq**, geba syllabic graph, used for *bbuq*, to shoulder responsibility.
9. **Jjiuqnal-sheello**, the sacred mountain.
10. **gv**, egg, used phonetically for *gv*, top.
11. **mee**, heaven.
12. **me**, negation.
13. **liulliu**, to shake.
14. **kee**, foot.
15. **ddiuq**, the earth.
16. **me**, negation.
17. **zheelddoq**, to wiggle.

Transcription

Ddvperq-seiggee / bbuq
white conch lion / oversee
Haisheeq-**coq**ssei / bbuq
golden elephant / oversee
Jjeqga-naqbbv / bbuq
deity / oversee
Jjiuqnal-sheello / **gv** / nee / **mee** / dvl / mee / juq / **liulliu**
sacred mountain / top / topicalizer / heavens / prop up / heavens / side / not / shake
kee / nee / **ddiuq** / tvl / ddiuq / juq / **me** / **zheelddoq**
foot / topicalizer / earth / step / earth / side / not / wiggle

Scharten translation

A lion named, Ndu-p'her and a oliphant, Nyeh-kae-na-pu comes also and have much strength to help. K'uen-luen, the mountain is now finished and still there is no voice in heaven.

New translation

The white-as-conch lion, the golden elephant kept, and Jjeqga-naqbbv were there to watch over the mountain. The tip of the mountain touched heaven and did not shake, and its foot reached the earth and did not shake.

Notes

Now that the beings who guard the mountain have been enumerated, the mountain has finally been stabilized. Scharten refers to the sacred mountain of the Naxi as "K'uen-luen" (Chinese Kunlun 崑崙), which seems to be a Sinicizing translation of the *axis mundi*. In Chinese mythology Kunlun was the source of the Yellow River, although today it refers specifically to a mountain chain along the northern edge of the Tibetan Plateau. Graphs 13 and 17 denote a vibration represented by several wavy lines; these lines are not strictly individual graphs but can be attached to objects to indicate that they are shaking, or wiggling, or vibrating, etc.

8-10

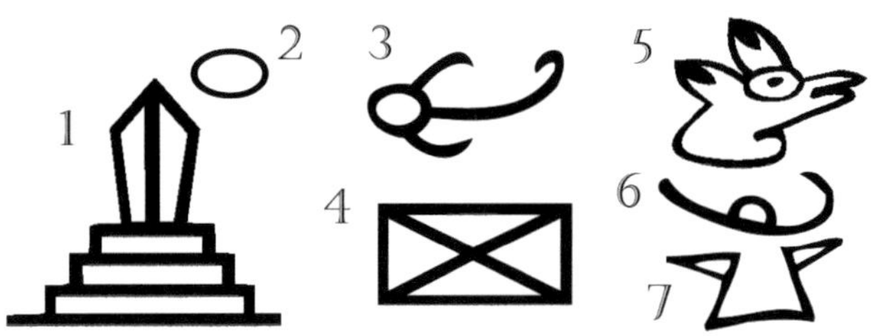

Graph-by-graph

1. **Jjiuqnal-sheello**, the sacred mountain.
2. **gv**, egg, used phonetically for *gv*, top.
3. **e**, a breath emerging. Used phonetically for first syllable of *ecei*, at first.
4. **cei**, salt, used phonetically for second syllable of *ecei*, at first.
5. **zzi**, a jackal, used phonetically to indicate "the people" in general.
6. **me**, negation.
7. **tvq**, a bucket, used phonetically for *tv*, emerge.

Transcription

Jjiuqnal-sheello / **gv** / ecei / **zzi** / me / tv
sacred mountain / top / at first / people / not / emerge

Scharten translation

Also with the finishing there were no men on earth.

New translation

At first, there were no people on the sacred mountain.

Notes

We can see an interesting scribal error on the manuscript in this panel: the heavens have been written atop the mountain, but then crossed out. The author probably had gotten so used to writing the heavens above the mountain on this page (in panels 5 and 9) that it had become something of a habit.

9-1

Graph-by-graph

1. **leigaiq**, a crow. Here read **cilli**, a wagtail.
2. **perq**, white.
3. **tvq**, a bucket, used phonetically for *tv*, emerge.
4. **me**, negation.
5. **bee**, an artemisia leaf, used phonetically for *beeq*, convention.
6. **tv**, to emerge.
7. **me**, negation.
8. **loq**, plowtail, used phonetically for the verb "to be capable" (auxiliary).

Transcription

cilli / **perq** / see / **tv**
wagtail / white / first / appear
cilli / perq / nee / perq / beeq / perq / lee / tv / bbeq zeel
wagtail / white / topicalizer / white / convention/ white / custom / appear / want
perq / lee / ku / bbeq zeel / **me** / naq / me / tal tal
white / custom / set / want / not / black /not / possible
berller / so cei / ddee / ddie / naq
throat / piece / one / bit / black
naq / beeq / me / waq / mei
black / convention / not / to be / end particle
perq / **beeq** / perq / lee / **tv** / **me** / **loq**
white / convention / white / custom / emerge / not / able

Scharten translation

A white bird is created, and want to fly to a white place, but he cant, for he has a black spot at his breast.

New translation

At first there came a white wagtail. This wagtail wanted to embody the qualities associated with that colour [kindness and purity]. But alas it could not, for it had a black spot on its throat. Even if it was not to be a paragon of blackness, it could not be a paragon of whiteness.

Notes

The Naxi *perq*, white, represents all the good things in life: justice, forthrightness, purity etc., while black represents negative qualities such as uncleanliness and wickedness. Before the birth of man, there first appeared these animals atop the mountain that wished to be emissaries for these qualities. All translations (including Scharten's) agree that the wagtail appears first, followed by a crow, but the manuscript clearly shows in this panel a crow, with the wagtail appearing in the following panel.

9-2

Graph-by-graph

1. **cilli**, a wagtail. Here read **leigaiq**, a crow.
2. **naq**, black.
3. **tvq**, a bucket, used phonetically for *tv*, emerge.
4. **zee**, to tie (a knot), used phonetically for *zeel*, to want.
5. **perq**, white
6. **bee**, an artemisia leaf, used phonetically for *beeq*, convention.
7. **tv**, to emerge.
8. **me**, negation.

Transcription

tee ggv / **leigaiq** / **naq** / nee / naq / beeq / naq / lee / **tv** / bbeq **zeel**
later / crow / black / topicalizer / black / convention / black / custom / appear / want
naq / lee / ku / bbeq zeel / me / perq / me / taltal
black / custom / set / want / not / white /not / possible
ddv / lei / mail / cei / soq / bee / perq

feather / particle / tail / part / three / measure word / white
perq / **beeq** / perq / lee / me / waq / mei
white / convention / white / custom / not / to be / end particle
naq / beeq / naq / lee / **tv** / **me** / loq
black / convention / black / custom / emerge / not / able

Scharten translation

Then a black crow comes, and want to fly to a black place, but he cant, for he has a white spot in his wings.

New translation

Then came a black crow who wanted to embody blackness. But alas it could not, for it had three white tail feathers. Even if it was not to be a paragon of whiteness, it could not be a paragon of blackness.

Notes

The black crow (graph 1) appears almost identical to the graph for a wagtail, *cilli* , which is usually written with the graph for white above it. In this case, however, the "white" is swapped out for *naq*, "black".

9-3

Graph-by-graph

1. **pei'leiq**, a butterfly (in flight).
2. **perq**, white.
3. **tvq**, a bucket, used phonetically for *tv*, emerge.
4. **bbei**, snow, here used semantically for *cee*, winter, together with graph 5 below for *cee seel hei*, "three months of winter".
5. **seel**, three.
6. **tv**, to emerge.
7. **her**, wind.

8. **bbu**, hillside.
9. **xel**, geba syllabic graph *xe*, used here for *xel*, to be blown on the wind. The geba graph is a graphic and phonetic loan from the Chinese *xia* 下.
10. **bee**, artemisia, used phonetically for *beeq*, convention.
11. **me**, negation.
12. **loq**, plowtail, used phonetically for the verb "to be capable".

Transcription

tee ggv / **pei'leiq** / **perq** / lei / **tv**
later / butterfly / white / again / emerge
pei'leiq / tv / me / gvl / **cee seel** hei / nieq / **tv**
butterfly / emerge / not / able / winter three months / in / emerge
ddv / ceeq / ga / me / yi
wing / thin / power / not / have
cee / her / perq / nee / muq / muq / lei / **bbu** / nieq / **xel**
winter / wind / white / topicalizer / blow / blow / come / again / hillside / on / on the wind
xel / **beeq** / xel / lee / me /waq
on the wind / convention / on the wind / custom / not / be
perq / beeq / perq /lee / tv / **me** / **loq**
white / convention / white / custom / emerge / not / capable

Scharten translation

Then a white butterfly comes and want also to fly, but it cant, for it is born in the winter, and its wings has no strength. The north wind comes and drives it away.

New translation

Then came a white butterfly, but it did not know how to be born, and was born in winter. Its thin wings had no strength, and it was buffeted around the hillsides by the winter wind. Being so at the mercy of the wind was not the custom, and so it could not be a paragon of whiteness.

Notes

Now the butterfly appears in all its beauty (literally so on the page, depicted in full, wings outstretched mid-flight). Graph 9 is an interesting geba graph that is a direct loan from Chinese *xia* 下 (down), and stands for the syllable *xel*, something like "blown on the wind".

9-4

Graph-by-graph

1. **chualwa**, an ant.
2. **tvq**, a bucket, used phonetically for *tv*, emerge.
3. **me**, negation.
4. **gv**, garlic, used phonetically for *gvl*, to be able.
5. **ruq seel hei**, "summer three months" i.e., summer, a compound graph with each syllable accounted for.
6. **tv**, to emerge.
7. **chualwa**, ant.
8. **cee**, a ghost that died from hanging, used phonetically for *ceeq*, thin.
9. **ga**, good.
10. **me**, negation.
11. **dda**, strike, pierce, used phonetically for *dda*, lake.
12. **jjiq**, water.
13. **mai**, tail.
14. **rer**, willow (?), used phonetically for *rer*, to move.
15. **chualwa**, ant.
16. **naq**, black.
17. **tv**, emerge.

Transcription

tee ggv / **chualwa** / **naq** / lei / **tv**
later / ant / black / again / emerge
chualwa / naq / nee / naq / beeq / naq / lee / tv / bbeq zeel
ant / black / topicalizer / black / convention / black /custom / emerge / want
chualwa / tv / **me** / **gvl** / **ruq seel hei** / nieq / **tv**
ant / emerge / not / able / summer / in / emerge
teel / **ceeq** / **ga** / **me** / yi
waist / thin / power / not / have
ruq / jji / naq / nee / bi
summer / water / black / topicalizer / wash away
dda jjiq / **mai** / nieq / **rer** / sseif / rer / heq / me / ddoq

lake water / tail / in / move / where / move / go / not / see
rer / beeq / rer / lee / me / waq / mei
move / convention / move / custom / not be / final particle
naq / beeq / naq / lee / **tv** / me / loq
black / convention / black / custom / emerge / not / capable

Scharten translation

Then a black ant comes, and want also to go a black place, but it cant, for it is born in the summer, and is not full grown, and has no power. The rains come and take it away.

New translation

Then came a black ant who wanted to be a paragon of blackness, but it also did not know how to be born, and was born in summer. Its thin waist had no strength, and it was washed away in the summer rain. It was moved this way and that by the waters. Being so at the mercy of the water was not the custom, and so it could not be a paragon of blackness.

Notes

In contemporary readings, Graph 14 is read *rul*, with the gloss “to stick”. I believe it depicts a willow, *rer*, and is used phonetically for the verb *rer*, to move. The second depiction of the ant (graph 7) shows a slightly elongated, thinner midsection when compared with graph 1.

9-5

Graph-by-graph

1. **ggeq**, a raised platform, semantically “on top of”.
2. **ko**, horns, used phonetically for *ko* “sound, voice”.
3. **tvq**, a bucket, used phonetically for *tv*, emerge.
4. **mi**, fire, used phonetically for *meeq*, beneath.
5. **sal**, breath.
6. **gguq**, to carry. Used phonetically (?) for *lvq*, warm.
7. **tv**, to emerge.
8. **ko**, sound.

9. **sal**, breath.
10. **bee**, artemisia, used phonetically for first syllable of *beebabbei*, "to make a change, transform".
11. **ba**, a frog's head, used phonetically for second syllable of *beebabbei*, "to make a change, transform".
12. **no**, milk. Graphic form derived from *perq*, white.
13. **chual**, six.
14. **tv**, to emerge.
15. **no**, milk (here one drop).
16. **dderq**, paper, used phonetically (?) for *ddee*, one.
17. **heel**, lake.
18. **sheeq**, yellow (like gold).
19. **heel**, lake.
20. **gguq**, storehouse, used phonetically for *gguq*, syllable in a name.
21. **tvl**, buttercream (in a dollop), used phonetically (?) for *tv*, to emerge.

Transcription

ggeq / nee / **ko** / ee / **tv** / **meeq** / nee / **sal** / lvq / **tv**
above / topicalizer / sound / good / emerge / below / topicalizer / breath / warm / emerge
ko / **sal** / nee / **beebabbei**
sound / breath / topicalizer / change
no / perq / seel / no / **tv**
milk / white / three / milk / emerge
no / perq / seel / no / nee / beebabbei
milk / white / three / milk / topicalizer / change
heel /sheeq / **ddee** / **heel** / tv
lake / yellow / one / lake / emerge
heel / sheeq / ddee / heel / beebabbei
lake / yellow / one / lake / change
Heel**sheeq-heelgguq** / **tv**
name / emerge

Scharten translation

From on high fog (mist) is coming and from beneath damp and when they come to gether, dew is falling on earth. This is changed in a great ocean, on which great waves are coming, which sound like thunder, which reaches heaven and from there is then heard a loud voice.

New translation

From above came a beautiful sound, and from below a warm breath. The sound and the breath came together to form into three drops of white milk, which in turn changed into a muddy lake. From the lake emerged Heelsheq-heelgguq.

Notes

In the source manuscript, a panel divider has been erased here, making this into one long panel. The appearance of some graphs in this panel are unusual, notably graph 6, which does not seem like a very close phonetic loan for the contemporary reading of *lvq*. Contemporary readings have the final section as three drops of milk producing three lakes instead of one, but the only way to account for graph 16 is as a phonetic loan for "one", which is a reading with which Li Lin-ts'an/He Cai concur (1978, 37). Graph 21 is a very unusual phonetic loan for *tv*, emerge, as we have up till now only seen the "bucket" graph used in this way. Graph 13, "six", is probably intended to be "three" written twice. It should also be noted that instead of the "milk" in contemporary readings which I adopt above, other translations (including Scharten's) agree on *rheeq*, "dew".

9-6, 9-7

Graph-by-graph

1. **mee**, heaven, used phonetically.
2. **gguq**, storehouse, used phonetically.
3. **tvq**, a bucket, used phonetically for *tv*, emerge.
4. **mee**, heaven, used phonetically.
5. **ssei**, flying ghost, used phonetically.
6. **cee**, kick, used phonetically.
7. **cherl**, generation (possibly representing an unbroken lineage of two generations).
8. **yuq**, sheep, used phonetically.
9. **cherl**, generation.
10. **tv**, to emerge.

Transcription

Heelgguq-**meegguq** / **tv**
name / emerge
Meegguq-**meessei** / cherl / tv
name / generation / emerge
Meessei-**cee**ceeq / **cherl** / tv
name / generation / emerge

Ceeceeq-cee**yuq** / **cherl** / **tv**
name / generation / emerge

Scharten translation
By and by the following generations had come on earth: A-ze-meh-ze, is one an other Meh-ze-t'seh-t'seh. An other: T'seu-yü-t'su-chü...

New translation
Then came Heelgguq-meegguq, followed by the generation of Meegguq-meessei. Then came the time of Meessei-ceeceeq, followed by the generation of Ceeceeq-ceeyuq.

Notes
We now have a list of the ancestors of mankind. Li Lin-ts'an suggests eleven total generations, Scharten has only six. While He Yuncai and He Fayuan list nine, I believe there are ten represented in Scharten's manuscript. The important thing to note is the naming convention. Lo Ch'ang-P'ei (1945) has shown that the Naxi, like most Tibeto-Burman peoples, historically used the naming system of genealogical patronymic linkage. The general feature of such a system is that the names of the father and the son overlap, specifically the last one or two syllables of the father's name become the first syllables of the son's name, and the system continues like this from generation to generation. If we examine the Ming dynasty genealogy of the Mu kings of Lijiang, we discover that the record of the legendary first twelve generations of the Naxi rulers clearly follows the pattern identified by Lo as A B C D – C D E F – E F G H: Coqssei-leel'ee's father (sixth generation) is transcribed as Bixian-caoxian 比羡草羡, and Coqssei-leel'ee himself as Caoxian-liweiwei 草羡里為為 (adopting the final two syllables). These ancestral names clearly indicate a concrete connection to family genealogy.

9-8

Graph-by-graph

1. **juq**, crow (of a rooster), used phonetically.
2. **cherl**, generation.

3. **tvq**, a bucket, used phonetically for *tv*, emerge.
4. **ssei**, flying ghost, used phonetically.
5. **cherl**, generation.
6. **tv**, to emerge.

Transcription
Ceeyuq-cee**juq** / **cherl** / **tv**
name / generation / emerge
Ceejuq-zzee**ssei** / **cherl** / **tv**
name / generation / emerge

Scharten translation
N/A

New translation
Afterwards came the time of Ceeyuq-ceejuq, followed by the generation of Ceejuq-zzeessei

Notes
Scharten does not appear to have translated these two generations.

9-9

Graph-by-graph
1. **zzi**, a jackal. Used phonetically.
2. **cherl**, generation.
3. **tvq**, a bucket, used phonetically for *tv*, emerge.
4. **coq**, an elephant, used phonetically.
5. **cherl**, generation.
6. **tv**, to emerge.

Transcription
Zzeessei-**zz**issei / **cherl** / **tv**
name / generation / emerge
Zisei-**coq**ssei / **cherl** / **tv**
name / generation / emerge

Scharten translation
...an other: ‘Chü-rze-chi-rze
Chi-re-tso-rze, one generation,...

New translation
And then was the time of Zzeessei-zissei, and after that Zisei-coqssei.

10-1

Graph-by-graph

1. **Coqssei-leel'ee**, the Naxi culture hero.
2. **cherl**, generation.
3. **tvq**, a bucket, used phonetically for *tv*, emerge.
4. **wa**, five.
5. **bbeiggv**, brothers (a pictographic depiction of two boys, *sso*).
6. **tv**, to emerge.

Transcription

Coqssei-leel'ee / cherl / tv
name / generation / emerge
Leel'ee / **wa** / **bbeiggv** / yi / teiq / nee / **tv**
name / five / brothers / topicalizer / static aspect particle / subject marker / emerge

Scharten translation

..., T'so-rze-leh-gheh is still an other geration.
From this last generation five brothers are born.

New translation

Finally it was the time of Coqssei-leel'ee, and from this generation five "Leel'ee" brothers were born.

Notes

The Naxi culture hero Coqssei-leel'ee is the final generation of the sequence, and it is at this point that the narrative begins to gather steam. Graph 1 is a variant of the Coqssei-leel'ee name, with the horned head and the elephant's trunk phonetic markers indicating the first syllable, *Coq*, elephant.

10-2

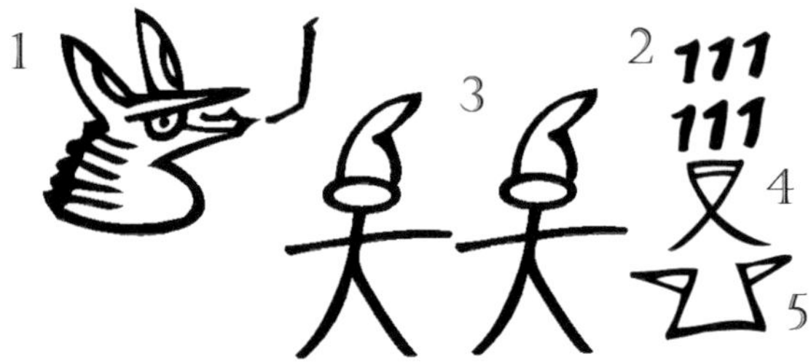

Graph-by-graph

1. **juq**, bray, as a donkey. Used phonetically.
2. **chual**, six.
3. **meiheiq**, sisters (pictographic representation of two women, *mil*).
4. **mei**, female.
5. **tvq**, a bucket, used phonetically for *tv*, emerge.

Transcription

Juqmil / **chual** / **meiheiq** / yi / teiq / nee / **tv**
name / six / sisters / topicalizer / static aspect particle / subject marker / emerge

Scharten translation

And six daughters.

New translation

And six Juqmil sisters were also born.

Notes

By simplifying, Scharten gets across in three words what the Naxi requires six graphs for. It is also possible to read graph(s) 3 as "*mil*", i.e. the second syllable of Juqmil, the proper name of these sisters.

10-3

Graph-by-graph

1. **Coqssei-leel'ee**, here only the final two syllables are read.
2. **wa**, five.
3. **aiq**, fight, here used phonetically for first syllable of *aiqloq*, mate.
4. **derl**, knot, used phonetically for second syllable of *aiqderl*, partner.
5. **tvq**, a bucket, used phonetically for *tv*, emerge.

Transcription

Leel'ee / **wa** / bbeiggv / **aiq**loq / zo / me / jju
name / five / brothers / mate / verb nominalizer / not / have
meiheiq / aiq**derl** / **tv**
sisters / partner / come

Scharten translation

They were all living together.

New translation

The five Lee'ee brothers had nobody to partner up with, so they paired up with their sisters.

Notes

The graph for "Coqssei-leel'ee" is used again (graph 1), but this time it is merely read as "leel'ee", the final two syllables of the name which act as an appellation for the five brothers.

10-4

Graph-by-graph

1. **juq**, bray, as a donkey. Used phonetically.
2. **chual**, six.
3. **meiheiq**, sisters (pictographic representation of two women, *mil*).
4. **mei**, female (i.e., first syllable of *meiheiq*).
5. ?, compound of *jjiq*, house, *ddeiq*, to have sexual intercourse, and *chel*, unclean.

Transcription

Juqmil / **chual** / **meiheiq** / bbuqloq / zo / me / jju
name / six / sisters / pair / static aspect particle / not / have
bbeiggv / bbuqderl / **tv**
brothers / partner / come

Scharten translation

One day they committed adultery, one with another.

New translation

The five Juqmil sisters had nobody to partner up with, so they paired up with their brothers.

Notes

The sources here often show slightly euphemistic translations of graph 5, a composite which depicts the incestuous act in graphic detail: a man having sexual intercourse with a woman (in this case brother and sister) inside a house, with unclean emissions above their heads. *Ddeiq*, to copulate, is a vulgar term. He Guisheng's reading has this act as simply "become a pair", echoing the previous panel, but ignoring graph 5. In this case, *chel*, the unclean energy gathering in the rafters, is not read: it is a foreshadowing of the pollution that emerges in the next panel as a result of incest. In Scharten's translation, however, we have a more direct rendition: "adultery, one with another". "Adultery" could be conceived of as the combination of the graph for "sexual intercourse" and "unclean".

10-5

Graph-by-graph

1. **mee**, heaven.
2. **ddiuq**, the earth.
3. **zzee**, walls, fortifications, used semantically to indicate a village.
4. **we**, a house, indicating a fortified settlement.
5. **lee**, farmland, something growing on top of the earth.
6. **dder**, a bamboo mat, used phonetically for *dder*, a rich field.
7. **chel**, perhaps an intestine, unclean.
8. **chel**, unclean.
9. **nieq**, a kind of grass, used phonetically for *nieq*, to pollute, make dirty.

Transcription

mee / neif / **ddiuq** / **zzee** / neif / **we** / lerq**lee** / **dder**'lee / la / **chel** / nee / **niel** / lei / heq
heaven / and /earth / village / and / hamlet / farmland / fertile fields / also / unclean / ablative case marker / pollute / particle / go

Scharten translation

Because of this, heaven and earth and fields were defiled.

New translation

And the heavens, the earth, all the villages and hamlets, all the fields and grasslands were defiled and polluted.

Notes

Graphs 7 and 8 are both *chel*, unclean, while He Guisheng reads it only once. Graph 9 could also be *chel*, in which case the reading would feature *chel* as a verb after each noun, e.g., *mee chel ddiuq chel*… (heaven was defiled, earth was defiled…).

10-6

Graph-by-graph

1. **hal**, night. An upside-down moon.
2. **so**, the dry roots of a dead tree, broken wood, or perhaps a scale with a weight attached. Used phonetically for *soq* morning.
3. **me**, negation.
4. **see**, the basket of the life god. Used phonetically for *see*, to know.
5. **ni**, the sun. Used semantically for "daytime".
6. **hal**, night.
7. **me**, negation.
8. **seel**, a wild grass, used phonetically for *see*, to know.
9. **zzerq**, a tree, used phonetically for *zeel*, modal particle.

Transcription

hal / neif / **soq** / **me** / **see**
dusk / and /dawn / not / know
ni / neif / **hal** / **me** / **see** / ye / **zeel**
sun / and / night / not / know / declarative particle / modal particle

Scharten translation

Their conduct was so bad, that they didn't know, when it was night, nor day even didn't know, which day it was.

New translation

They didn't know dusk from dawn, nor did they know day from night.

Notes

Graphs 4 and 8 are two different ways of writing *see*, to know. Different graphs are used presumably to add variety to the writing.

10-7

Graph-by-graph

1. **zzerq**, a tree.
2. **ggeq**, a raised platform, used semantically, on top of.
3. **noq**, lichen which hangs in long streamers from trees.
4. **la**, a tiger, claws raised.
5. **me**, negation.
6. **ta**, geba syllabic graph, representing *tal*, to be able.
7. **zzerq**, a tree.
8. **mi**, fire, used phonetically for *miq*, below.
9. **jjiq**, a watercourse.
10. **niq**, a fish.
11. **shuq**, an otter, paw raised.
12. **rherq**, to shake, used phonetically for *rher*, to swim.
13. **me**, negation.
14. **ta**, geba syllabic graph, representing *tal*, to be able.

Transcription

zzerq / **ggeq** / **noq** / yi / rhee / neif / **la** / co / **me** / **tal** / ssei / zeel
tree / top / lichen / grow / leopard / and / tiger / jump / not / able / final particle / modal particle
zzerq / **miq** / **jjiq** / yi / **ni** / neif / **shuq** / **rher** / **me** / **tal** / ssei / zeel
tree / below / water / grow / fish / and / otter / swim / not / able / final particle / modal particle

Scharten translation

For this reason a panther came, but he couldn't enter in.
Because of their bad behaviour many things happened, at the feet of a tree there came much water, and the fish and otter couldn't live in it, for it streamed too quickly.

New translation

And long lichen grew down from the treetops, so that the leopards and the tigers could no longer leap.

And water swelled up around the roots of the trees, so that the fish and the otter could no longer swim.

Notes
Note how in graphs 4 and 11, the tiger and the otter, the foot is raised. This indicates the action being made, i.e. for the tiger, leaping, and for the otter, swimming. Graph 3 in the manuscript is an unusual variant; He Guisheng reads it as *noq*. It is a kind of lichen that hangs down for the trees and is considered unclean. Its growth in this panel, hindering the animals, is a reflection of the sin of adultery.

10-8

Graph-by-graph

1. **jjuq**, a mountain.
2. **she**, geba syllabic graph *she* (graphic and phonetic loan from Chinese shang 上), used for *she*, sound.
3. **tvq**, a bucket, used phonetically for *tv*, emerge.
4. **chel**, unclean (not read).
5. **loq**, valley. Possibly also *cee*, spring, used phonetically for *ceeq*, come (past).
6. **loq**, valley (variant).
7. **loq**, valley (variant). Possibly also *cee*, spring, used phonetically for *ceeq*, come (past).
8. **ku**, door, used phonetically for first syllable of *kuka*, a ripping sound.
9. **ka**, bitter, used phonetically for second syllable of *kuka*, a ripping sound.
10. **tv**, to emerge.

Transcription
ggeq / nee / **jjuq**naq / seel**she** / **tv** / lei / cee
above / location marker / great mountain / crashing sound / emerge / again / came
meeq / nee / **loq**naq / **kuka** / **tv** / lei / cee
below / location marker / great valley / ripping sound / emerge / again / came

Scharten translation

A high mountain came down and splited the earth.

New translation

On high the great mountains cracked with a thunderous snap and down below the valleys split with a cacophonous roar.

Notes

Graph 5, 6 and 7 can all be considered variants of *loq*, valley, either with the dots depicting a larger volume of water (5 and 7), or with the cliffside included (6 and 7). Because "valley" is only read once, it instead makes sense to view graphs 5 and 7 as the graph for natural spring, *cee* (in which case the dots represent the bubbling up of water at a spring), used as a rebus for the verb *ceeq* ("came", most often depicted via *cee* , the ploughshare).

10-9

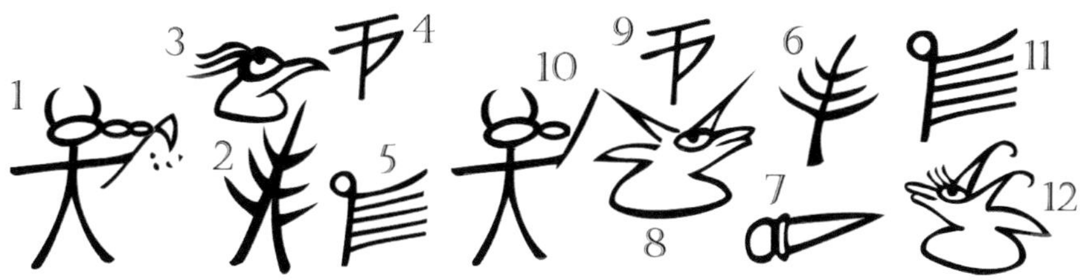

Graph-by-graph

1. **Coqssei-leel'ee**, Naxi culture hero, here holding an axe.
2. **zzerq**, a tree.
3. **hua**, silver pheasant.
4. **perq**, white.
5. **hoq**, ribs, used phonetically for *hoq*, slow.
6. **to**, pine tree.
7. **zhul**, awl, used phonetically for *zhul*, forest.
8. **yeq**, sheep.
9. **perq**, white.
10. **lvl**, to herd (a man holding a herding stick), here the shepherd is recognizably Coqssei-leel'ee.
11. **hoq**, slow.
12. **seiq**, goral, used phonetically for *seiq*, a modal particle.

Transcription

Coqssei-leel'ee sso / **zzerq** / ggv / **hua** / **perq** / hal
name (+ epithet "manly") / tree / top / silver pheasant / white / nest
hal / bbee / niel / **hoq** / seiq / wei / zeel
nest / go / self / slow / modal particle / emphatic / modal particle
tozhul / **yeq** / **perq** / **lvl**
pine forest / sheep / white / herd
lvl / bbee / niel / **hoq** / **seiq** / wei / zeel
herd / go / self / slow / modal particle / emphatic / modal particle

Scharten translation

One of the sons of T'so-rze-le-hgeh went to call his chickens, but he didn't call them in the right time. He also went to the mountain to call his sheep, but he came too late.

New translation

The brothers went to where the white pheasant was nesting atop the tree, and wanted themselves to nest there, but alas, they were too slow.
They then went to where the white sheep were herded in the pine forests, and wanted themselves to herd the sheep there, but alas, they were too slow.

Notes

The translations vary for this panel. McKhann writes how "Leel'ee-jiqggv and Leel'eekuaggv (two of the brothers)" are performing the actions (1992, 96), while He Guisheng simply reads the figure as Coqssei-leel'ee. The elephant trunks on the heads of these figures can suggest either the brothers in general (as in my translation) or Coqssei-leel'ee himself. Graph 10 is an example of how the dongba script can merge graphic elements to convey more information, the graph is nominally read *lvl*, to herd, showing a figure holding a herding stick, but in the manuscript the figure's head is changed to indicate the identity of the herder, despite this name not being read out. Scharten translates the final epithet "*sso*" (boy/man), often appended to Coqssei-leel'ee's name, as one of his "sons", whereas it is simply used to indicate that he is a paragon of male virtues. While undoubtedly a mistake, it is clear evidence that Scharten was translating directly from the Naxi, with no Chinese interference.

11-1

Graph-by-graph

1. **Coqssei-leel'ee**, Naxi culture hero, here holding a hand plough.
2. **leil**, cattle.
3. **leeq**, plough, furrow.
4. **me**, negation.
5. **gv**, ginger, used phonetically for *gv*, to be able.
6. **perq**, white, used phonetically for the first syllable of the place name, Perqye-ddvgv.
7. **goq**, alpine meadow, here not read, used graphically to indicate the place named above.
8. **Dduq**, male deity.
9. **Seiq**, female deity.
10. **kee**, foot (belonging to Dduq).
11. **bbuq**, pig.
12. **shee**, lean meat, used phonetically for *sheeq*, yellow.
13. **gelpv**, to turn over. The graph probably indicates a field with grass on top, turned upside down.
14. **ni**, sun, used semantically to indicate the daytime.
15. **hal**, an upturned moon, indicating nighttime.

Transcription

Coqssei-leel'ee sso / **leilleeq** / **me** / **gv**
name (+ epithet "manly") / plough / not / able
Perqye-ddvgv / we / gv / nee / **Dduq** / **Seiq** / **kee**tvl / lei / leeq / hee
place name / village / top / location marker / deity / deity / foot / again / plough / come
me / heeq / Dduq / me / heeq
not / peace / deity / not / peace
Dduq / Seiq / nee / **bbuq** / **sheeq** / keel
deity / deity / topicalizer / pig / yellow / release
kvl / lei / leeq / mei / soq / **gelpv**
evening / particle used before verbs / plough / emphatic / morning / turn over
ni / lei / leeq / mei / **hal** / gelpv
daytime / particle used before verbs / plough / emphatic / nighttime / turn over

Scharten translation

The son was also not able to plough his field. All because of his bad behaviour. He went now to a place, where the gods were gathered together and in that time, the god, Ndu-se, let loose a wild pig. That which was ploughed in the day time, the pig came to destroy it.

New translation

The brothers could not plough their land, so they went to Perqye-ddvgv, by the feet of the gods Dduq and Seiq, to plough the land there. This angered Dduq, who released a yellow pig. The fields ploughed in the evening were by morning all turned over, and the fields ploughed in the morning were by evening all turned over.

Notes

In this panel the brothers once again find themselves in trouble: they cannot plough their land, so they go to the land of the gods Dduq and Seiq to plough (to a village right at the very feet of the gods, no less), and this angers those deities, no doubt classic believers in the "not in my back yard" philosophy. They release a pig to overturn all the freshly ploughed soil. This "overturning" of the soil is depicted in graph 13, in what I believe to be a graphic depiction of a field, and below it a field inverted, that has not made it into the dictionaries. He Guisheng calls the pig "*bbuq mei nvl hiuq*", "O red-mouthed pig", but the manuscript has a rebus for yellow (graph 12), which I believe is indicative of the colour in this case. Scharten simply calls it a "wild pig".

11-2

Graph-by-graph

1. **Coqssei-leel'ee**, Naxi culture hero, here holding a trap (a form of pole lasso).
2. **ngvq**, silver.
3. **haiq**, gold.
4. **jiuq**, a hunting pole.
5. **soq**, morning.
6. **hal**, night.

7. **me**, negation.
8. **liuq**, to look (a pair of eyes looking at something).

Transcription

Leel'ee-kojiq sso / Leel'ee-kogv sso
name (+ epithet "manly") / name (+ epithet "manly")
ngvq / perq / dvlzhul / bvl
silver / white / pole trap / take
haisheeq / beilzeiq / bvl
golden yellow / trap / take
bbuq / sheeq / jiuq / lei / keel
pig / yellow / trap /again / set
soq / rheeq / teiq / lei / jiuq
morning / time / static aspect / again / place a trap
hal / rheeq / teiq / **me** / dder
evening / time / static aspect / not / hit

Scharten translation

The son is now very sorry and he takes a silver trap with a golden hook to catch the wild pig in the night time, but it is impossible, for he is in his hol

New translation

The brothers took silver and gold lasso traps and set them in order to catch the yellow pig. The traps set up in the morning were checked in the evening, but they were empty.

Notes

Graph 8, *liuq* "to look", is a bit of an anomaly; other versions have the verb "*dder*", to hit (i.e. nothing hit the trap). It could easily however be taken as *liuq*, to see, preceded by a negation, because as the traps are empty, the brothers could not have seen anything. He Guisheng now reads the same Coqssei-leel'ee graph (graph 1) as two of his brothers, Leel'ee-kojiq and Leel'ee-kogv. He notes that *dvlzhul* and *beilzeiq* are both hunting tools, the former designed to catch an animal's head, the latter an animal's foot.

11-3

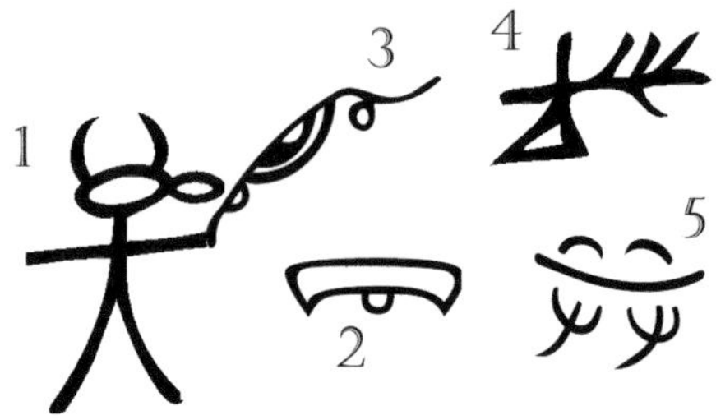

Graph-by-graph

1. **Coqssei-leel'ee**, Naxi culture hero, here holding a trap (a form of pole lasso). Not read.
2. **hal**, night.
3. **jiuq**, a hunting pole used as a trap.
4. **soq**, morning.
5. **liuq**, to look.

Transcription

hal / rheeq / teiq / lei / **jiuq**
night / time / static aspect / again / put a trap
soq / rheeq / lei / **liuq** / keel
morning / time / static aspect / look / go

Scharten translation

In the morning he want to intice him, but it was also impossible, for the pig had gone to the mountain.

New translation

The next morning, they went to look at the traps set up the previous evening.

Notes

We are now building up to the big catch, but Scharten seems to be translating a different version of the story than is presented on the page: she talks about how the pig was the previous evening in its hiding hole, and how the next morning it has gone off to a mountain, evading the traps. In fact, the final verb (graph 5) indicates that we are about to "see" the catch in the following panel.

11-4

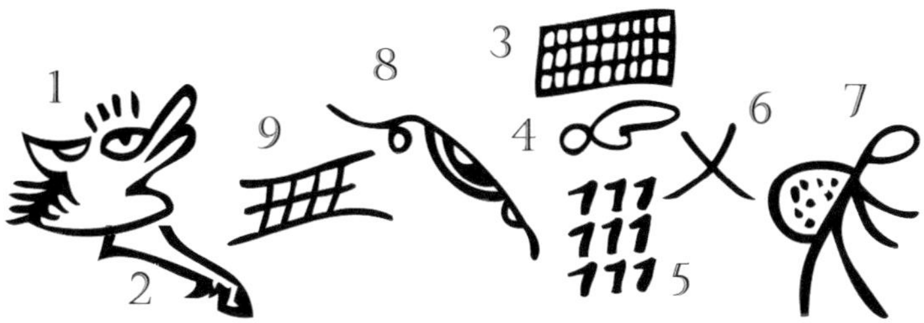

Graph-by-graph

1. **bbuq**, pig.
2. **kuabbei**, hoof (not read).
3. **tobvl**, a stretch of cotton cloth, used phonetically (?) for *bvq*, first syllable of *bvqshee*, cured meat.
4. **shee**, lean meat, second syllable of *bvqshee*, cured meat.
5. **ggv**, nine.
6. **cei**, ten.
7. **gguq**, to carry on the back.
8. **jiuq**, hunting pole.
9. **dder**, a bamboo mat, used phonetically for *dder*, to hit (a target)

Transcription

bbuq / sheeq / tee / **ggv** / **cei** / ggv / **gguq** / yi / gge / ddee / pul
pig / yellow / it / nine / ten / nine / carry / have / genitive / one / measure word
Coqssei-leel'ee / **jiuq** / gv / **dder** / lei / ceeq
name / trap / top / hit / again / come

Scharten translation

Afterwards he was able to intice him in the twilight, by putting a string around his legs. After killing it had nine loads of lean meat and ten loads of fa[t]

New translation

That yellow pig, so heavy that it weighed the equivalent of ninety-nine loads of cured meat, fell into the brothers' trap.

Notes

The poor pig's front trotter gets trapped, and the brothers have their prize: a pig that weighs the equivalent of 99 loads of meat, one "load" being what one could feasibly carry on one's back (see graph 7). He Guisheng doesn't mention graphs 3 and 4, which together I believe stand for *bvqshee*, cured meat, and add colour to the description of the pig's size. Scharten's translation provides a clue here: her version suggests that the pig was killed, offering up nine loads of lean meat and ten loads of fatty meat. The story can be expanded here with details not present in the writing: Coqssei-leel'ee does not wish to kill the pig, but his brothers do. An argument occurs, leading to the unfortunate, sacrilegious accident that is depicted in the following panel.

11-5

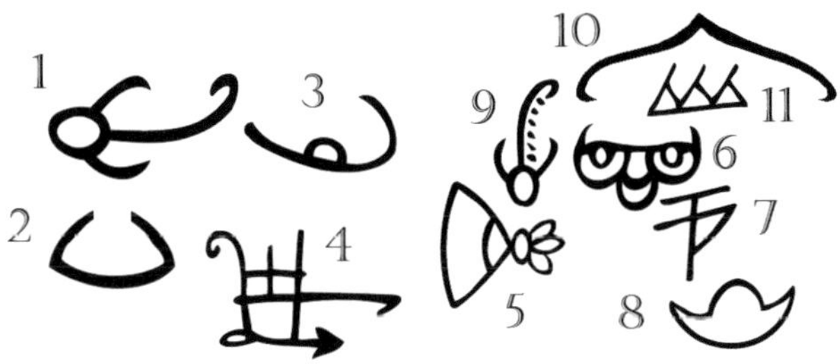

Graph-by-graph

1. **e**, a mouth emitting sound (not read).
2. **ko**, horns (probably simplified). Used phonetically for third syllable in the name Leel'ee-kogv.
3. **me**, negation.
4. **dv**, ploughshare.
5. **Dduq**, a male divinity, here having fallen down onto his side.
6. **ngvq**, silver.
7. **perq**, white.
8. **to'lo¸** a ritual headwear.
9. **ler**, to call or shout.
10. **mee**, heaven.
11. **mi**, fire, used phonetically for *mi*, to hear.

Transcription

Leel'ee-**kogv** / tee / **dv**'leeq / **me** / gvl
name / him / plough / not / able
epv / gv / niuq / diu
grandfather / head / on / strike
epv / **ngvq** / **perq** / **to'lo** / gv / niuq / dder
grandfather / silver / white / headdress / head / on / hit (a target)
ngvq / perq / to'lo / ke
silver / white / headdress / break

Dduq / **ler** / **mee** / **mi** / heq
deity / call / heaven / listen / go
meeggv-leegeel / niulniul / ggv / lei / heq
heaven and earth crack / shake / like / again / go

Scharten translation
The spirit of mankind, Ndu-se took a plough, but he fell and his silver myther was nearly broken. He cried and his voice went up to heaven.

New translation
So Leel'ee-kogv took up a plough, but he could not use it, and he struck grandfather Dduq on the head, breaking his silver headdress. Dduq cried out, such a cry that it was as if the universe itself was shaking, and the sound carried up to the heavens.

Notes
It is unclear what graph 1 refers to, possibly the brother Leel'ee-kogv, or possibly Dduq, who is here named as the "grandfather" (i.e. the "*e*" of "*epv*"). He Guisheng does not read it. Graph 2 is probably a very simplified *ko* , referring to the above brother who in his carelessness strikes the god Dduq on the head: he falls over (depicted in graph 5, lying on its side), his fancy hat in pieces on the floor, and lets out a mighty bellow.

11-6

Graph-by-graph
1. **cee**, a ploughshare.
2. **me**, negation.
3. **gv**, garlic, used for *gvl*, to be able.
4. **elnai**, grandmother, a female head with long hair. Here read Seiq, female divinity.
5. **haisheeq**, gold.
6. **meeltv**, a walking stick.
7. **me**, negation.
8. **qer**, to break. A broken stick.

9. **Seiq**, female divinity.
10. **ler**, to call out.
11. **ddiuq**, the earth.
12. **mi**, fire, used phonetically for *mi*, to hear.

Transcription

Leel'ee-kojiq / tee / **cee**'leeq / **me** / **gvl**
name / him / plough / not / able
Seiq / niuq / lei / diu
deity / on / again / strike
haisheeq / **meeltv** / gv / niuq / dder
gold / walking stick / on / come / hit
haisheeq / meeltv / **me** / **qer** / la / wecei / qer / lei / heq
gold / walking stick / not / break / also / almost / break / again / go
Seiq / **ler** / **ddiuq** / **mi** / heq
deity / call / earth / listen / go
ddiuq / geel / niuniu-salsal / ggv / lei / heq
earth / quiver / shake / like / again / go

Scharten translation

The spirit of the women took the iron cault of the plough and fell. Her gol-staff nearly broke. She cried and her voice went to the earth.

New translation

Then another brother, Leel'ee-kojiq, took up a plough, but he again could not use it, and he knocked down the goddess Seiq, almost breaking her golden walking stick. Seiq cried out, such a cry that it was as if the world itself was shaking, and the sound carried down to the earth.

Notes

Just as Dduq was struck by the incompetent brothers, now Seiq is unlucky enough to get in the way of an out-of-control plough. Her walking stick almost breaks, and she cries out in pain and anger. Scharten's "cault" is graph 1, the ploughshare; she likely means "coulter", a blade that cuts into soil ahead of a ploughshare. Graph 4 clearly depicts a grandmother, but He Guisheng simply reads the graph as "Seiq", the deity's name (in a reversal of the situation in the previous panel). Graphs 5 and 6 act as a compound, the "gold" superimposed upon the walking stick, indicating its colour.

11-7

Graph-by-graph

1. **Coqssei-leel'ee**, name of the Naxi culture hero.
2. **liuq**, to look, two eyes, looking.
3. **she**, geba syllabic graph, used for *shel*, to speak.
4. **Dduq**, male deity, lying on his side as if afflicted, here read *epv*, grandfather.
5. **bbeeq**, to be infertile. Not read, possibly semantically indicating illness.

Transcription

Coqssei-leel'ee / nee / **liuq** / lei / **shel** / mei
name / topicalizer / look / particle / speak / particle
epv / **gguq** / leel / me / gguq / zeel
grandfather / ill / or / not / ill / modal particle
epv / leel / gguq / neel / gguq / mei / o / yel / bbeq
grandfather / if / sick / particle / sick / emphatic / cupping therapy / give / can
epv / cer / leel / me / cer / zeel
grandfather / hot / or / not / hot / modal particle
epv / leel / cer / neel / cer / mei / kee / **yel** / bbeq
grandfather / if / hot / particle / hot / emphatic / acupuncture / give / can

Scharten translation

The son of T'so-rze-le-geh asks Ndu, who is laying on the ground: are you ill, I will heal you. Have you swellings, I will prick in them. Are you dirty, I will clean you. Are your clothing torn, I will sew them.

New translation

And so Coqssei-leel'ee looked at Dduq and asked, "Are you sick? If so, I will perform cupping therapy for you. Are you too hot? If so, I will perform acupuncture on you."

Notes

A very small (yet quite vertically dense) panel of five graphs yields 36 words in recital by He Guisheng, and this is still briefer than Scharten's translation, which contains four different questions from Coqssei-leel'ee instead of He's two. In the manuscript, what is written is Coq looking at Dduq and speaking, noticing that he is sick, but none of the ailments and suggested treatments are written. The first suggestion is cupping therapy, Naxi *o*, which has a very vivid graph, , a person holding the upturned cup and inside it the sucking force. Graphs 5 and 6 are quite unusual geba syllabics; they probably stand for the verb "to give", i.e. what Coqssei-leel'ee, as a paragon of virtue, intends to do for the injured deities. *Yel* is more commonly depicted as a rebus with the graph for tobacco, *yeq* .

11-8

Graph-by-graph

1. **mee**, variant graph for heaven.
2. **Dduq**, male deity, here speaking.
3. **she**, geba syllabic graph, used for *shel*, to speak
4. **Coqssei-leel'ee**, Naxi culture hero.
5. **leel**, a louse, used phonetically for the first syllable of Leel'ee, the five brothers.
6. **wa**, five.
7. **aiq**, fight, here used phonetically for first syllable of *aiqloq*, mate.
8. **juq**, bray, as a donkey. Used phonetically for the furst syllable of Juqmil, the six sisters.
9. **mil**, girl or daughter.
10. **chual**, six.
11. **ddeiq**, sexual intercourse (vulgar), here read via euphemism.

Transcription

Mee'leel**dduq** / epv / nee / lei / **shel** / mei
Name of deity / grandfather / topicalizer / again / say / emphatic
Coqssei-leel'ee sso
Name (+ epithet "manly")
Leel'ee / **wa** / bbeiggv / **aiq**loq / zo / me / jju

name / five / brothers / mate / verb nominalizer / not / have
meiheiq / aiqderl / bbei / seiq / zeel
sisters / partner / make / final particle / modal particle
Juqmil / chual / meiheiq / bbuqloq / zo / me / jju
name / six / sisters / pair / static aspect particle / not / have
bbeiggv / bbuqderl / bbei / seiq / zeel
brothers / partner / make / final particle / modal particle

Scharten translation

Ndu, the father of heaven replied. you are five brothers and six sisters and you have played adultery with one an other.

New translation

To which Dduq of heaven and earth replied, "Coqssei-leel'ee, the five Leel'ee brothers have committed adultery with the six Julmiq sisters."

Notes

Dduq is here given his full name, Mee'leeldduq, or Dduq of heaven and earth. In fact, Rock notes of the existence of a variant name, Mee'leeldduq-gvperq, "literally the Ndu[1] with the white head" (1972, 39). A longer rendition by He Guisheng has Dduq first praise Coqssei-leel'ee for saying nice things to him, and suggesting that this means Coqssei-leel'ee is someone who is kind of heart, before moving on to critiquing the adultery. Dduq is clearly a proponent of giving compliments before criticism.

11-9

Graph-by-graph

1. **mee**, heaven.
2. **chel**, perhaps an intestine, unclean.
3. **ddiuq**, the earth.
4. **zzee**, walls, fortifications, used semantically to indicate a village.

5. **we**, a house, indicating a fortified settlement.
6. **lee**, farmland, something growing on top of the earth.
7. **chel**, perhaps an intestine, unclean.
8. **dder**, a bamboo mat, used phonetically for *dder,* a rich field.
9. **bbi**, sun.
10. **chel**, unclean.
11. **leiq**, moon.

Transcription

mee / **chel** / **ddiuq** / chel / jju / lei / heq
heaven / unclean / earth / unclean / have / again / go
zzee / chel / **we** / chel / jju / lei / heq
village / unclean / settlement / unclean / have / again / go
lee / **chel** / **dder** / chel / jju / lei / heq
farmland / unclean / fields / unclean / have / again / go
bbi / **chel** / **lciq** / chcl / jju / lci / hcq
sun / unclean / moon / unclean / have / again / go

Scharten translation

Because of the you have defiled heaven and earth, the sun and moon and stars

New translation

Because of this, heaven and earth have been defiled, along with the villages and town, the farms and the fields, and the sun and the moon.

Notes

I follow the manuscript with the transcription and include the villages, the farmland and fertile fields, while He Guisheng separately mentions the stars and the planets. His reading is also more portentous, containing the warning: "Within three days, the sun and moon will go dark, the gods will wail, and nobody will be able to tell day from night."

12-1

Graph-by-graph

1. **Coqssei-leel'ee**, Naxi culture hero.
2. **sso**, boy, man. Repeated three times, here indicating *bbeiggv*, brothers.
3. **wa**, five.
4. **Dduq**, male deity, here speaking (*shel*).
5. **ee**, svastika. Used phonetically for *ee*, good.
6. **me**, negation.
7. **xi**, person (lying down, afflicted).

Transcription

Coqssei-leel'ee sso / Leel'ee / **wa** / **bbeiggv**
name + epithet (manly) / name / five / brothers
Mee'leel-**dduq**zzee / nee / lei / **shel** / mei
deity / topicalizer / again / speak / emphatic
sso / **ee** / shel / **me** / **piuq**
man / good / say / not / suffer loss

Scharten translation

Ndu, exert them and saith: if you hearken unto my voice, you will not eat bitterness

New translation

And Dduq said to the brothers: "A good man will not suffer."

Notes

He Guisheng has Dduq's speech as addressed specifically to Coqssei-leel'ee, reminding him of the upcoming calamity that will befall mankind (no matter how virtuous he himself may be): "you are kind and wise; but no matter how diligent the good man is, humanity will come to an end". Graph 8 is a prone person, and could be the semantic element of the graph *gguq*, to fall ill. I use "*piuq*" in the transcription because Scharten has "eat bitterness" (a literal translation of a Chinese term for suffering, *chiku* 吃苦), Rock notes the meaning "suffer loss" as one translation for *piuq* (1963, 234).

12-2

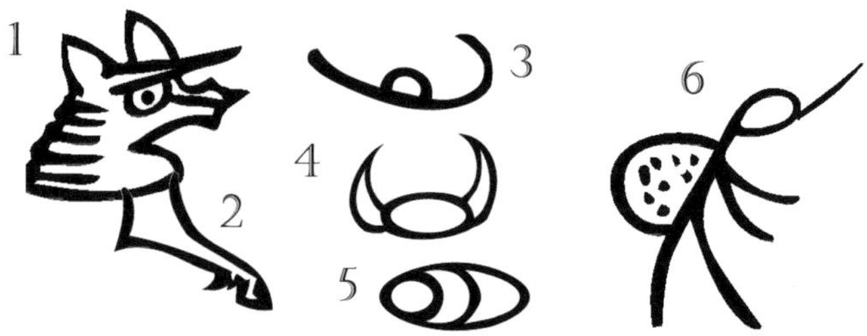

Graph-by-graph

1. **gguqchuq**, a fast horse.
2. **kua**, hoof.
3. **me**, negation.
4. **ko**, horns, used phonetically for ko, voice or message.
5. **jji**, yeast for brewing rice wine, used phonetically for *jji*, to walk (?).
6. **gguq**, to carry (a load on the back).

Transcription

gguqchuq / **kua** / xisaq
horse / hoof / nimble
req / **me** / her / lee / seiq
grass / not / green / come / final particle

Scharten translation

Like a horse hears to his masters voice, it will not suffer.

New translation

No matter how nimble the horse on its feet, the grass will not grow green again.

Notes

This panel lacks a direct translation. The transcription of this panel closely follows a reading by He Guisheng, but the reading seems almost to ignore the words on the page itself, hence graphs 4, 5 and 6 not appearing in the transcription. Scharten's translation is perhaps closer, translating "voice" (graph 4) and "suffer" (graph 6), but her version does not account for graph 5 (to walk). When quizzed about graph 5, He Guisheng offered up an alternate translation: "the impending calamity causes the horses to be lame, and the people carrying burdens can no longer walk", but this was not part of the initial reading, and also does not account for graph 4. The correct interpretation therefore remains something of an enigma.

12-3

Graph-by-graph

1. **Coqssei-leel'ee**, Naxi culture hero.
2. **bberq**, a yak, here being slaughtered.
3. **laq**, hoof.
4. **perq**, white.
5. **ggaiq**, sword, together with the animal, this graph is read *kol*, "to slaughter".
6. **ee**, animal skin.
7. **zhul**, awl.
8. **ceeq**, a ghost, used phonetically for *ceeq*, thin.
9. **keeq**, string.
10. **zheel**, crops.

Transcription

Coqssei-leel'ee sso
name + epithet ("manly")
bberq / shuaq / **laq** / **perq** / **kol**
yak / gelded / hoof / white / slaughter
bberq / **ee** / rherqddvq / daiq
yak / skin / pouch / tie
zhul / **ceeq** / **keeq** / bbiu / reeq
awl / thin / string / thick / tie
zheeq / lerl / xi / lerl / keel
grain / variety / hundred / variety / put

Scharten translation

He commands him then to kill a yack and use the skin for a leather sack. when you sew it, be sure to use a small needle and strong string.

New translation

Dduq said to Coqssei-leel'ee, "Kill a yak with a white hoof, and sew its skin into a pouch. Make sure to use a thin awl and coarse string. Then put all the kinds of grain inside."

Notes

Dduq now instructs Coqssei-leel'ee on the creation of a mini "ark" to survive the impending calamity. The verb for slaughter, *kol*, is a compound of the blade over the cattle's neck. In the manuscript, it becomes a larger diorama, with Coqseei-leel'ee depicted holding the blade over the animal's head.

12-4

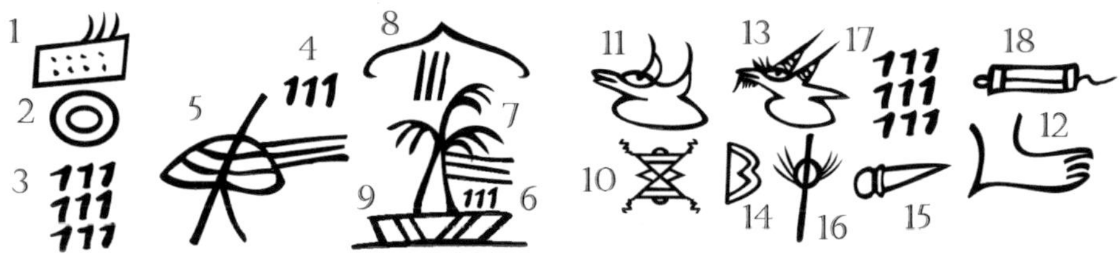

Graph-by-graph

1. **seel**, a kind of grass used to make straw sandals.
2. **ma**, butter, used phonetically for *maq*, fine.
3. **ggv**, nine.
4. **see**, three.
5. **xiul**, cypress tree, three ropes tied to it.
6. **lee**, a fir tree, three ropes tied to it.
7. **see**, three.
8. **mee**, heaven, three ropes tied to its vault.
9. **ddiuq**, the earth (not read).
10. **haisheeq**, gold.
11. **kee**, a dog.
12. **kee**, a foot, used phonetically for *keel*, to put.
13. **ceel**, a goat.
14. **zeimaq**, flint.
15. **zhul**, awl, used semantically for *ggaiq*, sword (?).
16. **zheeq**, crops.
17. **ggv**, nine.
18. **kvq**, a box (according to Rock), or a mouth harp, according to Fang, used phonetically for *kuq*, inside.

Transcription

seel / **maq** / **ggv** / erq / zeiq
straw / fine / nine / rope / use

see / bbaq / **xiul** / niuq / pai / lei / fai
three / lengths / cypress / on / tie / again / go
see / bbaq / **lee** / niuq / pai / lei / fai
three / lengths / fir / on / tie / again / go
see / bbaq / **mee** / niuq / pai / lei / fai
three / lengths / heaven / on / tie / again / go
haisheeq / **kee**ni / **keel** / lei / fai
gold / yellow / small dog / put / again / go
haisheeq / **ceelto** / keel / lei / fai
gold / small goat / put / again / go
haisheeq / **zeimaq** / keel / lei / fai
gold / flint / put / again / go
haisheeq / **ggaiq** / tal / keel / lei / fai
gold / sword / sharp / put / again / go
zheeq / lerl / **ggv** / lerl / la / **kuq** / lei / keel / lei / fai / la / zeel
crop / kind / nine / kind / also / inside / particle used before verbs / put / particle used before verbs / go / and / do

Scharten translation
Put on the sack nine ropes, three fastened in heaven, three on earth at a cedar tree; further put in it a golden dog, a silver sheep and nine other things.

New translation
"Now get nine straw ropes, [tie them onto the sack], and fasten three ropes to a cypress, three to a fir tree, and three to heaven. Inside the sack, put a golden dog, a golden goat, a golden fire striker and sharp sword, as well as nine kinds of grain."

Notes
The instructions continue. Many sources have the ropes that secure the survival pouch as "iron chains", but here graph 1 clearly indicates a kind of grass. The ropes are shown using numerals as well as ideographic depictions attached to the various objects. We then see a selection of important things to be taken inside the pouch (all of which are gold), including animals, seeds and some tools. Graph 14 looks almost like a bow; I believe it to be a variant form of *zeimaq* , flint.

12-5

Graph-by-graph

1. **Coqssei-leel'ee**, Naxi hero, in this case representing his two (wicked) brothers.
2. **kuaq**, bad.
3. **me**, negation.
4. **bbuq**, pig.
5. **sheel**, meat, used phonetically for *sheeq*, yellow.
6. **ggaiq**, sword, used semantically for *kol*, to slaughter.
7. **ee**, an animal skin.
8. **sal**, breath or air.
9. **bbei**, a farm tool, representing "to do or make".

Transcription

Leel'ee-kogv / Kojiq / sso / neeq / zzee / gvl
Name / name / man / you / pair / measure word
kuaq / bbei / gai / nee / jjuq
bad / do / before / topicalizer / have
ee / lei / jjuq / **me** / ddu
good / again / have / not / custom
bbuq / **sheeq** / ddee / pul / **kol**
pig / yellow / one / measure word / slaughter
bbuq / **ee** / rherqddvq / daiq
pig / skin / leather pouch / tie
goq / bbiu / keeq / ceeq / reeq
needle / thick / string / thin / sew

Scharten translation

The bad ones hear also to the words of the old father of heaven and when they returned home, they killed a pig, used its skin for a bag and sewed the sack with a big needle and fine thread.

New translation

"Now you two, Leel'ee-kogv and Leel'ee-kojiq, you have done bad deeds which shall not be rewarded. Go and kill a yellow pig, and tie its skin into a yellow sack, then sew it with a thick needle and fine thread."

Notes

This panel was originally separated from 12-4, but the divider has been crossed out and two graphs written on top, possibly *ggeqzzo* 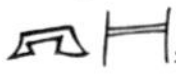, meaning "to add [on top]"; so, on top of the previous panel we have this panel, this could simply mean "following on". Now the two wicked brothers get a slightly different set of instructions (intended, by cruel trick of the gods, not to save them from impending doom). The first two of these intentionally wrong instructions are to kill a yellow pig, and to tie the leather pouch with a thick needle but fine thread. Graph 2, *kuaq*, meaning "bad", could be understood as a phonetic in the name of one of the brothers, alternatively, in combination with graph 3, could stand for the following in Rock: "Ndu said...that he was a **bad** man, that he could **not** obey or listen" (1952, 680; emphasis used to highlight the meaning of the two graphs). Scharten's "the bad ones" could also be a translation of "*kuaq mei*", whereby the negation *me* would be a rebus for *mei*, a topicalizer. Two words here are written but not read by He Guisheng, graphs 8 and 9, which I suggest (looking at He Cai's reading [1978, 18] of a similar written panel) can be interpreted as an instruction to inflate the pouch with air.

12-6

Graph-by-graph

1. **seel**, a kind of grass used to make straw sandals.
2. **ma**, butter, used phonetically for *maq*, fine.
3. **wa**, five.
4. **bbei**, a farm tool, representing "to do or make".
5. **erq**, rope (two lengths of rope are depicted here). Read as *bbaq*, lengths.

6. **bbee**, a chestnut tree.
7. **erq**, rope (two ropes are depicted here). Read as *bbaq*, lengths.
8. **to**, a pine tree.
9. **perq**, white.
10. **erq**, a rope. Read as *bbaq*, a length.
11. **mee**, heaven.
12. **ddiuq**, the earth.
13. **rherqddvq**, a leather sack, here suspended between heaven and earth (not read).

Transcription

seel / **maq** / **wa** / erq / **bbei**
straw / fine / five / rope / make
ni / **bbaq** / **bbee** / niuq / pai / lei / fai
two / lengths / chestnut / on / tie / again / go
ni / **bbaq** / **to** / **perq** / niuq / pai / lei / fai
three / lengths / pine / on / tie / again / go
ddee / **bbaq** / **mee** / neif / **ddiuq** / liul / pai / lei / fai
one / length / heaven / and / earth / between / tie / again / go

Scharten translation

Put on the sack five strings, two fatened at a chestnut tree, two at a fir tree and one between heaven and earth.

New translation

"Now get five straw ropes, [tie them onto the sack], and fasten two ropes to a chestnut tree, two to a white pine, and the final rope between heaven and earth."

Notes

This is the only version of this text (that I know of) which suggests that Dduq instructed the other brothers to use only five ropes, as opposed to Coqssei-leel'ee's nine. Nine is a more auspicious number in Naxi. He is here intentionally sabotaging the other brothers.

12-7

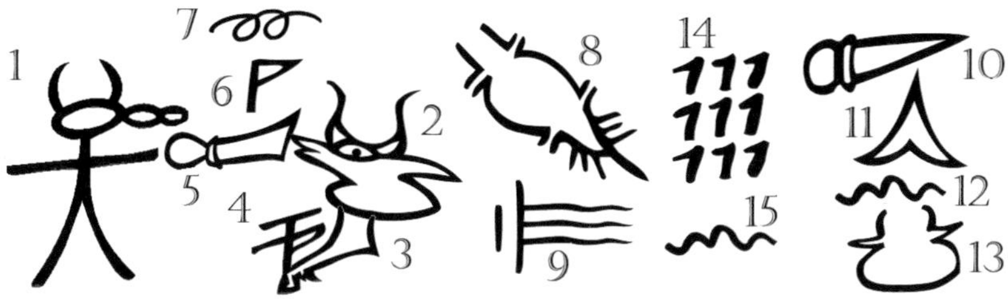

Graph-by-graph

1. **Coqssei-leel'ee**, Naxi culture hero.
2. **bberq**, a yak, here being slaughtered.
3. **laq**, hoof.
4. **perq**, white.
5. **ggaiq**, sword, together with the animal, this graph is read *kol*, "to slaughter".
6. **goq**, a needle, used phonetically for *goq*, "home".
7. **lei**, geba syllabic graph, used for *lei*, "to go back" (?).
8. **ee**, animal skin.
9. **sal**, breath or air.
10. **zhul**, awl.
11. **ceeq**, a ploughshare, used phonetically for *ceeq*, "thin".
12. **keeq**, string.
13. **bbv**, a deep pot, used phonetically for *bbiu*, "thick".
14. **ggv**, nine.
15. **keeq**, string, although perhaps "rope" is meant.

Transcription

Coqssei-leel'ee sso
name + epithet ("manly")
Mee'leeldduq / epv / nee / seiq / shel / seiq / lei / bbei
deity / grandfather / topicalizer / how / say / how / again / do
bberq shuaq / **laq** / **perq** / **kol**
yak / hoof / white / slaughter
bberq / **ee** / rherqddvq / daiq
yak / skin / pouch / tie
zhul / **ceeq** / **keeq** / **bbiu** / reeq
awl / thin / string / thick / tie

Scharten translation

The son of T'so-re-le-geh, the good one, hears after the words of the old father of heaven. When he has returned home, he kills a yack, whose legs were a little white. He makes of the skin a sack, uses a thin needle and strong thread and put nine ropes to it.

New translation

And Coqssei-leel'ee listened to the instructions of grandfather Dduq. After returning home, he killed a yack with a white front hoof, and he made a leather pouch out of its skin [inflating it with air]. He tied the sack with a thin awl and strong thread, and then fixed nine ropes to it.

Notes

Again, there are elements here that appear in the written manuscript that do not feature in a contemporary reading. Notably, graphs 6 and 7, what looks like a needle and thread, but in fact are a rebus for "home" and a syllabic graph for "return", which is, in fact, part of Scharten's translation: "returned home"; graph 9, which may indicate the air being blown into the sack to inflate it; and graphs 14 and 15, the nine ropes (although the graph for "thread" is again used).

13-1

Graph-by-graph

1. **ggv**, nine (not read).
2. **erq**, rope (three ropes are depicted here).
3. **xiul**, a cypress tree.
4. **erq**, rope (three ropes are depicted here).
5. **lee**, a fir tree
6. **erq**, rope (three ropes are depicted here).
7. **mee**, heaven.
8. **ddiuq**, the earth.
9. **haisheeq**, gold (a gold brooch).
10. **ceel**, a goat.
11. **kee**, a foot, used phonetically for *keel*, to put
12. **kee**, a dog
13. **aiq**, a chicken.
14. **zeimaq**, flint.
15. **rer**, knife.
16. **zheeq**, crops.
17. **ggv**, nine.
18. **kvq**, a box or a mouth harp, used phonetically for *kuq*, inside.

Transcription

see / bbaq / **xiul** / niuq / lei / pai / seiq
three / lengths / cypress / on / again / tie / modal particle
see / bbaq / **lee** / niuq / lei / pai / seiq
three / lengths / fir / on / again / tie / modal particle
see / bbaq / **mee** / niuq / lei / pai / seiq
three / lengths / heaven / on / again / tie / modal particle
haisheeq / **ceel**to / teiq / nee / **keel**
gold / small goat / static aspect / topicalizer / put
haisheeq / **kee**ni / teiq / nee / keel
gold / small dog / static aspect / topicalizer / put
haisheeq / **aiq**zerf / teiq / nee / keel

gold / small chicken / static aspect / topicalizer / put
haisheeq / **zeimaq** / teiq / nee / keel
gold / flint / static aspect / topicalizer / put
haisheeq / **rer**bbei / teiq / nee / keel
gold / sharp knife / static aspect / topicalizer / put
zheeq / lerl / **ggv** / la / **kuq** / lei / keel
crop / kind / nine / also / inside / particle used before verbs / put

Scharten translation
Three were fastened to heaven, three on earth at a cedar tree; he puts in it a golden dog, a silver sheep and nine other things.

New translation
He took those nine ropes, and tied three to a cypress, three to a fir tree, and three to heaven above. Inside the sack, he put a golden goat, a golden dog, a golden chicken, as well as flint, a knife, and nine kinds of seed.

Notes
The first three graphs of this panel are found at the end of the previous page (page 12). Coqssei-leel'ee follows the instructions to the letter in this repetitive panel. Scharten reads graph 17 as indicating nine kinds of thing in total, whereas it is likely attached to the graph for "crops", suggesting that our protagonist will have plenty of options for growing food after the calamity. Note that other versions use the numeral ten, not nine.

13-2

Graph-by-graph

1. **Coqssei-leel'ee**, Naxi culture hero. Here referring to his two wicked brothers.
2. **kuaq**, bad.
3. **me**, negation, here used phonetically for *mei*, an emphatic particle.
4. **goq**, a needle, used phonetically for *goq*, "home".

5. **lei**, geba syllabic graph, used for *lei*, “to go back” (?).
6. **bbuq**, pig.
7. **sheeq**, meat, used phonetically for *sheeq*, yellow.
8. **ggaiq**, sword, together with the animal, this graph is read *kol*, “to slaughter”.
9. **xi**, man, here not read (merely indicating a person doing the slaughter, see graph 8).
10. **ee**, animal skin.
11. **sal**, breath or air.
12. **zhul**, awl.
13. **bbv**, a deep pot, used phonetically for *bbiu*, “thick”.
14. **keeq**, string, although perhaps “rope” is meant.
15. **ceeq**, a ploughshare, used phonetically for *ceeq*, “thin”.

Transcription
Leel’ee-kogv / Leel’ee-kojiq / sso / ni / gvl / **kuaq** / **mei** / la
name / name / epithet, man / two / ones / bad / emphatic / also
Mee’leeldduq / epv / nee / seiq / shel / seiq / lei / bbei
deity / grandfather / topicalizer / how / say / how / again / do
bbuq / **sheeq** / ddee / pul / **kol**
pig / yellow / one / measure word / slaughter
bbuq / **ee** / rherqddvq / daiq
pig / skin / pouch / tie
zhul / **bbiu** / **keeq** / **ceeq** / reeq
awl / thick / string / thin / tie

Scharten translation
The bad ones hear also to the words of the old father of heaven and when they returned home, they killed a pig, used its skin for a bag and sewed the sack with a big needle and fine thread.

New translation
And the two wicked brothers listened to the instructions of grandfather Dduq. After returning home, they killed a yellow pig, and made a leather pouch out of its skin [inflating it with air]. They tied the sack with a thick awl and thin thread.

Notes
The “bad” brothers now follow the incorrect instructions. Again, Scharten translates graphs 4 and 5 as “returned home”, graphs that are not present in contemporary manuscripts and readings.

13-3

Graph-by-graph

1. **ceel**, goat.
2. **haisheeq**, gold.
3. **kee**, dog.
4. **aiq**, chicken.
5. **zheeq**, grain.
6. **ggv**, nine.
7. **bbiuq**, flour, used phonetically for *bbeeq*, many (or possibly semantically, the flecks representing a multitude).
8. **yeq**, tobacco, used phonetically for *ye*, an exclamation.

Transcription

haisheeq / **ceel**to / teiq / nee / keel
gold / small goat / static aspect / topicalizer / put
haisheeq / **kee**ni / teiq / nee / keel
gold / small dog / static aspect / topicalizer / put
haisheeq / **aiq**zerf / teiq / nee / keel
gold / small chicken / static aspect / topicalizer / put
zheeq / lerl / **ggv** / la / kuq / lei / keel
crop / kind / nine / also / inside / particle used before verbs / put

Scharten translation

They put in it, gold, a sheep and nine kinds of grain.

New translation

Inside, they placed golden animals: a small goat, a small dog and a chicken, as well as nine kinds of grain.

Notes

The final two graphs, flour that perhaps represents the idea of many things being put into the sack and a final exclamation, do not feature in the contemporary readings. Scharten also omits these, and once again cuts down the content of the translation by omitting two of the animals that are written.

13-4

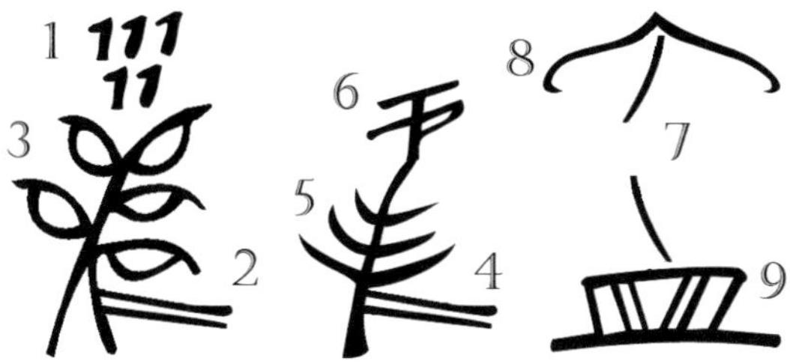

Graph-by-graph

1. **wa**, five.
2. **erq**, rope (two ropes are depicted here, the actual numeral is not written).
3. **bbee**, cypress.
4. **erq**, rope (two ropes are depicted here).
5. **to**, pine tree.
6. **perq**, white.
7. **ddee**, one (rope).
8. **mee**, heaven.
9. **ddiuq**, earth.

Transcription

seel / maq / **wa** / **erq** / zeeq
straw / fine / five / rope / use
ni / bbaq / **bbee** / niuq / lei / pai / seiq
two / lengths / chestnut / on / again / tie / modal particle
ni / bbaq / **to** / **perq** / niuq / lei / pai / seiq
three / lengths / pine / on / again / tie / modal particle
ddee / bbaq / **mee** / neif / **ddiuq** / liul / lei / pai / seiq
one / length / heaven / and / earth / between / again / tie / modal particle

Scharten translation

They put on it five strings, two fastened at a chestnut tree, two at a fir tree and one between heaven and earth.

New translation

Then they used five straw ropes, tying two to a cypress, two to a pine tree, and one in between heaven and earth.

Notes

Cypress and fir are traditionally considered to be trees growing at higher altitudes, chestnut and pine grow at lower altitudes. This is a hint at whose sack will survive the flood, and whose will not.

13-5

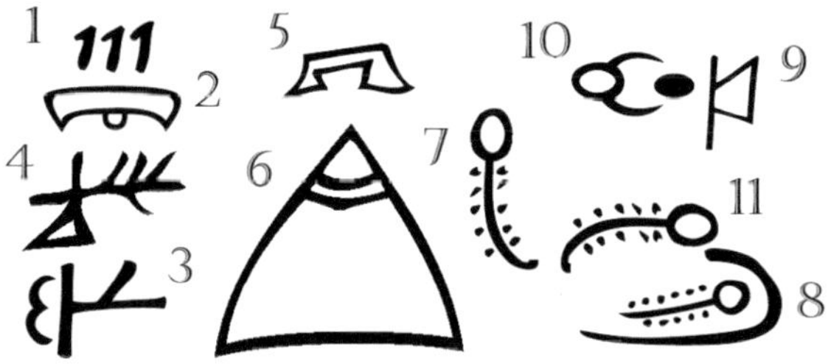

Graph-by-graph

1. **seel**, three.
2. **ha**, night, a moon facing down.
3. **yi**, geba syllabic graph, used for *yi*, numerous.
4. **soq**, morning.
5. **ggeq**, a raised platform, "on top".
6. **jjuq**, mountain.
7. **cee**, spring, used phonetically for *ceeq*, come (past).
8. **loq**, valley.
9. **ku**, door, used phonetically for first syllable of *kuka*, a ripping sound.
10. **ka**, bitter, used phonetically for second syllable of *kuka*, a ripping sound.
11. **cee**, spring, used phonetically for *ceeq*, come (past).

Transcription

seel / **ha** / **yi** / **soq** / ggv
three / night / numerous / morning / have
ggeq / nee / **jjuq**naq / seelshe / tv / lei / **ceeq**
above / location marker / great mountain / crashing sound / emerge / again / came
meeq / nee / **loq**naq / **kuka** / tv / lei / **ceeq**
below / location marker / great valley / ripping sound / emerge / again / came

Scharten translation

Three days after the high mountain came down and splitted the earth.

New translation

After three days and nights, the great mountains on high cracked with a thunderous snap and the great valleys below split with a cacophonous roar.

Notes

The prophecy comes to fruition: the earth splits with a thunderous roar.

13-6

Graph-by-graph

1. **to**, pine tree.
2. **perq**, white.
3. **mee**, heaven.
4. **ggv**, lightning striking the earth.
5. **jiq**, cloud.
6. **perq**, white.
7. **ggv**, nine.
8. **Coqssei-leel'ee**, Naxi hero, here indicating one of his brothers.
9. **bbee**, chestnut tree.
10. **lee**, the earth (archaism).
11. **ggv**, strike (as lightning). Here striking upwards at the tree, in fact *bi* is read, to sweep away (as in a flood).
12. **Coqssei-leel'ee**, Naxi hero, here indicating one of his brothers.
13. **zheenaq**, black soil.
14. **sher**, seven.
15. **me**, negation
16. **ddoq**, to see.

Transcription
to / **perq** / **mee** / niuq / **ggv**
pine / white / heaven / above / lightning strike
jiq / **perq** / **ggv** / diul / gol
cloud / white / nine / layer / in
Leel'ee-kojiq / tee
name / him
sseif / pil / sseif / yeq / hee / me / ddoq / ye / zeel
where / lose / where / hide / go / not / see / exclamation / final particle
bbee / hiuq / **lee** / nee / bi
chestnut / red / earth / topicalizer / flush away
Leel'ee-kogv / tee
name / him
zheenaq / **sher** / diul / gol
black soil / seven / layer / in
sseif / pil / sseif / yeq / hee / **me** / **ddoq**
where / lose / where / hide / go / not / see

Scharten translation
Heaven was opened and much rain came on earth. and lightning.
Through the lightning the ropes of the bas ones broke and their sacks fell in deep places.

New translation
Lightning from heaven struck the white pine, and Leel'ee-kojiq, in the ninth layer of clouds, was struck to who knows where. Water rushed from the ground and swept away the red chestnut, and Leel'ee-kogv, in the seventh layer of the earth, was swept to who knows where.

Notes
Now the wicked brothers are scattered by lightning and floods. The rushing water spoken of in the oral text is displayed using a lightning graph (graph 11). The bottom section of graph 4, the ground being struck by the lightning bolt, could be a depiction of the sack tied to the trees, hence Scharten's mention of the sack falling into deep ravines.

13-7

Graph-by-graph

1. **Coqssei-leel'ee**, Naxi hero.
2. **bbuq**, hill.
3. **sheeq**, yellow, used phonetically for *sheel*, new.
4. **ku**, door, used phonetically for "place".
5. **tv**, appear.
6. **ggv**, nine.
7. **hei**, month.
8. **Coqssei-leel'ee**, Naxi hero.
9. **ggaiq**, sword.
10. **ee**, skin, in this case indicating the leather sack.
11. **ggeq**, platform, used phonetically for *gge*, associative particle.
12. **pu**, to open, an open eye.
13. **wai**, left, a figure pointing to their left (and not the reader's left).
14. **liuq**, to look.
15. **gguq**, horse (archaic).
16. **me**, negation.

Transcription

Coqssei-leel'ee sso / **bbuq** / **sheel** / ddee / bbu / **ku** / yi / lei / **tv** / niuq
name + epithet (manly) / hill / new / one / hill / place / modal particle / come / arrive / emphatic
ggv / **hei** / tv / seiq / zeel
nine / months / arrive / modal particle / modal particle
Coqssei-leel'ee sso
name + epithet (manly)
teel / gol / **ggaiq** / lei / shu
waist / in / sword / come / draw
bberq / **ee** / rherqddvq / herl / bbei / **gge** / lei / **pu**
yak / skin / sack / cut / do / particle / come / open
wai / juq / ddee / **liuq** / neiq
left / side / one / look / particle
gguq / ddee / pul / **me** / ddoq
horse / one / measure word / not / see

Scharten translation

The bag of the good one arrived at a high mountain and remains there for nine months. At the end he takes his knife and cut the string. He looks and doesn't see any bird.

New translation

Coqssei-leel'ee floated to the top of a new hill, and after nine months he took up his sword from his waist and cut the sack open. He looked to his left, but did not see a single horse.

Notes

We see the survival of Coqssei-leel'ee, who emerges from his protective sack after nine months (other versions say seven months and seven days). Scharten calls him the "good one", which suggests the usage of the epithet "*ee*" (good) instead of "*sso*" (manly). She also translates the horse as "bird". The graph "*pu*" (graph 12), an open eye, as well as its semantic meaning of "open", can, when read in the third tone, *pul*, be used as an enumerator for eggs, cows, sheep, wild animals, as well as human body parts. It is used like this in the final intonation unit above, although it is not written.

14-1

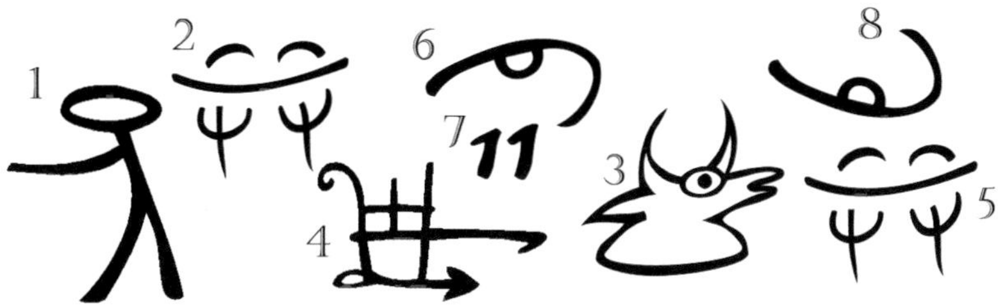

Graph-by-graph

1. **yiq**, right, a figure pointing to their right.
2. **liuq**, to look.
3. **lei**, cow. First syllable of **lei'lee**, farm cattle.
4. **lee**, to plough or furrow, second syllable of *lei'lee*, farm cattle.
5. **ddoq**, to see.
6. **me**, negation.
7. **ni**, two, used phonetically for *ni*, able.
8. **me**, negation (not read).

Transcription

yiq / juq / ddee / **liuq** / neiq
right / side / one / look / particle
lei'lee / ddee / wuq / **ddoq** / **me** / **ni** / ye / zeel
farm cattle / one / measure word / see /not / able / modal particle / emphatic

Scharten translation

He looks to the other side and there is none, who ploughs the field.

New translation

He looked then to his right, but did not see a single head of cattle.

Notes

On the manuscript, graph 1 (*yiq*, right) seems to have been originally miswritten simply as a person, *xi*, which has been corrected to reflect the person pointing to their right. Two negations are written, but contemporary readings only include one.

14-2

Graph-by-graph

1. **jjuq**, mountain.
2. **zee**, to tie, as in a knot (represented by a bundle of string, tied in the centre). Used phonetically for *zeel*, a modal particle.
3. **loq**, a valley.
4. **hol**, eight, used phonetically for *hol*, deep.
5. **ceeltoq**, goat, here seen bleating.
6. **zzijjeq-la'ler ddiuq**, the vast earth on which the people live.
7. **req**, grass.
8. **herq**, green (like turquoise).
9. **piq**, a shoulder blade, used phonetically for *pil*, to be lost.
10. **me**, negation.
11. **yeq,** tobacco, used phonetically for *ye*, sentence final particle.
12. **zee**, to tie, used phonetically for *zeel*, a modal particle.

Transcription

ggeq / juq / ddee / liuq / neiq
up / side / one / look / dynamic aspect
jjuq / yi / shua / seiq / ye / wei / zeel
mountain / particle / high / modal particle / final particle / particle / modal particle
meeq / juq / ddee / liuq / neiq
down / side / one / look / dynamic aspect
loq / yi / **hol** / seiq / ye / wei / **zeel**
valley / particle / deep / modal particle / final particle / particle / modal particle
haiq / **ceeltoq** / yi / ddee / bbaq / neiq
gold / goat / particle / one / call out / dynamic aspect
zzijjeq-la'ler ddiuq
the vast earth
jil / nieq / **req** / **herq** / zzee
small / time / grass / green / eat
niel / gge / guq / gge / req / herq / seel / der / sseiq / **pil** / hee / **me** / ddoq / **ye** / **zeel**

my / genitive / mouth / genitive / green /grass /three / measure word / where / lose / go / not see / final particle / modal particle

Scharten translation

In some places mountains have come, and other places deep valeys, where the rivers are streaming. This is the earth. He sees a sheep and saith to it: why do you bleet? The sheep answers: when I was young, I had grass to eat. When I got big, there is no grass and I want it.

New translation

High mountains soared overhead, and deep valleys plunged down below. In a high pasture, the golden goat bleated: "When I was small, I had green grass to eat, now there is nothing for me to eat, and I don't know where it has gone."

Notes

The transcription here is truncated; in fact, Coqseei-leel'ee is asking the goat "Why do you bleat so?", and the goat is responding to this question. Graph 6 represents the oral formula, *zzijjeq-la'ler ddiuq*, which can also be written with the first syllable, *zzi* (jackal, but used as a rebus for mankind), as a phonetic component: . Note graphs 7 and 8, which have in the manuscript formed an ideographic compound, the turquoise gem atop the blade of grass that look together like a flower in bloom, but actually indicate lush green shoots. Graph 4, a rebus for *hol*, deep, can be written with a phono-semantic compound , featuring the earth and a valley, inside which the numeral eight (*hol*) acts a phonetic.

14-3

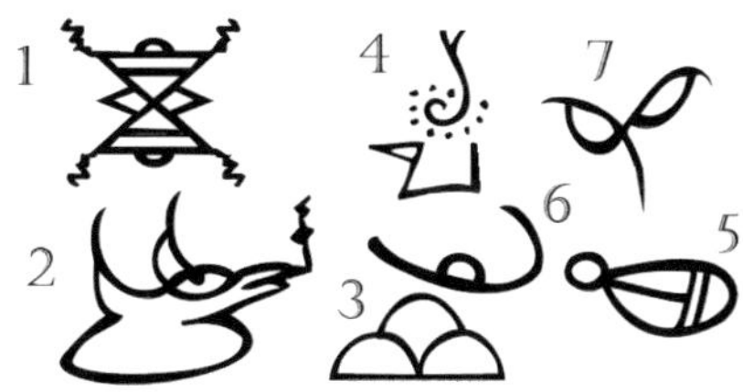

Graph-by-graph

1. **haiq**, gold.
2. **kee**, a dog, barking.
3. **lv**, stone, here used phonetically for *lvq*, to bark.
4. **no**, milk, being here poured into a container (not read).
5. **piq**, a shoulder blade, used phonetically for *pil*, to be lost.
6. **me**, negation.
7. **yeq**, tobacco, used phonetically for *ye*, sentence final particle.

Transcription

haiq / **kee**ni / yi / ddee / **lvq** / neiq
gold / small dog / particle / one / bark / dynamic aspect
goq / shua / goq / gv / perq
alpine meadow / high / meadow / on / white
jil / nieq / **no** / nee / xiq
small / time / milk / topicalizer / raise
guq / gge / no / yiq / seel / ddie / sseiq / **pil** / hee / **me** / ddoq / **ye** / zeel
mouth / genitive / milk /fragrant /three / drops / where / lose / go / not see / final particle / modal particle

Scharten translation

Now he sees a golden dog and he hears him barkening and saith to him: Why do you barken? The dogbreplies: when I was young, I had milk to drink and now there is none. Therefor I barken. Look for milk, that I may drink.

New translation

On a high alpine meadow, the golden dog barked. "When I was small, I was raised on milk. Now there is no milk and I don't know where it has gone."

Notes

The graph for milk (graph 4) is slightly different in the original manuscript, where it contains the symbol for white, hence "white milk". While the dog is depicted barking (graph 2), the actual verb used for bark is represented by the rebus, stones (graph 3).

14-4

Graph-by-graph

1. **haiq**, gold.
2. **aiq**, chicken, clucking.
3. **ju**, geba syllabic graph for *juq*, to crow (written twice).
4. **chua**, rice, in a container.
5. **perq**, white.
6. **piq**, a leg bone, used phonetically for *pil*, to be lost.
7. **me**, negation.
8. **yeq**, tobacco, used phonetically for *ye*, sentence final particle.
9. **me**, negation (not read).

Transcription

goq / shua / lee / naq / zzerq / kee / tvl
alpine meadow / high / fir / black / tree / foot / on
haiq / **aiq**zerf / yi / ddee / **juq** / neiq
gold / small chicken / particle / one / crow / dynamic aspect
jil / nieq / **chua** / nee / xiq
small / time / rice / topicalizer / raise
guq / gge / chua / **perq** / seel / liu / sseiq / **pil** / hee / **me** / ddoq / **ye** / zeel
mouth / genitive / rice / white / three / grains / where / lose / go / not see / final particle / modal particle

Scharten translation

Now he sees a golden chicken. It begins to cackle ans he asks: why do you cackle? The chicken replies: when I was young, I had rice to eat and now nothing. For this I cacle, look for rice, that I may eat.

New translation

By the foot of a black fir tree, the golden chicken clucked. "When I was small, I was raised on rice. Now there is no white rice and I don't know where it has gone."

Notes

As in the previous two panels, this is a dialogue between our hero and the animal: he hears their cries and asks why they are making such a commotion. Scharten's translation also has each animal direct Coqssei-leel'ee to go looking for food with a command. Graph 9 is an additional negation that appears to simply not be read at all.

14-5

Graph-by-graph

1. **zzijjeq-la'ler ddiuq**, the vast earth.
2. **zzi**, the people of the world, the jackal head, *zzi*, acts as a phonetic.
3. **bberqlerq**, a fly.
4. **see**, wool. Used phonetically for the first syllable of *seesaq*, weave (as in webs).
5. **siuq**, lead, as in the metal, used phonetically for the second syllable of *seesaq*, weave (?).

Transcription

Zzijjeq-la'ler ddiuq
the vast earth where the people live
zzi / me / jjuq / mei / ddiuq
people / negation / have / possessive / land
bberqlerl / keeq / **seesaq**
fly / thread / weave

Scharten translation

At that time there were no people on the globe, only flies and muskites.

New translation

There were no people inhabiting the vast wide earth, only flies hanging from cobwebs.

Notes

Most sources have *sa* 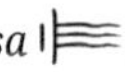 for graph 5, but here *siuq* is used. The fact that there is nothing but dead flies stuck in cobwebs indicates that the world is now empty and abandoned.

14-6

Graph-by-graph

1. **gguq**, horse (archaic).
2. **me**, negation.
3. **ddiuq**, earth.
4. **zer**, grass (growing atop the earth).
5. **herq**, turquoise-green.

Transcription

zzijjeq-la'ler ddiuq
the vast earth where the people live
gguq / **me** / lvl / mei / **ddiuq**
horse / negation / husbandry / possessive / land
req / **herq** / kv / derlder
grass / green / head / interwoven

Scharten translation

Neither was there any beast, only much grass.

New translation

And nor were there any horses being reared, only clumps of overgrown green grass strewn across the land.

Notes

Again, we have a scene of desolation: no animals, only overgrown grass.

14-7

Graph-by-graph

1. **Coqssei-leel'ee,** Naxi hero, here seen walking.
2. **ngv'lv**, snow mountain. Literally "silver rock", the silver (seen in the graph beneath the peak) is a metaphor for the snow.
3. **to**, pine tree.
4. **o**, bone, here read *wu*, inside.
5. **me**, negation.
6. **ko**, horn of an animal, used phonetically for *ko*, sound or voice.
7. **bbei,** a farm tool, used phonetically for *bbei,* to do or make.

Transcription

Coqssei-leel'ee sso
name + epithet
ngv'lv / **to**zhul / **wa** / yi / lei / tv / nieq
snow mountain / pine forest / in / emphatic / again / arrive / time
sso / ee / zzee / **me** / jjuq
man / good / companion / not / have
sso / **ko** / sso / zzee / **bbei**
man / voice / man / companion / make

Scharten translation

T'so-le-rze-geh, his son, came to a mountain with snow. He had no companion. He makes his voice his companion.

New translation

And so Coqssei-leel'ee came to a pine forest amidst the snowy peaks. There was nobody there to accompany him, so he made his own voice his companion.

Notes

In the manuscripts, some intonation units can be represented by just one graph, and the third unit here is representative of this: a simple negation (graph 5) is enough to tell us that there is nobody around to accompany our hero. Scharten continues to translate the epithet "*sso*" as "son", but our hero has at this point not taken a wife or conceived children. "He made his own voice his companion" can perhaps be taken as our hero now starting to talk or sing to himself to stave off the boredom of being the only person left on earth.

14-8

Graph-by-graph

1. **jji**, to go or travel, a figure moving with their feet (in this case, over a watercourse). Not read.
2. **jjiq**, water. In this case, indicating a river.
3. **gv**, garlic, rebus for *gv*, in. Not read.
4. **mai**, tail (of an animal). Here used semantically for the lower reaches of a river.
5. **gguq chuq**, a fast horse.
6. **tvq**, bucket, possibly used phonetically for *tvl*, to step on or trample.

Transcription

Cherllv-dda**jjiq** / **mai**
name of a river / tail
gguq chuq / zzee / me / jjuq
fast horse / companion / not / have
tvl / lvl / wu / zzee / bbei
step on / around / self / companion / make

Scharten translation

He has not any horse to ride on. He thinks my legs, I will consider as my horse.

New translation

He then came to the lower reaches of the Cherllv-dda river, but there were no fast horses to accompany him, so he took his own legs as his companions.

Notes

Scharten omits the name of the river. He Guisheng suggests the name in the translation above, while Li Lin-ts'an has "Ruallo-ddajjiq" (1978, 44). The graph for bucket, *tvq*, is called into use as a rebus for *tvl*, to trample, which could in this case be written with the following phono-semantic compound: .

14-9

Graph-by-graph

1. **Coqssei-leel'ee**, Naxi hero, here wearing a wool cloak, his pronounced feet suggesting he is travelling.
2. **ddaq**, a loom, indicating the verb "to weave".
3. **see**, wool, here a woolen cloak is meant.
4. **see**, three.
5. **leesee**, arrow.
6. **leemei**, bow (with arrow notched).

Transcription

Coqssei-leel'ee sso
name + epithet
see / **ddaq** / see / leel / neiq
wool / weave / wool / twist / dynamic aspect
see / perq / jjissei / muq
wool / white / travel clothes / wear
see / ji / **leesee** / bul
three / hand-length / arrow / take
see / chee / **leemei** / bul
three / arm span / bow / take

Scharten translation

He wears a skin goat and has a bow with three arrows.

New translation

He wove a white woolen cloak to wear on his travels, and took with him a bow that stretched to three arm spans in length, with an arrow three hand lengths long.

Notes

The graph showing Coqssei-leel'ee wearing his woolen cloak is a combination of the first three intonation units: we know from the head that the figure is meant to be our protagonist, he is wearing his new clothes, and his feet suggest that he is travelling, i.e. that the clothes are his travel wear. Scharten translates the numeral as related to the number of arrows, while He Guisheng suggests that it indicates the size of the arrows. The point here is that this is a giant-size bow and arrow, befitting a superhuman figure.

14-10

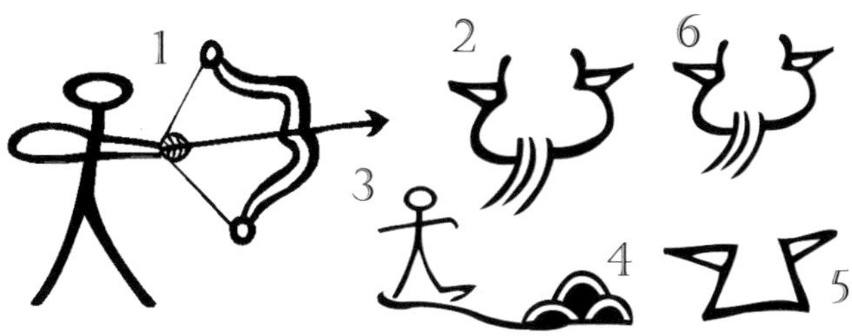

Graph-by-graph

1. **kai**, to shoot, a figure holding a notched bow.
2. **bvl**, a colander, used phonetically for *bvl*, to while away (time).
3. **jji**, to travel, a figure, travelling. Here not read.
4. **lv naq**, black stone.
5. **tvq**, bucket, used phonetically for *tvl*, to stroll.
6. **bvl**, a colander, to while away (time).

Transcription

see / **kai** / nil / **bvl** / neiq
arrow / shoot / days / while away / dynamic aspect
lv / gul / **tvl** / **bvl** / neiq
stones / throw / stroll / while away / dynamic aspect

Scharten translation

Because he has no work, he takes his bow and arrow. Also sometimes he takes stones and play with them.

New translation

He shot his bow and threw stones to while away the time [as he was travelling].

Notes

Graph 3, a person travelling, is not read, but it indicates that it is because his journeys are tedious that our hero has to occupy himself by firing his bow and throwing stones. The stones as written are black, but this does not appear in the reading. This is all because the land is now desolate, there is nobody around for him to talk to. Therefore, like an aimless child, he throws stones and shoots his arrows at nothing in particular.

14-11

Graph-by-graph

1. **Coqssei-leel'ee**, Naxi hero.
2. **goq**, an alpine meadow. The needle in the centre, *goq*, acts as a phonetic component.
3. **lee**, a fir tree.
4. **nimei**, the sun (also read simply *ni*).
5. **liu**, a spear, used phonetically for *liul*, middle.
6. **meelkeeq**, smoke, seen here rising from a fire.

Transcription

Coqssei-leel'ee sso
name + epithet
goq / shua / **lee** / naq / zzerq / kee / tvl / yi / lei / tv / nieq
meadow / high / fir / black / tree / foot / by / copula / again / arrive / time
goq / shua / lee / naq / zzerq / kee / tvl / nee / hiul
meadow / high / fir / black / tree / foot / by / topicalizer / stand
meeq / gge / la'ler ddiuq / nieq / ddee / liuq / neiq
below / genitive / vast earth / on / one / look / dynamic aspect
nimei / ni / **liul**ggv
sun / day / middle

meelkeeq / liu'o / ddee
smoke / spear / big
mee / nieq / lei / me / zhul
sky / on / again / not / connect

Scharten translation

Afterwards he comes to a forest and he sees something, which in the daytime like a smoke.

New translation

Coqssei-leel'ee came to a black fir tree atop a high meadow. In the middle of the day, he stood under the tree and looked down at the earth. Thereupon he saw a shaft of smoke only as thin as a spear handle, and the smoke did not reach up to the heavens.

Notes

Scharten's rendition of this panel translates all the graphs, but an oral performance includes more intonation units that flesh out the scene. Graph 5, the spear, could be taken to represent "middle" (as a rebus), or as a metaphor for the thin column of smoke that he spies from his high vantage point, or indeed it may represent both ideas. The metaphor suggests that there are no more people: signs of life can hardly be seen.

15-1

Graph-by-graph

1. **huq**, night, the moon casting its light (also read *hal*).
2. **mi**, fire.
3. **aiq**, chicken.
4. **bbuq**, hill, used phonetically for *bbu*, light.
5. **mee**, heaven, variant graph.
6. **Dduq**, Naxi deity representing the male principle, here speaking.
7. **she**, geba syllabic graph, used for *shel*, to speak.
8. **zzi**, jackal, used phonetically for *zzi*, the people.
9. **coq**, elephant, used phonetically for coq, mankind.
10. **me**, negation.
11. **zzijjeq-la'ler ddiuq**, the vast earth upon which the people live, here not read.

Transcription

huqmei / huqcee / ko
night / middle of the night / in
mizeil / **aiq** / perq / ddee
flames / chicken / white / big
mee / nieq / lei / me / **bbu**
sky / on / again / not / bright
Mee'leel-Dduq / epv / nee / **shel**
deity / grandfather / topicalizer / say
zzi / qu / **coq** / qu / **me** / jjuq / seiwei / zeel
people / kind / man / kind / not / have / end / modal particle
zzi / qu / coq / qu / zhul / bbee / zeel
people / kind / man / kind / continue / go / modal particle

Scharten translation

In the night time it is like a flame as the crest of a chicken. The god of heaven, Ndu, saith to him when there were not yet any men on earth...

New translation

In the middle of the night he saw flames only as big and bright as a rooster's comb, and they did not light up the sky. And then grandfather Dduq said, "Mankind is no more; yet mankind must live on".

Notes

Graph 4, *bbuq* (hill, hillside) is an interesting rebus. It is used for Naxi *bbu*, bright, to suggest that the fire is not lighting up the night sky, but there is an ideograph for "bright" that could have been used: . It is difficult to suggest that the "hillside" graph was used for aesthetic purposes; it was probably just the first "*bbu*" that came to the mind of the dongba who wrote this manuscript.

15-2

Graph-by-graph

1. **ser o**, a tree trunk, literally "tree bone".
2. **gv**, nine.
3. **siul**, lead, used phonetically for *siuq*, kind or sort.
4. **paidvq**, wooden puppet.
5. **me**, negation.
6. **gv**, garlic, used phonetically for *gvl*, to be able.
7. **zzi**, jackal, used phonetically for *zzi*, the people.
8. **coq**, elephant, used phonetically for *coq*, mankind.
9. **bbei**, to do or make (here not read).
10. **me**, negation.
11. **ga**, good (from Tibetan *ka*).

Transcription

ser o / **gv** / **siuq** / ddal
trunk / nine / kind / chop
paidvq / gv /zo / ddal
puppet / nine / set / chop
ser xi / shel / **me** / **gvl**
wooden man / speak / not / able

zzi / qu / **coq** / qu / zhul / **me** / **ga** / ye / zeel
people / kind / man / kind / continue / not / able / sentence final particle / modal particle

Scharten translation
...I prepared nine kind of wood, from which I prepared a wooden man, which couldn't do any thing, so it couldn't be reckoned as man

New translation
"So I chopped nine kinds of tree trunk to fashion into nine sets of wooden puppets, but they could not speak, and so mankind was not able to live on."

Notes
This panel reveals Dduq's plan to propagate the human race: make wooden puppets and hope that (via magic) they turn into real people. Unfortunately, this doesn't happen. He Guisheng's retelling is much more involved, and has Dduq test Coqssei-leel'ee by telling him not to untwine the newly-made puppets for nine days and nine nights. The idea is that after this period, the puppets will come to life. Poor Leel'ee was lonely and starved of companionship, and he did not wait out the whole nine days and nights, and untied the puppets, only for them to remain wooden and lifeless.

15-3

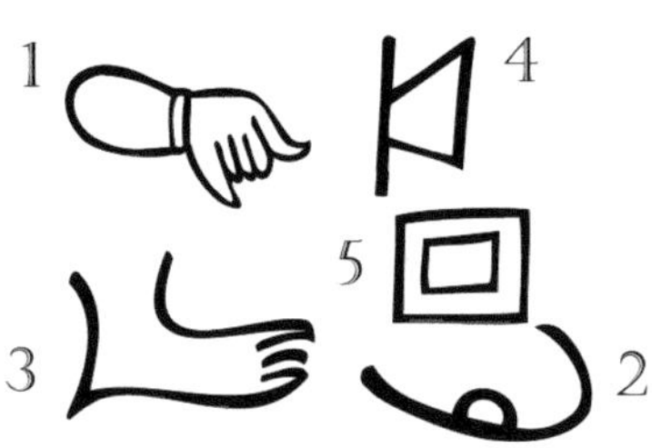

Graph-by-graph
1. **laq**, hand.
2. **me**, negation.
3. **kee**, foot.
4. **ku**, door, used phonetically for *ku*, mouth.
5. **dal**, box, used phonetically for *dal*, to speak.

Transcription
laq / zzeeq / chu / gvl / yuq / **me** / gvl
hand / have / extend / able / hold / not / able

kee / zzeeq / chu / gvl / jji / me / gvl
foot / have / extend / able / travel / not / able
ku / zzeeq / hal / gvl / **dal** / me / gvl
mouth / have / open / able / speak / not / able

Scharten translation
It had hands, but couldn't work; it had feet, but couldn't walk; it had a mouth, but couldn't speak.

New translation
The wooden puppets had hands but were not able to hold objects, they had feet but were not able to walk along, they had mouths that were not able to form words.

Notes
Once again, the negation (graph 2) is written only once but used in all three intonation units. Scharten's translation seems to suggest there is only one puppet, but as we shall see, a number were created.

15-4

Graph-by-graph
1. **ggaiq**, a sword, used here semantically to indicate *siul*, "to kill". Perhaps a loan from the Tibetan *sod*, to kill.
2. **aiq**, cliff, the chicken head acts as a phonetic marker.
3. **mu**, a kind of water demon, often associated with the *eeq* demons (who are wives of the *mu*).
4. **bee**, artemisia, used phonetically for *bee*, to change.

Transcription
ser / xi / paidvq / ddee / zo / **siul** / lei / **aiq** / nieq / gul
wood / man / puppet / one / set / kill / again / cliff / in / throw
aiq / loq / e-bbeeq / **mu** / yi / **bee** / lei / heq

cliff / in / name / water demon / copula / change / again / go

Scharten translation

I took it and threw it on a mountain, and it was changed in an acho.

New translation

So Dduq killed one set of wooden puppets and threw them into the cliffs, where they changed into the *e-bbeeq* demons.

Notes

Graph 1, *siul* "to kill", is usually a sword accompanied by the phonetic *siuq*, originally meaning "lead". While the graph for the demons used in the manuscript is *eeq*, the wives of the *mu*, the *mu* are in fact meant (and are the ones that appear in other published manuscript sources).

15-5

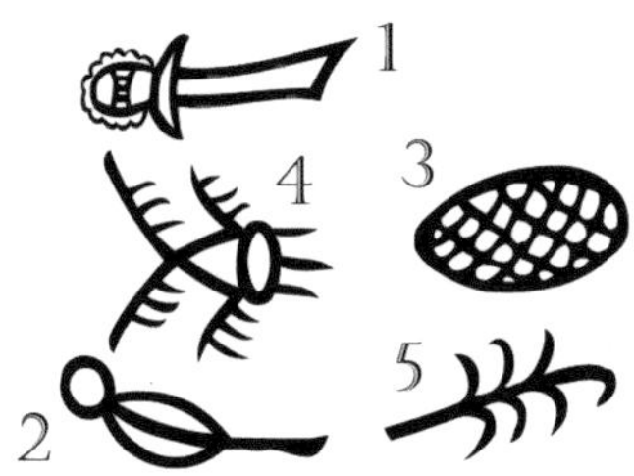

Graph-by-graph

1. **ggaiq**, a sword, used here semantically to indicate *siul*, "to kill". Perhaps a loan from the Tibetan *sod*, to kill.
2. **jjiq**, water, a watercourse flowing down from its source.
3. **mu**, a winnowing tray, used phonetically for *mu*, a kind of water demon.
4. **eeq**, a water demon.
5. **bee**, artemisia, used phonetically for *bee*, to change.

Transcription

ser / xi / paidvq / ddee / zo / **siul** / lei / **jjiq** / nieq / gul
wood / man / puppet / one / set / kill / again / water / in / throw
jjiq / gge / **mu** / nei / **eeq** / yi / **bee** / lei / heq
water / genitive / water demon / and / water demon / copula / change / again / go

Scharten translation

I cut an other and threw it in the water, and it was changed in the spirit of the waters.

New translation

Then he chopped up another set, and threw them into the water, where they changed into the *mu* and *eeq* water demons.

Notes

Here the winnowing tray (graph 3) is used for the *mu* demons, instead of the graph that depicts them visually; presumably graph 4, read *mu* in the previous panel, is now read *eeq* (the companions to the *mu*), its original pronunciation.

15-6

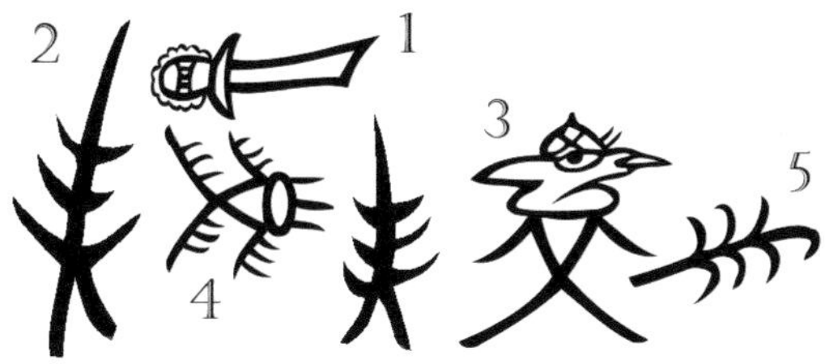

Graph-by-graph

1. **ggaiq**, a sword, used here semantically to indicate *siul*, "to kill". Perhaps a loan from the Tibetan *sod*, to kill.
2. **bbi**, forest (a number of trees, in this case, only two, separated by graph 4).
3. **coqpv**, name of a demon. It has the body of a demon, but the head of an elephant (which in this case is a phonetic marker, *coq*).
4. **eeq**, a kind of water demon, here read *mu* (another kind of water demon).
5. **bee**, artemisia, used phonetically for *bee*, to change.

Transcription

ser / xi / paidvq / ddee / zo / **siul** / lei / **bbi** / nieq / gul
wood / man / puppet / one / set / kill / again / forest / in / throw
bbi / gge / **coqpv** / **mu** / yi / **bee** / lei / heq
forest / genitive / demon / water demon / copula / change / again / go

Scharten translation

I cut an other and it was changed in the evil spirit of the woods.

New translation

Then he chopped up another set and threw them into the forest, where they changed into the *coqpv* demons.

Notes

Of the *coqpv*, McKhann notes, "I do not know who these demons are. They are not identified in any of the dictionaries of Naqxi pictographs". They indeed do not appear in Rock's compendia of demon names, or indeed any Chinese language dictionary of the dongba script. We can surmise from the context (and Scharten's translation) that these demons live in forests. The graph for forest (graph 2) seems like a variant of *bbi*, forest , which has the graph for to twist, *bbiq*, a person twisting thread, as a phonetic component, in between the semantic component of two trees. In this case the prone demon is placed in between the trees.

15-7

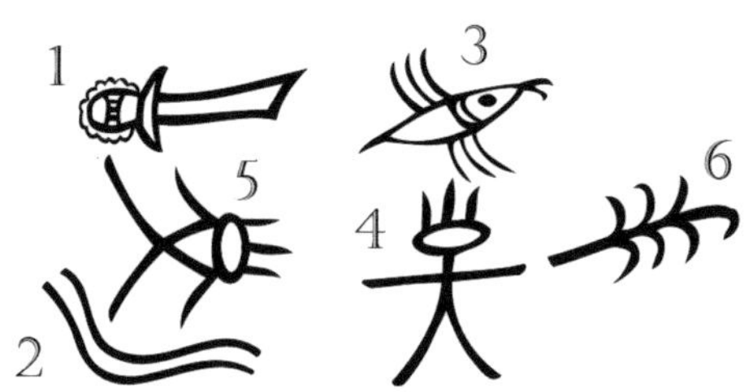

Graph-by-graph

1. **ggaiq**, a sword, used here semantically to indicate *siul*, "to kill". Perhaps a loan from the Tibetan *sod*, to kill.
2. **zhee**, a road.
3. **leel**, a louse, used phonetically for the name of a malevolent spirit.
4. **ceeq**, a ghost, usually one who has died from hanging.
5. **mu**, a kind of water demon.
6. **bee**, artemisia, used phonetically for *bee*, to change.

Transcription

ser / xi / paidvq / ddee / zo / **siul** / lei / **zhee** / nieq / gul
wood / man / puppet / one / set / kill / again / road / in / throw
zhee / gge / leelceeq/ **mu** / yi / **bee** / lei / heq
road / genitive / kind of ghost / water demon / copula / change / again / go

Scharten translation

I cut an other and it was thrown on the road and and it was changed in a hunting evil spirit.

New translation

Another set were killed and thrown onto the road, where they turned into the *leelceeq* spirits.

Notes

Scharten's translation is informative, for she suggests that this spirit, the *leelceeq*, is associated with hunting. The word leel in Naxi is a term for the spirit of the hunt. Graph 5 has finally morphed from *eeq* into *mu*. As another reminder of the indeterminacy of the Naxi ritual texts, He Guisheng reads graph 2, road, as a rebus for *zhee*, soil, i.e. thrown into the soil. I follow Scharten's translation.

15-8, 15-9

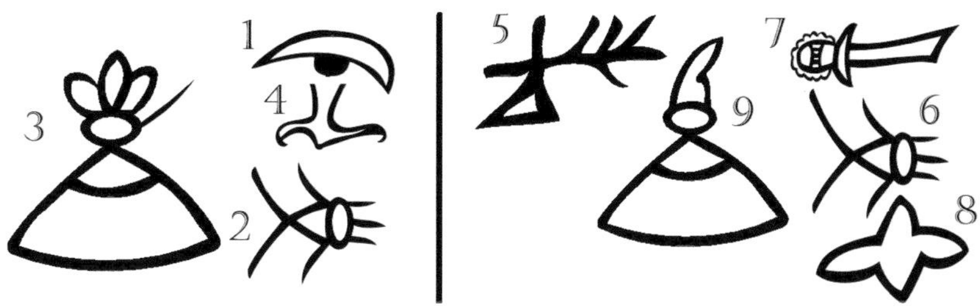

Graph-by-graph

1. **huq**, night, a moon facing down (to the earth).
2. **mu**, a kind of water demon.
3. **Dduq**, Naxi deity, the male principle.
4. **sseeq**, to catch (a claw opened as if about to catch onto something).
5. **so**, a scale with a weight attached, used phonetically for *soq*, morning.
6. **mu**, a kind of water demon.
7. **ggaiq**, a sword, used here semantically to indicate *siul*, "to kill". A composite graph, considered together with graph 8.
8. **siul**, lead. When accompanied with graph 7, sword, it is not read, and merely acts as a phonetic marker.
9. **Seiq**, Naxi deity, the female principle.

Transcription

huq / yi / **mu** / zzo / **Dduq** / nee
Night / copula / demon / suppress / deity / topicalizer / suppress
mu / **sseeq** / Dduq / nee / sseeq
demon / catch / deity / topicalizer / catch
soq / yi / **mu** / **siul** / **Seiq** / nee / siul
morning / copula / demon / kill / deity / topicalizer / kill

mu / siul / Seiq / jer / dder
demon / kill / deity / as / mission

Scharten translation
In the night the god fo heaven, Ndu, goes and kills the evil spirits.
In the daytime the god of earth kills the bogeys.

New translation
In the night, the god Dduq went to catch the demons. In the daytime, the goddess Seiq took upon the mission to kill the demons.

Notes
Now that Dduq has accidentally created all the above kinds of ghosts and demons, he, together with his "better half", Seiq, take it upon themselves to rid the world of them, each doing so at the particular time of day with which they are traditionally associated. Despite being separated by graph 6, graphs 7 and 8 should be taken as one composite graph, a phono-semantic compound, *siul*, with the semantic component being a sword, the phonetic component the metal, lead. In this way all three graphs become a compound indicating the meaning of "killing demons".

15-10

Graph-by-graph
1. **Dduq**, Naxi deity, the male principle
2. **Coqssei-leel'ee**, Naxi hero.
3. **zzeeqggu**, to discuss (two figures talking).
4. **sso**, man.
5. **mil**, woman.
6. **dvq**, thousand.
7. **xi**, hundred.
8. **ka**, bitter, something bitter entering a mouth. Used phonetically for *ka*, good.
9. **jjef**, scales. Used phonetically for *jjeq*, bad (poor, miserable).
10. **dvq**, thousand.

11. **sso**, man, seated.
12. **mil**, woman, seated.
13. **ka**, good, not read (?).

Transcription

Mee'leel-**Dduq** / epv / neif / **Coqssei-leel'ee** / lei / **zzeeqggu**
Dduq (in heaven) / grandfather / and / name / again / discuss
sso / **mil** / **dvq** / dvq / jjuq
man / woman / thousand / thousand / have
dvqdvq / **xixi** / jjuq
thousand upon thousand / hundred upon hundred / have
Jjiceil / sal / **ka** / sal / **jjeq** / gge
place name / judge / good / judge / bad / genitive
dvq / **sso** / dvq / **mil** / teeq / niuq / teiq / zzeeq / seiqwei / zeel
thousand / man / thousand / woman / this / in / static aspect / live / exclamation / modal particle

Scharten translation

The god of heaven saith now to T'so-rze-geh's son: on earth there are thousands and hundreds of influences, which bring the lovers together. When you like to be betrothed, there is an opportunity.

New translation

Grandfather Dduq and Coqssei-leel'ee talked with one another. Dduq said, "There are many hundreds and thousands [of deities] at Jjiceil, in this place there are men and woman of all kinds, good and bad."

Notes

Our hero Coqssei-leel'ee, having roamed the earth alone for quite some time, is now feeling exceptionally lonely. Then Dduq reveals to him that at a certain place reside many gods, and that he can go there to choose a partner. This is essentially him saying to Leel'ee, "there are plenty of fish in the sea", only in this case the sea is "Jjicei", a locale that, according to He Guisheng, lies in the cliffs of "Ye'lee-ekee" (and the fish are in fact divine beings).

16-1

Graph-by-graph

1. **Dduq**, Naxi deity, the male principle, here speaking.
2. **she**, geba syllabic graph, used for *shel*, to speak.
3. **mee**, the heavens.
4. **shuaq**, high, an ideograph.
5. **geeq**, stars.
6. **mil**, woman (here two women).
7. **mil**, woman (not read, used to indicate the one with vertical eyes).
8. **mie zeeq**, vertical eyes. This is an ideograph not used in other books, the vertical arrangement of the eyes is represented within the graph itself.
9. **mil**, woman (not read, used to indicate the one with horizontal eyes).
10. **mie lerq**, horizontal eyes. In fact, this graph is simply *mie*, eyes, but only in contrast with graph 8 is this read with the adjectival modifier.
11. **o**, turquoise. Here read *waq*, to propagate.
12. **ddv**, wing, here used phonetically for the first syllable in *ddvceiq*, celestial robe.
13. **me**, negation.
14. **ddv**, wing, here used for *ddvceiq*, celestial robe.

Transcription

Mee'leel-**Dduq** / epv / nee / lei / shel / mei
Dduq (in heaven) / grandfather / topicalizer / again / speak / modal particle
Meeshuaq-geeqaiq bbvq
place name
mee / **mil** / **mie zeeq** / **mie lerq** / ni / gvl / jjuq
heaven / woman / vertical eyes / horizontal eyes / two / measure word / have
ssi / yi / mie / zeeq / ssi
pretty / copula / vertical eyes / pretty
waq / yi / mie lerq / waq / meeq / zeel
propagate / copula / horizontal eyes / propagate / should / modal particle
mie zeeq / **ddv**cei / kvq / **me** / niq
vetical eyes / celestial robe / invite / not / want
Coqssei-leel'ee sso / mie lerq / **ddv**cei / kvq / bbeq / ddee / naiq / zeel
name + epithet / horizontal eyes / celestial robe/ invite / come / one / must / modal particle

Scharten translation

The god heaven saith further: under heaven there is a clifft, where are two heavenly women. One of them her eye-brows are nice, but her heart is not good. The other her eye-brows are not nice looking, but her heart is good as gold.

You must not take the feathers of the wings, whci belong to the one, whose heart is not right, but take them from the one, whose heart is right.

New translation

Dduq continued: "Under heaven, by the starry cliff, there are two celestial women, one with vertical eyes and one with horizontal eyes. The one with vertical eyes is pretty, but the one with horizontal eyes can propagate humanity. Do not marry the one with vertical eyes, Coqseei-leel'ee, you must marry the one with horizontal eyes."

Notes

Thus begins a classic episode in Naxi myth: the progenitor of mankind takes a wife, but not without an initial mishap. Dduq reveals to our hero that he can choose a bride from among the female divinities, and introduces two in particular, differentiated by their eyes. One has vertical eyes (i.e. stacked one atop the other, signifying superiority and a hierarchical relationship, see Mckhann 1992, 103), the other more "human" horizontal eyes. He Guisheng suggests that the second intonation unit contains a place name, while Scharten translates it literally as a cliff "under heaven". Additionally, graph 11 has two interpretations: *waq*, to propagate, or *o*, meaning precious or good (hence, a good heart, but not a pretty face, Scharten's "good as gold"). "Inviting the celestial robes" is here a metaphor for bringing a divine wife into the home; note Scharten's literal translation of "feathers", suggesting that these divine women have wings like angels.

16-2

Graph-by-graph

1. **Coqssei-leel'ee**, Naxi hero.
2. **mil**, woman (not read, used to indicate the one with vertical eyes).
3. **mie zeeq**, vertical eyes (not read).
4. **ssi**, beautiful (as a flower).
5. **mil**, woman (not read, used to indicate the one with horizontal eyes).

6. **mie lerq**, horizontal eyes (not read).
7. **o**, turquoise, possibly meaning "good" (not read).

Transcription

Coqssei-leel'ee sso / nee / ddeeq / pa / me / gguq
Naxi hero + epithet / heart / big / face / not / compare
pa / **ssi** / **mie** / me / gguq
face / pretty / eyes / not / compare

Scharten translation

New translation

Coqssei-leel'ee then thought to himself, "A kind heart is nothing compared to a pretty face, and a pretty face is nothing compared to pretty eyes."

Notes

Coqssei-leel'ee is nothing but an archetypal man, and he is quick to dismiss kind heartedness in order to swoon over a pretty face, particularly a beautiful pair of (vertical!) eyes. Scharten takes this panel as a simple statement that the vertical-eyed goddess was pretty, and the horizontal-eyed goddess was "good" (graph 7), which formed part of the translation for the previous panel. He Guisheng reads this part as the famous Naxi aphorism and satirical paean to good looks: "*laq peel nee me gguq, nee ddeq pa me gguq, pa ssi mie me gguq*" (clever hands are nothing compared to a kind heart, which is nothing compared to a pretty face, which is nothing compared to beautiful eyes), which I preserve in the translation, despite Scharten's rendition being closer to the written text. Note graph 4, "pretty", which is a flower with a couple of extra fronds, no doubt to indicate a particularly beautiful bloom.

16-3

Graph-by-graph

1. **Coqssei-leel'ee**, Naxi hero.
2. **nee**, heart, used phonetically for *nee*, topicalizer.
3. **mil**, woman (not read, used to indicate the one with horizontal eyes).
4. **mie lerq**, horizontal eyes.
5. **ddv**, wing, here used phonetically for the first syllable in *ddvceiq*, celestial robe.
6. **me**, negation.
7. **kvl**, sickle, used phonetically for *kvq*, to invite.
8. **mil**, woman (not read, used to indicate the one with vertical eyes).
9. **mie zeeq**, vertical eyes.
10. **ddv**, wing, here used phonetically for the first syllable in *ddvceiq*, celestial robe.
11. **kvl**, sickle, used phonetically for *kvq*, to invite.
12. **Coqssei-leel'ee**, Naxi hero, here not read, merely indicating who is doing the inviting (i.e. holding the sickle).
13. **ciq**, shoulder, (a shoulder blade), used phonetically for *ceeq*, to come (past tense).

Transcription

Coqssei-leel'ee / nee
Naxi hero / topicalizer
mie lerq / **ddv**cei / **me** / **kvq** / bbei
horizontal eyes / celestial robe / not / invite / do
mie zeeq / **ddv**cei / **kvq** / bel / **ceeq**
vertical eyes / celestial robe/ invite / bring / came

Scharten translation

T'so-rze-le-geh's son takes the feathers of the one, who is nice looking, and they two become a pair.

New translation

Coqssei-leel'ee then brought the girl with vertical eyes to be his wife, not the girl with horizontal eyes.

Notes

The choice is now made, for better or worse. Certain renditions of this story have the action here being not "inviting" the celestial woman to be our hero's bride, but instead the "stealing" of a bride (McKhann 102).

16-4

Graph-by-graph

1. **Coqssei-leel'ee**, Naxi hero.
2. **Mee mil mie zeeq**, celestial woman with vertical eyes.
3. **jjiq**, a house, used semantically for "family".
4. **yuq**, to give birth, a woman in childbirth, not read.
5. **mie zeeq**, vertical eyes, here not read, indicating which woman is giving birth.
6. **seel**, a kind of grass, used phonetically for *seel*, to be alive, to revive (in this case, to be born).
7. **to**, pine tree.
8. **bbee**, chestnut tree.

Transcription

Coqssei-leel'ee / neif / **mee** / **mil** / **mie zeeq** / tee / ni / gvl
Naxi hero / and / heaven / woman / vertical eyes / they / two / measure word
dallu / ddee / **jjiq** / bbei
come together / one / family / make
ddee / la / ddee / der / **seel** / **to** kee / **bbee** kee / seel
one / again / one / foetus / born / pine root / chestnut root / born

Scharten translation

When they came home. She gave birth, but the child were like roots of a fir tree

New translation

Coqssei-leel'ee and the celestial woman with vertical eyes made a home together. She gave birth, but the children were like the roots of the pine tree and the chestnut tree.

Notes

Having chosen poorly, Coqssei-leel'ee now reaps the consequences. His new bride cannot give birth to human children. Scharten mistranslates pine tree as fir tree and the tree roots in the readings are not depicted on the page.

16-5

Graph-by-graph

1. **yuq**, to give birth, a woman in childbirth, not read.
2. **seel**, a kind of grass, used phonetically for *seel*, to be alive, to revive (in this case, to be born).
3. **ggvq**, a bear.
4. **bbuq**, a pig.
5. **yuq**, to give birth, not read.
6. **seel**, to be born.
7. **reeq**, a snake.
8. **ba**, a frog.
9. **yuq**, to give birth, not read.
10. **seel**, to be born.
11. **yuq**, a monkey.
12. **aiq**, a chicken.

Transcription

ddee / la / ddee / der / **seel** / **ggvq** / der / **bbuq** / der / seel / lei / ceeq
one / again / one / foetus / born / bear / foetus / pig / foetus / born / again / come
ddee / la / ddee / der / **seel** / **reeq** / der / **ba** / der / seel
one / again / one / foetus / born / snake / foetus / frog / foetus / born
yuq / der / **aiq** / der / **seel**
monkey / foetus / chicken / foetus / born

Scharten translation

The second time, they were like a bear and a pig.
The third like a frog and snake, and afterwards like an ape and wild chicken.

New translation

And again she gave birth, to a bear and a pig, and once more to a snake and frog, and then to a monkey and a chicken.

Notes

The non-human offspring keep on coming, with three more pairs. The verb given by He Guisheng in all intonation units is *yuq* (graphs 1, 5, 9), to be born, not *seel* (graphs 2, 6, 10). It's interesting that both appear in this manuscript.

16-6

Graph-by-graph

1. **Dduq**, Naxi deity.
2. **she**, geba syllabic graph, used for *shel*, to speak.
3. **zzi**, jackal, used phonetically for *zzi*, the people.
4. **coq**, elephant, used phonetically for *coq*, mankind.
5. **zhul**, a grebe, a diving bird. The wavy line atop its head indicates air rising up after they have dived into the water. Used phonetically for *zhul*, to copulate or propagate.
6. **me**, negation.
7. **ga**, good (from Tibetan *ka*).

Transcription

Mee'leel **Dduq** / epv / nee / **shel**
deity / grandfather / topicalizer / say
zzi / qu / **coq** / qu / **zhul** / **me** / **ga** / ye / zeel
people / kind / man / kind / propagate / not / good / sentence final particle / modal particle

Scharten translation

The god of heaven saith to him: your wife give birth to such things, which cant be counted as men's descendants.

New translation

[Ater Leel'ee returned to Dduq,] Dduq said to him: "Your wife is unable to propagate mankind."

Notes

Our hero returns to the grandfatherly deity, Dduq, for advice. Dduq informs him that he will not be able to have human children with this wife that he has chosen. Note graph 5, the innocuous little grebe, which is a stand in for *zhul* which is, according to Rock, the spirit of fertility in Naxi (as well as the spirit of copulation), the very essence of transmission which ensures that the human race endures.

16-7

Graph-by-graph

1. **to**, a pine tree.
2. **bbee**, a chestnut tree.
3. **seel**, a kind of grass, used phonetically for *seel*, to be alive, to revive (in this case, to be born).
4. **bbu**, a hillside.
5. **ggvq**, a bear.
6. **bbuq**, a pig.
7. **bbi**, forest (two trees indicating many).

Transcription

Coqssei-leel'ee sso
name + epithet ("manly")
sso / ee / dal / me / see
man / good / say / not / know
sso / piuq / jju / seiq / yi
man / suffer / have / modal particle / emphatic
to / der / **bbee** / der / **seel**
pine / foetus / chestnut / foetus / born
to / **bbu** / kul / neiq / heel / lei / pil / fai / laq

pine / hill / place / in / throw / again / cast away / go / suggestion particle
ggvq / der / **bbuq** / der / seel
bear / foetus / pig / foetus / born
bbi / ddeeq / bbvq / neiq / heel / lei / pil / fai / laq
forest / large / place / in / throw / again / cast away / go / suggestion particle

Scharten translation
Because you have sinned and now you have to bring the roots of the trees to the mountains; the bear and the wild pig to the woods;

New translation
"Coqseei-leel'ee," said Dduq, "you have not listened to my words, and now you suffer. As for the pine and chestnut offspring, take them to the mountains, and cast them away. As for the bear and pig offspring, take them to the great forest, and cast them away."

Notes
The first intonation units, Dduq's admonition to Leel'ee, are not written, merely recited by the dongba. In fact, most of the syntactic words in this panel are missing: the final intonation unit of nine syllables is represented by only the forest (graph 7). Contemporary readings suggest that the pine and chestnut be cast away in a pine forest, but graph 4 clearly indicates a hill or mountain, so I follow Scharten's translation here in making the mountains explicit, and to differentiate from the following intonation unit, where the forest is explicitly written.

17-1, 17-2

Graph-by-graph

1. **reeq**, a snake.
2. **ba**, a frog's head, a frog.
3. **seel**, a kind of grass, used phonetically for *seel*, to be alive, to revive (in this case, to be born).
4. **jjiq**, water.
5. **herq**, green (as turquoise).
6. **yuq**, a monkey.
7. **aiq**, a chicken.
8. **see**, used phonetically for *seel*, to be born.
9. **aiq**, cliff.

Transcription

reeq / der / **ba** / der / **seel**
snake / foetus / frog / foetus / born
jjiq / **herq** / ko / neiq / heel / lei / pil / fai / laq
water / green / place / in / throw / again / cast away / go / suggestion particle
yuq / der / **aiq** / der / **seel**
monkey / foetus / chicken / foetus / born
aiq / shua / ko / neiq / heel / lei / pil / fai / laq
cliff / high / place / in / throw / again / cast away / go / suggestion particle

Scharten translation

the frog to the water. The ape and the chicken to the clifft.

New translation

"As for the snake and the frog offspring, take them to the green waters and cast them away. As for the monkey and the chicken offspring, take them to the high cliffs and cast them away."

Notes

He Guisheng's recitation has the snake foetus being discarded amongst the cave of the black rocks: "*lv naq ko*". Both He Guisheng and He Cai read graph 5, turquoise, as part of a place name. He Cai recalls it as "*waq jjiq shul*", the turquoise here read *waq*. I take it as a simple adjective as per the adjacent panels (great forest, high cliffs, etc.).

17-3, 17-4

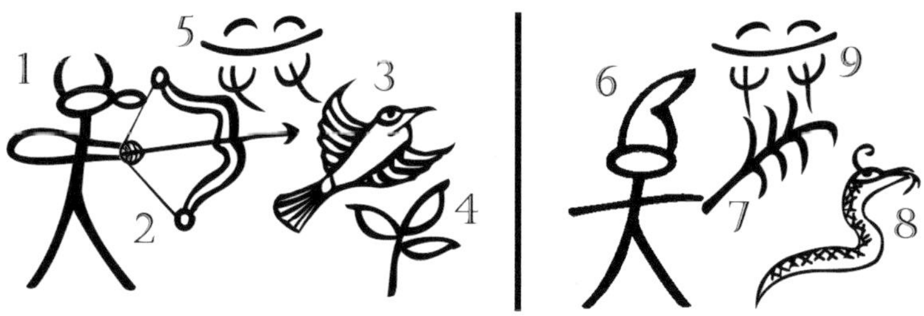

Graph-by-graph

1. **Coqssei-leel'ee**, Naxi hero.
2. **kail lee**, bow and arrow.
3. **vlssi**, a bird (here not read). This graph can also be read *zzeq*, to fly.
4. **rer**, willow, used phonetically for *ruq*, an enemy.
5. **ddoq**, to see.
6. **mil**, a woman. Here read *bbeeq* (archaic term for woman).
7. **bee**, an artemisia branch.
8. **reeq**, a snake.
9. **ddoq**, to see.

Transcription

Coqssei-leel'ee sso
name + epithet ("manly")
Mee'leel Dduq / epv / nee / seiq / shel / seiq / lei / bbei
deity / grandfather / topicalizer / how / say / how / particle / do
zhuaq / yi / **kail lee** / kail zo / bul

man / copula / arrows / bow / take
ruq / ddoq / ruq / siul / neiq
enemy / see / enemy / kill / dynamic aspect
bbeeq / yi / ddiuq / ceeq / **bbaigvq** / bul
woman / copula / stick / thin / broom / take
reeq / ddoq / reeq / bbaiq / reeq / siul / neiq
snake / see / snake / sweep / snake / kill / dynamic aspect

Scharten translation
T'so-rze-le-geh's son met his enemy. He takes his bow and kills him.
His wife mets also her ennemy. She takes a trap and kills her.

New translation
Coqssei-leel'ee did as he was instructed by Dduq. Then, on the road, the man took his bow and arrow, and, seeing his enemy, shot him dead. The woman took her branch of artemisia, and, seeing a snake, swept it away.

Notes
The first two intonation units, where Leel'ee is related as following the previous instructions, are not written down. What happens in these two panels is somewhat cryptic and requires a little explanation. Rock's translation is terse: "When he saw her [his enemy] he killed her on the mountain, when the girl saw the snake she killed it in the valley" (1952, 681). McKhann writes in a footnote that the Chinese translation by He Yuncai appears incorrect, saying that "Coq chanced upon a female snake or a demoness in the form of a snake", while his manuscript clearly shows a woman (as does the Scharten manuscript). In the translation McKhann refers to, only He Fayuan's Chinese is incorrect, the Naxi reading and interlinear translation are accurate. The contemporary readings have the two main figures in these panels as archetypal "man" and "woman", while Coqseei-leel'ee and his future wife are probably meant. The panels are perhaps not to be taken too literally, according to He Guisheng. The bird-like "enemy" of man and the snake encountered by woman are there to represent the dangers of the natural world – after all, the creatures that resulted from the union of Leel'ee and his vertical-eyed wife have now been returned to the cliffs and forests and waters at Dduq's behest. What this means is that mankind now has the custom of taking a bow and arrow for protection, while a woman will take a stick or broom (or indeed, as indicated in the panel, an artemisia branch) when walking the wilds, in case she encounters a snake on the path. They are not therefore to be understood as enemies in the traditional sense, or even demons, but simply the dangers one might encounter in the wild.

17-5

Graph-by-graph

1. **mil**, woman, here seen ascending (*ddo*).
2. **mie zeeq**, vertical eyes.
3. **shuq**, iron (as in an iron axe), used phonetically for *shuq*, to search for. Not read (?).
4. **mee**, the heavens.
5. **ggeq**, a raised platform or bench, used phonetically for *ggeq*, on top of.
6. **ddoq**, a ritual slat representing the *ddoq* demons. Used phonetically for *ddo*, to climb.

Transcription

mee / **mil** / **mie zeeq** / yi
haven / girl / vertical eyes / copula
mee / shuaq / ku / nieq / lei / ddiul / **ggeq** / lei / **ddo** / heq
sky / high / place / in / particle / chase / on / particle / climb / go

Scharten translation

T'so-rze-le-geh's son, he is good man, but he has no good wife. The god of heaven tells him, when you want one, you must climb up to heaven.

New translation

The vertical-eyed wife was then made to climb back up to the heavens.

Notes

There are two interpretations of this panel, and whoever wrote it was obviously in two minds. The figure to the left (graph one) is either a woman or Coqssei-leel'ee, and you can see where the headdress of the woman has been turned into Leel'ee's horns, and the vertical eyes have been turned into the familiar trunk. Scharten's translation uses this revision. He Guisheng's reading follows the original, i.e., it is his wife being made to return to heaven. Of course, the axe in hand (graph 3) is only read if we follow Scharten's rendition, i.e., Leel'ee is being instructed to search for a wife in heaven. Because the following panel includes the horizontal-eyed woman, I translate according to He Guisheng's reading. Graph 6, *ddo*, is a rebus for "climb", but it is quite superfluous, the original graph being a raised foot and a slope: . The dongba could have simply drawn the line representing slope instead of this graph.

17-6

Graph-by-graph

1. **Coqssei-leel'ee**, Naxi hero.
2. **shuq**, iron (as in an iron axe), used phonetically for *shuq*, to search for.
3. **mee**, the heavens.
4. **ddoq**, a ritual slat representing the *ddoq* demons. Used phonetically for *ddo*, to climb.
5. **ceil**, leaf (two leaves), used phonetically for *ceil*, first syllable in Ceilheeq-bbvbbeq.
6. **hee**, teeth, used phonetically for *heeq*, second syllable of Ceilheeq-bbvbbeq.
7. **mil**, woman, here seen moving over the earth, final epithet attached to name Ceilheeq-bbvbbeq.
8. **bbuq**, pig, used phonetically for *bbuq*, partner.
9. **shuq**, to search for.
10. **ddiuq**, the earth.
11. **ssaq**, a planet, seen as a malevolent demon that causes eclipses. Used phonetically for *ssaq*, to come down.

Transcription

sso / ee / zzee / me / jjuq
man / good / partner / not / have
Coqssei-leel'ee sso
Naxi hero + epithet ("manly")
zzee / **shuq** / **mee** / la / **ddo**
partner / search / heaven / also / climb
heiq / yi / mee / gge / ku / nieq / lei / wul / heq
god / copula / sky / on / place / in / particle / return / go
Ceil-heeq bbvbbeq **mil**
Naxi heroine + epithet ("womanly")

mil / ee / **bbuq** / me / jjuq
woman / good / partner / not / have
bbuq / **shuq** / **ddiuq** / **ssaq** / cee
partner / search / earth / descend / come

Scharten translation

He wnt and he mets a good person, who has no good husband. Her name is: T'se-hgheh beh-beh-mi. She has to go to earth.

New translation

And Coqssei-leel'ee, the good man who had no partner, climbed up to the divine heavens to search for a new wife. The good divine woman Ceilheeq-bbvbbeq had no partner, so she descended to the earth to find one.

Notes

Our hero now ascends to the heavens to find another bride, and in the second half of the panel our heroine, Ceilheeq-bbvbbeq (with the horizontal eyes), is named for the first time (see graph 5). While Leel'ee goes up to find a divine wife, she descends to find a human husband. They are about to meet halfway. Scharten's translation has them meeting already here in this panel, but the meeting occurs at a specific, mythologically important location in the next panel. While graph 5 is a representation of a leaf, used phonetically for the first syllable of the name ("Ceil"), they are reduplicated here perhaps in reference to her horizontal eyes. Fang and He record a graph with the leaf in the woman's hand (1981, 363): . Graph 6 is an extra phonetic clue, the teeth, *hee*, used for the second syllable of the name, Ceilheeq-bbvbbeq.

17-7

Graph-by-graph

1. **perq**, white.
2. **naq**, black.
3. **lee**, land (fields).

4. **zhul**, awl, used phonetically for *zhul*, to link or connect.
5. **Seeqka'lomuqbbaq**, name for the plum tree that grows at the threshold of the earthly and ghostly realms.
6. **ni**, two.
7. **laqjjuq**, bracelet, used phonetically for *jju*, to have.
8. **hol**, eight.
9. **bvl**, a colander, used phonetically for the second syllable of *gobvl*, to meet (to meet someone on the road).
10. **sso**, man, here walking.
11. **mil**, woman, here walking.
12. **zhul**, awl, used phonetically for *zhul*, to connect, second syllable of *zzeeqzhul*, to come together.

Transcription
perq / **naq** / **lee** / gai**zhul**
white / black / land / meet
Seeqka'lomuqbbaq
name of a plum tree
ni / ni / qiuqqiuq / bbaq
two / two / opposite / bloom
ni / zzeeq / ee / mei / ddeeq / derl / ggv
two / together / good / possessive / one / pair / become
ni / hiul / ee /mei / ddeeq / toq / ggv / lei / heq
two / stand / good / possessive / one / pair / particle / go
ni / neif / qiuq / go**bvl**
want / and / need / meet
sso / lei / **mil** / zzeeq**zhul**
man / paticle / woman / come together

Scharten translation
She arrives to a place, where heaven and earth come to gether wnd the white prune trees spring up, which every eight months blossom twice. At that plce they met one an other.

New translation
At the place where the white and the black lands meet, there grows a plum tree that blossoms twice a year. The two flowers faced one another, the wants and desire came together, man and woman stood facing one another and then joined together as a pair.

Notes
The manuscript here shows a tree full of flowers (*bbaq* 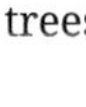). The Seeqka'lomuqbbaq is in fact supposed to be a plum tree, *seeqka* (not the "prune trees" of Scharten). This tree straddles

the border between the black land and the white land, the yang and the yin, the sun and moon. According to legend, the flowers on one side of the tree are black, on the other they are white; Fang shows a graph that reflects this dichotomy:  (1981, 162), one tree with a dual nature. Some manuscripts have the tree growing in the middle of the "land/earth" (graph 3), splitting it in two. This is the only manuscript of the ones I have encountered which includes the detail of the blooms appearing twice every eight months (as per Scharten's translation, see graph 8). Others simply say that the tree blooms twice every year (which McKhann [1992, 103] suggests is connected to the twice-yearly performance of the Sacrifice to Heaven rite). Contemporary readings of this manuscript simply skip this detail; He Guisheng makes a note that the syllable *hol*, eight, could be a phonetic for *hiul*, to stand, as the two stand facing one another (graphs 10 and 11). The poetic language at the end speaks of the two lovers meeting like the flowers on the tree.

17-8

Graph-by-graph

1. **Coqssei-leel'ee**, Naxi hero.
2. **go**, a crane.
3. **perq**, white.
4. **heiq**, a god, seated in heaven.
5. **mee**, the sky, the heavens.
6. **kvq**, a box, used phonetically for *kvq*, inside.
7. **tvq**, a bucket, used phonetically for *tv*, emerge.

Transcription

Coqssei-leel'ee sso
name + epithet ("manly")
Ceilheeq-bbvbbeq /gge
name / possessive
go / **perq** / ddv / gol / zeel
crane / white / wing / in / hide
zzeiq / lei / **heiq** / yi / **mee**gge / **kvq** / nieq / **tv**
fly / particle / god / copula / up in heaven / in / demonstrative pronoun / arrive

Scharten translation

T'so-rze-le-hgeh's son flys to heaven under the wings of a white storck.

New translation

Coqssei-leel'ee then hid under the wing of Ceilheeq-bbvbbeq's white crane, and flew up into the palace of the gods in heaven.

Notes

Ceilheeq-bbvbbeq is not written, and Scharten merely translates what is on the page: our hero tucks himself under the wing of a white stork (in what makes for a vivid composite, see graphs 1 and 2), and arrives in heaven. Other versions have Ceilheeq-bbvbbeq transforming herself into the white stork, or suggest that as a divine woman she has the wings of a white stork. The actual reading is not clear on this point, there is merely a possessive marker.

17-9

Graph-by-graph

1. **Zzee'laq-epv**, Naxi ancestor god.
2. **perq**, white, here used phonetically for pv, final syllable in Zzee'laq-epv.
3. **jjiq**, house.
4. **ggv**, nine.
5. **Coqssei-leel'ee**, Naxi hero, here seated (hiding inside the house).
6. **ke**, geba phonetic graph, used for *kel*, basket.
7. **Zzee'laq-epv**, Naxi ancestor god.
8. **kvl**, night. The moon, casting light.
9. **yuq**, sheep. The lines surrounding the graph suggest that it is shaking out of fear.
10. **derq**, a headless demon, used phonetically for *derl*, to close.
11. **loq**, plowtail. Used phonetically for *loq*, inside.
12. **so**, a scale with a weight attached. Used phonetically for *soq*, morning (not read, see next panel).
13. **loq**, inside (not read, see next panel).

Transcription

mee / gge / **Zzee'laq-epv** / ku / nieq / tv
heaven / possessive / deity / place / demonstrative pronoun / arrive
Zzee'laq-epv / gge / **jjiq** / ddee / **ggv** / zhual / ku / nieq / tv
deity / possessive / house / big / nine / inner chamber / place / demonstrative pronoun / arrive
Coqssei'leel'ee sso
name + epithet ("manly")
meel / sheeq / **kel**pieq / lvl / lei / ji
bamboo / yellow / basket / cover / particle / put
Zzee'laq-epv / gge / **kvl** / gge / bbv**yuq** / kuq / **derl** / bbiuq**loq** / zherq / ye /zeel
deity / possessive / night / possessive / sheep / inside / close / pen / afraid / sentence final / modal particle

Scharten translation

When he arrives there, the house with seven rooms is opened for him and hides himself under a big basket. In the evening, Nzu la-a-p'u, his father in law, comes to bring his sheep home, but the nearer they come home, the more they get frightened.

New translation

In the abode of the gods, Coqssei-leel'ee arrived at the celestial mansion of Zzee'laq-epv, father of his celestial bride. He hid under a yellow bamboo basket. In the night, Zzee'laq-epv wished to close his sheep in the pen, but they were frightened of something.

Notes

In this panel we can see Coqssei-leel'ee's father-in-law, Zzee'laq-epv, who will become a central character in the story. He is depicted as a robed deity with a tiger's head. This does not mean that he has the head of a tiger, it merely indicates the second syllable of his name: *laq*. As with Dduq, the final two syllables mean "grandfather". The mansion (graph 3) is a wonderful collage: we see the large beams and rafters, and the number nine indicates it has nine inner chambers (i.e., this is a large palace). Scharten writes "seven rooms", both nine and seven indicate the idea of "many" in Naxi. Our hero can be seen covering himself with a basket, which I believe is a geba graph. The basket, *kel*, can be written in dongba script like this: 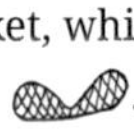.

The sheep sense something is amiss (there is a human trespassing in the divine realm), hence they begin to quake with fear. The final two graphs here (12 and 13) are connected to the next panel and are therefore not read just yet.

17-10, 17-11

Graph-by-graph

1. **so**, a scale with a weight attached. Used phonetically for *soq*, morning.
2. **yuq**, sheep (not read).
3. **kee**, a dog, here seen barking (*lvq*).
4. **lv**, stone, used phonetically for *lvq*, to bark.
5. **sse**, to sharpen a blade, combination of sword and stone (i.e. a whetstone).
6. **ser**, wood, used phonetically for *sse*, to sharpen.
7. **mil**, woman (representing our heroine, Ceilheeq-bbvbbeq.
8. **nee**, heart, used phonetically for *nee*, topicalizer.
9. **Zzee'laq-epv**, Naxi ancestor god.

Transcription

soq / gge / bbvkee / keel / bbiuq**kee** / goqloq / **lvq** / ye / zeel
morning / possessive / domestic dog / put / pen / inside / bark / sentence final / modal particle
kvl / gge / ggaiq / **sse** / neiq
night / possessive / sword / sharpen / dynamic aspect
soq / gge / ggaiq / caq / neiq
morning / possessive / sword / rub / dynamic aspect
Ceilheeq-bbvbbeq nee
name / topicalizer
Zzee'laq-epv / lei / milddo
deity / particle / ask
kvl / gge / ggaiq / sse / seiq / bbei / sse / neiq / zeel
night / possessive / sword / sharpen / how / do / sharpen / dynamic aspect / modal particle
soq / gge / ggaiq / caq / seiq / bbei / caq / neiq / zeel
morning / possessive / sword / rub / how / do / rub / dynamic aspect / modal particle

Scharten translation

In the morning he want to loose his dog, but the more he wants to do it, the more th dog begins to barken.

Nzu-la-a-p'u takes now a knife and begins to sharpen it. T'se hgeh-beh-beh-mi asks her father: why do you sharpen your knife?

New translation

In the morning he wished to put the household dogs in their pen, but they were barking at something. And so Zzee'laq-epv sharpened his sword during the day and during the night. His daughter Ceilheeq-bbvbbeq asked him, "Why are you sharpening your sword day and night?"

Notes

The reading of this panel begins with *soq gge*, "of the morning", and perhaps could be taken to be the final two graphs of the previous panel, *soq loq*, "in the morning". Graph 1, *soq* ("morning") is probably a repetition. The dogs of the divine household are also uneasy; they are having their "*fee fi fo fum*" moment, for they too sense the presence of our hero. On alert, Zzee'laq-epv begins to sharpen his blade. Graph 5 is an ideographic compound of a bladed weapon and stones, indicating the act of sharpening a blade on a whetstone. The following graph, graph 6, is a tree, *ser*, read as *ssc*, to sharpen. It acts merely as a reminder of the pronunciation of the previous word, and should not be read twice. In this way, graphs 5 and 6 could be taken together as a phono-semantic compound, the first graph being the semantic component, the latter supplying the phonetic clue.

18-1

Graph-by-graph

1. **kvl**, evening, a moon facing downward.
2. **yuq**, sheep. The lines surrounding the graph suggest that it is shaking out of fear, i.e. *zherq*, to quiver.
3. **derq**, a headless demon. Used phonetically for *derl*, to close.
4. **so**, a scale with a weight attached. Used phonetically for *soq*, morning (not read, see next panel).
5. **kee**, a dog, here seen barking (*lvq*).
6. **yuq**, sheep (not read).
7. **lv**, stone, used phonetically for *lvq*, to bark.
8. **sse**, to sharpen a blade, combination of sword and stone (i.e. a whetstone).

Transcription

Zzee'laq-epv / lei / shel / mei
deity / particle / say / particle
kvl / gge / bbv**yuq** / kuq / **derl** / biuq / dal / **zherq** / ye / zeel
night / possessive / household sheep / in / close / pen / adverb of degree / fear / sentence final particle / modal particle
soq / gge / bbv**kee** / bbiuq / kee / goq / dal / **lvq** / ye / zeel
night / possessive / household dogs / pen / put / in / adverb of degree / fear / sentence final particle / modal particle
ggaiq / **sse** / chee / bbei / sse / neiq / zeel
sword / sharpen / this / way / sharpen / dynamic aspect / modal particle
ggaiq / caq / chee / bbei / caq / neiq / zeel
sword / rub / this / way / rub / dynamic aspect / modal particle

Scharten translation

He answers: in the evening, when I want to shut up the sheep, the begin to bleat and in the morning, when I want to loose my dog, he begins to barken. Becuase of this I sharpen my knife.

New translation

And Zzee'laq-epv replied to her, "In the evening, the sheep in the pen were startled, and in the morning the dogs in the kennel were barking, this is why I am sharpening my blade."

Notes

The text as written is a simple repetition: the events of the evening and the morning surrounding the sharpening of the blade, the central action; there is however a subtext here that McKhann translates: "There is an earthborn man hiding around here somewhere, and I mean to kill him" (1992, 105). The animals are uneasy because they smell man, and the deity knows this.

18-2

Graph-by-graph

1. **mil**, woman, here speaking. Used semantically for Ceilheeq-bbvbbeq.
2. **ceil**, leaf (two leaves), used phonetically for *ceil*, first syllable in Ceilheeq-bbvbbeq.
3. **hee**, teeth, used phonetically for *heeq*, second syllable of Ceilheeq-bbvbbeq.
4. **she**, geba syllabic graph, used for *shel*, to speak.
5. **sse**, to sharpen a blade, combination of sword and stone (i.e. a whetstone).
6. **nei**, amaranth leaf, used phonetically for *neif*, and.
7. **me**, negation.
8. **ta** or **ddu**, geba syllabic graph. If the former, it will be connected with graph 5, *ggaiq ta*, to sharpen a blade. If the latter, it will be used phonetically for *dder*.
9. **Zzee'laq-epv**, Naxi ancestral deity.
10. **me**¸negation.
11. **ggaiq**, sword. Possibly used semantically for *siuq*, to kill.

Transcription

Ceilheeq-bbvbbeq / nee / lei / **shel** / mei
name / topicalizer / particle / say / particle
epv / ggaiq / **sse** / **neif** / ggaiq / caq / la / **me** / **dder**
grandfather / sword / sharpen / and / sword / rub / again / not / need

Scharten translation

The girl saith then to her father: please, dont do that.

New translation

So Ceilheeq-bbvbbeq said, "Father, there is no need for you to sharpen your sword so. Do not kill [him]."

Notes

He Guisheng does not read the final three graphs: the ancestor deity himself, a negation, and a sword. This could be understood as a request not to kill with the sharpened blade, although the verb "to kill", *siuq*, is usually accompanied by a graph that is phonetically used.

18-3

Graph-by-graph

1. **ddiuq**, the earth.
2. **Coqssei-leel'ee**, Naxi hero, here representative of mankind in general.
3. **me**, negation.
4. **kel**, bamboo basket, used phonetically for *ke*, to be evil.
5. **wuq**, a slave. Visually a bowl that has no cover.
6. **puq**, to escape; a slave running.

Transcription

zzijjeq-la'ler **ddiuq** / bbei lei bbeil ceeq ssee
the vast earth / the people of the world
seepei / **me** / **ke** / mei
chieftain / not / evil / particle
wuqjuq / keel / la / chee / me / **puq**
slave shackles / release / also / this / not / escape

Scharten translation

On the earth there is a man, T'so-rze-le-hgeh's son. He is not very clever. Let him come here to be our servant.

New translation

"On the vast earth where the people live, if the masters are not evil, their slaves will not run away."

Notes

Contemporary readings offer different understandings of this particular episode when compared with Scharten's translation. While Scharten sees it as a specific suggestion relating to our hero, i.e. "there's a man on the earth who can be our slave", other readings see it as a statement of a more general truth: if a master is kind, their slaves won't try to escape. This latter interpretation relies upon a negation not written, but as we have seen, it would hardly be an unusual situation for a negation to be missing.

18-4

Graph-by-graph

1. **lv**, stones.
2. **cei**, salt, here used phonetically for *cer*, to warm, phonetic component for graph 3.
3. **mi**, fire, used semantically for *cer*, to warm, semantic component to graph 2.
4. **bbaiq**, a bee.
5. **bbaiq**, (another) bee.

Transcription

lv / me / **cer** / mei / **bbai** / me / bber
stone / not / hot / topicalizer / bee / not / migrate
lv / cer / **bbai** / bber / ceeq
stone / hot / bee / migrate / come

Scharten translation
The bees, they have a king and they have to listen, so he will listen to me.

New translation
"If the stones are not hot, the bees will not move; they will move when the stones get hot."

Notes
Scharten's translation talks of a "king" of the bees, which appears nonsensical unless we consider that she has mistaken the slave-owning "chieftain" of the previous panel with the bees in this panel. In fact, it is a continuation of the parable: slaves don't run away if they are well-treated, bees don't flee if their home remains safe. Graphs 2 and 3 together form a phono-semantic compound, *cer*, to warm up.

18-5

Graph-by-graph
1. **goq**, alpine meadow, inside of which is a needle, *goq*, which acts as a phonetic marker.
2. **lee**, fir tree.
3. **naq**, black.
4. **Coqssei-leel'ee**, Naxi hero, in fact here depicted as a slave, with outstretched foot and hand.
5. **laq**, hand, possibly used phonetically for *la*, second syllable of *wuqla*, slave.
6. **mil**, woman, here used in place of the heroine Ceilheeq-bbvbbeq (not read).
7. **laq**, hand, here perhaps used semantically for the verb *ddee*, to obtain (i.e. I obtained a slave).

Transcription
goq / shua / **lee** / **naq** / zzerq / kee / tvl
meadow / high / fir / black / tree / foot / at
wuqla / zherwuq / ddee / gvl / ddee
slave / slave/ one / measure word / obtain

Scharten translation
Like a Chinese juniper we will do the work, hand in hand.

New translation

"At the foot of the black fir tree on the high alpine meadows, I obtained a slave."

Notes

Scharten seems to take the pronounced hands on this page literally, as man and woman working hand in hand. This is always the danger with approaching the Naxi texts literally: what you see is not necessarily what you get. The contemporary readings agree that this is a follow up to the parables about slaves and bees in the previous two panels; our heroine is persuading her father to not kill the trespassing human, spinning him a story about how he is a slave that will be useful to the household.

18-6

Graph-by-graph

1. **mee tv**, good weather, a sun shining in the sky.
2. **tvq**, a bucket, used phonetically for second syllable of *mee tv*.
3. **xi**, ear of rice.
4. **chua**, rice (in a bowl).
5. **Coqssei-leel'ee**, Naxi hero, holding an ear of rice (not read).
6. **zherl**, bone, used phonetically for *zher* to make (someone do something).

Transcription

mee tv / liu / qi / liu / seiq / **zher** / tal / zeel

clear day / grain / protect / grain / dry / make / can / modal particle

Scharten translation

When it is nice weather, he can dry our grains in the sun.

New translation

"When the sun is shining, we can make him dry our grain,"

Notes

The word(s) used for grain in the written manuscript are paddy rice and cooked rice in a bowl (graphs 3 and 4 respectively), however the readings use the more general term *"liu"* for grain. McKhann's translation adds some extra context to the bride service expected of Coqssei-leel'ee: "You won't always be healthy. If you get ill, he can wait on you" (1992, 106).

18-7

Graph-by-graph

1. **heeq ggee**, rain, rain falling from the sky. Here read **mee zza**, overcast.
2. **ni**, sun, semantic loan for "day".
3. **jjiq**, water.
4. **shuq**, iron, an axe (held by Coqssei-leel'ee), phonetic loan for *shu*, to sort out.
5. **xiq**, ear of rice.
6. **zherl**, bone, used phonetically for *zher* to make (someone do something).

Transcription

mee zza / jjiq / shu / xiq / zzeel / **zher** / la / tal
clear day / water / sort out / rice / dig / make / again / can

Scharten translation

When it is raining, he can dig out the drains.

New translation

"When the weather is bad, we can make him clear the drains and dig the fields,"

Notes

Graphs 1 and 2 could be read *"heeqggee gge nilwaq"*, "rainy day", but most readings have instead *mee zza* (overcast), , as the opposite of *mee tv* (clear skies) in the previous panel. Coqssei-leel'ee is seen holding the tool (graph 4) to clear out the drains, which are represented by the graph for water (graph 3).

18-8

Graph-by-graph

1. **Zzee'laq-epv**, Naxi ancestral deity.
2. **she**, geba syllabic graph, used for *shel*, to speak.
3. **ggee**, to chew, used phonetically for *ggeeq*, to be true.
4. **ceil**, leaf, used phonetically for *ceil*, first syllable in Ceilheeq-bbvbbeq.
5. **mi**, fire used phonetically for mil, woman.
6. **mil**, woman.
7. **ser**, wood, perhaps used for *meel sheeq*, yellow bamboo.
8. **kvq**, mouth harp.
9. **ddoq**, to look.

Transcription

Zzee'laq-epv / lei / **shel** / mei
deity / again / say / particle
ggeeq / la / ggeeq / jilmi
true / and / true / believe
Ceilheeq-bbvbbeq / **mil**
name / woman
seiqgge / ddee /gvl / mei
what / one / measure word / nominalizer
meelsheeq / **kvq** / nee / kuq
yellow bamboo / mouth harp / topicalizer / play
ku / kuq / bulbbel / ddee / **ddoq** / lv'laq / zeel
harp / play / bring / one / look / come / modal particle

Scharten translation

Her father hearing the words of his daughter, saith to her: your words are like true words. T'se-greh-buh-buh-mi calls now T'so-rze-le-hgeh's son.

New translation

Then Zzee'laq-epv spoke: "This is true. Ceilheeq-bbvbbeq, daughter, what kind of man is this? Play the yellow bamboo mouth harp and bring him here for me to see."

Notes

The deity Zzee'laq-epv is suddenly very interested in having a man about the house to do all his menial tasks, and asks for a meeting. The Naxi have a custom of playing the yellow bamboo mouth harp to welcome guests, so the suggestion that he be welcomed with the playing of such an instrument (graph 8) indicates that he is very enthusiastic about the idea.

18-9

Graph-by-graph

1. **ggv**, nine.
2. **jjiq**, water.
3. **cherl**, generation, used phonetically for *cher*, to wash.
4. **perq**, white.
5. **ggv**, nine.
6. **maq**, yak butter.
7. **hoq**, a constellation, the seven stars of Ursa major. Used phonetically for *ho*, first syllable of *ho'lo*, smooth and shiny.
8. **loq**, a plowtail, used phonetically for second syllable of *ho'lo*, smooth and shiny.

Transcription

ggv / hoq / **jjiq** / nee / **cher**
nine / measure word / topicalizer / wash
perq / ddeeq / gulgul / bbei
white / big / clean / make
ggv / lul / **maq** / nee / maq
nine / measure word / yak butter / topicalizer / rub
bbu / ddeeq / **ho'lo** / seiq
shiny / big / smooth / modal particle

Scharten translation

He saith: first I will wash me in nine different streams, that I may be clean. I will use nine pieces of soap, that I may be shiny.

New translation

So Coqssei-leel'ee washed himself in nine streams until he was all white and clean, and rubbed himself with nine pieces of yak butter until he was all smooth and shiny.

Notes

Our hero lathers himself up to be presented to his divine future father in-law. Scharten has "soap" for graph 6, yak butter, but I believe the latter translation better fits the final adjective, "shiny" (graphs 7 and 8). Graph 3 ("to wash") is a phonetic loan, it may also be written with a phono-semantic compound of a figure applying water to the hands, and a smaller version of the graph (perhaps representing decayed or rotten wood) as a phonetic component: .

19-1

Graph-by-graph

1. **Coqssei-leel'ee**, Naxi hero, here shown walking.
2. **ggaiq**, sword, knife.
3. **mil**, woman, seen walking, representing Ceilheeq-bbvbbeq (not read).
4. **yegoq**, home. Literally "tobacco needle", the two graphs seen inside the frame of a house.
5. **tv**, to arrive.
6. **Zzeeq'laq-epv**, ancestral deity.
7. **liuq**, to look.
8. **laq**, hand.
9. **be**, sole of the foot.
10. **sai**, blood, perhaps representing a drop (*tiel*) of blood, presaging the next panel (not read).
11. **berl**, comb, used phonetically for *berl*, line (e.g. on a palm).
12. **me**, negation.
13. **zzee**, wall, used phonetically for *zzeeq*, to have.

Transcription

Coqssei-leel'ee / nee
Naxi hero / topicalizer
shu / perq / **ggaiq** / tal / ggv / jjiq / gv / nee / ssaq
iron / white / sword / sharp / nine / measure word / ladder / on / topicalizer / go down
Zzee'laq-epv / **yegoq** / **tv** / lei / ceeq
deity / home / arrive / particle / come
Zzee'laq-epv / nee / **liuq** / mei
deity / topicalizer / look / particle
mu**be** / **laq**bbe / tai / **berl** / ddee / berl / **me** / **zzeeq**
sole / palm / bottom / line / one / line / not / have

Scharten translation

She brings hin now to her father's home. He uses his knife as a bridge to enter in. The father looks to his son in law and he looks to his head, his hand and feet. There are no lines.

New translation

Now Coqssei-leel'ee walked along the ladder of nine sharp iron swords to get to the house of Zzee'laq-epv. Zzee'laq-epv looked at the palms of Coqssei-leel'ee's hands and the soles of his feet, and did not see any lines.

Notes

Graphs 1 and 2 show in microcosm the freedom of resizing the graphs. Coqseei-leel'ee ascends to the heavenly palace on a ladder of nine (i.e. many) sharp swords. This is depicted by one single oversized sword, atop which we see the graph representing our hero, striding forwards purposefully. Upon reaching the palace, Zzee'laq-epv engages in a spot of palmistry, inspecting our hero's palms and soles, but finds nothing to see.

19-2

Graph-by-graph

1. **laqzheeqgvl**, fingernail
2. **sai**, blood.
3. **me**, negation.
4. **yi**, geba syllabic graph, used for *yi*, to flow.
5. **sai**, blood.
6. **me**, negation.

Transcription

laqzheeqgvl / nieq / ddee / liuq / nee
fingernail / on / one / look / topicalizer
sai / ddee / tiel / **me** / **yi**
blood / one / drop / not / flow
keezheeqgvl / nieq / ddee / liuq / nee
toenail / on / one / look / topicalizer
sai / ddee / tiel / **me** / yi
blood / one / drop / not / flow

Scharten translation
He looks to the nail of his hands and feet and there is no blood in them.

New translation
Zzee'laq-epv looked at his fingernails and toenails, and didn't see any blood.

Notes
Graph 1, as depicted in the written manuscript, shows a very pronounced fingernail protruding from the hand. This is the only manuscript tradition I have seen among the published versions that includes this detail; the others refer to a hand more generally. Note here the two depictions of "blood", one pictographic (a drop of blood, graph 2), one much more abstract (graph 5). Because Coqssei-leel'ee had to cross a ladder of sharp blades to get to the divine palace, he should by all accounts have blood on his hands and feet. According to McKhann, Naxi mythology has it that this act of crossing the sharp swords is the origin of the lines on people's hands and feet (1992, 106).

19-3

Graph-by-graph

1. **Zzee'laq-epv**, ancestor deity.
2. **she**, geba syllabic graph, used for *shel*, to speak.
3. **kel**, bamboo basket, used phonetically for *kee*, second syllable of the place name Ekee'lvqlei bbu.
4. **bbu**, slope, hill, used in place names (here not read).
5. **lv**, stone, third syllable of the place name Ekee'lvqlei bbu.
6. **lei**, roe, fourth syllable of the place name Ekee'lvqlei bbu.
7. **bbu**, slope, hill, used in place names.
8. **see**, father. A seated figure with a phonetic component on his head (*ser*, wood).
9. **rherq**, power. The etymology of the graph is, according to Fang, is "unclear" (354)
10. **ddeeq**, large. Perhaps representing the fruit of a kind of laurel.
11. **Coqssei-leel'ee**, Naxi hero, the graph here represents the idea of a son, and is read *sso*.
12. **rherq**, power.
13. **me**, negation.

Transcription

Zzee'laq-epv / lei / **shel** / mei
deity / again / speak / particle
neeq / qu / seiq / qu / zeel
you / race / what / race / modal particle
Ekee'lvqlei bbu
place name
see / **rherq** / **ddeeq** / mei / **sso** / **rherq** / ddeeq / **me** / zail
father / power / big / topicalizer / son / power / big / not / pass down

Scharten translation

The father saith then, your father, Ae-k'eh-lu-le-mbu, had a big spirit, but he has not given any of his spirit to you.

New translation

Zzee'laq-epv then said, "What kind of person are you? At the slopes of Ekee'lvqlei, the father has great power, but does not pass it down to his son."

Notes

Graph 4 seems to be mistakenly written; it appears again in the following intonation unit where it should be read (as graph 7). Contemporary readings all have the final part here as a kind of boast, where Coqssei-leel'ee reveals his great heritage, but here with Scharten's translation (and in Li Lin-ts'an's) we have the ancestral deity pointing out our hero's deficiencies, i.e., the son does not live up to the father.

19-4

Graph-by-graph

1. **Coqssei-leel'ee**, Naxi hero.
2. **nvl**, heart, with a visible artery.
3. **ni**, two, used phonetically for *nil*, first syllable of *nilsaq*, happy, satisfied.
4. **sal**, breath, used phonetically for second syllable of *nilsaq*, happy, satisfied.

5. **Zzee'laq-epv**, ancestor deity.
6. **me**, negation.
7. **seeq**, three, used phonetically for *see*, to know.
8. **bbiu**, to separate, to be distinct. Visually two piles of flour being separated.
9. **ni**, fish. Used phonetically for *ni*, to want.
10. **me**, negation.
11. **yeq**, tobacco leaf, used phonetically for *yel*, to give.
12. **so**, a scale with a weight attached, used phonetically for *so*, high mountain.
13. **bbu**, slope, hill, used in place names.
14. **jjiq**, water.
15. **me**, negation.

Transcription
Coqssei-leel'ee sso / **nvl** / mei / me / **nilsaq**
name + epithet / heart / topicalizer / not / happy
Zzee'laq-epv / me / see / bbiu / mei / **ni / me / yel** / ye / zeel
deity / not / know / separate / nominalizer / want / not / give / emphatic / modal particle
Zzee'laq-epv / lei / shel / mei
deity / again / speak / particle
zzijjeq-la'ler ddiuq
the vast earth
so / bbu / gv / ye / **jjiq / me** / yi / ye / zeel
high / slopes / place / declarative particle / water / not / slow / emphatic / particle / modal particle

Scharten translation
T'so-rze-le-hgeh covets the spirit of his father, but he saith: we dont give flour to the fishes, neither can water run up the mountains.

New translation
Hearing this, Coqssei-leel'ee was unhappy. Zzee'laq-epv did not want to give away his daughter to this outsider, and so he said, "On the vast green earth, the water does not flow in the high mountains,"

Notes
Scharten translates graphs 8 and 9 quite literally, as flour and fish: hence her translation "give flour to the fishes". Clearly this makes little sense, and both graphs can be interpreted as rebuses. The most likely explanation is that the dongba who interpreted the graphs for her was not the author of this book, hence could not explain this passage (most contemporary readings do not include these graphs, and He Guisheng had to read this several times before arriving at the reading above). *Bbiu*, "to separate" can be depicted as two circular objects being separated 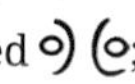; the manuscript shows flour being separated as it is a near-homophone (*bbiuq*).

19-5, 19-6

Graph-by-graph

1. **lv**, stones.
2. **zzerq**, tree, used phonetically for *zzeeq* to grow, to exist.
3. **me**, negation.
4. **zzerq**, tree, used phonetically for *zzeeq* to grow, to exist.
5. **to**, pine tree.
6. **lee**, fir tree.
7. **zzijjeq-la'ler ddiuq**, the vast green earth on which the people live.
8. **bee**, artemisia leaf.
9. **me**, negation.

Transcription

lv / **zzeeq** / gv / ye / lv / **me** / **zzeeq** / ye / zeel
stone / exist / place / declarative particle / stone / not / exist / emphatic / modal particle
to / zzeeq / **lee** / zzeeq / gv /ye / to / neif / lee / me / zzeeq / ye / zeel
pine / grow / fir / grow / place / declarative particle / pine / and / fir / not / grow / emphatic / modal particle
zzijjeq-la'ler ddiuq
the earth where the people live
beeceil / lei / **me** / her
artemisia / again / not / green

Scharten translation

A common fir tree is not like a Chinese juniper.
An artemisia is not like dry grass.

New translation

"Where there should be stones, there are no stones, and the pine and fir trees do not grow where they should grow; on the vast earth, the artemisia is no longer green."

Notes

It is worth pointing out that the manuscript page seems to be referring to lots of different kinds of wood: the word "tree" is repeated twice (graphs 2 and 4), then we have two specific kinds of tree, the fir and the pine (graphs 5 and 6). In fact, the first two "trees" are merely rebuses associated with the stones, i.e. *zzeeq*, to exist: "where the stones **exist**, there are no stones **existing**". In the first panel, one negation is used for both intonation units. In the second panel, the key word, "green" (the artemisia is no longer green, the human world has lost its lustre), is not written.

19-7

Graph-by-graph

1. **zzi**, jackal, used phonetically for *zzi*, "the people".
2. **zzeeq**, a seated figure, semantically "to live".
3. **sal**, breath.
4. **me**, negation.
5. **zzeeq**, a seated figure, to live.
6. **mil**, woman, daughter.
7. **bbuq**, pig, used phonetically for *bbuq*, wife.
8. **me**, negation.

Transcription

zzi / zzeeq / sal / me / zzeeq

people / live / breath / not / live

mil / bbuq / me / jjuq / seiq / wei / zeel

daughter / wife / not / have / finished action / exclamation / modal particle

Scharten translation

You are of the earth and because of this reason, I cant give you my daughter as your wife.

New translation

"There are no people living on the earth; you cannot have my daughter as your wife."

Notes

Graph 7, breath, here means something akin to "signs of human life", there is no human breath left on the earth, it has already become a deserted land to be forsaken.

19-8

Graph-by-graph

1. **mil**, woman, daughter.
2. **ni**, fish, used phonetically for *ni*, to want.
3. **me**, negation.
4. **yeq**, tobacco, used phonetically for *yel*, to give.
5. **zee**, to tie (a knot), used phonetically for *zeel*, modal particle.

Transcription

nge / **mil** / neeq / **ni** / **me** / **yel** / **zeel**
I / daughter / you / want / not / give / modal particle

Scharten translation

What you wish, I can't give you.

New translation

"You want my daughter, but I will not give her to you."

Notes

Zzee'laq-epv is now emphatically repeating himself: you cannot have the girl.

20-1

Graph-by-graph

1. **Zzee'laq-epv**, ancestral deity, here seen speaking.
2. **Coqssei-leel'ee**, Naxi hero, holding an axe (graph 3).
3. **bbei**, to do, used semantically to indicate *ddaiq*, capable.
4. **kel**, basket, here used phonetically for *keq*, hard-working.
5. **ni**, two, used phonetically for *ni*, to want.
6. **ggv**, nine.
7. **bbu**, hill. Used semantically to indicate a mountain forest, *xiq*.
8. **cerl**, to chop down. An axe felling a tree.
9. **me**, negation.
10. **ta**, geba syllabic graph, used for *tal*, to be able.

Transcription

Zzee'laq-epv / lei / **shel** / mei
deity / again / speak / particle
Coqssei-leel'ee sso
Name + epithet
ddaiq / la / neeq / ddaiq / ye
capable / also / you / capable / exclamation
keq / la / neeq / keq / ye
hard-working / also / you / hard-working / exclamation
ddaiq / mei / sso / neel / **ni**
capable / nominalizer / man / topicalizer / want
ggvcerqggv / **xiq** / **cerl** / mei / epv / gainiuq / ji / lu / zeel
ninety-nine / forested hills / chop / nominalizer / grandfather (me) / before / place / come / modal particle
Coqssei-leel'ee / lei / shel / mei
name / again / speak / particle
ddee / ni / ddee / xiq / cerl / **me** / **tal**
one / day / one / mountain / chop / not / able

Scharten translation

The father saith further to him: when you are an able man, you go and cut nine trees. The boy thinks, that thing I can never do.

New translation

And he said further, “Coqssei-leel’ee, you claim to be capable and hard-working, if you want to be such a man, go and clear ninety-nine forested hillsides, and place the trees before me [in one day’s time].”
Coqssei-leel’ee then said, “I couldn’t do even one hillside in a day!”

Notes

Now begin the many trials of Coqssei-leel’ee. The first task is to chop down the trees on ninety-nine hillsides and place the timber before the ancestor deity, all in one day’s time. Of course, such a task is impossible, and our hero knows it. The manuscript is quite idiosyncratic here, with *ddaiq* being represented by graph 3, a man holding a tool, *bbei*, a semantic loan, instead of a man holding a flag,  (*ddaiq*, “general”) which is the more common phonctic loan (and indeed which appears later on this page).

20-2

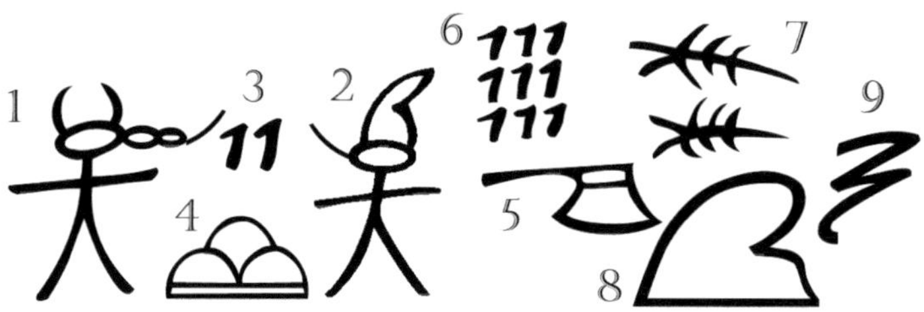

Graph-by-graph

1. **Coqssei-leel’ee**, Naxi hero, here seen speaking
2. **Ceilheeq-bbvbbeq**, the divine daughter.
3. **ni**, two, used phonetically for *ni*, to want.
4. **lv**, stone, used phonetically for second syllable of *miqlv*, husband and wife.
5. **zeil**, axe.
6. **ggv**, nine.
7. **ser**, wood (two trees), here semantically representing *xiq*, forested hill.
8. **bbu**, hill, used semantically together with graph 7 to indicate a forested hill, *xiq*.
9. **ji**, geba syllabic graph, used for *ji*, to put.

Transcription

Coqssei-leel'ee sso
name + epithet
Ceilheeq-bbvbbeq mil / **ni** / gvl
name + epithet / two / ones
nilyi / bbeeqzhuaq / lei / zzeeqggue
daytime / partner / particle / discuss
huqyi / miq**lv** / lei / seeddv
nighttime / husband and wife / particle / consider
Ceilheeq-bbvbbeq mil
name + epithet
neeq / ee / lei / seeddv
heart / soul / particle / consider
sal / jjeq / ddee / sal / tv
plan / good /one / measure word / emerge
zeil / ga / **ggv**cerqggv / zhuq / bvl
axe / good / ninety-nine / measure word / take
ggvcerqggv / **xiq** / ku / niuq / **ji**
ninety-nine / forested hill / place / go / put

Scharten translation

He talked the matter over with his wife. She command him to take nine very sharp knives and hang them at nine trees.

New translation

And so he discussed the matter with Ceilheeq-bbvbbeq for some time. An idea then came to Ceilheeq-bbvbbeq, and she told him: "Take ninety-nine sharp axes and put them in the mountain forests."

Notes

Scharten continues to translate the "nine" literally, while other versions take it as shorthand for ninety-nine; in any case both numbers can be understood simply as "many". Graph 9, *ji*, is a geba syllabic graph, although its shape is slightly unusual. Fang records it as  (1981, 429).

20-3

Graph-by-graph

1. **qiq**, muntjac.
2. **lei**, roe.
3. **see**, wool or felt cloak.
4. **per**, geba syllabic graph, used for *perq* in *seeperq*, white wool.
5. **bbu**, hill.
6. **yil**, sleep.
7. **yi**, geba syllabic graph, used for *yi*, as in *yilyi*, to sleep.
8. **zeil**, axe.
9. **ggv**, nine.
10. **ser**, wood, here semantically representing *xiq*, forested hill.
11. **seiq**, goral, used phonetically for *sei*, completed action marker.

Transcription

Coqssei-leel'ee sso
name + epithet
qiq / **lei** / sso / me / waq
muntjac / roe / small / not / be
seeperq / ggv / lullu
white woolen cloak / body / cover
bbu / toq / lei / **yilyi**
hill / behind / particle / sleep
soqni / la / meeseel
tomorrow / also / morning
ddee / liuq / lei / liuq / keel
one / look / particle / look / go
zeil / ga / **ggv**cerqggv / zhuq / nee
axe / good / ninety-nine / measure word / topicalizer
ggvcerqggv / **xiq** / cerl / **sei** / zeel
ninety-nine / forested hill / chop / completed action / modal particle

Scharten translation

He himself doesn't do any work and sleeps like a roebuck. The axes do the work and cut the nine trees.

New translation

Although Coqssei-leel'ee was not a muntjac or a roe, he went to the mountain and slept there, covering himself with a white woolen blanket. The next morning, he took one look and saw that the axes had chopped down all the trees.

Notes

While this manuscript makes it seem like the axes somehow became animated and chopped down all the trees themselves, other versions suggest that it is the work of the myriad insects while Coqssei-leel'ee sleeps: "Mumbling in his sleep, he asked the white butterflies and the black ants to come help him" (McKhann 1992, 108). I list graph 3 as a pictographic depiction of a cloak, although the graph in the manuscript has a triangular shape, somewhat reminiscent of the syllabic geba graph *sso*, . Coqssei-leel'ee lets the axes do the work for him as he sleeps. Highlighting the difficulties of reading the Naxi texts here are the three animal heads: the first two, the muntjac and the roe, are to be read literally as those animals, while the final head, the goral (graph 11), is a rebus indicating that the chopping down of the trees has been completed. The first task is over.

20-4

Graph-by-graph

1. **Coqssei-leel'ee**, Naxi hero.
2. **ni**, two, used phonetically for *ni*, to want.
3. **me**, negation (not read?).
4. **yeq**, tobacco, used phonetically for *yel*, to give.
5. **Zzee'laq-epv**, ancestor deity.
6. **mil**, daughter.
7. **me**, negation.

Transcription
Coqssei-leel'ee / nee / Zzee'laq-epv / niuq / lei / shel / heq
name / topicalizer / deity / toward / again / speak / go
wal / mil / ngeq / **ni** / ngeq / **yel** / lu'laq / zeel
you / daughter / I / want / I / give / come / modal particle
Zzee'laq-epv / lei / shel / mei
deity / again / speak / particle
ngeq / **mil** / neiq / yel / **me** / tal
I / daughter / dynamic aspect / give / not / able

Scharten translation
The boy saith: give me the girl. The father answers him: what you want, I cant give you.

New translation
Coqssei-leel'ee returned to Zzee'laq-epv and said, "Give me your daughter", but the deity replied, "I will not give you my daughter."

Notes
A simple dialogue is shown here, Coqssei-leel'ee requesting the girl's hand in marriage, the girl's father refusing once again. The first negation, graph 3, is perhaps mistakenly written, and is not read. Another possible reading might have the ancestor deity first say "what you want, I won't give, I won't give you my girl", *neeq ni nee ngeq me yel zeel, ngeq mil neiq yel me ta*.

20-5

Graph-by-graph
1. **Coqssei-leel'ee**, Naxi hero, here holding a flag, representing the word *ddaiq*, courageous or capable (see 2 below).
2. **ddaiq**, a man holding a flag, i.e. courageous, capable.
3. **ggv**, nine.
4. **ser**, wood (two trees), here semantically representing *xiq*, forested hill
5. **jjil**, a fire, "to burn".

6. **ddee**, one
7. **me**, negation.

Transcription

Coqssei-leel'ee sso
name + epithet
ddaiq / mei / sso / neel / waq
courageous / nominalizer / man / want / be
ggvcerqggv / **xiq** / **jjil** / mei / epv / gainiuq / ji / lu / zeel
ninety-nine / forested hills / burn / nominalizer / grandfather (me) / before / place / come / modal particle
Coqssei-leel'ee / lei / shel / mei
name / again / speak / particle
ddee / ni / ddee / xiq / jjil / **me** / tal
one / day / one / mountain / chop / not / able

Scharten translation

When you are a clever man, go and burn nine trees.

New translation

"Coqssei-leel'ee, if you're so courageous, go and burn down the ninety-nine forested hills and bring [the ashes] before me [in one day's time]."
Coqseei-leel'ee said, "I couldn't burn one in just one day."

Notes

Now we see the second trial: Coqssei-leel'ee must burn down the forests.

20-6

Graph-by-graph

1. **Coqssei-leel'ee**, Naxi hero, here seen speaking
2. **Ceilheeq-bbvbbeq**, the divine daughter.

3. **ni**, two, used phonetically for *ni*, to want.
4. **lv**, stone, used phonetically for second syllable of *miqlv*, husband and wife.
5. **ggv**, nine.
6. **ser**, wood (two trees), here semantically representing *xiq*, forested hill.
7. **jjil**, a fire, "to burn" (not read).
8. **ji**, geba syllabic graph, used for *ji*, to put.

Transcription

Coqssei-leel'ee sso
name + epithet
Ceilheeq-bbvbbeq mil / **ni** / gvl
name + epithet / two / ones
nilyi / bbeeqzhuaq / lei / zzeeqggue
daytime / partner / particle / discuss
huqyi / miq**lv** / lei / seeddv
nighttime / husband and wife / particle / consider
Ceilheeq-bbvbbeq mil
name + epithet
neeq / ee / sal / jjeq / ddee / sal / tv
heart / soul / plan / good / one / measure word / emerge
zeimaq / **ggv**cerqggv / tvq / bvl
pine torch / ninety-nine / measure word / take
ggvcerqggv / **xiq** / ku / niuq / **ji**
ninety-nine / forested hill / place / go / put

Scharten translation

He talks again with the girl and she gives him the following advice: take nine firs ticks and put them under nine trees.

New translation

Coqssei-leel'ee then returned to Ceilheeq-bbvbbeq and the two of them discussed for some time. An idea then came to Ceilheeq-bbvbbeq, and she told him: "Take ninety-nine pine torches and put them in the mountain forests."

Notes

While graph 7 re-iterates the task, i.e. that the forests now have to be burned, contemporary readings (and indeed Scharten's translation) do not include this verb. The implication is that the pine torches, what would have been the only source of light in the Naxi households of old, will burn down all the trees. Of the pine torches, Goullart writes "*Mingtze* — the rosin-impregnated pine splinters — were another important item, always necessary for illumination, and for lighting the home fires. As there were endless pine forests all around it was easy enough for any villager to gather them and to bring them to town for sale, either on horses or on his, or his wife's, back. In the morning there was always a column of fragrant pine-wood smoke rising above the city" (1957, 30).

20-7

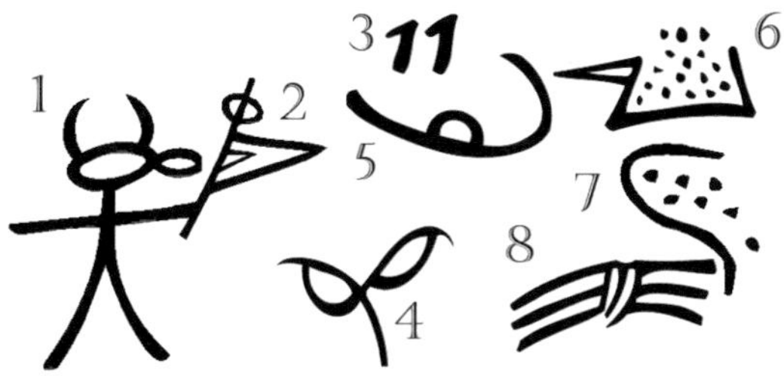

Graph-by-graph

1. **Coqssei-leel'ee**, Naxi hero, here holding a flag, representing the word *ddaiq*, courageous or capable (see 2 below).
2. **ddaiq**, a man holding a flag, i.e. courageous, capable.
3. **ni**, two, used phonetically for *ni*, to want.
4. **yeq**, tobacco, used phonetically for *yel*, to give.
5. **me**, negation.
6. **ruaq**, to measure millet, used semantically for *lerl*, seeds.
7. **pvl**, to sow (seeds being tipped out of a container).
8. **zee**, to tie (a knot), used phonetically for *zeel*, a modal particle.

Transcription

Coqssei-leel'ee sso
name + epithet
ddaiq / la / neeq / ddaiq / ye
capable / also / you / capable / sentence final particle
ngeq / mil / neeq / **ni** / **yel** / **me** / tal
I / daughter / you / want / give / not / able
ddaiq / mei / sso / neel / waq
capable / topicalizer / man / want / be
ggvcerqggv / xiq / **lerl** / **pvl** / epv/ gainiuq / ji / lu / **zeel**
ninety-nine / forested hill / seed / sow / grandfather / before / put / come / modal particle

Scharten translation

Although you are so clever, I cant give you, which you want. Show me, that you are more clever then this, take nine seeds and put them in ine pieces of grouns.

New translation

"Coqssei-leel'ee you are a capable man, but I can't give you my daughter, which is what you want. If you are so capable, go and sow seeds to replant the ninety-nine forests."

Notes

Quite a lot has been truncated in between this panel and the previous one. Coqssei-leel'ee took the pine torches and went again to the mountain forests, where those torches did all the work of burning the trees down (although he was in fact sleeping the whole time). He then returns to the ancestral deity to claim his prize. We pick the story up at this point: he is being set another task, to replant the forests that have just been burned down. Graph 6, grain in a measuring container, is used simply to depict the idea of seeds. Graph 7, to sow, is more usually written with a figure performing the action: .

20-8

Graph-by-graph

1. **Coqssei-leel'ee**, Naxi hero.
2. **ddee**, one.
3. **ruaq**, to measure millet, used semantically for *lerl*, seeds.
4. **pvl**, to sow (seeds being tipped out of a container).
5. **zee**, to tie (a knot), used phonetically for *zeel*, a modal particle.
6. **ser**, wood (two trees), here semantically representing *xiq*, forested hill
7. **xi**, rice, here used semantically to represent *lerl*, seeds.
8. **pvl**, to sow (seeds being tipped out of a container).
9. **me**, negation.
10. **ta**, geba syllabic graph, used for *tal*, to be able.

Transcription

Coqssei-leel'ee / lei / vq / mei
name / again / think / particle
ddee / mei / sso / nee / **lerl** / **pvl** / **zeel**
one / particle / man / topicalizer / seeds / sow / modal particle

ggvcerqggv / **xiq** / **lerl** / **pvl** / sei / **me** / **tal**
ninety-nine / forested hills / seeds / sow / finish / not / able

Scharten translation
He thinks, one piece of ground is difficult to sow, how shall I do nine.

New translation
Coqssei-leel'ee thought to himself, "One man cannot sow the seeds, how can I do so for ninety-nine forests?"

Notes
Tasked with sowing grain over the burned forests, Coqssei-leel'ee once again doubts that he has the ability to do so. The manuscript seems to follow Scharten's translation (i.e., the numeral refers to one piece of land, not one man), but I follow the contemporary readings. Graph 7, rice, makes it apparently clear what kind of grain is being used to re-plant the charred landscape, but none of the readings make it so explicit.

20-9

Graph-by-graph
1. **Coqssei-leel'ee**, Naxi hero, here holding a flag, representing the word *ddaiq* (see graph 2 below).
2. **ddaiq**, a man holding a flag, i.e. courageous, capable (not read).
3. **ggv**, nine.
4. **ser**, wood, here semantically representing *xiq*, forested hill.
5. **ruaq**, to measure millet, used semantically for *lerl*, seeds.
6. **pvl**, to sow (seeds being tipped out of a container).
7. **zzee**, many, numerous; perhaps a leaf or grass with dots representing the idea of many (Li 2001, 196), Rock (1963, 105) suggests that the original meaning of the graph has been lost (not read).
8. **seiq**, goral, used phonetically for *sei*, completed action marker.

Transcription
Coqssei-leel'ee / nee
name / topicalizer
ggvcerqggv / **xiq** / **lerl** / **pvl** / **sei** / zeel
ninety-nine / forested hill / seeds / sow / completed action / modal particle

Scharten translation
He goes and does it.

New translation
Coqssei-leel'ee finished sowing the seeds across ninety-nine forests.

Notes
Another very concise panel – especially in Scharten's translation – which is much more elaborate in certain oral readings. Coqseei-leel'ee manages to sow the seeds by using ninety-nine seed baskets and waiting for the ants and butterflies to help him do all the work as he sleeps.

20-10

Graph-by-graph
1. **Zzee'laq-epv**, ancestor deity.
2. **mil**, daughter.
3. **ni**, two, used phonetically for *ni*, to want.
4. **yeq**, tobacco, used phonetically for *yel*, to give.
5. **me**, negation.

Transcription
Zzee'laq-epv / lei / shel / mei
deity / again / speak / particle
ngeq / **mil** / neeq / **ni** / **yel** / **me** / tal
I / daughter / you / want / give / not / able

Scharten translation
The father; although you so clever as this, I cant give you what you want.

New translation
And Zzee'laq-epv said once again, "I can't give you my daughter whom you so desire."

Notes
A repetitive panel that we have seen several times already in slight variations (e.g. 19-8, 20-4).

21-1

Graph-by-graph

1. **Coqssei-leel'ee**, Naxi hero, here holding a flag, representing the word *ddaiq*, courageous or capable (see graph 2 below).
2. **ddaiq**, a man holding a flag, i.e. courageous, capable.
3. **me**, negation (not read).
4. **ggv**, nine.
5. **fai**, to overturn (hands being turned over). Used phonetically for *fai*, go (imperative).
6. **kvl**, to harvest, a sickle cutting a plant.
7. **ddee**, one.
8. **xi**, an ear of rice, used semantically for *lerl*, seed.
9. **me**, negation.
10. **ta**, geba syllabic graph, used for *tal*, to be able.

Transcription

Coqssei-leel'ee sso
name + epithet
ddaiq / mei / sso / neel / waq
courageous / nominalizer / man / want / be
ggvcerqggv / xiq / **kvl** / mei / epv / gainiuq / ji / fai / zeel
ninety-nine / forested hills / harvest / particle / grandfather (me) / before / place / go / modal particle
ddee / mei / sso / nee / **lerl** / kvl / zeel
one / particle / man / topicalizer / seeds / harvest / modal particle
ggvcerqggv / xiq / lerl / kvl / sei / **me** / **tal**
ninety-nine / forested hills / seeds / harvest / finish / not / able

Scharten translation

You have also to reap the harvest of these nine pieces. He thinks: however will I be able to do such a thing.

New translation

"If you are so capable, go to those ninety-nine planted forests and harvest all the plants." Coqssei-leel'ee thought to himself, "I am but one man, I cannot harvest all those plants".

Notes

The first three graphs of this panel appear at the end of page 20. We have another task being set, and Coqssei-leel'ee once again doubting his ability to complete it. The graphs here are unusual. Once again, there are two negations where readings supply only one. Graph 5 is very rare and does not appear in the Naxi script IME, I have therefore used the graph as it appears in Li (2001, 50). The graph is seen only in Baidi as a loanword for Chinese *fan* 翻 (to turn over), although it is here used phonetically for the imperative: "Go!". Graph 6, to reap or harvest, is normally written with the sickle cutting an ear of rice, but in this case the plant is the graph *zzee*, which can be used to represent the idea of "many", the numerous dots having that association (Coqssei-leele'ee has to harvest a lot of plants).

21-2

Graph-by-graph

1. **Coqssei-leel'ee**, Naxi hero, here seen speaking
2. **Ceilheeq-bbvbbeq**, the divine daughter.
3. **ni**, two, used phonetically for *ni*, to want.
4. **lv**, stone, used phonetically for second syllable of *miqlv*, husband and wife.
5. **ddaq**, a sickle.
6. **ggv**, nine.
7. **ggv**, nine.
8. **kvl**, a sickle cutting a plant, to harvest.
9. **seiq**, goral, used phonetically for *sei*, completed action marker.

Transcription

Coqssei-leel'ee sso

name + epithet

Ceilheeq-bbvbbeq mil / **ni** / gvl

name + epithet / two / ones
nilyi / bbeeqzhuaq / lei / zzeeqggue
daytime / partner / particle / discuss
huqyi / miq**lv** / lei / seeddv
nighttime / husband and wife / particle / consider
ddaq / ga / **ggv**cerqggv / liu / bvl
sickle / good / ninety-nine / measure word / take
ggvcerqggv / xiq / **kvl** / **sei** / zeel
ninety-nine / forested hill / harvest / completed action / modal particle

Scharten translation

He goes to the girl to talk over the matter with her. She gives him the following advice: you must take nine sticks and put them in the nine pieces of ground and the harvest shall be done.

New translation

Coqssei-leel'ee then went back to Ceilheeq-bbvbbeq and the two of them discussed once more. She told him: "Take ninety-nine sickles with you to the ninety-nine forests and the harvest will be finished."

Notes

What Scharten translates as "sticks" are clearly sickles in the manuscript. The Naxi sickle does not have a pronounced curved blade, but is long and serrated, as in graph 5. After this panel, the implication is that Coqssei-leel'ee goes and completes this task as instructed.

21-3

Graph-by-graph

1. **Zzee'laq-epv**, ancestor deity.
2. **mil**, daughter.
3. **ni**, two, used phonetically for *ni*, to want.
4. **yeq**, tobacco, used phonetically for *yel*, to give.
5. **me**, negation.

Transcription
Zzee'laq-epv / lei / shel / mei
deity / again / speak / particle
ngeq / **mil** / neeq / **ni** / neeq / **yel** / la / **me** / tal
I / daughter / you / want / you / give / also / not / able

Scharten translation
The father of heaven saith: even now I cant give you, what you want.

New translation
And Zzee'laq-epv said once again, "Again, I can't give you my daughter whom you so desire."

Notes
See panel 20-10 for an explanation, this panel is essentially the same.

21-4

Graph-by-graph
1. **Coqssei-leel'ee**, Naxi hero, here holding a flail (see graph 4).
2. **ddee**, one.
3. **zzee**, many (many leaves), used semantically for *zheeq*, crops.
4. **lal**, to thresh (with a flail).
5. **xi**, an ear of rice, used semantically for *zheeq*, crops.
6. **laq**, hand, used phonetically for *lal*, to thresh.
7. **me**, negation.

Transcription
Coqssei-leel'ee / lei / vq / mei
name / again / think / particle
ddee / mei / sso / nee / **zheeq** / **lal** / zeel
one / particle / man / topicalizer / crops / thresh / modal particle

ggvcerqggv / xiq / **zheeq** / **lal** / sei / **me** / tal
ninety-nine / forested hills / crops / thresh / finish / not / able

Scharten translation
This time you have to give me the grains of the nine pieces of ground.

New translation
Coqssei-leel'ee thought to himself, "One man cannot thresh the grain, how can I do so for that of ninety-nine forests?"

Notes
These are the continued instructions of the ancestor deity, to now thresh the newly reaped grains. The manuscripts shows our hero holding what looks to be a herding stick, but according to He Cai, can be read as *lal*, to thresh, so, a threshing flail. Contemporary readings have the deity instead asking Coqssei-leel'ee to count the grains that have been reaped.

21-5

Graph-by-graph
1. **Coqssei-leel'ee**, Naxi hero, here holding a flag, representing the word *ddaiq*, courageous or capable (see 2 below).
2. **ddaiq**, a man holding a flag, i.e. courageous, capable.
3. **ddiuq**, long stick, used semantically for *geellee*, threshing flail.
4. **ggv**, nine.
5. **zzee**, many, here indicating semantically the grain to be threshed (?).
6. **seiq**, goral, used phonetically for *sei*, completed action marker.

Transcription
Coqssei-leel'ee sso
name + epithet
ddaiq / mei / sso / neel / waq

capable / topicalizer / man / want / be
geellee / **ggv**cerqggv / liu / bvl
flail / good / ninety-nine / measure word / take
ggvcerqggv / **zheeq** / ku / niuq / ji / **sei** / zeel
ninety-nine / crops / place / go / put / completed action / modal particle

Scharten translation

The boy speaks again with the girl about it and she gives him the advice: to put nine flails in the nine pieces of ground. T'so-rze-le-hgeh's son goes himself to the field and does work.

New translation

Coqssei-leel'ee then went back to Ceilheeq-bbvbbeq and the two of them discussed once more. She told him: "Take ninety-nine flails with you," and so he went and put them by the crops.

Notes

The threshing flails of He Cai and Scharten seem to be simply herding sticks (see *lvl* 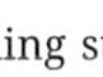, to herd). Rock does not offer an individual graph for this tool, but does show a compound ideogram for *lal*, to thresh: . Fang (278) shows the following graph: .

21-6

Graph-by-graph

1. **lashergual**, grain-drying rack.
2. **muq**, winnowing basket.
3. **muq**, see above.
4. **bul**, to take. A figure holding an object with both hands, in this case the figure is Coqssei-leel'ee.
5. **jil**, scissors, used phonetically for *jil*, to carry on the back.
6. **rua'lerq**, a neighing horse.
7. **her**, wind.
8. **perq**, white.

9. **her**, wind.
10. **naq**, black.
11. **ruaq**, to measure millet, used semantically to indicate measuring grain that is *mei*, plump (the grains inside the container are larger).
12. **ruaq**, to measure millet, used semantically to indicate measuring grain that is *me mei*, not plump (the grains are smaller).
13. **piq**, leg, used phonetically for *piq*, to distribute.

Transcription

nilni / la / meseel
next day / also / morning
bbemei / **lashergual** / keetvl
very large / drying rack / before
muq / ddee / **muq** / jil / **bul**
winnowing tray / large / winnowing tray / small / take
jilgguq / **rua'lerq** / bbei
carry / horse / make
wai / nee / **her** / **perq** / tv / yiq / nee / **her** / **naq** / tv
left / topicalizer / wind / white / emerge / right / topicalizer / wind / black / emerge
mei /nei / me / mei / chu**piq** / chu**ruaq** / neiq / lei / ji
plump / and / not / plump / distribute / count / dynamic aspect / again / put

Scharten translation

He takes a fan and separates the grain form the chaff, the white seed from the black.

New translation

Coqssei-leel'ee took a large and a small winnowing tray, and used a horse to carry the grain to a very large drying rack. From the left a white wind whipped up, and from the right came a black wind. The winds arranged the grain into two piles: the plump grains and the wizened grains.

Notes

The grain has been threshed, and now it has to be dried and brought before the ancestor deity. The gain drying rack (graph 1) is a large wooden stand upon which the grain is placed so it can dry in the sun. The two winnowing trays on the page are different in size: one large and one small. The divine winds whip up and separate the good grains from the bad; this separation can be seen in both the phonetic loan graph, *piq*, to distribute, and in the curved lines that separate the two containers of grain, this graph could be read *bbiu* 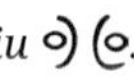. Scharten writes of a "fan"; I believe she is mistranslating graph 13, *piq* (a "fan" in Naxi is *piqceilperq*).

21-7

Graph-by-graph

1. **ggv**, nine.
2. **zzee**, many, used semantically to indicate *lerl*, the many seeds that have been harvested.
3. **lerl**, seeds, here three grains (*seel liu*) are depicted.
4. **bbei**, half (grains cut in half are shown).
5. **chualwa**, an ant.
6. **seel**, three. Indicating the three halves.
7. **yi**, geba syllabic graph, used for *yi*, to have.
8. **to'leef**, a dove, with pronounced crop (muscular pouch).
9. **yi**, geba syllabic graph, used for *yi*, to have.

Transcription

ggvcerqggv / rhu / gge / **lerl** / lei / epv / gainiuq / ji / keel
ninety-nine / kinds / of / seeds / again / grandfather / before / put / go
epv / laq / zeeq / laq / qerq / neiq
grandfather / hand / raise / hand / bend / dynamic aspect particle
me / zeeq / **seel** / liu / zzee**bbeiq** / jjuq / sei / ye
not / count / three / measure word / half ones / have / final particle / emphatic
Ceilheeq-bbvbbeq / lei / shel / mei
name / again / say / particle
zzeebbeiq / **chualwa** / teel / niu / **yi** / hee / seiq
half ones / ant / waist / on / have / go / modal particle
seel / liu / waher-t**o'leef** / berller / gv / niu / **yi** / hee / seiq
three / measure word / turtledove / pouch / place / on / have / go / modal particle
lerl / seel / lerl / me / zeeq
seeds / collect / seeds / not / count
me / zeeq / jjuq / seiq / ye
not / count / have / modal particle / emphatic

Scharten translation

The father of heaven counts the grains. There were three and three halves too less. Three were in the stomac of a dove and the three halves in the stomac of an ant.

New translation

The ninety-nine grains were placed before the grandfather deity. He then counted them on his hands, but three and three halves of grain were missing. At this, Ceilheeq-bbvbbeq said, "The three halves are on the abdomen of the ant, the three seeds are in the pouch of the turtledove. When we collected the seeds, we did not count them, and that's why some have not been counted."

Notes

The grains are counted, but some are missing. To be specific, three grains and three half grains, as depicted visually on the page. This is an example of the Naxi script showing an idea visually, disconnected from the spoken language (there's no conventional graph for "half-grains"). The manuscript shows the full body of the turtledove (graph 8). Contemporary readings elaborate on Scharten's rendition, with Ceilheeq-bbvbbeq here offering up an excuse as to why the number of grains falls short.

21-8

Graph-by-graph

1. **Zzee'laq-epv**, Naxi ancestor deity.
2. **lerq**, to call out. A head, speaking in a loud voice ("loud" is depicted by the extra dots). The head is wearing the crown of the gods.
3. **lerl**, seeds, here three grains (*seel liu*) are depicted.
4. **bbei**, half (three grains cut in half are shown).
5. **me**, negation.
6. **ddoq**, to see.

Transcription

epv / nee / **lerq** / gge / **seel** / liu / zzee**bbeiq** / lei / **me** / **ddoq**

grandfather / topicalizer / speak / genitive / three / measure word / half ones / particle / not / see

teel / gv / jju / sei / zeel
this / place / have / final particle / modal particle

Scharten translation

—

New translation

And the grandfather deity called out: "Those missing three and three halves of grain that we couldn't find, there they are!"

Notes

Scharten does not translate this panel. Once again, while the proper graph for the ancestor deity is written, the reading refers to him only as *epv*, grandfather. Gaph 2, *lerq*, call out, is interesting: it can be written in several different ways. The first is a person, calling out: ; the second is simply the head (or mouth): ; and the third is shown in the manuscript, a head with a divine crown, reminiscent of the deity Dduq, who we recall in panel 11-5 was depicted as calling out to heaven in a scene that presages the great flood.

21-9

Graph-by-graph

1. **to'leef**, a dove.
2. **peiqddaq**, a weaving loom.
3. **Coqssei-leel'ee**, Naxi hero, holding a bow.
4. **kailzo**, a bow.
5. **ceiqggu**, a shuttle (for a loom).
6. **lerl**, seeds, here three grains (*seel liu*) are depicted.
7. **tvq**, a bucket, used phonetically for *tvl*, to get.
8. **Coqssei-leel'ee**, Naxi hero, holding a thread.
9. **peiqddaq**, a loom (not read)
10. **kee**, thread.
11. **chualwa**, an ant.
12. **seel**, three.

13. **chuq**, pearls, used phonetically for *chuq*, fast.
14. **tvq**, a bucket, used phonetically for *tv*, to emerge.

Transcription
nilni / la / meseel
next day / and / morning
waher **to'leef** / tee / zzeiq / lei / **peiqddaq** / dol / gv / hal / lei / ceeq
turtledove / it / fly / particle / loom / top / place / perch / again / come
Coqssei-leel'ee / nee / kaillee / **kailzo** / bul
hero / topicalizer / arrows / bow / take
kail / bbee / seeq / lerller / me / bbee / seeq / lerller
shoot / want / thee / aim / not / want / three / aim
Ceilheeq-bbvbbeq / **ceiqggu** / bul
name / shuttle / take
laq mai meeltv / ddee / diu / neeq
elbow / one / hit / particle
kail / neiq / lerl / daldal
shoot / and / aim / together
waher to'leef / berller / niuq / dder
turtledove / crop / on / hit
seel / **liu** / **tvl** / lei / epv / gainiu / lei / ji / keel
three / measure word / get / come / grandfather / before / again / put / go
zzeebbeiq / chualwa / teel / niu / yi / ye / zeel
half ones / ant / waist / on / have / sentence final / modal particle
Coqssei-leel'ee / nee
name / topicalizer
gguq / mai / **kee** / ceeq / seel / keeq / bul
horse / tail / thread / thin / three / strands / take
chualwa / teel / lei / zee
ant / waist / again / tie
me / peel / peel / lee / kakaq / gv
not / broken / broken / particle / the same / like
seel / liu / zzeebbiq / **chuq** / **tv** / seiq
three / measure word / half ones / fast / emerge / modal particle

Scharten translation
T'so-rze-le-hgeh's son takes a bow and arrow and kills the dove, n which stomac the three are found. Afterwards he takes the hair of a horse tail and bind with them the stomac of the ant and very soon the three halves come out.

New translation

The next morning, the turtledove perched atop Ceilheeq-bbvbbeq's loom. Coqssei-leel'ee took up his bow and arrow and aimed at the bird but could not get a good shot. With the shuttle of her loom, Ceilheeq-bbvbbeq knocked into Coqssei-leel'ee's elbow, and he shot the arrow, hitting the bird in its crop. They got the three grains and put them before the grandfather deity. The three halves were in the stomach of the ant, so Coqssei-leel'ee got three threads made from the hair of a horse's tail, and tied it around the ant's waist. It was as if the ant's midsection would break, and just like that, the three halves emerged.

Notes

This is a famous section of the story that is often used as an example of the ideographic, mnemonic nature of the writing: quite a lot of what is read is not actually written (see Li 2001, 44; Fang 1981, 504). Coqssei-leel'ee hesitating to shoot because he cannot get a good aim is not written down, and the fact that the ant's midsection appears to be breaking apart is also not written. Some versions have the turtledove perching on a fence, but here it is clearly seen perching on a loom. There is a second loom (graph 9), that seems to indicate that perhaps the thread used by Coqssei-leel'ee to tie up the ant comes from said loom, but the readings (including Scharten's translation) make it explicit that it is hair from a horse's tail, and the loom is not mentioned again. The dividing line between this panel and the previous one (21-8) has been removed, and a graph written over the divide (graph 5, Ceilheeq-bbvbbeq's shuttle). Li Lin-ts'an shows this panel in a more ideographic way, with Ceilheeq-bbvbbeq figured using the shuttle to prod Coqssei-leel'ee's elbow:  (Li, *ibid*). Perhaps graph 5 was added later to make the scene clearer.

21-10

Graph-by-graph

1. **Coqssei-leel'ee**, Naxi hero.
2. **ni**, two, used phonetically for *ni*, to want.
3. **yeq**, tobacco, used phonetically for *yel*, to give.
4. **Zzee'laq-epv**, Naxi ancestor deity.

5. **mil**, daughter.
6. **me**, negation.

Transcription
Coqssei-leel'ee / nee / lei / shel
name / topicalizer / again / speak
wal / gge / Ceilheeq-bbvbbeq / ngeq / **ni** / ngeq / **yel** / lu'laq / zeel
you / possessive / name / I / want / I / give / come / modal particle
Zzee'laq-epv / lei / shel / mei
deity name / again / speak / particle
nge / **mil** / neeq / ni / neeq / yel / la / **me** /tal
I / daughter / you / want / you / give / and / not / able

Scharten translation
The heavenly father saith: although I see, that you are clever, I cant give you the one, who you want.

New translation
Coqssei-leel'ee then said, "Give me your daughter who I want." To which Zzee'laq-epv replied, "I cannot give you my daughter as you wish."

Notes
Again, a familiar panel where Coqssei-leel'ee is once again denied. The manuscript sets this up as a dialogue, with the deity to the left and our protagonist to the right, and the daughter they are quibbling over in the middle. Scharten translates as a one-way speech.

22-1, 22-2

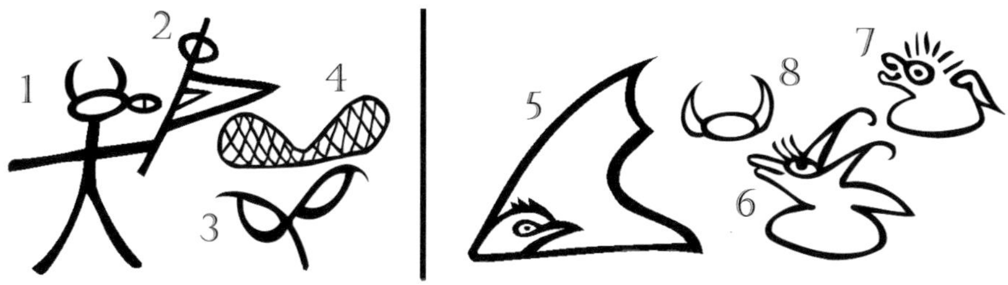

Graph-by-graph

1. **Coqssei-leel'ee**, Naxi hero, here holding a flag, representing the word *ddaiq* (see graph 2 below).
2. **ddaiq**, a man holding a flag, i.e. courageous, capable.
3. **yeq**, tobacco, used phonetically for *ye*, sentence final particle.
4. **kel**, basket, here used phonetically for *keq*, hard-working.
5. **aiq**, cliff. The chicken's head (*aiq*) provides the phonetic component.
6. **seiq**, a goral
7. **yuq**, monkey, used phonetically for *yuq*, to live.
8. **ko**, horns, used phonetically for *ko*, place (or possibly *kol*, to kill).

Transcription

Coqssei-leel'ee sso
name + epithet
ddaiq / la / neeq / ddaiq / **ye**
capable / too / you / capable / sentence final particle
keq / la / neeq / keq / ye / wei / zeel
hard-working / too / you / hard-working / sentence final / emphatic / modal particle
ddaiq / mei / sso / neel / waq
capable / possessive / man / want / be
azzeef / la / ni / gvl
us / also / two / ones
aiq / gge / **seiq** / **yuq** / **ko** / seiq / heeq / pabbaq / yuq / bbee / zeel
cliff / possessive / goral / live / place / goral / plump / present / get / go / modal particle

Scharten translation

"If you are clever, you have to go to the mountain, and get me a mountain sheep."

New translation

"Coqssei-leel'ee, if you are capable and hard-working, come with me to the mountain where the gorals live, and we will get one of the plump ones as a present."

Notes

The next task is set, but Zzee'laq-epv is still setting up our protagonist for failure. Graph 8 is used phonetically for perhaps "*ko*" as in a place, or mountain cave, but it could also indicate *kol*, to kill (the task is to kill a plump mountain sheep).

22-3

Graph-by-graph

1. **Coqssei-leel'ee**, Naxi hero, here seen speaking
2. **Ceilheeq-bbvbbeq**, the divine daughter.
3. **ni**, two, used phonetically for *ni*, to want.
4. **lv**, stone, used phonetically for second syllable of *miqlv*, husband and wife.
5. **ko**, horns, used phonetically for *ko*, half (*huqko*, middle of the night).
6. **me**, negation.
7. **ko**, horns, used phonetically for *ko*, half (*huqko*, middle of the night).
8. **Coqssei-leel'ee**, Naxi hero.
9. **seiq**, a goral.
10. **yuq**, monkey, used phonetically for *yuq*, to live.
11. **ko**, horns, used phonetically for *ko*, cave or place.

Transcription

Coqssei-leel'ee sso
name + epithet
Ceilheeq-bbvbbeq mil / **ni** / gvl
name + epithet / two / ones
nilyi / bbeeqzhuaq / lei / zzeeqggue
daytime / partner / particle / discuss
huqyi / miq**lv** / lei / seeddv
nighttime / husband and wife / particle / consider
huq**ko** / huq / **me** / **ko**
middle of the night / night / not / middle
Coqssei-leel'ee sso

name + epithet
aiq / gge / **seiq** / **yuq** / **ko** / bbee / zeel
cliff / possessive / goral / live / place / go / modal particle

Scharten translation
Now the boy and the girl speaks again together and she saith to him: it is not the meaning of my father, that he wants a sheep, but htat hae wants to kill you.

New translation
The boy and the girl talked it over again. Then in the middle of the night Coqssei-leel'ee went off to the cliff where the goral lived.

Notes
Note here the difference between Scharten's translation and contemporary readings. While He Guisheng reads the repeated "horns" graph (graphs 5, 7 and 11) as borrowings for "half" or "cave" (depending on context), Scharten reads them as *kol*, to kill or slaughter. This makes some sense; for it is indeed the ancestor deity's plan to kill the protagonist.

22-4

Graph-by-graph
1. **ceil**, leaf, used phonetically for *ceil*, first syllable in Ceilheeq-bbvbbeq.
2. **mil**, woman, here the divine daughter.
3. A strange composite of **ser**, tree, **lv**, stone, and **see**, felt (the box-like covering).
4. **Zzee'laq-epv**, the ancestor deity in horizontal position, sleeping.
5. **aiq**, cliff. The chicken's head (*aiq*) provides the phonetic component.
6. **ggaiq**, sword.
7. **cal**, to bite, used phonetically for *caq*, sharp.

Transcription
Coqssei-leel'ee sso
name + epithet

Ceilheeq-bbvbbeq **mil** / ni / gvl
name + epithet / two / ones
serdvq / **see** / lvl / tvl
wood block / felt / cover / do
liuq / lei / Leel'ee / yil / zzo / bbei
look / particle / name / sleep / seem / do
epv / kee / mai / ji / laq / zeel
grandfather / foot / bottom / put / go / modal particle
epv / no / yi / see / cee / cee
grandfather / wake / emphatic / three / kick / kick
me / no / see / cee / cee
not / wake / three / kick / kick
serdvq / cee / lei / **aiq** / gol / rhuq
wood block / kick / particle / cliff / in / fall
serdvq / seiq / diu / tei / shee / ye
wood block / goral / hit / conjunction / die / final particle
Coqssei-leel'ee / **ggaiq** see / ggaiq **caq** / bul
name / sharp sword / sharp blade / take

Scharten translation

They both go together to the mountain to kill the sheep. The put their felt over a tree and take it to the side of the father. In the midnight the father pushes the tree down the mountain.

New translation

Together the two of them covered a wooden block with some felt so that it looked like a sleeping Coqssei-leel'ee, and put it by the feet of Zzee'laq-epv. In the night he kicked it down the cliff, and it hit and killed a goral. [Going down the mountain,] Coqssei-leel'ee took his sharp blade.

Notes

Quite a lot is happening in this panel, and not much is actually written down. Epv's plan is to kick Coqssei-leel'ee down the mountain while he sleeps, but our hero has other plans, and manages to complete the task set for him by dressing up a block of wood in felt (i.e. human clothes) and putting it by the feet of the deity at night, thus tricking him. Graph 4 above appears to be the tree covered in a square piece of felt. Other versions have the object as a stone wrapped in felt: 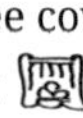 (Li 1978, 41), and it appears that the stone is also written in this manuscript, underneath the tree. A line seems to be emanating from Ceilheeq-bbvbbeq to her father's feet (from graph 2 to graph 4): this possibly indicates the action of placing the wooden block.

22-5

Graph-by-graph

1. **so**, a scale with a weight attached, used phonetically for *so*, tomorrow.
2. **seiq**, a goral. Here shown upside down, it has been killed by the falling block.
3. **mai**, an animal tail, used phonetically for **mai**, to attain.
4. **seiq**, a goral.
5. **shee**, meat.
6. **bul**, to take or bring. A figure holding something in both hands.
7. **ree**, a road. Here the road leads to a house.
8. **Coqssei-leel'ee**, Naxi hero.
9. **jji**, to walk, shown here by the pronounced foot striding forwards.
10. **yeq**, tobacco, used phonetically for first syllable of *yegoq*, home.
11. **goq**, needle, used phonetically for second syllable of *yegoq*, home.
12. **me**, negation.
13. **tvq**, bucket, used phonetically for *tv*, to arrive.
14. **tv**, to arrive.
15. **chuq**, pearls, used phonetically for *chuq*, quickly.

Transcription

so / seel / elmuniul
tomorrow / morning / very early
seiq / yuq / seiq / **mai** / seiq
goral / get / goral / attain / modal particle
seiq / **shee** / pabbaq / **bul**
goral / meat / present / take
epv / guq / **ree** / jji
grandfather / far / road / walk
Leel'ee / dvl / ree / **jji**
name / close / road / walk
epv / **yegoq** / **me** / **tv** / nee
grandfather / home / not / arrive / topicalizer

Leel'ee / yegoq / lei / tv / **chuq**
name / home / particle / arrive / quickly

Scharten translation

When it falls down, it will come down on the head of a sheep. He takes it and when he comes home, he prepares it for the father, for he is coming later, than he, because he takes an other road.

New translation

The next morning Leel'ee got the goral meat and took it with him. Epv took a longer road back home, and Leel'ee took the fast road, hence he arrived at home first.

Notes

There is quite the ideographic collage occurring on the manuscript page, with the central figure of Coqssei-leel'ee displaying several ideas at once: to take the meat, to walk on a road. Quite a lot of graphs are stuffed into the large graph for the home, within it are two phonetic loans that are commonplace for the pronunciation of this graph, alongside many other graphs suggesting that Epv does not make it back before Leel'ee (graphs 12 and 13, alongside a superfluous "bucket"). There is one more superfluous graph: another "meat" shown entering the home, in addition to the one in Leel'ee's hands (graph 5).

22-6

Graph-by-graph

1. **Zzee'laq-epv**, Naxi ancestor deity.
2. **bber**, a guest. A figure wearing the large hat of a traveller.
3. **ceil**, millet. Used phonetically for the first syllable of *ceiltv*, to host.
4. **tvq**, a bucket, used phonetically for the second syllable of *ceiltv*, to host.
5. **ha yi**, to have food (a steaming bowl of rice). Used semantically for *chuq zzee*, to eat dinner.

Transcription
Coqssei-leel'ee / nee / **Zzee'laq-epv** / niuq / lei / shel / mei
name / topicalizer / deity / toward / again / said / particle
epv / wal / gge / seiq / heeq / pabbaq / shuq / ceeq / seiq
grandfather / you / possessive / goral / plump / present / find / come / modal particle
bber / lei / lee / ddee / ni / bber / **ceiltv** / laq / zeel
guest / particle / come / one / day / guest / host / come / modal particle
bber / me / lee / ddee / ni / **chuqzzee** / chuqserl / bbei / laq / zeel
guest / not / come / one / day / eat dinner / dinner food / make / come / modal particle

Scharten translation
In the evening the father sits with his guests to the meal.

New translation
Coqssei'leel'ee then said to Zzee'laq-epv, "I have found the plump goral meat that you wanted. If you have guests during the day, you can serve them, if you do not have guests, you can eat it for dinner."

Notes
Scharten has this panel as a simple depiction of a meal, shared between the ancestor deity and his guest. Contemporary readings have it as dialogue from our protagonist, suggesting the uses to which the meat can go. Either way, the task is complete, and the deity has his food: the delicious, steaming goat meat (the goat freshly murdered by a falling tree).

22-7

Graph-by-graph
1. **Coqssei-leel'ee**, Naxi hero.
2. **mil**, daughter.
3. **ni**, two, used phonetically for *ni*, to want.
4. **yeq**, tobacco, used phonetically for *yel*, to give.
5. **me**, negation.

Transcription
Coqssei-leel'ee / nee / Zzee'laq-epv / niuq / lei / shel / heq
name / topicalizer / deity / toward / again / speak / go
wal / **mil** / ngeq / **ni** / ngeq / **yel** / lu'laq / zeel
you / daughter / I / want / I / give / come / modal particle
Zzee'laq-epv / lei / shel / mei
deity / again / speak / particle
ngeq / mil / neiq / yel / **me** / tal
I / daughter / dynamic aspect / give / not / able

Scharten translation
The father answers: although you have done all these things, I cant give you my daughter as wife.

New translation
Coqssei-leel'ee then said again, "Give me your daughter, whom I want." To which Zzee'laq-epv replied, "I cannot give you my daughter as you wish."

Notes
Coqssei-leel'ee comes away empty-handed once again.

22-8

Graph-by-graph
1. **Coqssei-leel'ee**, Naxi hero, here holding a flag, representing the word *ddaiq* (see graph 2).
2. **ddaiq**, a man holding a flag, i.e. courageous, capable.
3. **kel**, basket, here used phonetically for *keq*, hard-working.
4. **jjiq**, water.
5. **ko**, horns, used phonetically for *ko*, spring.
6. **ni**, fish.
7. **yuq**, monkey, used phonetically for *yuq*, to take.

8. **Coqssei-leel'ee**, Naxi hero, here seen holding the fish (not read).
9. **me**, negation (not read).

Transcription
Coqssei-leel'ee sso
name + epithet
ddaiq / la / neeq / ddaiq / ye
capable / too / you / capable / sentence final
keq / la / neeq / keq / ye / wei / zeel
hard-working / too / you / hard-working / sentence final / emphatic / modal particle
ddaiq / mei / sso / neel / waq
capable / possessive / man / want / be
azzeef / la / ni / gvl
us / also / two / ones
jjiqko / gv / niu / **ni** / heeq / pabbaq / **yuq** / bbee / zeel
spring / place / possessive / fish / plump / present / take / go / modal particle

Scharten translation
If you are really clever, bring me a fish.

New translation
"Coqssei-leel'ee, if you are so clever and hard-working, if that's the kind of person you wish to be, let us go down to the waters, and once there you can catch me a nice big fish."

Notes
The next plot is set in motion. Zzee'laq-epv wants to kick Coqssei-lee'ee into the water and drown him, and is using the request for a fish as a pretense. Graph 9, the negation, is perhaps mistakenly written and should not be read (or belongs to a kind of reading that neither Scharten nor I have been privy to). It is quite noticeable at this point that Scharten's translation is becoming ever more concise, leaving out lots of small details still present on the page (such as the water).

22-9, 22-10

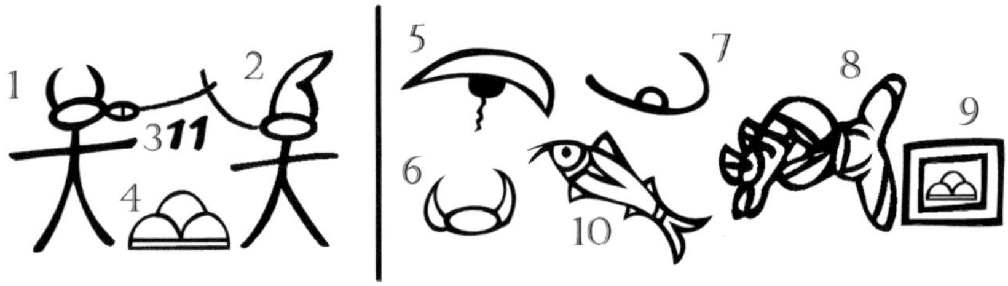

Graph-by-graph

1. **Coqssei-leel'ee**, Naxi hero, here seen speaking.
2. **Ceilheeq-bbvbbeq**, the divine daughter (here represented by the graph *mil*, woman).
3. **ni**, two, used phonetically for *ni*, to want.
4. **lv**, stone, used phonetically for second syllable of *miqlv*, husband and wife.
5. **huq**, evening or night, a moon shining.
6. **ko**, horns, used phonetically for *ko*, half (*huqko*, middle of the night).
7. **me**, negation.
8. **Zzee'laq-epv**, ancestral deity, here on his side, sleeping.
9. **lv**, stone, here supposedly covered in felt, *see*, although in actuality a box, *dal*, is depicted.
10. **ni**, a fish.

Transcription

Coqssei-leel'ee sso
name + epithet
Ceilheeq-bbvbbeq mil / **ni** / gvl
name + epithet / two / ones
nilyi / bbeeqzhuaq / lei / zzeeqggue
daytime / partner / particle / discuss
huqyi / miq**lv** / lei / seeddv
nighttime / husband and wife / particle / consider
huqko / huq / **me** / ko
middle of the night / night / not / middle
epv / jjiq / kee / yil
grandfather / water / foot / sleep
lv / naq / **see** / lullu
stone / large / felt / cover
epv / kee / mai / ji / laq / zeel
grandfather / foot / bottom / put / go / modal particle
ni / xi / jjiq / mai / daq / fai / la
fish / net / water / bottom / place / go / also

epv / no / yi / see / cee / cee
grandfather / wake / copula / three / kick / kick
me / no / see / cee / cee
not / wake / three / kick / kick
lv / cee / jjiq / niuq / rhuq
stone / kick / water / in / drop
ni / rherq / xi / niu / dder
fish / startle / net / in / hit

Scharten translation

The boy convers with his wife and she saith: my father dosnt want the fish, but he wants your life.

They take a stone, and cover it with their felt and put it at the side of the father. In the midst of night the father pushes the stone. It fells in the water and it kills a big stone.

New translation

Coqseei-leel'ee again conferred with Ceilheeq-bbvbbeq. In the middle of the night, Zzee'laq-epv slept by the river. They covered a big stone in a felt blanket and put it by his feet, and put a net in the water. Zzee'laq-epv woke and kicked the stone into the water, thinking it was Leel'ee. This startled the fish, which jumped right into the net.

Notes

Scharten again translates horns (graph 6) as *kol*, to kill, making the plot explicit: I think that its connection here with graph 5, *huq*, indicates that they together form *huqko*, middle of the night. The story of how the fish is killed is quite elaborate, and conveyed using only three graphs on the manuscript page. He Guisheng (as seen in the new translation above) relates how our hero places a net into the water to catch the fish, but this net is not seen in the manuscript, and Scharten's version has the stone directly killing the fish, indicating a simpler reading.

23-1, 23-2

Graph-by-graph

1. **ni**, fish.
2. **gguq**, to carry a load on the back. Here the figure is Coqssei-leel'ee.
3. **ceeq**, ghost, used phonetically for *ceeq*, to come (past tense).
4. **Zzee'laq-epv**, here seen walking.
5. **heel**, lake, used phonetically for *heel*, far.
6. **ree**, road.
7. **ddeeq**, big, used phonetically for *ddee*, to take.
8. **me**, negation.
9. **tvq**, bucket, used phonetically for *tv*, to arrive.
10. **Coqssei-leel'ee**, here seen walking.
11. **tv**, to arrive.
12. **chuq**, pearls, used phonetically for *chuq*, quickly.

Transcription

Coqssei-leel'ee sso
name + epithet
ni / heeq / pabbaq / **gguq**
fish / plump / present / carry
dvl / ree / loq / nee / **ceeq**
near / road / on / topicalizer / come
epv / **heel** / **ree** / **ddee**
grandfather / far / road / take
yegoq / **me** / **tv** / nee
home / not / arrive / topicalizer
Coqssei-leel'ee / yegoq / lei / **tv** / **chuq**
name / home / particle / arrive / early

Scharten translation

He takes the fish and want to present it to his father in law, but he comes later, for he dosnt take the straight way.
The son in law comes quicker home.

New translation

Coqseei-leel'ee carried the plump fish on his back, and took the short path home. Zzee'laq-epv took the long road home, and did not get there before Coqseeileel'ee, who arrived earlier.

Notes

The first three graphs appear on the last panel of the previous page, but they should be considered part of the first panel. Once again our hero takes the shortcut home, and gets there before the ancestor deity. Of particular note is graph 3, the ghost, which is used as a rebus for "came", i.e. by which road he came. In Li (1978) we see the same word depicted by the graph *ciq* , shoulder blade.

23-3

Graph-by-graph

1. **ni**, a fish.
2. **shee**, meat.
3. **bber**, a guest. A figure wearing the large hat of a traveller.
4. **ceil**, millet. Used phonetically for the first syllable of *ceiltv*, to host.
5. **ha**, a bowl of rice. Here not read, but representing dinner made for the guests.
6. **Zzee'laq-epv**, Naxi ancestor deity.
7. **shee**, meat (not read, representing the fish meat eaten for breakfast).
8. **ha**, rice, again not read, used semantically to represent breakfast (*chu*).

Transcription

Coqssei-leel'ee / nee / Zzee'laq-epv / niuq / lei / shel / mei
name / topicalizer / deity / toward / again / said / particle
epv / wal / gge / **ni** / **shee** / pabbaq / shuq / ceeq / seiq
grandfather / you / possessive / fish / meat / present / find / come / modal particle
bber / lei / lee / ddee / ni / bber / **ceil**tv / laq / zeel
guest / particle / come / one / day / guest / host / come / modal particle
bber / me / lee / ddee / ni
guest / not / come / one / day

epv / soq / gge / **chuccee** / bbei
grandfather / morning / possessive / breakfast / make

Scharten translation
And prepares the fish.
In the morning the father eats it.

New translation
Coqssei'leel'ee then said to Zzee'laq-epv, "I have found the fish meat that you wanted. If you have guests during the day, you can serve them, if you do not have guests, you can eat it for breakfast in the morning."

Notes
Originally two panels, I label this as one single panel because the central dividing line has been struck though on the original manuscript. The rice bowls, graphs 6 and 8, represent meals and are not to be read literally as "rice". Scharten ignores the guest entirely in her translation. As McKhann notes, when Coqssei-leel'ee talks of the fish and the goral as "presents", he is suggesting that they are "part of a brideprice that he must pay…in order to obtain the woman" (1992, 113). In Rock's translation, upon returning to the palace, Coqssei-leel'ee puts the fish in a pond and it is not cooked (1952, 684); presumably it was some kind of decorative fish.

23-4

Graph-by-graph

1. **Coqssei-leel'ee**, Naxi hero, here holding a flag, representing the word *ddaiq* (see graph 2 below).
2. **ddaiq**, a man holding a flag, i.e. courageous, capable.
3. **kel**, basket, here used phonetically for *keq*, hard-working.
4. **la**, a tiger.
5. **nil**, milk.
6. **seel**, three.
7. **biu**, container, here used semantically for *chaq*, to milk (milk being squeezed into a jug).

Transcription
Coqssei-leel'ee sso
name + epithet
ddaiq / la / neeq / ddaiq / ye
capable / too / you / capable / sentence final
keq / la / neeq / keq / ye / wei / zeel
hard-working / too / you / hard-working / sentence final / emphatic / modal particle
ddaiq / mei / sso / neel / waq
capable / possessive / man / want / be
la / **nil** / **seel** / tie / **chaq** / lu / zeel
tiger / milk / three / drops / squeeze / come / modal particle

Scharten translation
If you are clever, you have to go to the mountain and get me some milk of the tiger.

New translation
"Coqssei-leel'ee, if you are so clever and hard-working, if that's the kind of person you wish to be, then go and get three drops of tiger milk".

Notes
Another task is set, and while it's seemingly limited in scope (retrieve three drops of milk), the difficulty is significantly raised by the animal to be milked: a tiger. Some versions have Zzee'laq-epv asking our hero to milk a tiger and a leopard, only the tiger is present in this version.

23-5

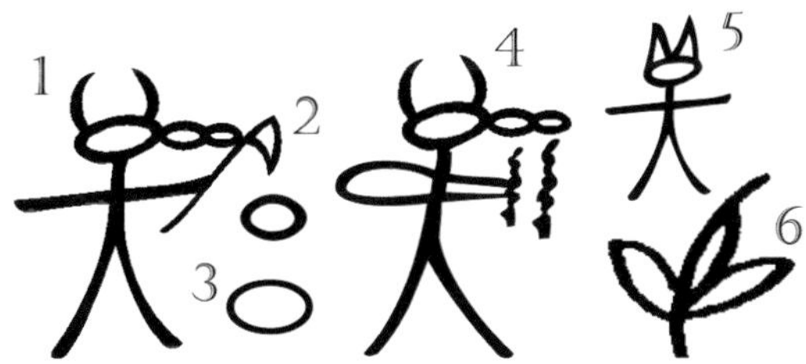

Graph-by-graph
1. **Coqssei-leel'ee**, Naxi hero, here holding a farm tool, representing the word *bbei* (see graph 2 below).
2. **bbei**, a farm tool, to do or make.
3. **gv**, egg, here used phonetically for *gvl*, to be able.

4. **bbiq**, to weave. Here the figure is Coqssei-leel’ee doing the weaving.
5. **zeiq**, a demon, used phonetically for *ssiq*, tight.
6. **rer**, willow, here used phonetically for *zeel*, modal particle (?).

Transcription
Coqssei-leel’ee / lei / shel / mei
name / particle / say / particle
bbei / lo / niul / **gvl** / sei / we / zeel
do / work / I / able / finished action / emphatic / modal particle
bbiq / lei / **ssiq** / mei / niul / gvl / sei / we / **zeel**
weave / again / tight / particle / I / able / finished action / emphatic / modal particle

Scharten translation
He thinks, he can do it myself and makes a rope,

New translation
Coqssei-leel’ee thinks to himself, “I can do this myself, like weaving a tight rope, I can do it!”

Notes
Now we see our protagonist’s hubris: “Piece of cake!”, he thinks to himself. McKhann translates the central image (graph 4) as “all the ropes have been tightened”, noting that the reference is “unclear” (1992, 113). He Guisheng explains the reference to weaving ropes as follows: having completed all the previous tasks, Coqssei-leel’ee thinks they’re as easy as twisting hemp fibers together to make a rope, so he can do this task himself. In other words, “making a rope” is a metaphor for performing an easy task.

23-6, 23-7

Graph-by-graph

1. **Coqssei-leel'ee**, Naxi hero.
2. **mil**, woman, here representing Ceilheeq-bbvbeeq.
3. **me**, negation.
4. **la**, a tiger.
5. **nil**, milk.
6. **seel**, three.
7. **chaq**, to milk (milk being squeezed into a jug).
8. **me**, negation.

Transcription

Coqssei-leel'ee sso / Ceilheeq-bbvbeeq **mil** / nee / **me** / shel
name + epithet / name + epithet / topicalizer / not / speak
bbeeqzhuaq / me / zzeeqggue
husband and wife / not / discuss
Coqssei-leel'ee sso / ddaiq / bbei / **la** / **nil** / **seel** / tie / **chaq** / heq
name + epithet / capable / do / tiger / milk / three / drops / squeeze / go
ddaiq / bbei / la / kee / da / me / loq
capable / do / tiger / place / arrive / not / able

Scharten translation

He dosnt confer with his wife
He afterall dosnt get the milk of the tiger,

New translation

Coqssei-leel'ee did not go to talk with Ceilheeq-bbvbeeq, and instead went off by himself to get the three drops of tiger milk. But he was not able to get close to that tiger.

Notes

The typical man, our hero decides that he does not need to discuss things with his better half, instead running off straight away to get the milk, without a plan. Graph 7, to milk, is a container (*biu*) with liquid falling into it. Fang (1981) does not record such a graph, but it can be found in Li (2001, 274).

23-8

Graph-by-graph

1. **dder**, a bamboo mat, used phonetically for *dder*, planted (as in a field).
2. **ddiuq**, the earth, used here semantically for *lee*, field.
3. **ddvq**, a wildcat.
4. **nil**, milk (being squeezed into a container).
5. **ddai**, a fox (note the pronounced tail).
6. **nil**, milk (being squeezed into a container).
7. **nil**, milk, possibly used semantically for *tie*, drop.
8. **seel**, three.
9. **biu**, container, here used semantically for *chaq*, to milk (milk being squeezed into a jug).

Transcription

dder / **lee** / keq / lee / zhul
planted / field / barren / field / between
ddvq / **nil** / **ddai** / **nil** / **seel** / **tie** / **chaq** / lei / ceeq
wildcat / milk / fox / milk / three / drops / squeeze / particle / come

Scharten translation

But gets the milk of a fox and a wild cat.

New translation

Coqssei-leel'ee went to the place in between the fertile fields and the barren ones, and there milked the fox and the wildcat, getting three drops of each.

Notes

Graphs 4 and 6 are technically two graphs in one, the container and the milk (i.e. *chaq*, to milk), but the container is merely decorative in this case and not read out. Coqssei-leel'ee hopes that the ancestor deity is not going to notice that it isn't tiger milk: after all, milk is milk, right?

23-9

Graph-by-graph

1. **Coqssei-leel'ee**, Naxi hero.
2. **nil**, milk.
3. **seel**, three.
4. **biu**, container, here not read.
5. **ciq**, shoulder blade, used phonetically for *ceeq*, to come.
6. **yeq**, tobacco, used phonetically for first syllable of *yegoq*, home.
7. **goq**, needle, used phonetically for second syllable of *yegoq*, home.
8. **tvq**, bucket, used phonetically for *tv*, to arrive.
9. **Zzee'laq-epv**, ancestor deity.
10. **nil**, milk.
11. **rherq**, power.
12. **ee**, a svastika, denoting the idea of "goodness", "good".

Transcription

Coqssei-leel'ee sso / ddvq / **nil** / ddai / nil / **seel** / tie / yu / lei / **ceeq**
Name + epithet / wildcat / milk / fox / milk / three / drops / take / particle / came
epv / **yegoq** / **tv**
grandfather / home / arrive
Zzee'laq-epv / la / niu / guq
deity / hand / in / pass
la / **nil** / **rherq** / ddeeq / **ee** / me / zeel
tiger / milk / power / large / goo / particle indicating certainty / modal particle

Scharten translation
T'so-rze-le-gheh's son takes it and wants to present it to his father in law.
When he comes home, the father looks to it.

New translation
Coqssei-leel'ee took the milk of the wildcat and the yak and brought it back to the divine household., where he gave it to Zzee'laq-epv, who said, "The milk of a tiger is very powerful and good".

Notes
Contrast graph 5 (shoulder blade) with graph 3 (ghost) of panel 23-1: both are phonetic loans for the past-tense verb "came", *ceeq*. There are no rules to follow about which graph to use; the ghost, *ceeq*, is a closer phonetic match, but the shoulder blade, *ciq*, is more commonly used in this manuscript. Scharten continues to mistake the epithet ascribed to our hero "*sso*", i.e. manly, for *sso*, "son".

23-10

Graph-by-graph
1. **nil**, milk. Not read.
2. **zzeeq**, a dzo, yak and cattle hybrid.
3. **bberq**, a yak.
4. **me**, negation.
5. **jil**, scissors, used phonetically for *jil*, to be frightened.
6. **nil**, milk. Not read.
7. **rua**, a horse.
8. **eey**, cattle.
9. **me**, negation.
10. **jil**, scissors, used phonetically for *jil*, to be frightened.

Transcription
zzeeq / neif / **bberq** / bbiuq / ddee / ji / neiq
dzo / and / yak / pen / one / put / dynamic aspect
zzeeq / lei / bberq / tee / we
dzo / also / yak / all / emphatic
almuq / **me** / **jil**see
a little / not / frightened
rua / neif / **ee** / bbiuq / ddee / ji / neiq
horse / and / cattle / pen / one / put / dynamic aspect
rua / lei / ee / tee / we
horse / also / cattle / all / emphatic
almuq / **me** / **jil**see
a little / not / frightened

Scharten translation
He puts the milk in the stable of a yak and bullock, but they dont take it; Afterwards he puts it in the stable of a horse and cow and they also dont take it

New translation
The milk was put into the pen where the dzo and yaks were kept, but they did not fear it even a little. Then it was placed into the pen where the horses and cattle were kept, but they also did not fear it even a little.

Notes
The milk is put to the test. He Guisheng does not read graphs 1 and 6, the milk, but they do appear as a reminder of what is being put into the animal pens. Scharten writes of the animals not "taking" the milk, this is the same as McKhann's "they ignored it" (1992, 113), which comes from the Chinese *zaiyi* 在意, to pay attention it, found in He Fayuan's translation (1986, 237). In all cases the interpretation appears to depend upon how one translated the Naxi *jilsee*. Li Lin-ts'an translates as *jingdong* 惊动 "to be startled" (1978, 68), a reading with which He Guisheng agrees. This makes some sense, as the previous panel talked of how "powerful" the tiger milk should be.

23-11, 23-12

Graph-by-graph

1. **nil**, milk. Not read.
2. **ceel**, a goat.
3. **yuq**, a sheep.
4. **me**, negation.
5. **jil**, scissors, used phonetically for *jil*, to be frightened.
6. **nil**, milk. Not read.
7. **kee**, a dog.
8. **bbuq**, a pig.
9. **me**, negation.
10. **jil**, scissors, used phonetically for *jil*, to be frightened.

Transcription

ceel / neif / **yuq** / bbiuq / ddee / ji / neiq
goat / and / sheep / pen / one / put / dynamic aspect
ceel / lei / yuq / tee / we
goat / also / sheep / all / emphatic
almuq / **me** / **jil**see
a little / not / frightened
kee / neif / **bbuq** / bbiuq / ddee / ji / neiq
dog / and / pig / pen / one / put / dynamic aspect
kee / lei / bbuq / tee / we
dog / also / pig / all / emphatic
almuq / **me** / **jil**see
a little / not / frightened

Scharten translation

In the stable of a sheep ad goat and they also dont take it.
Also he puts the milk in the stable of the dog, but he also is not afraid of it.

New translation

The milk was then put into the pen where the goats and sheep were kept, but they too did not fear it even a little. Then it was placed into the pen where the dogs and pigs were kept, but they also did not fear it even a little.

Notes

The milk is continued to be passed around all the animals, who are not afraid of such mundane milk.

24-1

Graph-by-graph

1. **nil**, milk. Not read.
2. **al**, a duck, the wavy lines indicate it is shaking with fear, and can indicate *rer*, to be scared.
3. **aiq**, a chicken.
4. **loq**, a plowtail, used phonetically for *lo*, inside.
5. **jil**, scissors, used phonetically for *jil*, to be frightened.
6. **so**, a scale with a weight attached, used phonetically for *see*, second syllable of *jilsee*, to be frightened.

Transcription

al / bbiuq / **aiq** / bbiuq / **lo** / yi / ddee / ji / neiq
duck / pen / chicken / coop / in / copula / one / put / dynamic aspect
al / **rer** / aiq / **rer** / **jilsee** / seiq / we / zeel
duck / scared / chicken / scared / frightened / modal particle / emphatic / modal particle

Scharten translation

Now he puts it in the stable of a duck and of a chicken and they are afraid.

New translation

Then the milk was put into the place where the ducks and chickens were kept, and they shook with fear.

Notes

The ducks and chickens are visibly very afraid of the milk: this is because chickens and ducks are the natural prey of the wildcats and foxes, so they can sense that this is the milk of their predators. When they smell it, they start to go wild.

24-2

Graph-by-graph

1. **Zzee'laq-epv**, ancestor deity.
2. **she**, geba graph, used for *shel*, to speak.
3. **la**, geba graph, used for *la*, tiger.
4. **nil**, milk.
5. **biu**, container, here not read.
6. **me**, negation.

Transcription

Zzee'laq-epv / lei / **shel** / mei
deity / particle / speak / nominalizer
ddaiq / bbei / **la** / **nil** / seel / tie / tee / **me** / waq
capable / do / tiger / milk / three /drops / it / not / is

Scharten translation

The father in law saith now: I see by this, that you have not taken tiger's milk.

New translation

And so Zzee'laq-epv said, "This is not the milk of the powerful tiger."

Notes

Note graph 3, a geba syllabic graph used instead of the pictograph of a tiger's head. This is merely used for convenience: it is simpler to write.

24-3

Graph-by-graph

1. **dder**, a bamboo mat, used phonetically for *dder*, planted (as in a field).
2. **ddiuq**, the earth, used here semantically for *lee*, field.
3. **zhul**, awl, used phonetically for *zhul*, between.
4. **ddvq**, a wildcat.
5. **ddai**, a fox (note the pronounced tail).
6. **nil**, milk (being squeezed into a container).
7. **biu**, container, here not read.
8. **chee**, the weight of a balance, used phonetically for *chee*, this/that.
9. **oq**, grain, often used phonetically for *oq*, thus, so, and by extension can be read *waq*, to be.

Transcription

dder / **lee** / keq / lee / **zhul**
planted / field / barren / field / between
ddvq / nil / **ddai** / **nil** / **tee** / **wa** / seiq
wildcat / milk / fox / milk / that / is / modal particle

Scharten translation

But it is milk of the fox and of the wild cat.

New translation

"It is in fact the milk of the wildcat and of the fox."

Notes

Graph 9, grain, is often used in place of *wa*  (five), a rebus for "to be". It is frequently seen on manuscript covers in the formulation "*wa mei*", meaning "this is the [book of]...".

24-4

Graph-by-graph

1. **Coqssei-leel'ee**, Naxi hero, here seen speaking
2. **Ceilheeq-bbvbbeq**, the divine daughter (here represented by the graph *mil*, woman).
3. **lv**, stone, used phonetically for second syllable of *miqlv*, husband and wife.
4. **ddaq**, a sickle with a serrated edge, used phonetically for *ddaq*, shade.
5. **aiq**, cliff.
6. **la**, tiger.
7. **ddaq**, a sickle, used phonetically for *ddaq*, shade.
8. **pu**, to open (as in an eye), used phonetically for *pul*, slope.

Transcription

Coqssei-leel'ee sso
name + epithet
Ceilheeq-bbvbbeq mil / ni / gvl
name + epithet / two / ones
miq**lv** / lei / zzeeqggue
husband and wife / particle / discuss
Ceilheeq-bbvbbeq mil / nee / lei / shel / mei
name + epithet / toipicalizer / particle / say / modal particle
daqpul / **aiq** / shuaq / gv
shaded slope / cliff / high / place
lasso / **daqpul** / jjuq
tiger cub / shaded slope / live

Scharten translation

Now the boy goes to talk with his girl, what to do. She saith: the little one of the tiger is at the side, where no sun is.

New translation

Coqssei-leel'ee discussed the matter with Ceilheeq-bbvbeq. She told him that in the high cliffs there is a shady slope where a young tiger lived.

Notes

Graph 4, the sickle, is here used as a rebus for *ddaq*, shade. We know that the shady place is high up in the mountains because the sickle is written over the top of graph 5, cliff.

24-5

Graph-by-graph

1. **la**, a tiger.
2. **bbaq**, sunshine, the sun's rays.
3. **bbu**, a hill, here used semantically for pal, slope.
4. **jjiu**, a cabbage. Used phonetically for *jjuq*, to have.
5. **chuq**, pearls, used phonetically for *chuq*, early.
6. **shee**, meat.
7. **shu**, geba syllabic graph, used for *shuq*, to search for. Possibly also *gee*, star.
8. **lv**, stones, used phonetically (?) for *ddu*, habit (see reading below), or used for its original meaning, stone.
9. **Coqssei-leel'ee**, Naxi hero.
10. **lv**, stones
11. **la**, tiger.
12. **diu**, to strike.
13. **la'ee**, tiger skin.
14. **muq**, to drape over the shoulder (here depicted by Coqssei-leel'ee wearing the tiger skin).
15. **la**, tiger.
16. **nil**, milk.
17. **seel**, three.
18. **biu**, container, here used semantically for *chaq*, to milk (milk being squeezed into a jug).

Transcription

la / mei / **bbaq** / **pal** / **jjuq**
tiger / mother / sunshine / slope / reside
la / mei / **chuq** / bbei / **shee** / **shuq** / **ddu** / waq / zeel
tiger / mother / early / do / meat / find / habit / is / modal particle

Coqssei-leel'ee sso / **lv** / naq / seel / lv / bul
name + epithet / stone / black / three / stones / bring
la / sso / gv / niu / **diu**
tiger / cub / head / on / hit
la'ee / ggu / niu / **muq**
tiger skin / body / on / drape
guq / nee / la / ler / **jilgguq** / see / juq / neiq
mouth / topicalizer / tiger / call / whistle / three / sounds / dynamic aspect
ddai / mei / la / hiuq / tee
courageous / possessive / tiger / red / it
sso / lerq / neiq / jilmi
cub / call / dynamic aspect / think
tei / niuq / tv / lee / zaq
here / in / arrive / come / will
laq / nee / **la** / **nil** / **seel** / tie / **chaq** / lu / la
hand / topicalizer / tiger / milk / three /drops / squeeze / come / particle

Scharten translation
The mother tiger goes to the place, where the sun is, to warm herself. Now take a stone and kill the little one and take the skin and put it on and go near the mother tiger and she will think, it is her little one and you will be able to take her milk.

New translation
And the mother tiger lived on the sunny side of the mountain, and it was her habit to go off early to look for meat. Coqssei-leel'ee took with him three black stones. He hit the tiger cub on the head and killed it. He covered his body with the tiger skin, then he whistled three times in imitation of the tiger cub's call. The ferocious red tiger mother, thinking it was her cub calling, came running over, and so Coqssei-leel'ee was able to milk it, getting three drops of tiger milk.

Notes
A long panel that features quite a lot of action; as with some previous panels this serves double duty as both Ceilheeq-bbvbbeq's instructions and the actual actions carried out by our hero after receiving them. The second intonation unit, relating the tiger mother's habit of looking for meat according to He Guisheng, could also be interpreted as the proper name of a slope where there is a great rock that can be used to kill the tiger cub: "Bbisheelgeechuq" (McKhann 1992, 114); in this interpretation, graphs 5, 6 and 7 are all used as rebuses. For Rock, graph 7 may be *geeq*, stars, used literally: "take rocks the size of stars" (1952, 684) are the instructions given to our hero. Much hinges on what is interpreted as a rebus, and what is to be read literally. Scharten, perhaps wisely, simply does not translate these graphs. Graph 4, the cabbage, is often used as a rebus for the verb "to have"; although in this manuscript we have also seen the bracelet, *laqjjuq* , used for this purpose. Of particular note here are

graphs 14 and 15, a very distinctive way of showing the tiger skin and how Coqssei-leel'ee wore it over his shoulders. It is also possible to make out the sounds coming from his mouth and that of the tiger; presumably the latter is the call of the tiger, and the former is Coqssei-leel'ee's imitation of it.

24-6

Graph-by-graph

1. **Coqssei-leel'ee**, Naxi hero. Here seen bringing the milk into the house, hands outstretched.
2. **nil**, milk.
3. **seel**, three.
4. **biu**, container, here not read.
5. **jjiq**, house, not read.
6. **goq**, needle, used phonetically for the second syllable of *yegoq*, home.
7. **tvq**, a bucket, used phonetically for *tv*, to arrive.

Transcription

Coqssei-leel'ee sso
name + epithet
la / **nil** / **seel** / tie / yuq / lei / epv / ye**goq** / **tv**
tiger / milk / three / drops / bring / come / grandfather / home / arrive
Zzee'laq-epv / la / niu / guq
deity / hand / in / pass

Scharten translation

He goes home and gives it to the father in law.

New translation

Coqssei-leel'ee returned to the ancestral deity's house and gave him the three drops of tiger milk.

Notes

Our hero returns with the correct milk in hand. Graph 5 is the house, acting as an ideographic compound: the words inside indicating that the milk has been brought into the home.

24-7

Graph-by-graph

1. **nil**, milk (not read).
2. **ddeeq**, large.
3. **zzeeq**, a dzo (visibly shaking).
4. **bberq**, a yak (visibly shaking).
5. **nil**, milk (not read).
6. **rua**, a horse (visibly shaking).
7. **nil**, milk (not read).
8. **ee**, cattle, a cow (visibly shaking).

Transcription

la / nil / rherq / **ddeeq** / ee / me / zeel
tiger / milk / power / big / good / possessive / modal particle
zzeeq / neiq / **bberq** / bbiuq / **ddee** / ji / neiq
dzo / and / yak / pen / once / put / dynamic aspect
zzeeq / rherq / bberq / rherq / chee / lo'lo
dzo / scared / yak / scared / this / tremble
rua / neiq / **ee** / bbiuq / ddee / jji / neiq
horse / and / cattle / pen / once / put / dynamic aspect
rua / rherq / ee / rherq / chee / lo'lo
horse / scared / cattle / scared / this / tremble

Scharten translation

The father put it in the stable of the yak and bullock and they fear for it very much.
Also in the stable of a horse and cow and the also fear with great fear.

New translation

Then Zzee'laq-epv put the powerful tiger milk into the pen where the dzo and the yak were kept, and they trembled with fear, likewise the horses and cattle were very afraid of it.

Notes

Whereas these animals had been very much unperturbed by the milk of fox and wildcat, this tiger milk is a different story: the animals are agitated and shake with fear. The wavy movement lines that surround the animals indicate this (and can be considered to be the written form of *rherq*, to be scared).

24-8

Graph-by-graph

1. **nil**, milk (not read).
2. **ceel**, a mountain goat (visibly shaking).
3. **nil**, milk (not read).
4. **yuq**, a sheep (visibly shaking).
5. **nil**, milk (not read).
6. **kee**, a dog (visibly shaking).
7. **nil**, milk (not read).
8. **bbuq**, pig (visibly shaking).

Transcription

ceel / neiq / **yuq** / bbiuq / **ddee** / ji / neiq
goat / and / sheep / pen / once / put / dynamic aspect
ceel / rherq / yuq / rherq / chee / lo'lo
goat / scared / sheep / scared / this / tremble
kee / neiq / **bbuq** / bbiuq / ddee / jji / neiq
dog / and / pig / pen / once / put / dynamic aspect
kee / rherq / bbiuq / rherq / chee / lo'lo
dog / scared / pig / scared / this / tremble

Scharten translation

Now he puts it in the stable of the pig and dog and the same with them.

New translation

Then it was put into the pen where the goats and sheep were kept, and they trembled with fear, as too did the dogs and the pigs.

Notes

The parallel panels continue with more animals that had previously been unafraid. Scharten completely omits the goats and sheep from her translation. In the top right corner of the panel on the manuscript page there is a crossed out negation; this clearly belongs in the next panel, hence its removal.

24-9

Graph-by-graph

1. **nil**, milk (not read).
2. **al**, a duck.
3. **aiq**, a chicken.
4. **me**, negation.
5. **jil**, scissors, used phonetically for *jil*, to be frightened.
6. **so**, a scale with a weight attached, used phonetically for *see*, second syllable of *jilsee*, to be frightened.

Transcription

al / bbiuq / **aiq** / bbiuq / **lo** / yi / ddee / ji / neiq
duck / pen / chicken / coop / in / copula / one / put / dynamic aspect
almuq / **me** / **jilsee**
a little / not / frightened

Scharten translation

Afterwards he put it by the dick and chicken and they are not afraid.

New translation
Then it was put into the pen where the ducks and chickens were kept, and they were not even a little bit afraid.

Notes
The ducks and the chickens are not afraid (the tiger is not their natural predator) – once again graph 6, *so*, seems to be used as a phonetic borrowing for *see* despite the different final vowel sound.

24-10

Graph-by-graph
1. **Zzee'laq-epv**, ancestor deity.
2. **she**, geba graph, used for *shel*, to speak
3. **Coqssei-leel'ee**, Naxi hero, here holding a flag, representing the word *ddaiq* (see graph 4 below).
4. **ddaiq**, a man holding a flag, i.e. courageous, capable.
5. **bbei**, a farm tool, indicating the verb "to do or make" (not read).

Transcription
Zzee'laq-epv / lei / **shel** / mei
deity / particle / speak / nominalizer
Coqssei-leel'ee sso / **ddaiq** / mei / sso / neel / waq / ye / zeel
name + epithet / capable / particle / man / are / emphatic / modal particle

Scharten translation
Now the father saith to his son in law:

New translation
The ancestor deity then said to him: "Coqssei-leel'ee, you truly are a capable man."

Notes

Zzee'laq-epv praises our protagonist once more, but is still not ready to allow him to marry into his family. Graph 5 is not read, and is present seemingly to reinforce the idea that our hero is very capable and hard-working, the word *bbei*, to do, indicating that he "gets things done". Scharten does not translate this line of dialogue.

25-1

Graph-by-graph

1. **la**, a tiger.
2. **nil**, milk.
3. **biu**, container, here not read.
4. **seel**, three.
5. **seiq**, a goral, used phonetically for *seiq*, a modal particle.

Transcription

la / nil / seel / tie / waq / seiq / we / zeel
tiger / milk / three / drop / this / is / modal particle

Scharten translation

"...by this I see, that you got truly the milk of a tiger."

New translation

"This really is three drops of tiger's milk."

Notes

A straightforward panel, the familiar goral's head used as a modal particle to indicate a currently relevant state (see Pinson 2012, 338). Note here the use of "three" as a numeral, and contrast with its use in the next panel.

25-2

Graph-by-graph

1. **Coqssei-leel'ee**, Naxi hero (not read).
2. **Zzee'laq-epv**, ancestor deity.
3. **seel**, three, used phonetically for *see*, to recognise.
4. **seel**, three, used phonetically for *see*; reduplicated *see* also meaning to recognise.
5. **bbiu**, to separate (two containers, separated in the middle).

Transcription

Zzee'laq-epv / tee / me / **seesee** / **bbiu** / mei
deity / him / not / recognise / separate / particle

Scharten translation

The son saith: when I divide the different drops of milk, are you then willing to give me your daughter?

New translation

Zzee'laq-epv did not recognise Coqssei-leel'ee, as he was not of the clan.

Notes

The versions here differ: Scharten takes graph 5 literally, as "separating [the milk]" (supported by the graph itself, as the objects being separated are the milk in the containers), whereas He Guisheng understands it to indicate that Coqssei-leel'ee is "separate" from him and his daughter, as Leel'ee is a man, and they are gods. Scharten's interpretation doesn't make much logical sense. Why would they be separating the milk? If we consider graphs 3 and 4 (absent from Scharten's translation), *seesee* (to recognise), the meaning seems to support He Guisheng's contemporary reading. Leel'ee is different, a man apart, he is not recognised as worthy. This only again serves to highlight the difficulty of reading a manuscript tradition with which you are unfamiliar; the "three" graphs here are not numerals, as in the previous panels, but instead used phonetically, and the all-important negation, "does **not** recognise", is simply not written at all!

25-3, 25-4

Graph-by-graph

1. **Zzee'laq-epv**, Naxi ancestor deity, words coming from his mouth.
2. **she**, geba syllabic graph (phono-graphic borrowing from Chinese *shang*, 上), used for *shel*, to speak.
3. **mil**, daughter.
4. **ni**, two, used phonetically for *ni*, to want.
5. **yeq**, tobacco, used phonetically for *yel*, to give.
6. **me**, negation.
7. **Coqssei-leel'ee**, Naxi hero.
8. **qiul**, to cut through, used phonetically for *qu*, kind or race.
9. **siul**, lead (the metal), used phonetically for *siuq*, what.

Transcription

Zzee'laq-epv / lei / **shel** / mei
deity name / again / speak / particle
nge / **mil** / neeq / **ni** / neeq / **yel** / la / **me** / tal
I / daughter / you / want / you / give / and / not / able
Coqssei-leel'ee sso / neeq / **qu** / **siuq** / qu / zeel
name + epithet / you / race / what / kind / modal particle

Scharten translation

The father replies, even then I dont want to give you what you want, for after all, what kind of men are you?

New translation

Zzee'laq-epv said, "I will not give you my daughter, whom you desire. Coqssei-leel'ee, what kind of man are you?"

Notes

The two "z" marks on the top and bottom of the dividing line between these panels on the manuscript indicates that it is to be erased, probably because of the continuity error: the first two graphs to be read are the ancestral deity and the syllabic graph indicating the verb that begin the “second” panel. This is the deity once again denying our hero what he wishes, and then going on to ask him what sort of man he is – not with regards to his character (by this point Zzee’laq-epv believes him to be hard-working and capable), but with regards to his ancestors: the question is essentially “Are you from a good family?”. Graphs 8 and 9 look deceptively like the verb “to kill”, *siul*, a phono-semantic compound portrayed by the metal, lead (graph 9, the phonetic component) and a sword (the semantic component): . In this case, however, graph 8 is an awl punching through an object, not a sword, and the two words are separate.

25-5

Graph-by-graph

1. **Coqssei-leel’ee**, Naxi hero, the pronounced foot indicates movement. Perhaps here read *niel*, personal pronoun, “I”.
2. **ggv**, nine.
3. **mee**, sky.
4. **tvq**, bucket, here read *tv*, to emerge.
5. **qiul**, to cut through, used phonetically for *qu*, kind or race.
6. **Coqssei-leel’ee**, Naxi hero, the pronounced foot indicates movement, holding a farm tool, indicating the act of splitting the earth. Not read.
7. **sher**, seven.
8. **ddiuq**, the earth.
9. **ku**, to open (as in a door).
10. **qiul**, to cut through, used phonetically for *qu*, kind or race.

Transcription

Coqssei-leel’ee / lei / shel / mei
name / again / speak / particle
niel / yi / zhuaq / ee / **ggv** / luq / **mee** / **tv** / **qu**
I / exclamation / man / good / nine / brothers / sky / open / race
bbeeq / ee / **sher** / luq / **ddiuq** / **ku** / **qu**
woman / good / seven / sisters / earth / open / race

Scharten translation

The son saith: I am the descendant of one, who has opened nine water-dragons and seven high ways.

New translation

Coqssei-leel'ee said, "I am the descendant of the nine goodly brothers who opened up the heavens and the seven goodly sisters who opened out the earth."

Notes

Now begins the famous speech known to all Naxi, as Coqssei-leel'ee relates his lineage with more than a little bluster and bravado. He refers here to the nine brother gods and seven sister gods who created the earth. The manuscript shows Coqseei-leel'ee twice (graphs 1 and 6), while other traditions show the brothers and the sisters, the implication here is that Leel'ee is related to them. Scharten's translation goes awry; her reference to the water dragons is probably a mistranslation of *luq*, brothers, which she may have heard as *lvq*, dragon. Leel'ee is, it must be stressed, *not* related to the water dragons. This shows again how Scharten was translating from the oral performance of the text and not the manuscript itself.

25-6

Graph-by-graph

1. **Coqssei-leel'ee**, Naxi hero, the pronounced foot indicates movement. Not read.
2. **ggv**, nine.
3. **cerq**, ten.
4. **bbuq**, hill.
5. **loq**, muntjac, used phonetically for *lol*, to go over.
6. **ggeq**, raised platform (on top of), used phonetically for first syllable of *ggeqddeeq*, to praise.
7. **ddeeq**, large, used phonetically for second syllable of *ggeqddeeq*, to praise.
8. **qiul**, to cut through, used phonetically for *qu*, kind or race.
9. **Coqssei-leel'ee**, Naxi hero, the pronounced foot indicates movement. Not read.
10. **sher**, seven.

11. **cerq**, ten.
12. **bbuq**, hill.
13. **loq**, muntjac, used phonetically for *lol*, to go over.
14. **ggeq**, raised platform (on top of), used phonetically for first syllable of *ggeqddeeq*, to praise.
15. **ddeeq**, large, used phonetically for second syllable of *ggeqddeeq*, to praise.
16. **qiul**, to cut through, used phonetically for *qu*, kind or race.

Transcription

ggv / **cerq** / ggv / **bbuq** / **lol** / **ggeqddeeq** / mei / **qu**
nine / ten / nine / hill / cross / praise / genitive / race
sher / **cerq** / sher / ddiuq / **lol** / **ggeqddeeq** / mei / **qu**
seven / ten / seven / earth / cross / praise / genitive / race

Scharten translation

I have walked over ninety hills and people of seventy places have hounered me

New translation

"I am of the people who were praised for crossing the ninety-nine mountains, and the seventy-seven lands."

Notes

Graphs 3 and 11, "ten", *xi* +, is more commonly used for "one hundred" in Naxi, while ten, *ceiq*, is also commonly written as an 'x' instead of a cross: X. Li Lin-ts'an notes that both graphs are used interchangeably, and whichever number is meant depends on the individual dongba (2001, 270).

25-7

Graph-by-graph

1. **Coqssei-leel'ee**, Naxi hero. Not read.
2. **jjiq**, water, in this case, a river (*yi bbiq*) is meant.

3. **ku**, mouth, an upper and lower jawbone, here indicating an open mouth.
4. **no**, down, soft feathers, used phonetically for *nieq*, “in” (?).
5. **ggee**, to chew, here indicating *ggee* “to be full”.
6. **me**, negation.
7. **qiul**, to cut through, used phonetically for *qu*, kind or race.
8. **Jjiuqnal-sheello**, the sacred mountain.
9. **Coqssei-leel’ee**, Naxi hero. Not read.
10. **wa**, a bone.
11. **hoq**, ribs, here indicating *zherl*, joint.
12. **lo**, mouthful, an upper and lower jawbone, here indicating the act of eating a mouthful, different from graph 3 above.
13. **me**, negation.
14. **qiul**, to cut through, used phonetically for *qu*, kind or race.
15. **seel**, three.
16. **biu**, a filled container, indicating a measure (usually one litre).
17. **paq**, a jackal. Used phonetically for *pa*, to choke.

Transcription

yibbiq / **ku** / **neiq** / zoq / **ggee** / **me** / gvl / mei / **qu**
river / mouth / in / direct / full / not / able / genitive / race
sheello / mulmul / keel / gaq / me / tal / mei / qu
sacred mountain / bosom / put / tired / not / able / genitive / race
wa / seel / **zher** / nee / ddee / **lo** / go
bone / three / joints / topicalizer / one / mouthful / swallow
aiq / **me** / gvl / mei / **qu**
stuck in throat / not / able / genitive / race
bbiuq / **seel** / **biu** / nee / ddee / lo / mal / **pa** / me / gvl / mei / qu
flour / three / litres / topicalizer / one / mouthful / swallow / choke / not / able / genitive / raxe

Scharten translation

That K’uen-luen mountain I am able to put in my bosom. And when I drink the water of the Yang-tzeh, that will not fill my stomac. When I take three bushels of flour, even when I will not cough; when I take three brig bones, my throat will not be choked.

New translation

“I am of the people that can drink the Yangtze and still not feel full; who can keep the whole sacred mountain in their bosom and not feel tired, who can swallow three bones and not get them stuck in our throats, who can swallow three tonnes of tsamba and not choke.”

Notes

The boast continues. While only the graph for water or river is written, the Jinsha River (upper reaches of the Yangtze) is implied. Controversial here is the intonation unit about the sacred mountain (graph 8, Li Lin-ts'an's manuscript has a snow mountain, *ngv lv*). McKhann renders this "we can take the whole of Mt. Jjunalsheelloq into our vaginas, so that none of it sticks out" (1992, 115). His interpretation has in mind the "structural alternation between male and female" that recurs throughout the passage, though it should be noted that none of the other renditions actually use this word: Scharten has "bosom" (as does He Guisheng), He Cai renders it as "heart", while Rock writes "eat Mt. Sumeru" (1952, 684). For the measurement indicated by graph 16, this is normally considered as one litre, but I believe it is best rendered in English here as tonnes, as the context warrants exaggeration.

25-8

Graph-by-graph

1. **ggaiq**, sword, when in combination with graph 2, it is read *siul*, to kill.
2. **siul**, lead (the metal), used phonetically for *siul*, to kill.
3. **shee**, a prostrated figure, indicating *shee*, to die. The figure's head indicates that it is Coqssei-leel'ee.
4. **me**, negation.
5. **tal**, tower or pagoda, used phonetically for *tal*, to be able.

Transcription

siul / lei / **shee** / **me** / **tal** / mei / qu
kill / particle / die / not / able / genitive / race

Scharten translation

When one would like to kill me, they will not be able to do so. When they would beat me, it would not hurt me.

New translation

"I am of the people that cannot be killed, and cannot be struck down."

Notes

A whole intonation unit is missing in the written manuscript: a parallel to not being able to be killed is "*diu lei ggoq me tal mei qu*" (of the race that cannot be struck down). Unusually, for she normally sticks to what is on the page only, Scharten does translate this.

25-9

Graph-by-graph

1. **Coqssei-leel'ee**, Naxi hero, not read.
2. **sheeq**, lion, here the proper name **Ddvperq-seiggee** is meant (the lion who is white as a conch [see panel 7-6]).
3. **coq**, an elephant, here the proper name **Haisheeq-coqssei** is meant.
4. **Jjeqga-naqbbv**, a deity.
5. **qiul**, to cut through, used phonetically for *qu*, kind or race.

Transcription

Ddvperq'seiggee / qu
name / race
Haisheeq-coqssei / qu
name / race
Jjeqga-naqbbv / qu
name / race

Scharten translation

I am the descendant of a lion, and of an olihpant and of Dyeh-ka-nae-puh.

New translation

"I am the descendant of the white lion and the golden elephant, and of Jjeqga-naqbbv."

Notes

If we refer back to panel 7-6, we will see that these three figures were responsible for guarding the sacred mountain during its construction. Scharten simply translates the graphs literally – a lion (graph 2) and an elephant (graph 3), but when they are placed next to the figure of

Jjeqga-naqbbv (graph 4), we know that these are not ordinary beasts, but mythical animals of great strength and virtue.

25-10

Graph-by-graph

1. **Zzee'laq-epv**, ancestor deity, here speaking.
2. **she**, syllabic graph indicating *shel*, to speak.
3. **Coqssei-leel'ee**, Naxi hero, facing his interlocutor.
4. **ni**, sun, used semantically for *nil*, daytime.
5. **zzeeq**, to sit, used phonetically for *zzeeq*, male, first syllable of *zzeeqpv-bbuqpv*, "bride price".
6. **mil**, woman, used semantically for *bbuq*, female, third syllable of *zzeeqpv-bbuqpv*, "bride price".
7. **siul**, lead (the metal), used phonetically for *siuq*, what or kind.
8. **ciq**, shoulder blade, used phonetically for *ceeq*, to come.
9. **mee**, sky.
10. **geeq**, the stars.
11. **hu**, to drive (as in livestock), to herd.
12. **ceeq**, a ghost, used phonetically for *ceeq*, to come.

Transcription

Zzee'laq-epv / **shel**
deity name / speak
Coqssei-leel'ee sso / **nil** / gge / **zzeeq**pv-**bbuq**pv / **siuq** / bul / seiq / ruaq / **ceeq** /
name + epithet / daytime / genitive / bride price / what / bring / how / calculate / come
Coqssei-leel'ee / nee / shel / mei
name / topicalizer / speak / particle
zzeeqpv-bbuqpv / tee / **mee**bbvq / **geeq** / sherl / jju / me / nal
bride price / it / heaven above / star / full / have / genitive / but
hu / lei / mee / jerq / **ceeq** / me / tal / ye /zeel
drive / particle / sky / come / not / able / sentence final particle / modal particle

Scharten translation

The father answers then to his son, when you get married, what kind of presents can you give? The son replies: heaven is high and there are many stars. Because of this, the cows and sheep are not able to reach so high as this.

New translation

Zzee'laq-epv then asked, "Coqssei-leel'ee! With what do you bring as your bride price this day?"

To which Coqssei-leel'ee replied, "My bride price is as numerous as the stars in the sky; but I am not able to bring it up into the sky."

Notes

The bride price, *zzeeqpv-bbuqpv*, literally "male price female price", is now discussed. Coqssei-leel'ee claims that he has a very substantial bride price (usually livestock, hence the visual in graph 11 of our hero holding a stick to "herd" his gifts upward), but he cannot bring them up into the heavens where the gods reside. This is, one would think, quite a good excuse. He Guisheng reads the first verb as *milddo*, to ask, although graph 2, *shel*, clearly indicates "to speak". Graphs 8 and 12, a shoulder blade and a ghost with hair sticking on end, are both used as phonetic borrowings for the past tense of the verb, "to come".

26-1

Graph-by-graph

1. **yuq**, sheep.
2. **mee**, sky.
3. **hu**, to drive (as in livestock), to herd (the figure is Coqssei-leel'ee).
4. **me**, negation.
5. **ta**, geba syllabic graph, representing *tal*, to be able.
6. **ddiuq**, the earth (replete with lush grass, *ssee*).
7. **ngvq**, silver.
8. **haiq**, gold.
9. **gguq**, to carry on the back.
10. **me**, negation.
11. **ta**, geba syllabic graph, representing *tal*, to be able.

Transcription

ee / **yuq** / **mee** / bbvq / geeq / sherl / jju / me / nal
cow / sheep / sky / below / star / full / have / genitive / but
hu / lei / mee / jerq / ji / **me** / **tal** / ye /zeel
drive / particle / sky / put / not / able / sentence final particle / modal particle
ddiuq / jerq / **ngvq** / **haiq** / ssee / bbei / jju / me / nal
earth / on top / silver / gold / grass / do / have / genitive / but
gguq / bbei / mee / jerq / tv / **me** / **tal** / ye / zeel
carry / do / sky / om top / arrive / not / able / sentence final particle / modal particle

Scharten translation

Because of this, the cows and sheep are not able to reach so high as this. On earth there is much grass, gold and silver, but not able to bring as high as this.

New translation

"There are as many cows and sheep on the earth as there are stars in the sky, but they cannot be driven up into the heavens; there is as much gold and silver as grass on the ground, but it cannot be brought up into the heavens."

Notes

The first intonation unit here acts as a repetition or reinforcement of the last one in the previous panel, but the livestock is made more explicit. Not only is there much livestock, but there are great treasures too, but Coqseei-leel'ee cannot bring them up to offer as a bride price. For graphs 5 and 11 (*ta*), the syllabic graph is once again used in place of the "tower" graph, *tal*, to indicate the verb "to be able".

26-2

Graph-by-graph

1. **Zzee'laq-epv**, ancestor deity.
2. **she**, syllabic graph, used to represent *shel*, to speak.
3. **Coqssei-leel'ee**, Naxi hero.
4. **zzeeq**, to sit, used phonetically for *zzeeq*, male, first syllable of *zzeeqpv-bbuqpv*, "bride price".
5. **siul**, lead (the metal), used phonetically for *siuq*, what or kind.
6. **ruaq**, to measure millet (grains in a container), used phonetically for *ruaq*, to calculate, to count (as).
7. **ni**, sun, used semantically for *ni*, day.
8. **sher**, seven, used phonetically for *sherl*, part of the oral formula, *eni la sher ni*, "long, long ago".
9. **Coqssei-leel'ee**, Naxi hero.
10. **ddaiq**, to be capable.
11. **ggv**, nine.

12. **cerl**, to chop down (an axe chopping wood).
13. **zzeeq**, to sit, used phonetically for *zzeeq*, male, first syllable of *zzeeqpv-bbuqpv*, “bride price”.
14. **pv**, a bubble, used phonetically for *pv*, price (of an object), the second and fourth syllable of *zzeeqpv-bbuqpv*, “bride price”.
15. **chuq**, a string of carnelian beads, used phonetically for *chuq*, early.
16. **ruaq**, to measure millet (grains in a container), used phonetically for ruaq, to count (as), cover (the cost).

Transcription
Zzee’laq-epv / lei / **shel** / mei
deity name / again / speak / particle
Coqssei-leel’ee sso / nil / gge / **zzeeq**pv-bbuqpv / **siuq** / bul / seiq / **ruaq** / zeel
name + epithet / daytime / genitive / bride price / what / bring / how / calculate / particle
Coqssei-leel’ee / lei / shel / mei
name / again / speak / particle
e**ni** la **sher** ni
long, long ago
Coqssei-leel’ee / ngeq / **ddaiq** / bbei / **ggv** / cerq / ggv / xiq / **cerl**
name / I / capable / do / nine / ten / nine / forest / chop
zzeeqpv-bbuqpv / **chuq** / bbei / **ruaq** / seiq / zeel
bride price / early / do / count / modal particle / modal particle

Scharten translation
Further the boy saith: I dont know, what kind of presents you really want? I have done altready quite a lot, first of all I have cut down nine trees. Through this I have paid already enough.

New translation
To which Zzee’laq-epv said again, “What bride price did you bring this day?”
And Coqssei-leel’ee replied, “Before, I, Coqssei-leel’ee, was capable enough to chop down ninety-nine forests, and that already counts as a bride price.”

Notes
Graph 14 is the graph *pv*, originally depicting a bubble, here used to indicate *pv*, the price or value [of the bride price]. The graph is normally written with flared sides: 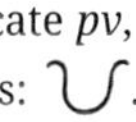. Li Lin-ts’an suggests that the inwardly curved “u” of the manuscript might be read *kueq* as a graph in the Eya area (2001, 286), but this is a Lijiang manuscript, hence the reading “*pv*”. The graph is not to be confused with the geba syllabic *piu*, which looks more like a “u”: 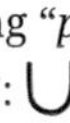.

26-3

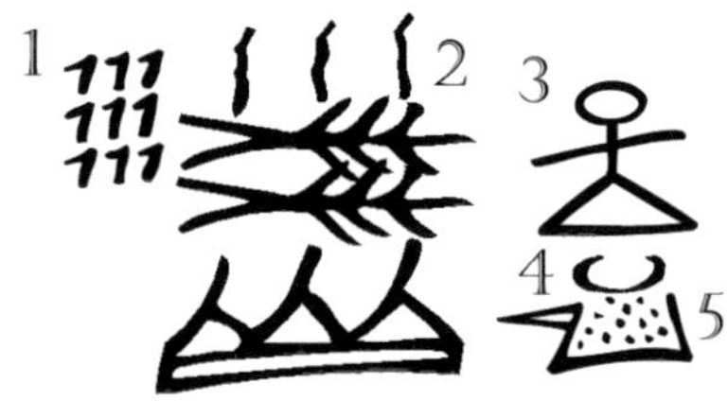

Graph-by-graph

1. **ggv**, nine.
2. **jjil**, to burn (in this case, trees being burned on a fire, smoke rising from the charred branches).
3. **zzeeq**, to sit, used phonetically for *zzeeq*, male, first syllable of *zzeeqpv-bbuqpv*, "bride price".
4. **pv**, a bubble, used phonetically for *pv*, price (of an object), thc second and fourth syllable of *zzeeqpv-bbuqpv*, "bride price".
5. **ruaq**, to measure millet (grains in a container), used phonetically for *ruaq*, to count (as), cover (the cost).

Transcription

ggv / cerq / ggv / xiq / **jjil**
nine / ten / nine / forest / burn
zzeeqpv-bbuqpv / me / ggvq / la
bride price / not / match / and
zzeeqpv-bbuqpv / chuq / bbei / **ruaq** / seiq / zeel
bride price / early / do / count / modal particle / modal particle

Scharten translation

I have burnt the wood of nine and through this I have paid enogh.

New translation

"I have burned down ninety-nine forests, and that already counts as the bride price."

Notes

Graph 2, *jjil* "to burn", is a modified ideographic compound. It is usually written with the graph for meat over the fire: . In this case, however, it is the trees being burned, so trees are substituted in place of the meat.

26-4

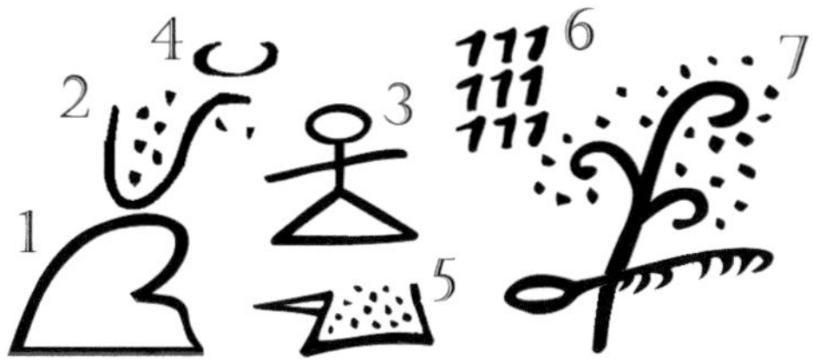

Graph-by-graph

1. **bbuq**, hill or slope, here perhaps referring to the forested hills, *xiq*.
2. **pvl**, to sow (seeds being tipped out of a container).
3. **zzeeq**, to sit, used phonetically for *zzeeq*, male, first syllable of *zzeeqpv-bbuqpv*, "bride price".
4. **pv**, a bubble, used phonetically for *pv*, price (of an object), the second and fourth syllable of *zzeeqpv-bbuqpv*, "bride price".
5. **ruaq**, to measure millet (grains in a container), used phonetically for *ruaq*, to count (as), cover (the cost).
6. **ggv**, nine.
7. **kvl**, a sickle cutting a plant, to harvest.

Transcription

ggv / cerq / ggv / **xiq** / **pvl**
nine / ten / nine / forest / burn
zzeeqpv-bbuqpv / me / ggvq / la
bride price / not / match / and
zzeeqpv-bbuqpv / chuq / bbei / **ruaq** / seiq / zeel
bride price / early / do / count / modal particle / modal particle
ggv / cerq / ggv / xiq / **kvl**
nine / ten / nine / forest / burn
zzeeqpv-bbuqpv / me / ggvq / la
bride price / not / match / and
zzeeqpv-bbuqpv / chuq / bbei / ruaq / seiq / zeel
bride price / early / do / count / modal particle / modal particle

Scharten translation

I have sown five pieces of land, and through this I have paid enough. Also I have harvested nine pieces of ground and also through this I have paid enough.

New translation

"And I have sown the land that was burned and harvested all ninety-nine forests again, and that already counts as the bride price."

Notes

Two parallel episodes of three intonation units each are represented by only seven graphs; the final three intonation units are derived from only the last two graphs.

26-5

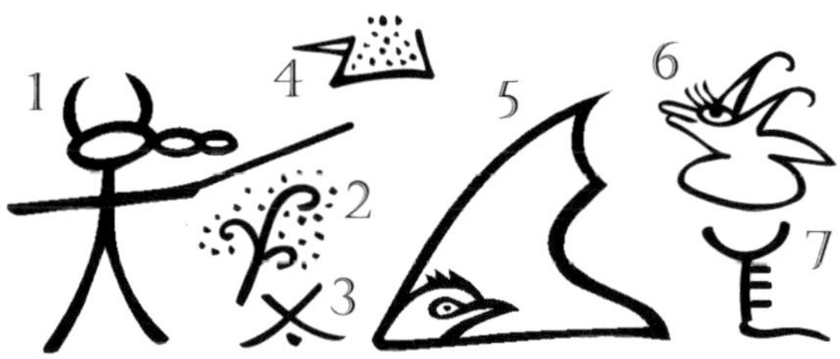

Graph-by-graph

1. **Coqssei-leel'ee**, Naxi hero, here holding a flail, read *lal*, to thresh.
2. **zzee**, many (many leaves), indicating the crops being threshed, not read.
3. **la**, geba syllabic graph, used for the particle *la*, and.
4. **ruaq**, to measure millet (grains in a container), used phonetically for *ruaq*, to count (as), cover (the cost).
5. **aiq**, cliff (the chicken's head acts as a phonetic marker).
6. **seiq**, goral, a kind of mountain goat.
7. **yu**, geba syllabic graph, read *yuq*, to catch.

Transcription

ggv / cerq / ggv / xiq / **lal**
nine / ten / nine / forest / thresh
zzeeqpv-bbuqpv / me / ggvq / **la**
bride price / not / match / and
zzeeqpv-bbuqpv / chuq / bbei / **ruaq** / seiq / zeel
bride price / early / do / count / modal particle / modal particle
aiq / la / **seiq** / **yuq** / keel
cliff / possessive / goral / catch / go
seiq / heeq / pabbaq / nee / chuqzzee-chuqserl / bbei

goral / plump / present / topicalizer / dishes / make
zzeeqpv-bbuqpv / ddee / tv / ruaq / seiq / zeel
bride price / one / piece /count / modal particle / modal particle

Scharten translation

I have threshed all the grain, I have caught a sheep at the mountain.

New translation

"And I have threshed all the grains, that already counts as the bride price, and I caught a goral in the mountains which was then made into a feast, and that counts as the bride price."

Notes

Graph 7 is an unusual variant of the geba phonetic *yu*, , with three prongs and an elaborate "tail" that looks somewhat similar to the Tibetan "u" vowel.

26-6

Graph-by-graph

1. **jjiq**, water, a river.
2. **ko**, horns (of an animal), used phonetically for *ko*, place.
3. **ni**, a fish.
4. **beil**, to fish, a figure holding a fishing rod (the figure is Coqssei-leel'ee), read here as *yuq*, to catch.
5. **zzeeq**, to sit, used phonetically for *zzeeq*, male, first syllable of *zzeeqpv-bbuqpv*, "bride price".
6. **ruaq**, to measure millet (grains in a container), used phonetically for *ruaq*, to count (as), cover (the cost).

Transcription

jjiq / ko / **ni** / **yuq** / keel
water / place / fish / catch / go
ni / heeq / pabbaq / nee / chuqzzee-chuqserl / bbei
fish / plump / present / topicalizer / dishes / make

zzeeqpv-bbuqpv / ddee / tv / **ruaq** / seiq / zeel
bride price / one / piece /count / modal particle / modal particle

Scharten translation
I have caught a fish and by this all I have already paid my debt.

New translation
"I caught a fish in the river which was then made into a feast, and that counts as the bride price."

Notes
Graph 3 is a vivid depiction of our protagonist actually catching the fish, but the action verb of fishing with a lure is not read. He Guisheng instead reads "*yuq*" (to catch), as in the previous panel.

26-7

Graph-by-graph
1. **Coqssei-leel'ee**, Naxi hero.
2. **la**, tiger.
3. **nil**, milk.
4. **seel**, three.
5. **biu**, container, used semantically for *cherl*, to squeeze, the milk being squeezed into a jug.
6. **zzeeq**, to sit, used phonetically for *zzeeq*, male, first syllable of *zzeeqpv-bbuqpv*, "bride price".
7. **pv**, a bubble, used phonetically for *pv*, price (of an object), the second and fourth syllable of *zzeeqpv-bbuqpv*, "bride price".
8. **ruaq**, to measure millet (grains in a container), used phonetically for *ruaq*, to count (as), cover (the cost).
9. **yuq**, monkey, used phonetically for *yuq*, "light".
10. **seiq**, goral, used phonetically for *seiq*, modal particle.
11. **ruaq**, to measure millet (grains in a container), not read.

Transcription

Coqssei-leel'ee / nee / lei / shel / mei
Naxi hero / topicalizer / particle / speak / particle
ddaiq / bbei / **la** / **nil** / **seel** / tie / **cherl**
capable / do / tiger / milk / three / drops / squeeze
zzeeqpv-bbuqpv / tee / niu / **ruaq** / seiq / zeel
bride price / it / come /count / modal particle / modal particle
kvl / gge / Dduq / epv / nee / shel
night / genitive / deity / grandfather / topicalizer / say
soq / gge / Seiq / ezzee / nee / shel
morning / genitive / deity / grandmother / topicalizer / say
ko / hei / tee / **yuq** / **seiq**
sound / ear / this / light / modal particle

Scharten translation

I caught the milk of a tiger and certainly the debt is all paid.

New translation

And Coqssei-leel'ee continued, "I milked three drops of milk from the powerful tiger, and that surely counts as the bride price." In the evening, Dduq spoke, and in the morning, Seiq spoke. And they were listened to.

Notes

The first part of this panel is straightforward; Coqssei-leel'ee is continuing to argue that all the feats he accomplished should be enough to win the hand of his bride-to-be. The second part (graphs 9 and 10) is more complicated, and Scharten omits it entirely. The major nouns and verbs here are not written: the deities Dduq and Seiq (not written) speak out, and they are listened to. Graph 11, *yuq*, represents *kohei yuq*, to listen to a message (literally "sound ear light", the sound enters the ears because it is "light"). This means that the deities have intervened to persuade Zzee'laq-epv – via gentle whisperings – to accept our protagonist. He has finally received the blessing of his father-in-law. It is a major turning point in the story, but depicted with one lone graph, *yuq*, (which happens also to be a phonetic borrowing!). To complicate matters even further, graph 11 is not read, and appears to serve no purpose. In McKhann's translation, we have "The good name of Dduq is carried on...Seil's good name is carried on" (1992, 116).

26-8

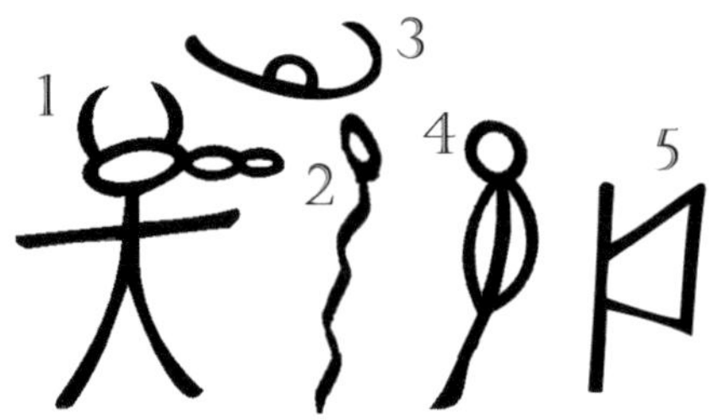

Graph-by-graph

1. **Coqssei-leel'ee**, Naxi hero.
2. **jjiq**, a stream, used phonetically for *jji*, clothing.
3. **me**, negation.
4. **jjiq**, water, a river.
5. **ku**, a door or gate, used phonetically for *kua*, natural spring.

Transcription

Coqssei-leel'ee sso
name + epithet
sso / ee / **jji** / **me** / jjuq
man / good / clothes / not / have
jji / shuq / bbee / dder /zeel
clothes / search / go / should / modal particle
la / jjuq / so / nee / jjuq
tiger / have / mountains / topicalizer / have
Zeiq**jjiq** / **kua** / nee / jjuq
place name, "clear water" / spring / topicalizer / have

Scharten translation

This good boy has not yet any clothing and wat to prepare his wedding garment.

New translation

The goodly Coqssei-leel'ee had no clothes to wear for his wedding, so he had to go and find some. In the deep mountains there was a tiger, who lived by the source of the clear river.

Notes

Scharten combines the final two graphs of this panel with the next panel on the following page. Having finally secured the blessings of Zee'laq-epv, the wedding must now be prepared. Clothing is the first item on the to-do list. Graph 2, what looks like a narrow stream (especially when next to graph 4, a broader waterway), is in fact a phonetic loan for "clothing", *jji*. The graph does not appear in Fang's dictionary, but Li Lin-ts'an provides the rebus meaning (2001, 41). The "clear water" is a specific place name, Zeiqjjiq, although the manuscript simply says "by the river".

27-1

Graph-by-graph

1. **la**, a tiger.
2. **ddoq**, to see.
3. **mil**, woman, here read *bbeeq*, archaic term for woman.
4. **me**, negation.
5. **gv**, garlic, used phonetically for *gvl*, to be able.

Transcription

la / **ddoq** / xi / me / jjuq
tiger / see / person / no / have
la / ddoq / **bbeeq** / nee / ddoq
tiger / see / woman / topicalizer / see
bbeeq / mieq / tal / nee / ddoq
woman / eyes / capable / topicalizer / see
la / kail / xi / **me** / **gvl**
tiger / shoot / person / no / able

Scharten translation

His girl has seen a tiger at the side of the rivermbut she is not able to hunt it.

New translation

Nobody could see the tiger except for the girl, whose eyes were good. Nobody was able to hunt the tiger.

Notes

Now the couple are working together to prepare for their marriage. Coqssei-leel'ee needs the tiger skin for his wedding clothes, and only his bride's eyesight is good enough to see where the tiger is.

27-2

Graph-by-graph

1. **la**, a tiger.
2. **kail**, a bow and arrow, to shoot.
3. **Coqssei-leel'ee**, Naxi hero, here read *zhuaq*, man.
4. **ba'laq**, clothes (the clothes are clearly made from the tiger's pelt, and worn by Coqssei-leel'ee).
5. **jiljuq**, saddle.
6. **ggaiq**, sword, possible a scabbard.
7. **ggaiq jji**, a scabbard.
8. **shel**, to speak, not read.
9. **biu**, container, not read (?).

Transcription

la / **kail** / **zhuaq** / nee / kail
tiger / shoot / man / topicalizer / shoot
zhuaq / ee / laq / tv / sso / nee / kail
man / good / hand / hard-working / man / topicalizer / shoot
la / ee / **ba'laq** / bbei
tiger / skin / clothes / make
la / ee / **jiljuq** / bbei
tiger / skin / saddle / make
la / ee / **ggaiqjji** / bbei
tiger / skin / scabbard / make
sso / ee / ji / hal / ddee
man / good / clothes / beautiful / get

Scharten translation

The boy takes now his arrow and bow and kills the tiger. He takes the skin, of which he makes a dress, a mat and a shade for his knife. The son has now prepared his garment.

New translation

Coqssei-leel'ee was the only one capable enough to shoot the tiger. He skinned it and made from the pelt his clothes, a saddle, and a scabbard. He then had beautiful clothes to wear.

Notes

A tiger skin cloak is the mark of a Naxi chieftain. The scabbard appears to be represented by two graphs: a sword (graph 6), and a sword covered in thorns (*qi*, graph 7). This may be an unusual example of a phono-semantic compound, thorns, *qi*, representing the syllable *jji*. Graphs 8 and 9 are perhaps errors, other versions have a bowl of rice, *ha*, and the "small river" graph over it (*ji hal*, beautiful clothing), somewhat reminiscent in form to that of graph 9 (liquid entering a container).

27-3

Graph-by-graph

1. **bbaq**, a flower, used semantically for *chul*, autumn, the season of flowering alpine plants.
2. **bbv**, a sheep, hoof outstretched.
3. **perq**, white (not read).
4. **goq**, alpine meadow, the symbol in the centre is a needle, *goq*, used as a phonetic.
5. **shuaq**, high, this is a simple ideograph, horizontal lines marking a height.
6. **ssaq**, planet, used phonetically for *ssaq*, down.
7. **jil**, scissors.
8. **pielkuaq**, bamboo sheep pen.
9. **wa**, five.
10. **geeq**, simplified form of graph 18, *geeq*, gall bladder, used phonetically for *ggeq*, catty (500g).
11. **see**, felt mat.
12. **perq**, white.
13. **guq**, ginger, used phonetically for gul, to throw.
14. **cerq**, ten.
15. **geeq**, simplified form of graph 18, *geeq*, gall bladder, used phonetically for *ggeq*, catty.
16. **leijji**, a ladder or notched log, used phonetically *leijji*, a pleated skirt.
17. **ddee**, one.

18. **geeq**, gall bladder, used phonetically for *ggeq*, catty.
19. **gumuq**, a hat.
20. **geeq**, gall bladder, used phonetically for *ggeq*, catty.
21. **pul**, to open, used phonetically for *pul*, half.
22. **bbeegeel**, a belt tied around the waist, usually wool or linen.
23. **mil**, woman.
24. **ji**, small river, used phonetically for *ji*, clothing.
25. **ha**, rice, used phonetically for *hal*, ample.

Transcription

Ceilheeq-bbvbbeq mil / bbeeq / ee / ji / me / jjuq
name + epithet / woman / goodly / clothes / not / have
chulmei / chul / seel / hei
autumn / autumn / three / months
chulji / **bbv** / **goq** / **shuaq** / nee / **ssaq**
autumn / sheep / meadow / high / topicalizer / down
pielkuaq / ggu / tiul / koq / nee / derl / lei / ji
sheep pen / nine / layers / in / topicalizer / close / particle / put
jil / tal / bbv / see / ggaiq
scissors / sharp / sheep / wool / cut
wa / **geeq** / **sse** / **perq** / **gul**
five / catties / felt mat / white / stretch out
cei / **ggeq** / **leijji** / gul
ten / catties / skirt / stretch out
ddee / **ggeq** / **gumuq** / gul
one / catty / hat / stretch out
ggeq / **pul** / **bbeegeel** / gul
catty / half / belt / stretch out
mil / ee / **ji** / **hal** / ddee
woman / good / clothes / ample / get

Scharten translation

Now the girl has not yet prepared her clothing. In the spring the sheep have nice wool; and she takes the wool, of which she makes the following: she uses five catties of wool for a mat; ten for a dress; one for a hat; and have a catty for a belt and the girl is satisfies.

New translation

Ceilheeq-bbvbbeq did not have good clothes to wear. In the three months of autumn the sheep come down from the high alpine meadows. The sheep are then put in the large bamboo pen. She sheared a sheep and used five catties of wool to make a felt mat, ten catties to make a skirt, one catty to make a hat, and half a catty for a belt. Thus, she had clothes to wear.

Notes

An unusually long panel wherein Ceilheeq-bbvbeeq prepares her traditional woolen garments; graph 8 (which has a left and right part either side of the sheep's hoof) depicts a large bamboo pen used to keep sheep and indicates where the sheep was enclosed when its wool was shorn. Graphs 10 and 11 are simplified forms of the gall bladder graph, *geeq* (graph 18). They resemble the geba syllabic graph *ko* △, which is a triangle, but the similarity is superficial in this case. There is a pictograph of meat on a scale that can be used for catty (500g): .

27-4

Graph-by-graph

1. **zzee**, geba syllabic graph.
2. **la**, geba syllabic graph.
3. **e**, geba syllabic graph.
4. **pv**, geba syllabic graph.
5. **nee**, geba syllabic graph.
6. **yeq**, tobacco, used phonetically for *yel*, to give.
7. **me**, negation.
8. **siul**, lead (the metal), used phonetically for *siuq*, things.
9. **laqjjuq**, bracelet, used phonetically for *jju*, to have.
10. **ngvq**, silver.
11. **kual**, a bowl.
12. **ggv**, nine.
13. **haiq**, gold.
14. **kual**, a bowl.

15. **sher**, seven.
16. **wa**, turquoise.
17. **kual**, a bowl.
18. **ggv**, nine.
19. **chuaq**, carnelian beads, jade.
20. **kual**, a bowl.
21. **sher**, seven.

Transcription

Zzee'laq-epv / nee
deity / topicalizer
yel / yi / **me** / yel / **siuq** / me / **jju**
give / emphatic / not / give / stuff / not / have
ngvq / **kual** / **ggv** / liu / yel
silver / bowl / nine / measure word / give
haiq / **kual** / **sher** / liu / yel
gold / bowl / seven / measure word / give
wa / **kual** / **ggv** / liu / yel
turquoise / bowl / nine / measure word / give
chuaq / **kual** / **sher** / liu / yel
carnelian / bowl / seven / measure word / give

Scharten translation

The father has not any objection any more and he gives them nine golden bowls and seven silver bowls, also nine of previous stone and seven of coral.

New translation

There was nothing that Zzee'laq-epv did not give to them [as a dowry]. Nine bowls of silver and seven of gold, nine bowls of turquoise and seven of carnelian.

Notes

The dowry is arrayed in all its splendour. The first five graphs are geba syllabic graphs that seem to have been written at a later date around the other graphs. They represent the four syllables of Zzee'laq-epv's name, followed by the topicalizer, *nee*. Graphs 6-9 contain a double negative when read, but only one negation is actually written. If you were to only read what is on the page, you would get something like "there was nothing given" – a bit of a difference!

27-5

Graph-by-graph

1. **leeq**, a plough.
2. **ee**, ox.
3. **ggv**, nine.
4. **yeq**, tobacco, used phonctically for *ycl*, to give.
5. **gel**, a rake.
6. **ee**, ox.
7. **sher**, seven.

Transcription

leeq / **ee** / **ggv** / pul / **yel**
plough / oxen / nine / measure word / give
gel / **ee** / **sher** / pul / yel
rake / oxen / seven / measure word / give

Scharten translation

Plough oxen nine pair, seven pair

New translation

Nine plough oxen and seven rake oxen were given.

Notes

Scharten translates these as "pairs", so 18 plough oxen etc., a reading supported by Rock (1952, 685). The numbers are associated with gender: nine for men, because ploughing was traditionally men's work and seven for women, because raking was women's work.

27-6, 27-7

Graph-by-graph

1. **zzai**, to ride (a figure riding a horse, the horse's hoof outstretched).
2. **ggv**, nine.
3. **yeq**, tobacco, used phonetically for *yel*, to give.
4. **jil**, to carry a load (as in a pack horse), a horse carrying a load.
5. **jil**, shears or scissors, used phonetically for *jil*, to carry a load.
6. **sher**, seven.
7. **biuq**, a dongba (here reciting a scripture).
8. **biuq**, to worship or perform a religious ceremony, a wooden ritual slat stuck in the ground.
9. **ggv**, nine.
10. **yeq**, tobacco, used phonetically for *yel*, to give.

Transcription

zzai / rua / **ggv** / pul / **yel**
ride / horse / nine / measure word / give
jil / rua / **sher** / pul / yel
load / horse / seven / measure word / give
biuqgvl / **ggv** / nvq / **yel**
dongba / nine / measure word / give

Scharten translation

Riding-horses nine, carrying horses seven.
Also nine sorcerers,

New translation

Nine riding horses and seven pack horses were given.
Nine dongba were given.

Notes

Several phonetics are used in these two panels to reinforce the pictographs (creating de-facto phono-semantic compounds): graph 5, *jil*, provides the pronunciation for graph 4, and graph 8, *biuq*, Provides the pronunciation for graph 7 (despite being somewhat more spatially removed). These are both redundant phonetic markers.

28-1, 28-2

Graph-by-graph

1. **mil**, woman, in this case when combined with graph 2, a female diviner, *paq*.
2. **perq**, white.
3. **sher**, seven.
4. **yeq**, tobacco, used phonetically for *yel*, to give.
5. **Zzee'laq-epv**, ancestor deity, here read phonetically as only "la" (tiger), first syllable of the name Lahiuq.
6. **qul**, lightning, a flash of lightning.
7. **ee**, svastika, denoting the adjective "good", or the verb "to be good at".

Transcription

paqgvl / **sher** / nvq / **yel**
female diviner / seven / measure word / give
Lahiuq / **qul** / zeeq / **ee** / mei / yel
name / lightning / calculate / good at / particle / give

Scharten translation

The father looks now for a good day, that they can marry.

New translation

Seven female diviners were given.
Lahiuq, who could divine the lightning, was given.

Notes

Graphs 1 and 2 can be combined more closely to form the following graph, , read *paq*, showing a seated diviner, the female analogue to the dongba ritualists. Graph 5 is the now-familiar Zzee'laq-epv, but here used merely for the *la* syllable, and points to another figure. Some dongba may read this figure as the deity himself, as in Rock, "Dzi-la-ä-p'u could reckon the 3Ts'ü (stars) well" (1952, 685), or indeed Scharten's rendition above. Graph 6 is a rarely seen graph, but it does appear in Li Lin-ts'an's dictionary (2001, 22), He Guisheng reads it as "*hiuq*", red.

28-3

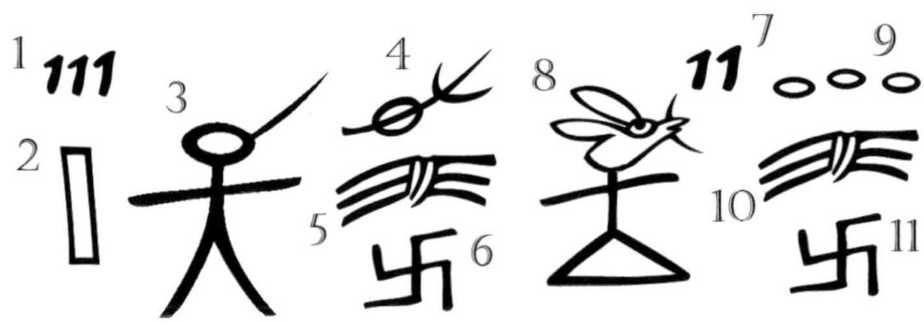

Graph-by-graph

1. **seel**, three, used phonetically for *see*, first syllable of the name Seetoq.
2. **do**, a wooden board, used phonetically for *toq*, second syllable of the name Seetoq.
3. **shel**, to speak, a figure speaking. Used to represent Seetoq, here not read.
4. **ssaq**, planet, a malevolent demon that causes eclipses in Naxi myth.
5. **zeeq**, to count (as in counting by tying knots, a knot is shown).
6. **ee**, svastika, denoting the adjective "good", or the verb "to be good at".
7. **ni**, two, used phonetically for *ni*, first syllable of the name Nilei.
8. **lei**, muskrat, used phonetically for *lei*, second syllable of the name Nilei.
9. **geeq**, stars.
10. **zeeq**, to count (as in counting by tying knots, a knot is shown).
11. **ee**, svastika, denoting the adjective "good", or the verb "to be good at".

Transcription

Seetoq / **ssaq** / **zeeq** / **ee** / mei / yel
name / planet / calculate / good at / particle / give
Nilei / **geeq** / **zeeq** / **ee** / mei / yel
name / stars / calculate / good at / particle / give

Scharten translation

There is man named: Seh-t'eo, who is able to distinguish the stars, which are bad; and an other man, named: Ni-le, who is able to distinguish the stars, which are good, and he asks them to look at them.

New translation

Seetoq, who could divine the planets, was given to them.
Nilei, who could divine the stars, was given.

Notes

More named characters who are good at divining various portents are gifted to the couple. In expanded versions of the story, these characters cast horoscopes to divine which path the bride and groom take to get down to the world below, but their first try is aborted because the horoscope was incorrect. "This interruption of the progress of the ancestors of the Na-khi people only emphasizes that even experts can make mistakes in casting horoscopes" (Jackson 1975, 230). Elements of this can be seen in Scharten's translation.

28-4, 28-5

Graph-by-graph

1. **Jji'aq**, people of Jji'aq, the central part of eastern Tibet.
2. **hal**, night, a moon, used semantically to indicate "day".
3. **zeeq**, to count (as in counting by tying knots, a knot is shown).
4. **ee**, svastika, denoting the adjective "good", or the verb "to be good at".
5. **Leibbv**, people of the Bai nationality.
6. **do**, wooden board, used phonetically for *dol*, to throw (dice or conch shells, when casting horoscopes).
7. **zhul**, an awl, used phonetically for zhul, to join together.
8. **ee**, svastika, denoting the adjective "good", or the verb "to be good at".
9. **yeq**, tobacco, used phonetically for *yel*, to give.

Transcription

Jji'aq / **hal** / **zeeq** / **ee** / mei / yel
people from Jji'aq / day / calculate / good at / particle / give
Leibbv / baiqmai / **tol** / **zhul** / **ee** / mei / **yel**
name / planet / calculate / good at / particle / give

Scharten translation

He asks an other one to look at the moon. This man is named: Ndyeh-a.
He asks also a Ming-chia to look for a good day.

New translation

A diviner from Jji'aq who could cast horoscopes for the days was given to them, as well as a Bai diviner who could divine by throwing the cowry shells.

Notes

Graph 1 represents a figure from the land of Jji'aq, Tibetan *rgya-sde*, in the centre of eastern Tibet (I do not believe it is a proper name of a person, as Scharten's translation suggests, especially when taken as parallel with the following panel: the divine couple are offered great diviners hailing from nearby ethnic groups). Rock says that the majority of the Jji'aq people "profess the Bon creed" (1952, 199). One of their deities is the sacred roc, the garuda, known also to the Naxi. Li Lin-ts'an notes that some dongba believed the Jji'aq to be from India. In the next panel the figure is from the Bai ethnicity, as seen by the headdress (perhaps how the Bai women traditionally wore their hair?). They are known for their method of divination which involves using two flattened cowry shells, blackened on one side, which are thrown into a bowl and interpreted in tandem with a book. The Bai diviner casting the cowry shells can be written thus:  (Li 2001, 97). Graph 7, *zhul*, suggests that they throw the cowry shells several times in succession when casting a horoscope.

28-6

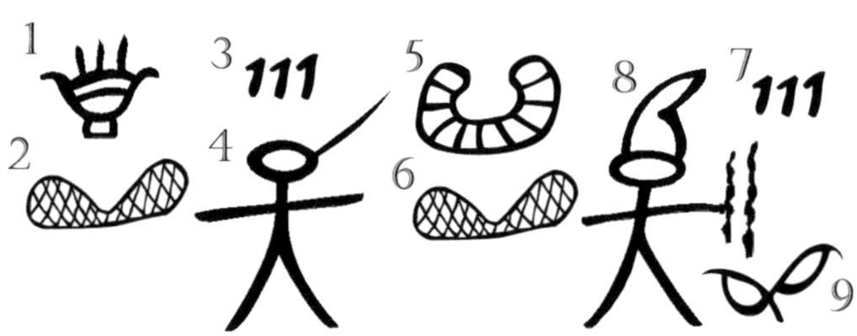

Graph-by-graph

1. **wuq**, bowl of rice used as an offering, used phonetically for *wu*, male slave.
2. **kel**, basket, here used phonetically for *keq*, hard-working.
3. **seel**, three.
4. **shel**, to speak, here indicating sso, man.
5. **laqjjuq**, bracelet, used phonetically for *jjuq*, female slave.
6. **kel**, basket, here used phonetically for *keq*, hard-working.

7. **seel**, three
8. **mil**, woman, here seen twisting threads together, *bbiq*, i.e. engaged in work.
9. **yeq**, tobacco, used phonetically for *yel*, to give.

Transcription
wu / **keq** / **seel** / **sso** / yel
male slave / hard-working / three / man / give
jjuq / **keq** / **seel** / **mil** / **yel**
female slave / hard-working / three / woman / give

Scharten translation
He ires three capable men and three capable women servants.

New translation
He also gave them three hard-working male slaves, and three hard-working female slaves.

Notes
Graph 4, meant to indicate *sso*, man, should simply be a stick figure, but the addition of the speech line makes this graph *shel*. The original composer of the manuscript has the habit of adding the speech lines to various figures, in this case it should not affect the meaning, and we can take it simply as *sso*, man.

28-7, 28-8

Graph-by-graph
1. **me**, negation.
2. **yeq**, tobacco, used phonetically for *yel*, to give.
3. **siul**, lead (the metal), used phonetically for *siuq*, things.
4. **yuq**, a sheep, used metonymically for *neeq*, livestock.
5. **ggv**, nine.
6. **yel**, to give

7. **halleiq**, a cat.
8. **hal**, evening, used phonetically for first syllable of *halleiq*, cat.
9. **qiul**, to cut through, used phonetically for *qu*, kind or race.
10. **me**, negation.
11. **yel**, to give.
12. **neeq**, livestock (different reading from graph 4 above).
13. **gv**, an egg, used phonetically for *ggv*, similar.
14. **tol**, a stone inlay or molding board, used phonetically for *toq*, behind.
15. **ciq**, a shoulder blade, used phonetically for *ceeq*, came.

Transcription
me / **yel** / **siuq** / me / jjuq
not / give / things / not / have
neeq / mei / **ggv** / siuq / **yel**
livestock / particle / nine / varieties / give
halleiq / **qu** / **me** / **yel**
cat / kind / not / give
halleiq / **neeq** / caq / **ggv**
wild cat / livestock / kind / similar
neeq / ko**toq** / nee / bber / lei / **ceeq**
livestock / behind / topicalizer / move / particle / came

Scharten translation
Not to give you anything, that will not do. I will give you nine kinds of domestic animals and no wild cats.
But after all the cat follows the annimals.

New translation
"I won't give you nothing". He gave them also nine kinds of livestock, but not the cat. The cat came following behind the animals anyway.

Notes
Graph 8, the moon facing down, normally indicates *hal*, evening. In this case it provides a phonetic clue for the first syllable of *halleiq*, cat (graph 7). In this case the two graphs can be understood as a single phono-semantic compound. While this version has the cat following along of its own accord, in some versions Coqssei-leel'ee carries it with him inside his new tiger skin coat.

28-9, 28-10

Graph-by-graph

1. **zheeq**, grain.
2. **mei**, originally denoting perhaps female reproductive organs, generally used to denote female, here used phonetically for *mei*, particle used in possessive constructions.
3. **xi**, one hundred.
4. **yeq**, tobacco, used phonetically for *yel*, to give.
5. **keeddvq**, a plant.
6. **ddvq**, a malevolent spirit, used here phonetically for the second syllable of the *keeddvq* plant.
7. **me**, negation.
8. **yeq**, tobacco, used phonetically for *yel*, to give.
9. **zheeq**, grain.
10. **gv**, an egg, used phonetically for *ggv*, similar.
11. **tol**, a stone inlay or molding board, used phonetically for *toq*, behind.
12. **ciq**, a shoulder blade, used phonetically for *ceeq*, came.

Transcription

zheeq / **mei** / **xi** / leel / **yel**
grain / particle / nine / varieties / give
keeddvq / leel / **me** /**yel**
plant / variety / not / give
keeddvq / **zheeq** / caq / **ggv**
plant / grain / kind / similar
zheeq / ko**toq** / nee / bber / lei / **ceeq**
grain / behind / topicalizer / move / particle / came

Scharten translation

Further he gives a hundred kind of grain, but not the little seed of the mustard tree.
But after all there was one between and it came up.

New translation

He then gave them a hundred kinds of grain, but not the seed of the *keeddvq*. But the *keeddvq* seed came following along with the grain anyway.

Notes

Quite what the *keeddvq* seed (graphs 5 and 6) refers to is contentious. Rock does not name the seed, transliterating as k'ö-ddv and calling it a weed, while Scharten uses "mustard seed". He Guisheng calls it in Chinese the *yebazi* 野坝子, a shrub in the mint family. McKhann's translation is "turnip" ("Secretly, Ceil took some turnip seeds with her under her fingernails" [1992, 118]), which is based on a reading of *keeq*, not *keeddvq*, but he explains that both turnip and mint represent abundance, as they produce a great many seeds.

28-11

Graph-by-graph

1. **Coqssei-leel'ee**, Naxi hero.
2. **bber**, to migrate, here indicated by a path of migration.
3. **kee**, a dog.
4. **me**, negation.
5. **see**, a die, use phonetically for *see*, to take.
6. **kvq**, a box (or possibly a mouth harp), used for *kvq*, inside.
7. **bbiu**, to divide (numerous objects represented by dots, being split up into two), used phonetically for *bbiuq*, outside.
8. **me**, negation.

Transcription

Coqsei-leel'ee sso
name + epithet
coq / **bber** / cee / tee / ni
people / migrate / come / this / day
coq / bber / **kee** / **me** / **see**
people / migrate / dog / not / take

kvq / **bbiuq** / **me** / ddubbiu
inside / outside / not / separate

Scharten translation
When they had the marriage, there was no dog and it was not possible to know the division between out and in side.

New translation
On the day Coqssei-leel'ee was going to make his journey, he did not bring a dog, and they could not differentiate between inside and outside.

Notes
In this panel we see the beginning of the titular migration of mankind: the figure representing humanity, Coqssei-leel'ee (graph 1), makes a journey (graph 2). This is the journey from the divine realm down to the human world. The distinction between inside and outside (of which the dog is the arbiter) refers to the distinction between family and outsiders, and guests and strangers, that is to say, who is kin.

29-1

Graph-by-graph

1. **sso**, man, here representing *coq*, mankind.
2. **kee**, a dog (being led on a leash).
3. **perq**, white.
4. **see**, a die, use phonetically for *see*, to take.
5. **kvq**, a box (or possibly a mouth harp), used for *kvq*, inside.
6. **bbiu**, to divide (numerous objects represented by dots, being split up into two), used phonetically for *bbiuq*, outside.

Transcription

coq / bber / **kee** / **perq** / lei / **see** / ceeq
people / migrate / dog / white / particle / take / come
kvq / **bbiuq** / lei / ddubbiu
inside / outside / particle / separate

Scharten translation

A white dog was brought in and they knew the division between in- and out-side.

New translation

Then he brought the white dog inside, and thus the division between inside and outside became clear.

Notes

Graph 1 can be read either as gender neutral *xi*, person, or *sso*, man. While the reading here is "*coq bber*", the migration of man, the figure is probably meant to identify Coqssei-leel'ee specifically, as he is the one making the journey as the first ancestor of mankind. The act of taking the dog is emphasized by the addition of the leash connecting man and dog, a detail that is not included in the oral performance.

29-2

Graph-by-graph

1. **mil**, woman, here representing Ceilheeq-bbvbbeq.
2. **aiq**, a chicken.
3. **me**, negation.
4. **bvl**, to carry (a figure holding an object in their outstretched hands).
5. **ni**, the sun, semantically *nil*, daytime.
6. **huq**, nighttime (a moon facing down).
7. **me**, negation.
8. **bbiu**, to divide.

Transcription

Ceilheeq-bbvbbeq **mil**
name + epithet
coq / ssaq / **aiq** / **me** / **bvl**
people / migrate (down) / chicken / not / carry
nil / **huq** / **me** / ddu**bbiu**
daytime / nighttime / not / separate

Scharten translation

He had no chicken and they did not know, the division between night and day.

New translation

When the people migrated down from the heavens, Ceilheeq-bbvbbeq did not carry a chicken, and so they did not know the difference between day and night.

Notes

The chicken (graph 2) is more accurately a cockerel, because it is the cockerel who rings in the dawn (hence allows people to differentiate between day and night). Graphs 1, 2 and 4 could be understood as a single compound graph: a woman (*mil*), carrying (*bvl*) a chicken (*aiq*). Through context we know that this woman is Ceilheeq-bbvbbeq.

29-3

Graph-by-graph

1. **mee**, sky, used phonetically for *meq*, down.
2. **aiq naq**, a black chicken, the black dot represents *naq*, black.
3. **bvl**, to carry (a woman holding an object in her outstretched hands).
4. **ni**, the sun, semantically *nil*, daytime.
5. **huq**, nighttime (a moon facing down).
6. **bbiu**, to divide.

Transcription

coq / ssaq / **aiq** / **naq** / lei / **bvl** / ceeq
people / migrate (down) / chicken / black / particle / bring / come
nil / **huq** / lei / ddu**bbiu**
daytime / nighttime / particle / separate

Scharten translation

A chicken was brought in and they knew night and day.

New translation

So they took a black chicken, and they knew the difference between day and night.

Notes

Graph 1, *mee*, is a variant of the graph for sky or heaven, . In this case, it is used as a rebus for *meq*, down/below, but the contemporary reading has *ssaq* (to go down) instead.

29-4

Graph-by-graph

1. **Coqssei-leel'ee**, Naxi hero.
2. **xulgel**, cypress branch.
3. **mitvq**, torch.
4. **me**, negation.
5. **qi**, thorn, used phonetically for *qil*, cold.
6. **ciq**, shoulder blade, used phonetically for *ceeq*, come.

Transcription

Coqssei-leel'ee sso
name + epithet
xulgel / **mitvq** / zheel
cypress branch / torch / light
bbuddeeq lulla / **me** / **qil** / bbei / lei / **ceeq**
bright and warm / not / cold / make / particle / come

Scharten translation

When they had the marriage, for every thing was made ready, they come down and the boy prepares a cedar torch, that when they sleep in the night, they may not get cold.

New translation

Coqssei-leel'ee lit a cypress torch, so that when they came it would be warm and bright.

Notes

The graph for the burning cypress torch does not exist in dictionaries; we can however find a graph for torch, *mitvq*, which is a piece of wood with "fire" on the end: . This would be a standardized compound ideogram. In the case of the source manuscript, the cypress branch is simply the graph for cypress tree, and the "fire" is *not* the commonly recognised pictograph of three triangles, but instead a more vivid drawing of flames.

29-5, 29-6

Graph-by-graph

1. **hal**, night, a moon facing down.
2. **hal**, a figure lying prone probably indicating *hal*, to roost (or rest).
3. **zherl**, joint or bone. Used phonetically for *zherq*, to make do, to cause.
4. **mil**, woman, here used semantically to represent *emei*, mother.
5. ?, unclear. A figure holding a smoking torch. Not read.
6. **kual**, a bowl, probably referring to a container for the torch, a brazier. Not read.
7. **bbi**, the sun, giving off its rays (this is the literary word for "sun").
8. **bbuq**, a hill or slope, used semantically for *niu*, place.
9. **hal**, night, a moon facing down.
10. **hal**, a figure lying prone probably indicating *hal*, to roost (or rest).
11. **ser**, wood, used phonetically for *seeq*, father.

Transcription

ddee / hal / leiq / niu / **hal** / **zherq**
one / night / moon / place / rest / make
leiq / yi / **emei** / ggv
moon / emphatic / mother / like
ddee / hal / **bbi** / **niu** / **hal** / zherq
one / night / sun / place / rest / make
bbi / yi / **eseeq** / ggv
sun / emphatic / father / like

Scharten translation

He wears a white hat and in the day time, he warms himself in the sun, which is like a father, looking after his child and in the evening he sleeps.

New translation

One night they arrived at the moon, and the moon was like a mother.
One night they arrived at the sun, and the sun was like a father.

Notes

Scharten does not translate the first panel. Graphs 1 and 2 in the first panel (and 9 and 10 in the second) are likely phono-semantic compounds – the moon, *hal*, providing the phonetic component and the prone figure the semantic element (to roost or rest). At this point the newlyweds are travelling to the world, but they make some stops on their way, first the moon and then the sun, the planetary bodies being compared to a mother and father respectively. The sun and moon give us warmth and light. In most versions the sun comes before the moon. In He Guisheng's reading, graph 5 is Coqssei-leel'ee holding the torch that was lit in panel 29-4, and is not read again. Scharten translates only the hat the figure in graph 5 is wearing. There is also the possibility that graphs 5 and 6 are both phonetics in a place name, *ssiuqkua ddiuq*, and the *ddiuq* (place) is referenced by the hillside (graph 8): see Rock (1952, 686).

29-7

Graph-by-graph

1. **Coqssei-leel'ee**, Naxi hero, here with an elephant's head providing the phonetic, *coq*.
2. **jjiq**, water, river. Part of a place name.
3. **bbuq**, a hill or slope, part of a place name.
4. **laq**, hand, used phonetically for *la*, also.
5. **tvq**, bucket, used phonetically for *tv*, arrive.
6. **mi**, fire, used phonetically for *meeq*, beneath, perhaps read semantically *ssaq*, descend.
7. **ssiuq**, a constellation
8. **ai**, geba syllabic graph, used for *aiq*, to fight.
9. **piul**, to spit.

Transcription

Coqssei-leel'ee sso
name + epithet
Ruiqjjiq / **bbuq** / **la** / **tv**
name / hillside / also / arrive
Ruiqjjiq / bbuq / nee / **ssaq**
name / hillside / topicalizer / descend

ssiuq / **aiq** / ssiuq / **piul** / neiq
constellation / fight / constellation / spit / dynamic aspect

Scharten translation

He comes to a place, named: Leh-hgeh-ndji-nkguh and meets stars, which prophecy, that rain shall come.

New translation

Coqssei-leel'ee arrived at Ruiqjjiq slope, from which he descended, and the constellations fought and spat.

Notes

Graph 8 looks like the graph for "ten", *ceiq*, , but is in fact a geba syllabic for *aiq*, to fight. "To fight" can also be represented pictographically thus: , two figures engaged in a fight with weapons. The constellations fighting and spitting (graph 9) is a metaphor for the rains that are to come in the next panel. It's possible that the constellation (graph 7) represents a place on the migratory route: in McKhann, Coqssei-leel'ee and his bride "arrived at [the good constellation] Ssiuqkuadduq and at [the evil constellation] Sotoqlahiuqkeeq" (1992, 119-120).

29-8, 29-9

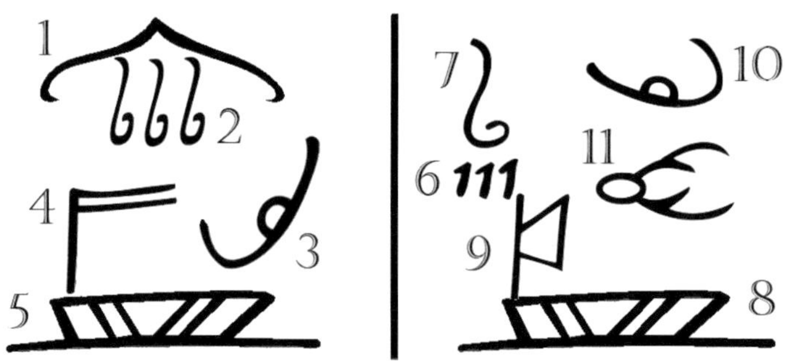

Graph-by-graph

1. **mee**, the heavens.
2. **heeq**, rain.
3. **me**, negation.
4. **shuaq**, high, an ideograph of a line with a mark denoting a high point.
5. **ddiuq**, the earth (not read).
6. **seel**, three.
7. **heeq**, rain (one drop), not read.
8. **ddiuq**, the earth.

9. **ku**, gate or door, used phonetically for *kul*, area.
10. **me**, negation.
11. **ggeeq**, to drop to the ground (a ripe fruit that has opened after falling to the ground), used phonetically for *ggeeq*, clean (impurities washed away).

Transcription
seel / ni / **mee** / lu'lu
three / days / sky / cloudy
seel / ni / **heeq**naq / ggeeq
three / days / heavy rain / fall
seel / ha / bbei / perq / ggeeq
three / nights / snow / white / fall
mee / jju / gul / **me** / **shuaq**
sky / have / outline / not / high
ddiuq / jju / **kul** / **me** / **ggeeq**
earth / have / area / not / clean

Scharten translation
The rains come and it is difficult to walk, because of this, there is nearly no dry place to walk.

New translation
For three days the sky clouded over, for three days the heavy rains fell, for three nights the white snow fell. The sky was not high, and the earth was not clean.

Notes
These two panels can be taken as parallel, showing how, now that our protagonists have reached the earth, they find it covered in impurity (this is indicated by the bad weather, and finally, the literal statement that the earth is unclean). Everything is shrouded and in flux. Scharten fixates on "walking", but there is no indication that this should be the interpretation. Her "no dry place to walk" could by extension be understood as the path being dirty. Graph 2, rain, is here read *heeqnaq*, "big rain". There is a graph for this, which depicts black rain (black being a phonetic component, *naq*, providing the meaning of "big"): . Graph 5, the earth, is the counterpart to the sky and is not read, it is written simply for aesthetic balance. It will be repeated (and this time read) in the next panel (graph 8). Graphs 6 and 7 appear to serve merely as reminders of the rains that have fallen in the previous panel.

29-10

Graph-by-graph

1. **chel**, impurity.
2. **jjiq**, river, or water.
3. **seel**, three.
4. **heeq**, rain, possibly read as *hoq*, a measure word for streams and rivers (i.e. each drop represents one stream).
5. **hiu**, wild animal. Similar to the roe deer, but without the pronounced whiskers.
6. **kua**, hoof, not read, possibly used semantically for *ssaq*, to descend.
7. **me**, negation.
8. **shuq**, an axe, used phonetically for *shuq*, to be clean.

Transcription

chel / **jjiq** / **seel** / **hoq** / shuq / me / ni
impure / water / three / measure word / clean / not / want
hiu / **ssaq** / ddiuq / **me** / **shuq**
female / possessive / wild beasts / descend / earth / not / clean

Scharten translation

When the rains come down, the water in the rivers, is not clear.

New translation

The impure water muddied the three rivers, the wild beasts came down and the world was unclean.

Notes

He Guisheng reads graph 1 and 2 together as *lei*, a grammatical particle, but Li Lin-ts'an suggests that they represent wild beasts coming down from on high. I follow Li for this panel.

A clear picture of the need for the purification rite begins to take shape, and in fact the four graphs to the left of this panel form a logical sequence: the dirty rain falls into three rivers. He Guisheng does not read "rain" at all (although it was probably part of the reading performed for Scharten, as she translates it). In the other English versions, this panel is simplified, for example "the streams grew muddy" (McKhann 1992, 120).

29-11

Graph-by-graph

1. **Coqssei-leel'ee**, Naxi hero.
2. **ree**, road.
3. **ddee**, one, used phonetically for *ddee*, obtain.
4. **me**, negation.
5. **ddeeq**, big, used phonetically for *ddee*, obtain.
6. **zzoq**, bridge, a plank over a river.

Transcription

Coqssei-leel'ee sso / neif / Ceilheeq-bbvbbeq mil / ni / gvl
name + epithet / and / name + epithet / two / measure word
jji / bbee / **ree** / **me** / **ddee**
walk / go / road / not / obtain
ggv / bbee / **zzoq** / me / **ddee**
cross / go / bridge / not / obtain

Scharten translation

He has no road to walk on, neither a bridge to cross the waters.

New translation

They had no road to walk on, and no bridge to cross the rivers.

Notes

While the manuscript only shows Coqssei-leel'ee, contemporary readings have the newlyweds mentioned together, in this case we could understand graph 1 as a metonym for the migrating couple. Graphs 3 and 5 can both be understood as phonetic loans for the same word: *ddee*, to obtain, i.e. they could find no roads or bridges as they traversed the migratory path.

30-1, 30-2

Graph-by-graph

1. **ni**, two, used phonetically for *ni*, first syllable of the name Nilei.
2. **lei**, muskrat (or a seated figure with a muskrat's head), used phonetically for *lei*, second syllable of the name Nilei.
3. **geeq**, stars.
4. **zeeq**, to count or calculate (as in counting by tying knots, a knot is shown).
5. **ee**, svastika, denoting the adjective "good", or the verb "to be good at".
6. **ji'lvl**¸ a weight on a sliding scale, used phonetically for *jji*, first syllable of Jji'aq (see graph 7).
7. **Jji'aq**, people of Jji'aq, the central part of eastern Tibet.
8. **hal**, night, a moon, used semantically to indicate "day".
9. **zeeq**, to count (as in counting by tying knots, a knot is shown).
10. **ee**, svastika, denoting the adjective "good", or the verb "to be good at".
11. **mei**, female (the female reproductive organs), used phonetically for *mei*, a nominalizer or topicalizer.

Transcription

Ni'lei / geeq / zeeq / ee / mei / geeq / liuq / zherq
name / stars / calculate / good at / nominalizer/ stars / look / order
Jji'aq / hal / zeeq / ee / mei / hal / liuq / zherq
people from Jji'aq / day / calculate / good at / nominalizer/ day / look / order

Scharten translation

...and also Ni-le to look to the good stars.
He asks also one else to look at the moon, named: Dyeh-a.

New translation

Also, Ni'lei, who divined the stars and a diviner from Jji'aq who could cast horoscopes for the days were made to perform their divinations.

Notes

These two panels are very similar to 28-3 and 28-4, with the same figures appearing. While those panels were showing how the diviners were gifted to the newlyweds, these panels show the diviners being made to take action and cast the horoscopes at which they are most proficient. "The art consisted of predicting good or bad omens on days of the eclipse depending upon which star was in the ascendant...The Na-khi never made any important decision without consulting the diviners or astrologists" (Jackson 1975, 230-231). This time around, the diviner from Jji'aq gets a phonetic marker (graph 6), and the seated figure plus the phonetic marker come together to form a phono-semantic compound.

30-3

Graph-by-graph

1. **Coqssei-leel'ee**, Naxi hero.
2. **ee hiuq**, a red cow. *Hiuq*, red, is depicted by the graph for "fire" placed inside the cow's head.
3. **maq**, butter.
4. **seel**, three.
5. **zeeq**, to count (as in counting by tying knots), used phonetically for *zeel*, modal particle.
6. **mil**, woman, used here semantically to denote Ceilheq-bbvbbeq.
7. **mi**, fire, used phonetically for *mil*, woman, epithet appended to Ceilheq-bbvbbeq.
8. **zzei**, wheat.
9. **shuq**, iron (depicted by an axe), used phonetically for *shuq*, clean and pure.
10. **seel**, three.
11. **biu**, container holding grain (in this case, flour, *bbiuq*), indicating a measurement, one litre.
12. **svq**, nature spirit, with a human head and torso and a snake's tail. Here seen speaking.
13. **chuq**, string of carnelian beads, used phonetically for *chul* (first syllable of *chulbajjil*, see graph 13).
14. **chulbajjil**, to burn incense for the gods and spirits, incense (cypress branch) burning on a stand with butter and flour. Here read *chulba*.

Transcription

Coqssei-leel'ee sso
name + epithet
ee hiuq / **maq** / **seel** / lv / bvl / **zeel**
red cow / butter / three / measure word, lump / bring / modal particle
Ceilheeq-bbvbbeq mil
name + epithet
zzei / **shuq** / **bbiuq** / **seel** / **biu** / lei / bvl
wheat / pure / flour / three litres / particle / bring
jjuq / tee / pul / neif / lo / ddvq / pul / niuq
mountain / this / side / and / valley / that / side / in
Saqddal-seepei / **svq** / neiq / lv / kee / **chulba** / bbei
mountain spirit / nature spirit / and / dragon / place / offer incense / do

Scharten translation

T'so-rze-le-hgeh's son takes three pieces of butter and T'se-hgeh-puh-puh-mi takes three bushels of flour and offers these to the water dragon.

New translation

Coqssei-leel'ee took three pieces of red cow butter, and Ceilheeq-bbvbbeq took three kilos of pure wheat flour. Then, amidst the mountains and valleys, they offered these to the mountain gods, the nature spirits and water spirits on an incense burner.

Notes

The diviners have chosen the right day to make the offering, and now we see the offerings that will help to rid the earth of the torrential waters. These are butter and flour. Together with a cypress branch, these are burnt on incense burners during purification ceremonies. These three items can be seen on the burner (graph 14), together this graph is read *chulbajjil*, which acts like a verb (to burn sacrificial incense). Graph 13 acts like a phonetic marker for this highly pictographic logograph. Graph 12 depicts the nature spirits, *svq*, who in Naxi legend are related to humanity (half-siblings with the same father but a different mother).

30-4, 30-5

Graph-by-graph

1. **mee**, the heavens.
2. **gv**, garlic, used phonetically for *gul*, outline.
3. **shuaq**, high, an ideograph of a line with a mark denoting a high point.
4. **ddiuq**, the earth (not read).
5. **ku**, gate or door, used phonetically for *kul*, area.
6. **ggeeq**, to drop to the ground (a ripe fruit that has opened after falling to the ground), used phonetically for *ggeeq*, clean (impurities washed away).
7. **Coqssei-leel'ee**, Naxi hero.
8. **zzoq**, bridge, a plank over a river.
9. **ddeeq**, big, used phonetically for *ddee*, obtain.
10. **ree**, road.

Transcription

mee / jju / **gul** / lei / **shuaq**
sky / have / outline / particle / high
ddiuq / jju / **kul** / lei / **ggeeq**
earth / have / area / particle / clean
Coqssei-leel'ee sso / neif / Ceilheeq-bbvbbeq mil / ni / gvl
name + epithet / and / name + epithet / two / measure word
ggv / bbee / **zzoq** / lei / **ddee**
cross / go / bridge / particle / obtain
jji / bbee / **ree** / lei / ddee
walk / go / road / particle / obtain

Scharten translation

They see the heaven is clearing, and the earth is drought and dry.
Now they walk further on and they have good ways and bridges over the stream.

New translation

The heavens cleared, and the earth became dry and clean. Then the two of them had bridges to cross the rivers and roads to walk upon.

Notes

The first panel is a resolution to panels 29-8 and 29-9, in that the rains have gone, and the waters have cleared, so it is now possible to look up to the vault of heaven. This time around we get a new rebus, ginger (graph 2), this word was read in panel 29-8 but not written. Now that there is no negation, there is extra space to accommodate this graph. The following panel is a resolution to 29-11 where our protagonists had nowhere to go, but now the offerings have been made, the path onwards is revealed.

30-6

Graph-by-graph

1. **bbuq**, pig.
2. **bbuq**, hill or slope, used phonetically for *bbuq*, acting as a phonetic marker for graph 1.
3. **kua**, hoof, here read *kee*, foot.
4. **perq**, white.
5. **dder**, a pond (but almost dried up, revealing gravel at the bottom), used phonetically for *dder*, wrong.
6. **seel**, a die with grass on top, a kind of grass used to make straw sandals, used phonetically for *shul*, to purify.
7. **aiq**, a chicken.
8. **perq**, white.
9. **dder**, a pond, used phonetically for *dder*, wrong.
10. **dvl**, a four-pronged stick with an egg inserted at its top, used during the sacrifice to heaven ceremony to ward off evil that descends from the sky. Used phonetically for *dvl*, to ward off.

Transcription

bbuq / naq / lul / **kee** / **perq** / nee / **dder** / lei / **shul**

pig / black / four / foot / white / topicalizer / wrong / particle / purify

juq / ddee / ee / **aiqperq** / nee / **dder** / lei / **dvl**
crow / large / good / cockerel / topicalizer / wrong / particle / ward off

Scharten translation

They take a pig, which has white feet and offer it to the mountain spirit, that their sins may be forgiven, and a white chicken, to the high road.

New translation

They offered a white-hoofed black pig in payment for their sins, and they offered a white cockerel to ward off wrongdoing.

Notes

In the original manuscript there was originally a panel divider separating the pig and the cockerel, but it has been removed. While it looks like the pig is leaping over a hill (graph 2), that hill actually serves as a phonetic marker for "pig"; both hill and pig are read *bbuq*. Graph 6, the grass read *seel*, could possibly be a rebus for the nature spirits, *svq* or *see*, and Scharten seems to read it this way. I take it as phonetic loan (although not an exact one) for *shul*. Graph 10 is a ritual instrument, in the manuscript it has an elongated line at its base, this could be an embellishment to fill space, although Scharten seems to understand it as "road".

30-7

Graph-by-graph

1. **Coqssei-leel'ee**, Naxi hero, here read Coq, as a metonym for the human race.
2. **ree**, road, here used semantically for *bber*, to leave, to go.
3. **ciq**, shoulder blade, used phonetically for *ceeq*, come.
4. **mil**, woman, here not read.
5. **ssaq**, planet, used phonetically for *ssaq*, down.
6. **ciq**, shoulder blade, used for *ceeq*, come.

Transcription
tee / gguq / **coq** / **bber** / coq / **ssaq** / meq / lei / **ceeq**
this / after / people / move / people / down / below / particle / come
bber / lei / zzijjeq-la'ler ddiuq / niuq / **ceeq**
move / particle / the wide earth / on / come

Scharten translation
They both now are going on.

New translation
And after that they migrated down, and arrived at the vast expanse of the earth.

Notes
This panel is split into two intonation units, we can see the two movement verbs (graphs 3 and 6) which end both sentences. There are two figures prominently written, clearly our newlyweds, but they are not read in contemporary readings, instead they together represent the people, coq, who are migrating down onto the earth. Finally, they have now arrived. Other versions have the arrival as a much more detailed affair, involving a number of stops along the way such as at the "Silver With Horns" village and "Gold With Eyes" village (McKhann 1992, 120-121).

30-8

Graph-by-graph
1. **Coqssei-leel'ee**, Naxi hero, here read *zhuaq*, man (archaic).
2. **jjiq**, house, in fact a felt tent is meant: *gvljji*.
3. **tvq**, bucket or container, used phonetically for *tvq*, to put up.
4. **mil**, woman, here read bbeeq, woman (archaic).
5. **shuq**, iron (represented by an axe), perhaps used phonetically for *xiuq*, incense.
6. **mi**, fire.
7. **kee**, foot, used phonetically for *keel*, to light.

Transcription
zhuaq / nee / gvl**jji** / lei / **tvq** / seiq
man / topicalizer / felt tent / particle / put up / modal particle
bbeeq / nee / **xiuqmi** / lei / **keel** / seiq
woman / topicalizer / incense fire / particle / light / modal particle

Scharten translation
They reach the earth. The boy, he puts up a tent and the girl, she prepares a fire.

New translation
The man erected the felt tent, and the woman lit the incense fire.

Notes
Tasks associated with traditional gender roles are here made clear; the man is responsible for putting up the tent, and the woman for lighting the fire. The fire, graphs 5 and 6, could actually be read as one graph, *shul* , to forge (i.e. an axe and a fire), but this is not the correct reading, and in fact is an excellent example of not being able to take the “pictographs” at face value. The axe is not to be read literally, but instead either phonetically, or perhaps simply as a stand-in for the idea of doing work in general.

30-9

Graph-by-graph
1. **eseeq**, father (a man with wood, *see*, on his head, acting as a phonetic).
2. **neeq**, domestic animals, used phonetically for seminal emissions.
3. **kua**, hoof, not read.
4. **chel**, unclean.
5. **niul**, to shake, a person trembling. Used phonetically for first syllable of *niulyi*, pollution.
6. **mil**, woman, here read *emei*, mother.
7. **oq**, beryl or turquoise gemstone, here used phonetically for *oq*, vaginal emissions.
8. **ssaq**, planet, used phonetically for *ssaq*, to go down, discharge.
9. **chel**, unclean.

10. **lv**, stone, perhaps used phonetically for *ddu*, as in *ddu yi*, will (?).
11. **gv**, garlic, used phonetically for *gvl*, will, to be able.

Transcription

eseeq / **neeq**bber / ree / yi / **chel** / nee / **niul**yi / gvl
father / seminal emissions / road / copula / unclean / topicalizer / pollution / will
emei / **oqssaq** / ree / yi / **chel** / nee / niulyi / **ddu** / yi / **gvl**
mother / vaginal emissions / road / copula / unclean / topicalizer / pollution / will / copula / will

Scharten translation

From this time, the father and also the mother do adultery.

New translation

The father's seminal emissions became unclean, and the mother's vaginal emissions became unclean.

Notes

Scharten talks of "adultery", which is a specific moral/spiritual interpretation of impurity. The manuscript itself merely indicates via euphemism that their reproductive systems become unclean. In *Coqbbertv* traditions that are not connected to the purification rite, the newlyweds become more nebulously ill. In this manuscript, their emissions specifically become "unclean" or *chel*, because they do not know the proper way to banish the impurities which need to be cleansed (this is, after all, a manuscript connected to the purification rite). *Neeq* and *oq*, the male and female emissions can also be understood together more abstractly as "wealth", or even a household comprising people and domestic and animals. While both intonation units associated with this panel can be considered parallel, some parts are written and some are not: *gvl* (graph 11), "to be able", appears in each intonation unit, but is written only once, while "unclean" appears twice (graphs 4 and 9). Graph 7 has appeared elsewhere as *waq*, turquoise, or *herq*, green, but is here read *oq* (also a greenish gemstone, but here phonetically vaginal emissions). All three pronunciations are valid readings of the graph.

31-1

Graph-by-graph

1. **perq**, white, a phonetic borrowing for Paiq, a god associated with the Tibetans.
2. **saiq**, a deity associated with the Bai people of Dali. In fact, it is here represented by the geba syllabic *xe*, graphic loan from Chinese *xia* 下.
3. **gga**, the god of victory. Depicted here by a battle flag.
4. **wuq**, commander, a high-ranking military official, depicted here by the phonetic, which is a bowl of rice used as an offering.
5. **chel**, unclean.
6. **niul**, to shake, a person trembling. Used phonetically for the first syllable of *niulyi*, pollution.
7. **gv**, garlic, used phonetically for *gvl*, will, to be able.
8. **o**, a protective deity.
9. **heiq**, a great god.
10. **chel**, unclean.

Transcription

gge / yi / **Paiq** / neif / **Saiq** / yi / chel / nee / niulyi / gvl
top / copula / deity / and / deity / copula / unclean / topicalizer / pollution / will
Gga / neif / **Wuq** / yi / **chel** / nee / **niul**yi / **gvl**
deity / and / deity / copula / unclean / topicalizer / pollution / will
O / neif / **Heiq** / yi / **chel** / nee / niulyi / gvl
deity / and / deity / copula / unclean / topicalizer / pollution / will

Scharten translation

They have six gods. Two, who open heaven and earth, two, who govern the earth, two, who nourish the earth.

New translation

Up high, the gods Paiq and Saiq became unclean, the gods Gga and Wuq became unclean, and the gods O and Heiq became unclean.

Notes

The first four graphs of this panel appear at the end of page 30, but this is to be considered a single panel. In fact, a panel divider has been removed here after graph 7, and before the final three graphs, most likely because they should be taken as part of the same panel. The impurity of the world is suffusing even the abode of heaven. The genesis of these six gods was related way back in the beginning of this manuscript, in panel 3-3. Note graph 2, which is more commonly written .

31-2

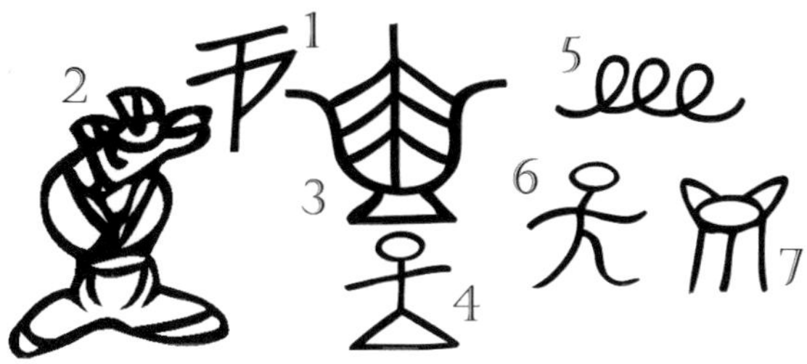

Graph-by-graph

1. **perq**, white, a phonetic borrowing for *pv*, first syllable of *pv'la*, house gods.
2. **Zzee'laq-epv**, ancestor deity with a tiger's head, used phonetically for second syllable of *pv'la*, house gods.
3. **Seel**, a basket representing the Naxi life god who protects the family.
4. **zzeeq**, to sit, used phonetically for *zzeeqgv*, altar.
5. **chel**, unclean.
6. **niul**, to shake, a person trembling. Used phonetically for first syllable of *niulyi*, pollution.
7. **gv**, garlic, used phonetically for *gvl*, will, to be able.

Transcription

pv'la / gga'la / yi / chel / nee / niulyi / gvl
deity / deity / copula / unclean / topicalizer / pollution / will
Seel / **zzeeq**gv / yi / **chel** / nee / **niul**yi / **gvl**
deity / altar / copula / unclean / topicalizer / pollution / will

Scharten translation

At the place of the god of marriage, named Suh, the peaple are not clean.

New translation

The house gods became unclean, and the altar of the life god became unclean.

Notes

The *pv'la* (graphs 1 and 2) are perhaps equivalent to the Tibetan *pho-lha* ཕོ་ལྷ, male deities that are traditionally numbered among the personal protective deities. While the graph for Zzee'laq-epv is used, it merely refers to the syllable "*la*", not the specific ancestor deity. He Guisheng notes that *pv'la gga'la*, taken together, indicate all the gods in general. Graph 3 is the Naxi life god, perhaps the same as the Tibetan *srog* སྲོག. This deity is said to live within this basket.

31-3

Graph-by-graph

1. **neeq**, domestic animals (represented by a cow's head).
2. **oq**, grain, the deity of the grain (represented by a pile of grain).
3. **zzi,** jackal, here used phonetically to represent humanity in general (the jackal's head is the head of a seated person).
4. **hoq**, a constellation, used phonetically for *Huaq*, name of an ancient tribe.
5. **chel**, unclean.
6. **niul**, to shake, a person trembling. Used phonetically for first syllable of *niulyi*, pollution.
7. **gv**, garlic, used phonetically for *gvl*, will, to be able.

Transcription

neeq / neiq / nol / zzeeqgv / yi / chel / nee / niulyi / gvl
domestic animals / and / deity of domestic animals / altar / copula / unclean / topicalizer / pollution / will
zheeq / neiq / **oq** / zzeeqgv / yi / chel / nee / niulyi / gvl
grain / and / deity of grain / altar / copula / unclean / topicalizer / pollution / will
zzi / neiq / **Huaq** / zzeeqgv / yi / **chel** / nee / **niul**yi / **gvl**
humanity / and / tribe / altar / copula / unclean / topicalizer / pollution / will

Scharten translation

In the stables of the cows, there were unclean things.

New translation

The domestic animals and the altar of their god became unclean, and the grains and the altar of the god of grain became unclean. The peoples of the world became unclean.

Notes

Several of the graphs in this panel are somewhat cryptic: graph 4 appears to be an interesting compound: a pile of grain, but atop the pile we can see what appears to be grain growing, i.e. the grain (*zheeq* ) and the god of grain (*oq* ) are turned into a compound. The graph appears similar to the graph for alpine meadow, *goq*: . Of the first four graphs, Scharten here translates only the first (domestic animals, cows). Graph 4, *hoq*, which is according to He Guisheng used to depict the name of an ancient tribe, looks very similar here to an alternate graph for water, *jjiq*. *Hoq* can also be written with the addition of horns at the top: .

31-4

Graph-by-graph

1. **ee**, a cow.
2. **yuq**, a sheep.
3. **pielkuaq**, bamboo sheep pen, here simply read *bbiuq*, pen.
4. **ceel**, a mountain goat.
5. **yuq**, a sheep.
6. **bbiuq**, pen (simplified). The dots inside the pen indicate many animals.
7. **chel**, unclean.
8. **niul**, to shake, a person trembling. Used phonetically for first syllable of *niulyi*, pollution.
9. **gv**, garlic, used phonetically for *gvl*, will, to be able.

Transcription

ee / xiq / **yuq** / xiq / **bbiuq** / yi / chel / nee / niulyi / gvl
cow / raise / sheep / raise / pen / copula / unclean / topicalizer / pollution / will
ceel / xiq / **yuq** / xiq / **bbiuq** / yi / **chel** / nee / **niul**yi / **gvl**
goat / raise / sheep / raise / pen / copula / unclean / topicalizer / pollution / will

Scharten translation

Also in the stable of yak and sheep.

New translation

The pens where the cows, sheep and goats were kept all became unclean.

Notes

Scharten does not translate the second intonation unit.

31-5

Graph-by-graph

1. **chuq**, a horse (archaic).
2. **pai**, to tie up, here represented by a rope and a peg.
3. **zo**, a wooden peg.
4. **leil**, a cow.
5. **pai**, to tie up, here represented by a rope only.
6. **koq**, a fence or trellis.
7. **aiq**, a chicken.
8. **zzo**, stand, here a chicken coop.
9. **bbuq**, a pig.
10. **bbiuq**, a pen, the dots indicate many animals.
11. **chel**, unclean.
12. **niul**, to shake, a person trembling. Used phonetically for first syllable of *niulyi*, pollution.
13. **gv**, garlic, used phonetically for *gvl*, will, to be able.

Transcription

chuq / **pai** / **zo** / **leil** / **pai** / **koq** / yi / chel / nee / niulyi / gvl
horse / tie / peg / cow / tie / fence / copula / unclean / topicalizer / pollution / will
aiq / hal / **zzo** / **bbuq** / xi / **bbiuq** / yi / **chel** / nee / **niul**yi / **gvl**
chicken / rest / coop / pig / raise / pen / copula / unclean / topicalizer / pollution / will

Scharten translation
And in the stable of horse, pig and chicken.

New translation
The pegs where the horses were tied and the fences where the cows were tied became unclean, as well as the chicken coops and the pig pens.

Notes
Scharten translated three of the four animals mentioned (leaving out the cattle, graph 4), although she doesn't render the actual location of the impurity, which is where the animals are being kept. The chicken coop, *zzo* (graph 8), is here written with a variant of its traditional form, which is a more parallel structure: 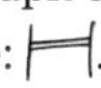.

31-6

Graph-by-graph
1. **Coqssei-leel'ee**, Naxi hero.
2. **mil**, woman, representing Ceilheeq-bbvbbeq. She has her hands up, as if dancing, and is wearing trousers.
3. **ssaq**, planet, used phonetically for *ssaq*, to go down.
4. **chel**, unclean.
5. **biuq**, to sacrifice (to the gods), a ritual stake placed in the ground.
6. **ddee**, one.
7. **ni**, sun, used semantically for *ni*, day.

Transcription
Coqssei-leel'ee sso
name + epithet
Ceilheeq-bbvbbeq **mil**
name + epithet
neeqbber / oq**ssaq** / ree / yi / **chel** / nee / niulyu / gvl
male emissions / female emissions / path / copula / unclean / topicalizer / pollution / will

gga / guaq / ceel / gga / lv / zeeq / lei / **biuq** / ceeq / gge / tee / **ddee / ni**
god of victory / stake / erect / god of victory / stone / put / particle / sacrifice / come / genitive / this / one / day

Scharten translation

T'so-rze-le-hgeh and T'se-hgeh-buh-buh-mi did wrong, and because of this, they want to offer.

New translation

The reproductive organs of both Coqssei-leel'ee and his bride Ceilheeq-bbvbbeq became unclean, and so, on the day of the sacrifice, they erected the victory stone and the victory stake.

Notes

The graph for trousers is depicted in Li (2001, 246) , but here they have been placed onto the legs of Ceilheeq-bbvbbeq (graph 2), probably as a decorative adornment.

Scharten's version is roughly similar, but suggests that their impurity is relating to moral wrongdoing, and her "offer" is a translation of graph 5, to sacrifice, which refers to the preparing of a ritual ground where offerings will be made to the spirits. In the manuscript, graphs 3 and 5 are placed on top of one another but belong to separate intonation units; this is somewhat unusual.

31-7

Graph-by-graph

1. **jil**, scissors, used phonetically for *jil*, small, or possible *jji*, to walk, as part of the noun phrase, *zzeilji-bbeyuq*, fleet-footed young slave.
2. **zzeilji-bbeyuq**, a fleet-footed young slave (a young person running along).
3. **Chelshul-jiqbber**, a dongba depicted with the head of a yak (*bber*, used phonetically), here speaking. He is the overseer of the *chelshul* purification ceremony.
4. **perq**, white.
5. **reeqlv**, a ceremonial altar made with white felt, adorned with a ploughshare.
6. **ngvq**, silver.

7. **haiq**, gold.
8. **waq**, turquoise.
9. **chuq**, carnelian beads.
10. **yiq**, to leak, water emerging from the bottom of a container, used phonetically for *yi*, first syllable of *yiddal*, ritual offerings.
11. **ddal**, an object within another; to place, or to put together. Used phonetically for second syllable of *yiddal*, ritual offerings.
12. **bbei**, a farm tool striking an object, to do or make.

Transcription
Zzeilji-bbeyuq / zherq
young slave / send off
Chelshul-jjiqbber / biubbvq / ddiul
name / ritualist / invite
see / **perq** / **reeqlv** / gge / lei / ceel
wool / white / altar / on / particle / erect
ngvq / **haiq** / **waq** / **chuq** / pv'la / **yiddal** / **bbei**
silver / gold / turquoise / carnelian / gods / offerings / make

Scharten translation
They send a servant, to invite a sorcerer, named T'she-su-ch-mbehr, to exel the devil for them. They prepare the following: on a white felt is placed an iron coult, gold, silver, precious stones and coral, all for an offering.

New translation
They sent a young slave, fleet of foot, to call on the ritualist Chelshul-jjiqbber. A white felt ritual altar was erected, and offerings of silver, gold, turquoise and carnelian were made.

Notes
Graphs 1 and 2 should probably be considered a single phono-semantic compound, the scissors acting as a phonetic. Fang shows the graph thusly: , i.e. with the familiar black face of the slave. Like many of the figures in this manuscript, the characters on this page appear with speech emerging from their mouths. This is merely decorative. Chelshul-jjiqbber, according to Rock, is a dongba who controls the demons of impurity (1972, 198). He Guisheng reads this dongba not as a single person, but as "three Chelshul-jjiqbber ritualists", which indicates that the name can also be used as a title, i.e. any ritualist proficient at this ceremony can be given this title, and three such persons were invited (although this detail is not present on the page). The offerings, *yiddal*, are in this case made to the ritualists, as payment for their work in performing the ceremony.

31-8

Graph-by-graph

1. **ggeq**, a raised platform or bench, used phonetically for *ggeq*, on top of.
2. **heiq**, great god.
3. **chua**, rice (grain in a bowl).
4. **perq**, white.
5. **mee**, heaven, used phonetically for *meq*, below.
6. **svq**, nature spirit, with a human head and torso and a snake's tail.
7. **kual**, wooden ritual slat.
8. **laka**, white poplar.
9. **meel**, bamboo.
10. **ggv**, nine.
11. **ddiuq**, earth, not read.

Transcription

ggeq / yi / **heiq** / zzeiq'ee / **chua** / **perq** / lei / ol
above / emphatic / deity / highland barley / rice / white / particle / scatter
meq / yi / **svq** / kual / lv / kual / meq / nee / ceel
below / emphatic / nature spirit / slat / dragon / slat / below / topicalizer / erect
sherqxi / muq**kual** / perq
seven hundred / wooden slat / white
waxi / muqkual / shuaq / lei / zeiq
five hundred / wooden slat / tall / particle / use
laka / ggv / bbi / zeiq
white poplar / nine / branch / use
meelceiq / **ggv** / wuq / zeiq
bamboo / nine / branch / use
svq / we / lei / ceel / seiq
nature spirit / village / particle / erect / modal particle

Scharten translation

To the god in high places white rice. At the water side they place sticks to be offered to the god of the water.

New translation

To the gods on high, they scattered white rice and highland barley. To the nature spirits down below, they put up the ritual slats: seven hundred white ones and five hundred tall ones. Nine branches of white poplar were used, as well as nine sticks of bamboo, and then the village of the nature spirits was complete.

Notes

Offerings of grain are made to the gods. Then the "village" of the nature spirits is erected to propitiate them. This construction involves wooden ritual slats, here read *kual*, but also known as *kolbiuq*. These are made from pine wood. He Guisheng adds the following: slats used to propitiate demons are flat, while *muqkual shuaq* have a pointed tip and are used to propitiate the gods. All the numbers in the reading are figurative: seven hundred, five hundred, nine; they all indicate the idea of "many". Contemporary readings add another branch to the construction of the "village": ninety-nine branches of Yunnan hazel (*Corylus yunnanensis*). Graph 11 simply represents the ground atop which the ritual occurs, and is not read.

32-1

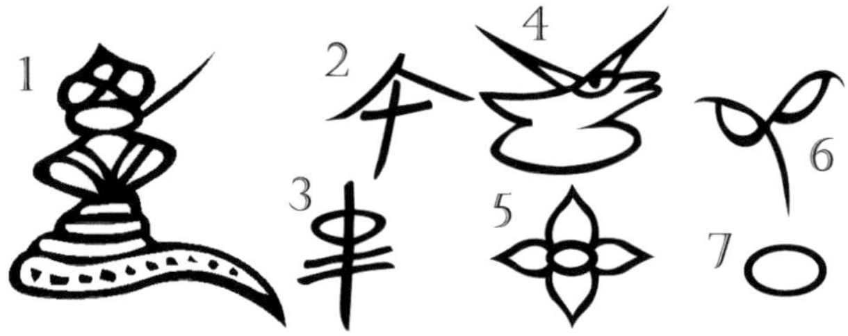

Graph-by-graph

1. **svq**, nature spirit, with a human head and torso, and a snake's tail. Here speaking.
2. **mee**, heaven, used phonetically for *meq*, below.
3. **liu**, a spear with a round, sharpened point. Used phonetically for *liul*, middle.
4. **neeq**, a cow, domestic animals, used phonetically for *neeq*, male seminal emissions.
5. **oq**, beryl or turquoise gemstone, here used phonetically for *oq*, vaginal emissions.
6. **yeq**, tobacco, used phonetically for *yel*, to give.
7. **gv**, egg, used phonetically for *gvl*, will, to be able.

Transcription

svq / we / ggv / we / **meq** / nee / **liul**
nature spirit / village / nine / village / below / topicalizer / middle
neeq / neiq / **waq** / yi / **yel** / yi / **gvl**
male emissions / and / female emissions / emphatic / give / copula / will

Scharten translation

They have now the hope, that these gods will bless them with sons and daughters.

New translation

Below, in the village of the nature spirits, they were given happiness.

Notes

The result of the offerings is the removal of impurities: the male and female emissions, which can be understood either generally as "happiness" or specifically as the ability to bear children, are given back to the husband and wife. Scharten's interpretation is clear: the gods will bless the couple with children.

32-2

Graph-by-graph

1. **Chelshul-jiqbber**, a dongba depicted with the head of a yak.
2. **chel**, unclean.
3. **biuq**, to sacrifice (to the gods), a ritual stake placed in the ground.
4. **shuq**, iron (represented by an axe), used phonetically for shul, to expel or smoke out.
5. **laqpal**, bundle of green branches, to be lit and smoke out demons.
6. **mi**, fire, used phonetically to represent *meq*, below.
7. **ceel**, a goat. Here read **Ceelbbaq-laso**, the name of the goat used in the purification ceremony.
8. **meq**, low flames, "below".
9. **pai**, to tie up, here represented by a rope and a peg.

Transcription

Jiqbber / biubbvq / **chel** / lei / **biuq** / chel / lei / **shul**
name / ritualist / impurity / particle / sacrifice / impurity / particle / expel
laqpal / **meq** / nee / zheel
stick bundle / below / topicalizer / light
Ceelbbaq-laso / **meq** / nee / **pai**
name / below / topicalizer / tie up

Scharten translation

T'she-su-chi-mbehr makes a torch of different wood and bind a black mountain sheep.

New translation

Chelshul-jiqbber then made sacrifices to expel impurity. He lit a bundle of sticks and tied up a black mountain goat.

Notes

We can now see the ritual taking place. The officiating dongba, the purification specialist Chelshul-jiqbber lights the green branches which burn with white smoke and drive out demons. Then a black goat is tied up. It will be sacrificed and offered to the demons. Rock states that a white goat is used (1952, 628). Graph 5 represents a bundle of branches (see Li 2001, 298), in the manuscript it appears that a willow branch is used, amongst others. Graph 6 could be taken as *meq*, a phonetic loan for "below", or *zheel*, a semantic loan for "to light (a torch etc.)". In any case, note how the "fire" graph has a variant in graph 8 specifically to depict lower flames. He Guisheng notes that "Ceelbbaq-laso" (graph 7) is a proper name given to the goat used in this sacrifice.

32-3

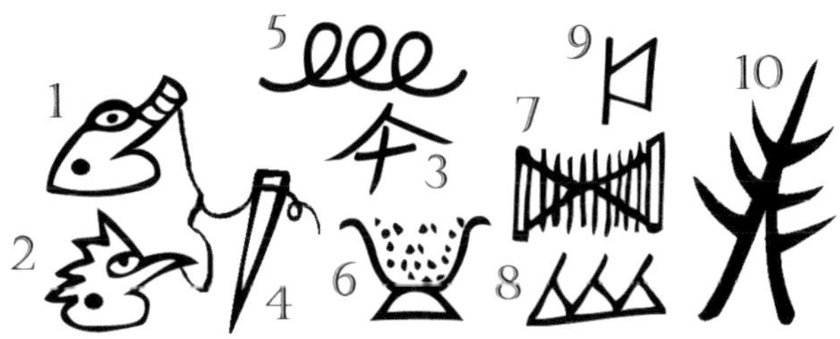

Graph-by-graph

1. **al naq**, a black duck, the black dot inside the head represents *naq*, black.
2. **aiq naq**, a black chicken, the black dot inside the head represents *naq*, black.
3. **mee**, heaven, used phonetically for *meq*, below.
4. **pai**, to tie up, here represented by a rope and a peg.
5. **chel**, impurity.
6. **gol naq**, black sacrificial rice.
7. **pei**, flax or hemp twine (here on a loom).
8. **meq**, low flames, "below".
9. **ku**, gate or door, used phonetically for *ku*, to arrange or spread out.
10. **zzerq**, a tree, here specifically a fir tree is meant.

Transcription

al naq / **aiq naq** / **meq** / nee / **pai**
black duck / black chicken / below / topicalizer / tie up
gol naq / meq / nee / ol
black sacrificial rice / below / topicalizer / scatter
pei / naq / **meq** / nee / **ku**
flax / black / below / topicalizer / spread out
zzerq / naq / meq / nee / ceel
tree / black / below / topicalizer / erect

Scharten translation

A black dug and a black chicken. He puts black grains on the place, where they want to exell evil spirit. He takes a piece of cloth, made from the hennep plant, as a bridge for the spirit. At the end of all things a fir tree is place

New translation

Down below, a black duck and black chicken were tied up, black sacrificial rice was scattered, and a black hemp cloth was spread out. A black fir tree was placed.

Notes

More elements of the ritual are here described, and Scharten's translation is very accurate. The duck and chicken are sacrificial offerings. The black rice is used to help expel the demons of impurity (although He Guisheng does not read graph 5, impurity). Note again two different ways of writing *meq* (graphs 3 and 8, used for diversity). The hemp/flax cloth (graph 7) is spread out on top of a bench where offerings a placed. During the ritual, the cloth represents a black bridge that the *chel* demons can use to cross over into this realm, accept the offerings, and be propitiated. The tree mentioned here (graph 10) is traditionally a fir belonging to the species *Abies Forrestii*, and is known as a "*chel* tree" that attracts the demons. The manuscript depicts a generic tree; there is a graph for the fir tree, *leel* , but it is not used here.

32-4

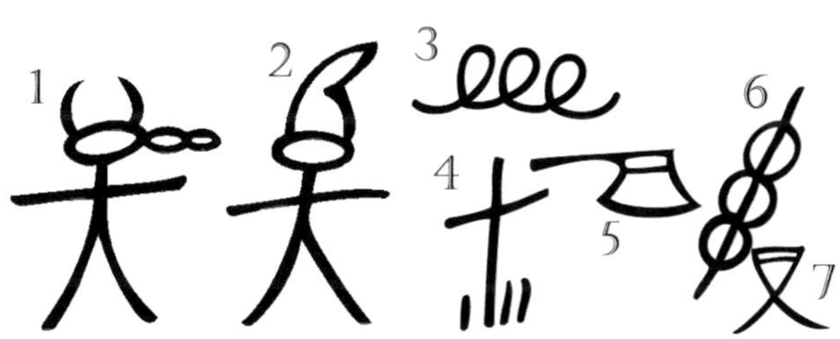

Graph-by-graph

1. **Coqssei-leel'ee**, Naxi hero.
2. **mil**, woman, here representing Ceilheeq-bbvbbeq, the divine daughter.
3. **chel**, impurity.
4. **biuq**, to sacrifice (to the gods), a ritual stake placed in the ground.
5. **shuq**, iron (represented by an axe), used phonetically for *shul*, to expel or smoke out.
6. **chuq**, carnelian beads, used phonetically for *chuq*, early.
7. **mei**, female reproductive organ, used phonetically for *mei,* modal particle.

Transcription
Coqssei-leel'ee / Ceilheeq-bbvbbeq / la
name / name / also
chel / biuq / chel / **shuq / chuq / mei** / yi
impurity / sacrifice / impurity / expel / early / particle / emphatic

Scharten translation
Although the boy and girl have done wrong,

New translation
Coqssei-leel'ee and Ceilheeq-bbvbbeq performed the ritual and expelled the impurity in a timely way.

Notes
The ritual is complete, and we will now see what the result is. The manuscript tells us via the word *chuq*, graph 6, that the ritual has been performed on time, and we know that it will therefore be efficacious. Scharten's translation is somewhat enigmatic and does not reflect a direct reading of the manuscript.

32-5

Graph-by-graph
1. **me**, negation.
2. **gguq**, a box or large container (for storing grain etc.), used phonetically for *gguq*, illness.
3. **cei**, salt, used phonetically for *cer*, to be hot.
4. **chel**, impurity.
5. **qi**, thorn, used phonetically for *qil*, to be cold.
6. **bbiu**, to separate (objects being separated into two piles).

Transcription
me / gguq / me / **cer / me / qil** / me / **bbiu** / gv / lei / heq
not / sick / not / hot / not / cold / not / separate / will / particle / go

Scharten translation

There is nothing any more, after that the devil has been expelled.

New translation

There was no longer any sickness, they would not be too cold or too hot, and they would no longer be apart.

Notes

This is a formulaic result of most ritual actions that can be found across many manuscript traditions. If the rites are conducted as tradition dictates, there will be no more illness or extreme temperatures, and all will be well for the beneficiaries. Note Scharten's invocation of the Christian idea of the "devil": while there are demons and ghosts in the Naxi tradition, they are by no means unequivocally evil beings.

32-6

Graph-by-graph

1. **perq**, white, a phonetic borrowing for Paiq, a god associated with the Tibetans.
2. **saiq**, a deity associated with the Bai people of Dali. In fact, it is here represented by the geba syllabic *xe*, graphic loan from Chinese *xia* 下.
3. **chel**, unclean.
4. **me**, negation.
5. **zherl**, bone joint, used phonetically for *zherq*, to cause or allow.
6. **gga**, the god of victory. Depicted here by a battle flag.
7. **wuq**, commander, a high-ranking military official, depicted here by the phonetic, which is a bowl of rice used as an offering.

Transcription

paiq / neif / **saiq** / la / **chel** / nee / niul / **me** / **zherq**
deity / and / deity / also / unclean / topicalizer / pollution / not / cause
gga / neif / **wuq** / la / chel / nee / niul / me / zherq
god of victory / and / commander / also / unclean / topicalizer / pollution / not / cause

Scharten translation

The name of the above six idols are: the first two, who open heaven and earth are named: P'her and Sae. The second two, who govern the earth, are named: Kae and Wu. They dont want, that there is any unclean thing on the earh

New translation

The gods Paiq and Saiq were no longer made to be unclean, the gods Gga and Wuq were no longer made to be unclean.

Notes

The impurities are cleansed, and the gods are also no longer polluted. The manuscript begins to list all the deities that were mentioned on the previous page. Scharten calla them "six idols", but she actually means six pairs or groups. Where she had previously only described their function, now she gives the names of these deities in full.

32-7

Graph-by-graph

1. **O**, a protective deity.
2. **Heiq**, a great god.
3. **chel**, unclean.
4. **me**, negation.
5. **zherl**, bone joint, used phonetically for *zherq*, to cause or allow.
6. **svq**, nature spirit, with a human head and torso and a snake's tail.
7. **lvq**, dragon, a water spirit, probably a loan word from Chinese *long* 龙.
8. **chel**, unclean.
9. **me**, negation.
10. **zherl**, bone joint, used for *zherq*, to cause or allow.

Transcription
O / neif / **Heiq** / la / **chel** / nee / niul / **me** / **zherq**
deity / and / great god / also / unclean / topicalizer / pollution / not / cause
svq / neif / **lvq** / la / **chel** / nee / niul / **me** / **zherq**
nature spirit / and / dragon / also / unclean / topicalizer / pollution / not / cause

Scharten translation
The third two, who govern the harvest, are named: O and He. They also don't want, that there is any thing unclean on the earth. T'u and Ndi, the gods of the waters, are of the same mind.,

New translation
The gods O and Heiq were no longer made to be unclean, the nature and water spirits were no longer made to be unclean.

Notes
More deities and spirits are cleansed. Scharten labels the latter two (graphs 6 and 7) as T'u and Ndi, these are unusual pronunciations that I cannot trace, for the graphs clearly show the *svq* serpent-tailed spirits and the *lvq* horned dragons that govern the waters.

32-8

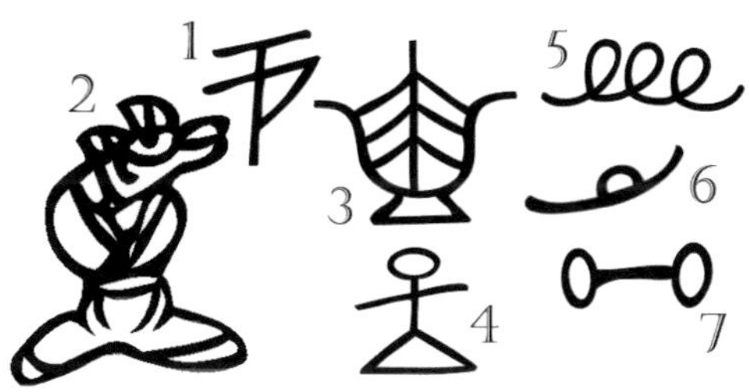

Graph-by-graph
1. **perq**, white, a phonetic borrowing for *pv*, first syllable of *pv'la*, house gods.
2. **Zzee'laq-epv**, ancestor deity with a tiger's head, used phonetically for second syllable of *pv'la*, house gods.
3. **Seel**, a basket representing the Naxi life god who protects the family.
4. **zzeeq**, to sit, used phonetically for *zzeeqgv*, altar.
5. **chel**, unclean.
6. **me**, negation.
7. **zherl**, bone joint, used phonetically for *zherq*, to cause or allow.

Transcription

pv'la / gga'la / yi / chel / nee / niul / me / zherq
deity / deity / copula / unclean / topicalizer / pollution / not / cause
Seel / **zzeeq**gv / yi / **chel** / nee / niul / **me** / **zherq** / bbei / seiq
deity / altar / copula / unclean / topicalizer / pollution / not / cause / make / modal particle

Scharten translation

The god of marriage, named Suh, doesnt want a filthy thing on the earth.

New translation

The house gods were no longer made to be unclean, the altar of the life god was no longer made to be unclean.

Notes

While He Guisheng reads three distinct deities or groups of spirits (the house gods, the gga'la victory spirits and the life god), Scharten only translates graph 3, the life god, represented by a bamboo basket. The Naxi *seel* is perhaps derived from the Tibetan *srog*.

33-1, 33-2, 33-3

Graph-by-graph

1. **we**, village, a village house.
2. **gv**, garlic, used phonetically for *gv*, top.
3. **kee**, a dog.
4. **shuq**, iron (as in an iron axe), used phonetically for to sit, used phonetically for *shul*, to cleanse.
5. **we**, village.
6. **mai**, tail, used phonetically for *mail*, end or bottom.
7. **bbuq**, a pig.
8. **geeq**, gallbladder, used phonetically for *geel*, to remove.
9. **cherl**, a generation (represented by a broken stick or a splitting branch, one generation into another), used phonetically for *cheef*, this or that.

Transcription

we / **gv** / me / shuq / **kee** / nee / **shul**
village / top / not / clean / dog / topicalizer / cleanse
we / **mai** / me / shuq / **bbuq** / nee / lei / **geel** / seiq
village / bottom / not / clean / pig / topicalizer / particle / remove / modal particle
cheefseil
like that

Scharten translation

On high they offer a dog and on earth they offer a chicken for the unclean things.

New translation

If the top of the village is unclean, a dog will cleanse the impurity. If the bottom of the village is unclean, a pig will remove the impurity.
And that's that.

Notes

Scharten's translation suggests that the animals are offered as sacrifices – but this is not the case. The final few panels relate how any remaining impurities can be sniffed out around the village: dogs have a keen sense of smell, so they can discover any impurities in the mountains above the village, and pigs can sniff out any impurities in the ground below the village. All hidden impurities are cleansed. The very final graph (graph 9) indicates the end of the book, and represents *cheefseil*, which can mean something like "and that's that", or perhaps even more concisely, "fin".

References

Andrews, Jim. 1923. "Letter from Likiang". *Confidence* 133, 88.

Bacot, Jacques, and Édouard Chavannes, eds. 1913. *Les Mo-so: Ethnographie des Mo-so, leurs religions, leur langue et leur écriture*. Leiden: E.J. Brill.

Chao, Emily. 2012. *Lijiang Stories: Shamans, Taxi Drivers, and Runaway Brides in Reform-Era China*. Seattle: University of Washington Press.

Fu, Maoji 傅懋勣. 1948. *Lijiang Mexie xiangxingwen "Gushiji" yanjiu* 丽江么些象形文'古事记'研究. Wuchang: Huazhong University.

Fu, Maoji 傅懋勣. 1982. "Naxizu tuhua wenzi he xiangxing wenzi de qubie 纳西族图画文字和象形文字的区别". *Minzu yuwen* 民族语文 1982, 1:1-9.

Fang, Guoyu 方国瑜, and He Zhiwu 和志武. 1981. *Naxi xiangxing wenzipu* 纳西象形文字普. Kunming: Yunnan renmin chubanshe.

Friedrich, Michael. 2023. "Lost in Translation? A Brief History of the Study of Dongba Manuscripts from its Beginnings to 1945". In *Bon and Naxi Manuscripts*, edited by Agnieszka Helman-Ważny and Charles Ramble, 269-348. Berlin: De Gruyter.

He, Jiren 和即仁. 2006. *Minzu yuwen lunwenji* 民族语文论文集. Kunming: Yunnan minzu chubanshe.

He, Xueguang 和学光. 2013. *Naqxi neif Habaq shelzoteeq (jjijizeiq)*, six volumes. Lijiang: Lijiangshi Naxi wenhua chuanxi xiehui.

Jackson, Anthony. 1975. "Floods, fertility and feasting". *Ethnos* 40:1-4, 212-243.

Jackson, Anthony. 1989. "Naxi Studies: Past, Present and Future." *New Asia Academic Bulletin* VIII, 133–147.

Koc, Robert. 1969. *Yü-Lung Shan: Gesang am Jade-Drachenberg*. Salzburg: Stifterbibliothek.

van der Laan, Cornelis. 2008. "Beyond the Clouds: Elize Scharten (1876–1965), Pentecostal Missionary to China", in *Pentecostalism in Context: Essays in Honor of William W. Menzies*, edited by Wonsuk Ma and Robert P. Menzies, 337-369. Sheffield: Sheffield Academic Press.

de Lacouperie, Terrien. 1894. *Beginnings of Writing in Central and Eastern Asia, or Notes on 450 Embryo-Writings and Scripts*. London: Nutt.

Leys, Simon. 2013. *The Hall of Uselessness: Collected Essays*. New York: New York Review Books.

Li, Guowen 李国文. 2007. *Li Guowen Naxixue lunji* 李国文纳西学论集. Beijing: Minzu chubanshe.

Li, Jingsheng 李静生. 2009. *Naxi dongba wenzi gailun* 纳西东巴蚊子概论. Kunming: Yunnan minzu chubanshe.

Li, Lin-ts'an 李霖燦. 1957. *Translations and annotations of Mo-so classics, six volumes* 麼些經典譯註六種. Taipei: China Series Publishing Committee.

Li, Lin-ts'an 李霖燦. 1978. *Translations and annotations of Mo-so classics, nine volumes* 麼些經典譯註九種. Taipei: China Series Publishing Committee.

Li, Lin-ts'an 李霖燦. 2001. *Naxizu xiangxing biaoyin wenzi zidian* 纳西族象形标音文字字典. Kunming: Yunnan minzu chubanshe.

Lo, Ch'ang-p'ei. 1945. "The Genealogical Patronymic Linkage System of the Tibeto-Burman Speaking Tribes". *Harvard Journal of Asiatic* Studies 8: 349–363.

McKhann, Charles. 1992. "Fleshing out the Bones: Kinship and Cosmology in Naqxi Religion", PhD thesis, University of Chicago, Department of Anthropology.

McKhann, Charles. 2017. "Crimes Against Nature: Kincest, Cosmology, and Conservation in Southwest China". *Anthropological Forum* 27:4, 382-401.

Michaud, Alexis, He Limin and Zhong Yaoping. 2017. “Nàxī 納西 language/Naish languages.” In *Encyclopedia of Chinese language and linguistics*, edited by Rint Sybesma, Wolfgang Behr, Yueguo Gu, Zev Handel, C.-T. James Huang, and James Myers, 144-157. Leiden: Brill.

Mueggler, Erik. 2011. *The Paper Road: Archive and Experience in the Botanical Exploration of West China and Tibet*. Berkeley: University of California Press.

Mueggler, Erik. 2022. “Divination and the scapular theory of writing in north Yunnan: graph, verse, page”. *Études mongoles et sibériennes, centrasiatiques et tibétaines [En ligne]* 53.

Pan, Anshi. 1998. “The Translation of Naxi Religious Texts.” In *Naxi and Moso Ethnography: Kin, Rites, Pictographs*, edited by Michael Oppitz and Elisabeth Hsu, 275-309. Zurich: Volkerdemuseum.

Pinson, Thomas (ed.). 2012. *Naqxi-Habaq-Yiyu Ceeqdiai*. Kunming: Yunnan minzu chubanshe.

Poupard, Duncan. 2018. “The Lady of Lijiang: Contextualising a Forgotten Missionary Translator of Southwest China”. *Bulletin of the John Rylands Library* 94:2, 95-114.

Prunner, Gernot. 1969. “The Kinship System of the Nakhi (SW-China) as Seen in Their Pictographic Script.” *Ethnos* 34: 100-106.

Rock, Joseph F. 1935. “The Story of the Flood in the Literature of the Na-khi Tribe”, *Journal of the West China Border Research Society* (Chengtu), 7: 64-80.

Rock, Joseph F. 1952. *The Na-khi Naga Cult and Related Ceremonies* (2 volumes). Rome: Istituto Italiano per il Medio ed Estremo Oriente.

Rock, Joseph F. 1955. *Zhimä Funeral Ceremony of the Na Khi of Southwest China*. Vienna: St. Gabriel’s Mission Press.

Rock, Joseph F. 1963. *A Na-Khi–English Encyclopedic Dictionary*. Rome: Instituto italiano per il Medio ed Estremo Oriente.

Rock, Joseph F. 1965. *Na-khi Manuscripts*, part 1. Wiesbaden: Franz Steiner Verlag.

Rock, Joseph F. 1972. *A Na-Khi–English Encyclopedic Dictionary*, Vol. 2. Rome: Instituto italiano per il Medio ed Estremo Oriente.

Rock, Joseph F. 2002. *Berichte, Briefe und Dokumente des Botanikers, Sinologen und Nakhi-Forschers: Mit einem Schriftenverzeichnis/herausgegeben von Hartmut Walravens*. Stuttgart: Steiner.

Tatsuo, Nishida. 1966. *Ikiteiru shōkei moji: Mosozoku no bunka* 生きている象形文字：モソ族の文化 (Living pictographic writing: Culture of the Moso people). Tokyo: Chūō Kōronsha 中央公論社. (Enlarged and revised ed., Ikiteiru shōkei moji. Tokyo: Gogatsu Shobō 五月書房, 2001.)

Wang, Yuanlu 王元鹿. 1988. *Hangu wenzi yu Naxi dongba wenzi bijiao yanjiu* 汉古文字与纳西东巴文字比较研究. Shanghai: East China Normal University Press.

Xi Yuhua 习煜华, Zhao Shihong 赵世红 (eds.). 2009. *Zhongguo shaoshu minzu yuanshi zongjiao jingji huibian (dongbajing juan)*. 中国少数民族原始宗教经籍汇编 (东巴经卷). Beijing: China Minzu University Press.

Xu, Duoduo. 2023. “Digital Approaches to Understanding Dongba Pictographs”. *International Journal of Digital Humanities* 4, 131-146.

Yang, Fuquan 杨福泉. 2012. *Dongbajiao tonglun* 东巴教通论. Beijing: Zhonghua shuju.

Yang, Zhengwen 杨正文. 2008.*Yang Zhengwen naxixue lunji* 杨正文纳西学论集. Kunming: Yunnan minzu chubanshe.

YNDXLSYJSMZZ Yunnan daxue lishi yanjiusuo minzuzu 云南大学历史研究所民族组. 1976. Zhongguo xinan gu Naxi wangguo 中国西南古纳西王国 [The ancient Nakhi kingdom of southwest China]. Kunming: Yunnan daxue.

YSMGZCGB Yunnansheng Shaoshu minzu guji zhengli chuban guihua bangongshi 云南省少数民族古籍整理出版规划办公室. 1986. Naxi dongba guji Yizhu (vol. 1) 纳西东巴古籍译注 (一). Kunming: Yunnan minzu chubanshe.

Yu, Suisheng 喻遂生. 2003. *Naxi dongbawen yanjiu conggao* 纳西东巴文研究丛稿. Chengdu: Bashu shushe.

Zhou, Rucheng 周汝诚. 1963. *Chongbantu* 崇搬图. Lijiang: Lijiang xian wenhuaguan.

Appendix 1

The Scharten manuscript

Collection Nationaal Museum van Wereldculturen. Coll.no. RV-4175-26

Cover page, see pp. 45-46

Page 1, see pp. 47-57

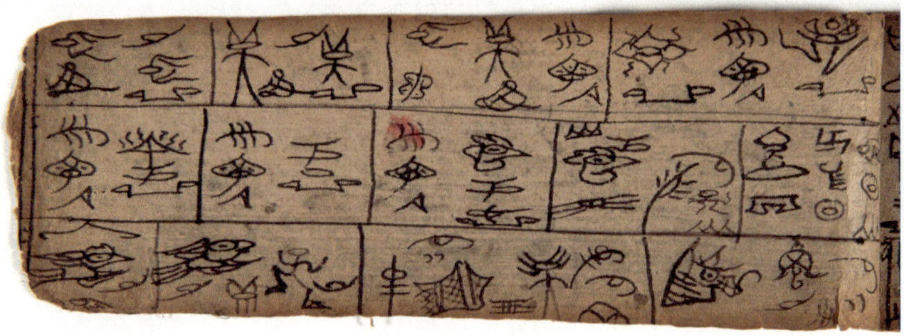

Page 2, see pp. 58-72

Page 3, see pp. 73-83

Page 4, see pp. 84-94

Page 5, see pp. 95-106

Page 6, see pp. 107-117

Page 7, see pp. 118-126

Page 8, see pp. 127-137

Page 9, see pp. 138-148

Page 10, see pp. 149-158

Page 11, see pp. 159-170

Page 12, see pp. 171-180

Page 13, see pp. 181-190

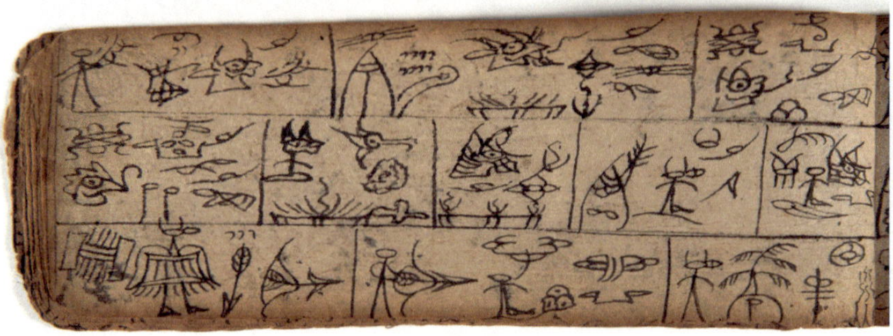

Page 14, see pp. 191-203

Page 15, see pp. 204-213

Page 16, see pp. 214-222

Page 17, see pp. 223-234

Page 18, see pp. 235-244

Page 19, see pp. 245-252

Page 20, see pp. 253-265

Page 21, see pp. 266-278

Page 22, see pp. 279-289

Page 23, see pp. 290-301

Page 24, see pp. 302-313

Page 25, see pp. 314-324

Page 26, see pp. 325-335

Page 27, see pp. 336-344

Page 28, see pp. 345-353

Page 29, see pp. 354-364

Page 30, see pp. 365-373

Page 31, see pp. 374-383

Page 32, see pp. 384-392

Page 33, see pp. 393-394

Appendix 2

The Scharten translation (sample)

Collection Nationaal Museum van Wereldculturen. Coll.no. RV-4175

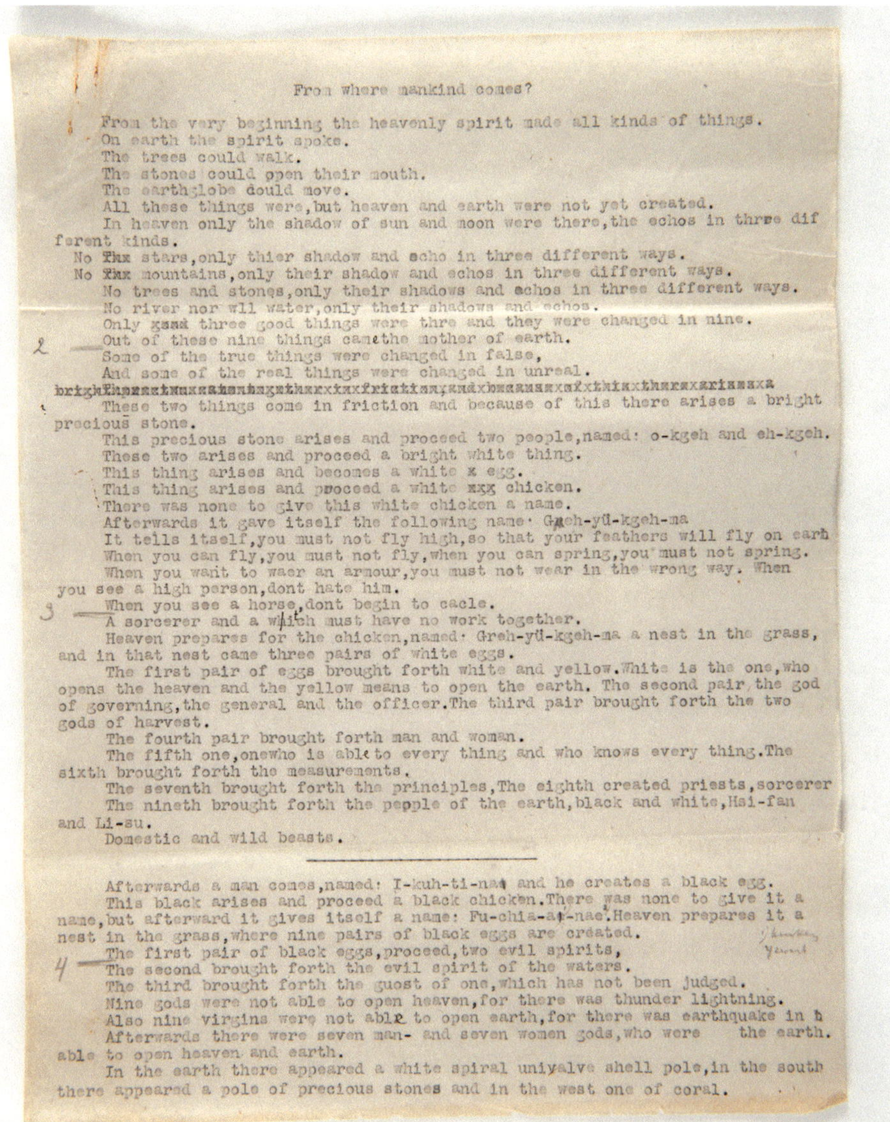

From where mankind comes?

From the very beginning the heavenly spirit made all kinds of things.
On earth the spirit spoke.
The trees could walk.
The stones could open their mouth.
The earthglobe dould move.
All these things were, but heaven and earth were not yet created.
In heaven only the shadow of sun and moon were there, the echos in three different kinds.
No stars, only thier shadow and echo in three different ways.
No mountains, only their shadow and echos in three different ways.
No trees and stones, only their shadows and echos in three different ways.
No river nor wll water, only their shadows and echos.
Only three good things were thre and they were changed in nine.
Out of these nine things came the mother of earth.
Some of the true things were changed in false,
And some of the real things were changed in unreal.
[illegible]
These two things come in friction and because of this there arises a bright precious stone.
This precious stone arises and proceed two people, named: o-kgeh and eh-kgeh.
These two arises and proceed a bright white thing.
This thing arises and becomes a white egg.
This thing arises and proceed a white chicken.
There was none to give this white chicken a name.
Afterwards it gave itself the following name: Greh-yü-kgeh-ma
It tells itself, you must not fly high, so that your feathers will fly on earh
When you can fly, you must not fly, when you can spring, you must not spring.
When you want to waer an armour, you must not wear in the wrong way. When you see a high person, dont hate him.
When you see a horse, dont begin to cacle.
A sorcerer and a witch must have no work together.
Heaven prepares for the chicken, named: Greh-yü-kgeh-ma a nest in the grass, and in that nest came three pairs of white eggs.
The first pair of eggs brought forth white and yellow. White is the one, who opens the heaven and the yellow means to open the earth. The second pair, the god of governing, the general and the officer. The third pair brought forth the two gods of harvest.
The fourth pair brought forth man and woman.
The fifth one, onewho is able to every thing and who knows every thing. The sixth brought forth the measurements.
The seventh brought forth the principles, The eighth created priests, sorcerer
The nineth brought forth the pepple of the earth, black and white, Hsi-fan and Li-su.
Domestic and wild beasts.

Afterwards a man comes, named: I-kuh-ti-nae and he creates a black egg.
This black arises and proceed a black chicken. There was none to give it a name, but afterward it gives itself a name: Fu-chia-a-nae. Heaven prepares it a nest in the grass, where nine pairs of black eggs are created.
The first pair of black eggs, proceed, two evil spirits,
The second brought forth the evil spirit of the waters.
The third brought forth the guost of one, which has not been judged.
Nine gods were not able to open heaven, for there was thunder lightning.
Also nine virgins were not able to open earth, for there was earthquake in the earth.
Afterwards there were seven man- and seven women gods, who were able to open heaven and earth.
In the earth there appeared a white spiral univalve shell pole, in the south there appeared a pole of precious stones and in the west one of coral.

Printed in the United States
by Baker & Taylor Publisher Services